AFTER
WORDS

AFTER WORDS

The
POST-PRIME MINISTERIAL SPEECHES

PJ KEATING

ALLEN&UNWIN
SYDNEY·MELBOURNE·AUCKLAND·LONDON

First published in 2011

Allen & Unwin
Sydney, Melbourne, Auckland, London

83 Alexander Street
Crows Nest NSW 2065
Australia
Phone: (61 2) 8425 0100
Fax: (61 2) 9906 2218
Email: info@allenandunwin.com
Web: www.allenandunwin.com

Cataloguing-in-Publication details are available
from the National Library of Australia
www.trove.nla.gov.au

ISBN 978 1 74237 759 9
ISBN 978 1 74237 923 4 (special edition)

Internal design by Lisa White
Index by Puddingburn
Set in 11.35/15.5 pt Electra LT by Bookhouse, Sydney
Printed and bound in Australia by Ligare Pty Ltd

10 9 8 7 6 5 4 3 2 1

CONTENTS

PART 2 INTERNATIONAL RELATIONS AND FOREIGN POLICY

PART 3 AUSTRALIAN AND INTERNATIONAL ECONOMIC POLICY

INTRODUCTION

Friedrich Schiller, the German philosopher, said: 'if man is ever
to solve the problems of politics in practice, he will have to approach it
through the problem of the aesthetic, because it is only through beauty
that man makes his way to freedom'.

Romantic and idealistic as that view may seem to some, the thought
is revelatory of the fact that the greater part of human aspiration has
been informed by individual intuition and privately generated passions,
more than it has through logic or scientific revelation. The moral
basis of our public life, our social organisation, has come from within
us—by aspiration and by light, not by some process of logical deduction.
Immanuel Kant referred to our inner impulses as 'the higher self', an
unconscious search for truth, going deeply into ourselves to establish
who we are and what we should be.

Beauty is about the quest for perfection or an ideal, and that quest
has to begin with aesthetic imagination—something informed by
conscience, carved by duty. Kant called it 'the inner command', the
ethical construct one creates to guide one from within.

But we need tools to mine good intentions: inspirations, ones which
await the creative spark, the source of all enlargement. Creativity is
central to our progress and to all human endeavour.

Music provides the clue: unlike other forms of art, music is not
representational—unlike the outcome of the sciences, it was never

discoverable or awaiting discovery. A Mahler symphony did not exist before Mahler created it. E.T.A. Hoffman, a contemporary of Beethoven's, famously said: 'music reveals to man an unknown realm, a world quite separate from the outer sensual world surrounding him, a world in which he leaves behind all feelings circumscribed by intellect in order to embrace the inexpressible'.

This is not to turn our back on reason. Or to argue that modernism, with all its secular progress through education, industrialisation, communications, transport and the centralised state, has not spectacularly endowed the world as no other movement before it.

But a void exists between the drum-roll of mechanisation with its cumulative power of science and the haphazard, explosive power of creativity and passion. Science is forever trying to undress nature while the artistic impulse is to be wrapped in it.

While these approaches are different—perhaps often diametrically opposite—they inform related strands of thinking in ways that promote energy and vision.

This is what I have found when these forces are contemplated in tandem. When passion and reason vie with each other, the emerging inspiration is invariably deeper and of an altogether higher form. One is able to knit between them, bringing into existence an overarching unity—a coherence—which fidelity to the individual strands cannot provide.

In the world I have lived in, the world of politics, political economy and internationalism, the literature exists in abundance. But what is far from abundant are the frameworks for the intuitive resolution of complex problems which require multi-dimensional solutions.

But from where do we glean this extra dimensionality?

For me, it has always been from two sources: policy ambition in its own right and from imagination—the dreaming. Policy ambition arising from Kant's higher self, and imagination promoted by those reliable wellsprings—music, poetry, art and architecture—blending the whole into a creative flux.

This collection of speeches reflects many of those interests and impulses—whether it be Jørn Utzon's Opera House or the imperative of liberal internationalism in foreign policy or Neoclassicism, the future of native title or the rise of China. Each is related in a wider construct which is part and parcel of the way I have viewed and thought about the world.

While the speeches are from the period after my prime ministerial life and period in government, the impulse in writing them came from the same framework and inclinations which informed my life in public office.

The speeches may be read individually or read together, subject to subject, idea to idea. Either way, a common thread informs them all. I trust this might be evident to the reader.

Paul Keating

PUBLISHER'S NOTE

FOLLOWING HIS DEPARTURE FROM PUBLIC office Paul Keating accepted public and private speaking invitations. This collection of speeches was given between 1996 and 2011; all were written by Paul Keating.

The original or delivery copies of these speeches are in the possession of the National Archives of Australia, along with dictation and handwritten drafts—including written re-drafts of major addresses. Notes, sometimes underpinning extemporaneous speeches, also reside with the Archive, as do transcripts.

The speeches are reproduced here as they were given, except where Paul Keating thought occasional amplification around particular points added clarity and value. Transcripts of speeches delivered extemporaneously have been edited with attention to punctuation and grammar.

HISTORY, CULTURE AND SOCIAL POLICY

1

BUILDING A MASTERPIECE
The Sydney Opera House
Sydney,
10 August 2006

*Paul Keating's lifelong interest in architecture and design encouraged
the editor of* Building a Masterpiece *to invite him to launch her book
in celebration of the fiftieth anniversary of Jørn Utzon's nomination
as winner of the NSW Opera House competition. Paul Keating sees
Utzon's Opera House as more art than architecture, describing the
design as timeless, earthy and utopian. He claims Utzon's creation is
not simply the greatest building of the twentieth century but one of the
greatest of all history.*

WHATEVER WAS PEDESTRIAN ABOUT SYDNEY, and God knows so much
has always been, we have always rejoiced in the extraordinary natural
beauty of its harbour and its maritime environs.

The high points of its built form—the colonial ones such as
Greenway's St James' Church and environs, Barnet's monumental
Bridge Street, St Mary's Cathedral and Sydney University—as well as
the twentieth-century residential and commercial buildings such as the
Astor, the AWA Tower and many others we could mention, could, in
one form or another, be seen in other cities around the world.

Sydney dropped the veil of me-tooism when it built the Harbour
Bridge. At the apogee of the industrial age, the Labor government of
New South Wales made the almighty gesture of spanning the north and

3

southern shores of the harbour with this utterly grand and monumental structure, book-ended by pairs of completely resolved granite pillars.

From that moment on, at least in world terms, that great arch defined Sydney and, for the most part, Australia, as the world had come to know it and indeed us.

It was Sydney's Eiffel Tower, its greatest engineering feat, and built in much the same manner.

But it was more than that. It was a declaration of the importance of the public domain and its primacy in the scheme of things. And in an era when one found one's identity in the common quotient with one's peers, it was cause for rejoicing of a kind that an insular and uncertain place, bound by the modesty of its circumstances, had not previously had.

In the sweep of any nation's history, 30 years is not a long time. But that was the time between the decision to go ahead with the construction of the Harbour Bridge and the decision to build the Sydney Opera House.

Perhaps not remarkable in itself, but remarkable, as it turned out.

Those 30 years took Australia from the age of iron and steel to the age of concrete, with all its beguiling plasticity.

Those 30 years, in Sydney at least, saw the advent of the steel-frame building and its Cubist march across the city's golden masonry.

'Free at last', cried the architects, 'of the limits imposed by brick and stone; now the sky is the limit'. As the First World War brought down the monarchies across Europe, from that point on, cities and their architects would celebrate the liberation by turning their backs on the decoration and forms which represented so much of the autocratic past.

Function, simplicity and utility took the ascendancy, while materials were employed in a form of exhibitionism which slaked from façades all remnants of the architectural forms and motifs that existed down through the ages.

Architecture in this mould, today, has many names; modernism and postmodernism come to mind. But whatever it is, it holds as uppermost, one single tenet: that everything that happened in architecture before it is irrelevant.

It was in and from this milieu that Jørn Utzon's revolutionary Opera House emerged—so completely and remarkably.

Not only does Utzon refuse to let the materials divine his design, he moulds them to a naturalism which his genius understood would allow him to draw from an entirely new order.

As surely as the gothic of the middle ages brought its rules and inspiration from nature's florilegium, Utzon's 'shells' drew their inspiration from nature and, in their building, from the perfection of nature's sphere. In one leap, Utzon bounded from the new modernism with its naïve geometry and stultifying righteousness, to an entirely new framework of his own creation.

Somewhere in the Utzon head came inspiration for this. For his building is, without doubt, more art than architecture. Some creativity in that brain of his, inspired by nature, or some set of passions, brought this conception into being.

Architecture is not an art. It is a taught medium. Students, certainly these days, sit down and learn rules. They then translate those rules to particular tasks. The tasks, at their best, have creativity about them; but, more often than not, only a modicum.

The artist, of course, knows no boundaries. Art is infinite. It is not deductable; it defies containment.

Utzon's building, like all great art, never weakens. No matter how often you see it or from what angle you look at it or in what light it is cast, it always hits you in the heart because it is simply so good.

It is, without any shadow of a doubt, the greatest building of the twentieth century and one of the greatest of all history. Because it devolves to a new and ingenious order which its creator himself divined.

It begs, I think, an important question: does everything truly great about architecture find its origin in nature? Or at least spring from it?

The ancient Egyptian orders with their bud-like, tension-filled capitals and the Greek ones with their relieved flowering represented the highest architectural ideals of all humanity and did so until the second quarter of the twentieth century. The Egyptians with their Pyramids built with a simplicity of form beyond improvement while the Greeks, with their temple pediments and logarithmic loggias, borrowed from nature's rules to instruct themselves in perfection. In progression, Rome's Pantheon gave the world its first half-hemisphere with its ocular view of the heavens.

Nature not only feeds us, it informs and inspires us. Could the judging panel in 1956 not understand that it was present at the creation of something new and utterly revolutionary? Something each judge recognised as being novel but possessing resonances each had experienced or could identify with?

Just as the Royal Society could not mistake the stodgy Turner in his ruffled black suitcoat and concussed top hat for the great and new art that was in his power, so, too, Ashworth and Saarinen and their fellows could not mistake real genius, no matter the modesty of its origin. For their perspicacity, we thank them sincerely.

As we especially thank Ove Arup for applying his creativity in seeing Utzon's conception to reality. Utzon, unlike Blondel or Ledoux, would not have survived on paper. Utzon had to go real. University students and graduates around the world would not, these days, be researching through the Sydney Opera House competition entries or debating why Utzon did not win, had Utzon not got to build his edifice. I doubt that he would even have ended up in texts about classicists, such as of Friedrich Gilly who, by the way, did a modernist reductive loggia in 1796 much more resolved than the one Utzon himself did here recently.

No, Utzon had to get his building into the sky.

He was in the form business. He was not in the music business. All this talk over the years about the tragedy of him not completing the interior belies the fact that what Utzon, more than anything else, would have wanted to see was those magic forms and silhouettes become a reality.

Like most people, I should have liked to have seen him execute his design through to completion. But I don't think many of the great buildings, whether they were Michelangelo's or Christopher Wren's, were turnkey jobs where the architect left an invoice at the end and was presented with an award. These master works were always a work in progress. In fact, Utzon's was relatively speedy.

In the age of autocracy it was possible to garner the civic authority to conceive and complete grand buildings of this kind. In our age of democracy, this is nigh on impossible, with governments coming and going, while the financial demands of the task soar. Most governments these days would wilt under a Sydney Opera House project. A building like this today would represent ten cross-city tunnels all rolled together, with works ministers back-pedalling for all they were worth.

That said, I would like to amplify a couple of things that, over the years, have occupied my mind about Utzon's concept at its core.

There is little doubt that the inspiration for the masterpiece came from nature.

The more horizontal organic shells of Utzon's original entry touching his podium lightly at their load-bearing apexes no doubt have their roots in nature. Light and seemingly hovering, the shells could almost be thought to flutter.

The problem was, they could not be built.

Because of their organic shape, the stresses within each shell were unpredictable and could not be measured.

It was, I believe, Arup's application to the task which pushed Utzon to rethink the practicability of his conception, so as to provide it with shell elements that could be built, owing to the fact that they would behave predictably: in other words, subject to an applicable order or set of governing principles.

This, no doubt, is where his vertical, heaven-sent shells came from.

It is to his everlasting credit that Utzon saw the sphere as providing him with a building geometry that was at once predictable, while capable of calibration for industrial reproduction.

Utzon's passage from his artistic conception to his spherical solution is as impressive and as real as architectural history's age-old journey from the primeval hut to the stylish, mathematical purity of the Parthenon.

Utzon's Opera House does not belong to any historical age, but is 'timeless, earthy and utopian', all at once.

I have no personal connection with the building save for four things.

I was at the opening and, of course, it was better to be there than not be there.

In another instance, I sat on the design committee of the new Parliament House in Canberra for seven years and from the Saarinen example in Utzon's selection, I did what I could to encourage IM Pei to join the judging panel. And, as it turned out, he played a similar role in turning up Aldo Giurgola's and Richard Thorp's winning design.

In yet another instance, one of Utzon's young collaborators, Peter Myers, approached me as Prime Minister about the withering state of Utzon's drawings and the body of work associated with Arup's engineering. I gave the government of New South Wales a grant of $6 million to preserve them.

Finally, I scurried across the quayside from a green double-decker bus in George Street to the building that was then only at podium stage, to hear the great basso voice of Paul Robeson standing in his herringbone coat with cap on head and hand at ear. He sang the great black spiritual songs that had made him famous and which seemed to come not from the bottom of his chest but from the earth underneath him.

And maybe if I can add one more.

I saw the USSR State Symphony Orchestra under the baton of Evgeny Svetlanov, with their battered and decaying instruments, lift Tchaikovsky's *Manfred Symphony* to a musical experience so profound as to make me ask the question: why could the Sydney Symphony Orchestra, with the greatest residence in the world, not sound like that? Seven years later, as Prime Minister, I took the opportunity to free the SSO from the stultifying bosom of the ABC and it has never looked back.

It is fitting and right that 50 years after the New South Wales Labor government launched the competition in 1956 for the new opera house, we should celebrate that event. An exercise in vision and community-building which, in this country, only comes from Labor governments.

But, what a wonderful opportunity to reflect on the genius who won the competition.

Utzon's building has no parallel in human history. Not only did it represent an endorsement of us as a people, a people whose community had come of age, in a much more parochial sense, it reconnected Sydney to its own harbour.

This book, *Building a Masterpiece*, edited by Anne Watson, is being published by the Powerhouse Museum to celebrate the fiftieth anniversary of that great undertaking.

I understand it was to be the frontispiece of an exhibition surrounding the project, which, sadly, never came about.

Nevertheless, there are gems contained here. Eugene Goossens's own vision of an opera house he campaigned for. Details of the unprecedented design and construction challenges including stories about the work site, its multiculturalism and industrial activism.

It talks also about the reconciliation between Utzon and the community of New South Wales, which, I must say, is an issue that has been way overdone. No one else at that time would have had the political patience or the funding to have built Utzon's design. Now, of course, many would, but not then.

Utzon made his appointment with history when he dropped his entry into the competition box. He should never forget this. But, neither should we.

2

A TIME FOR REFLECTION
Political Values in the Age of Distraction
The Third Annual Manning Clark Lecture,
Canberra,
3 March 2002

*Paul Keating uses the third Annual Manning Clark Lecture to
urge Australians to remain remote from 'the gated refuge of nothingness'
by restoring a proper moral basis to our politics. In the lecture he upbraids
the Howard government for its exclusionary refugee policies; its blatant
use of racism under the guise of freedom of speech; its assault on
institutions including the High Court and the Governor Generalship;
and its politicising and suborning of the public service and the Australian
Defence Force. Paul Keating also disavows John Howard's 'deputy sheriff'
strategy for Australia, urging an Australian, rather than American, foreign
policy and with it, a new 'Australian' century.*

MANY OF YOU HAVE BEEN attending the Weekend of Ideas, hosted over the past three days by Manning Clark House, of which this is the final session.

I am delighted to be part of it. Because out here, on the edge of Asia, a long way from major markets and natural groupings, ideas are all Australia has to shield itself from the harsh winds of global change.

Not military might, or a large population, or unique resources. Just ideas.

Ideas are what must sustain our democracy, nurture our community and drive our economy into new areas so we can cope with the challenges I will be talking about tonight.

I first met Manning Clark in the early 1980s.

I used to visit him in that little birdcage of a room on the roof of his house where he retired to think and write. That face of craggy desiccation looking out on Australia, a country which he did so much simply to interpret, but by his interpretation, to shape.

I was always amused by the view put about by some conservatives that Manning was the house historian of the Keating government. Anyone who spent time in his presence knew that he was no economic rationalist. He would have regarded financial-sector deregulation or tax reform with suspicion or indifference. And he was always much more mystical than Marxist.

But I'll come back to Manning and his contribution later.

I want to talk first about his great theme—Australia, and how we, with all our human foibles, come to terms with our lives on this continent.

After the election result was clear in 1996, I made the remark that when the government changes, the country changes.

I was making the unfashionable point that politics matter: that by their actions and words, our political leaders powerfully shape the sort of country Australia is.

I was saying that whatever voters might have been entitled to draw from the bland me-tooism of Liberal-policy pronouncements during that election campaign, Australia would be different afterwards.

And, six years on, it is more different than even I imagined.

The last time I spoke here at the National Library was in August 1993 at its twenty-fifth-anniversary dinner. I said then, partly by way of tribute to Sir John Gorton who had opened the Library, that I believed that change—some of which the Gorton government had set in motion—had 'won a resounding victory' in Australia.

I said: 'We have seen the remarkable growth of tolerant, creative cultural pluralism and all the riches this has brought Australia . . . the xenophobia has largely gone.'

11

Well, over the past five or six years there is no doubt that the reactionaries have fought back. The tolerance looks frailer and the xenophobia more robust.

From those first claims in the 1996 election that our national objective should be to become 'relaxed and comfortable' to the fear-mongering about borders in the 2001 campaign, this government has consistently looked both inward and backward.

The last campaign was fought overtly about closing the borders and keeping people out, but symbolically that idea has been the sustaining policy theme of the Howard years.

They have been trying to pull up the drawbridge, but they have failed to understand that moats cannot keep us safe anymore.

The period of reaction began with the flirtation with Hansonism and the pretence that the blatant racism was really all to do with freedom of speech.

We have seen, ever since, from the government and its coterie of columnists, the repetitive use of demonising language: 'the Aboriginal industry', 'welfare rorters', 'queue jumpers', 'political correctness', 'elites' and 'chattering classes'.

The emphasis is exclusionary. It's an effort in part to stigmatise those who are destitute or stateless as having somehow brought it upon themselves. The approach is a manifestation of the growing tendency of contented bourgeois societies all over the world to express their extremism around matters of inclusion and especially citizenship. Who is in and who is out. Who belongs to our community and who doesn't.

Much cleverer people than Pauline Hanson have since joined the game in Australia. People with fewer excuses than small shopkeepers in troubled regional towns.

For example, Professor Wolfgang Kasper told the readers of *Quadrant* a couple of months ago—*Quadrant* readers may be few in number, but they do know what they like—that Muslim immigrants to Australia brought unacceptably high 'transaction costs'. They are not People Like Us.

He was echoed in the press not long later by John Stone.

12

This was the central message behind that infamous advertisement during the last election campaign: 'We have the right to decide who comes to this country'.

Once the language has been debased and the people marginalised, it is much easier to convince voters that asylum-seekers are prepared to sacrifice their children or are terrorists. That it is acceptable in Australia for children to be locked away, out of sight, in desert camps and treated like prisoners.

The numbing effect of this is that we are at risk of becoming, as Manning once said, subjects in the kingdom of nothingness. Subjects of a post-Christian, post-Enlightenment world where there is no inspiration, no higher endeavour, little compassion and no belief beyond narrow self-interest. Like members of a gated community we pretend, in our comfortable urban solace, that all is well, including all around us.

Manning used to say that Australian public life broke into two groups: the enlargers, and the punishers and straighteners.

As the incarcerated asylum-seekers at Woomera can attest, this government is well and truly into the punishing and straightening game.

There has long been an inbuilt tension in Australian approaches to immigration; between the idea that our immigration policy is basically about patrolling our perimeter to keep people out and the reality that we need to attract good immigrants to help us develop the country, people who are doing us a service into the bargain.

It's the latter view that has to prevail. Televised pictures of asylum-seekers in camps and news reports of our treatment of refugees are doing us far more damage in terms of the message they send to skilled young people the world over than whatever spurious deterrent benefits they may be thought to have against so-called 'queue jumpers' or illegal immigrants. The notion that Australia is suspicious of foreigners is a damaging idea to put out in a world that is becoming smaller and more interdependent.

In few areas of policy has the change in Australia's view of itself been clearer than in the attitude the country brings to foreign policy generally and to Asia in particular.

Members of this government claimed that as Prime Minister, I was pursuing an Asia-only policy. Of course that was never true. We had a more effective relationship with the United States than the current Coalition has and a position with European governments of real standing.

But we did believe that all Australia's vital interests coalesced in Asia. That Australia needed to find its security in Asia, not from Asia. But it was always Australian interests we were talking about, not Asian ones.

The Howard government came to office proclaiming—more code— that Australia did not have to choose between its geography and its history. As though you can ever choose between those two fixed realities.

The only thing we *can* choose is our future, and this is where the country has been let down.

The current government brings to its relations with Asia a policy only of benign neglect and tokenism. They believed they could send one message to the outside world and another to the domestic audience. But in the information age, you can't get away with this duplicity.

From the time Gough Whitlam got the fire hose out to clean the postcolonial sludge from Australian foreign policy, an essential bipartisanship obtained in Australia about our view of the world.

The political parties might differ on ways and means of getting there, or about the handling of particular issues, but the direction we were headed in, the nature of Australian interests in the world, were agreed.

That bipartisanship fell apart with John Howard. The Howard government has subordinated foreign policy to domestic policy to an unprecedented and dangerous degree.

We've seen it in the jingoism after the Timor intervention, in the withdrawal from UN committees which had the temerity to criticise government policy. And it had its most recent manifestation in the *Tampa* and the 'Pacific Solution'—and isn't that phrase a good example of the capacity of this government to get political double-speak accepted in public discourse.

It was on view again in interesting ways during John Howard's latest visit to Jakarta. The visit where journalists in the press party were told it was all a success, while officials were insulting President Megawati and telling favourite journalists that the Prime Minister would probably never return there. One of the themes of press briefings during the visit—at least those that did not consist of gratuitous off-the-record insults to Indonesia and its leaders—was criticism of my alleged obsession with Indonesia.

The only obsession has been their obsession with me.

I believe the government's problems with foreign policy stem from its own insecurity; from a defensive and uncertain view of Australia and its place in the world. A sense that we should know our place, that we shouldn't get ideas above our station. A government that has little faith in Australians or what they are capable of.

We saw it clearly in John Howard's agreement to the assertion that Australia's role in the region was to be the Deputy Sheriff.

The *Deputy* Sheriff!

I'd have more respect for him if he'd wanted to pin the silver star on his own lapel and gallop off at the head of the posse. But that is not where Australia goes under the Howard regime.

The changes in Australia since 1996 have not just been in ways of thinking. Australia's institutions have also been eroded in dangerous ways.

There is something odd about Australian conservatives. It is that, in some important ways, they aren't conservatives at all.

Whatever else you say about conservative political philosophies, you can usually rely upon their followers to cherish institutions of state. It's true of the different brands of conservatism in Britain and the United States. Whether it's the American constitution or the British House of Lords, they want to keep and preserve them, to defend them from enemies and often from friends as well.

Out here, though, we've ended up with conservatives who treat the institutions of state with contempt.

From the High Court to the Australian public service to the Australian Defence Force to the nature of the Governor Generalship, the Howard government has been damaging those institutions rather than preserving them. Undermining them, not defending them.

The Coalition has a contemptuous disregard for convention—the etiquette—that has grown around us and which provides the binding for our social and political life.

Political parties and leaders are in most respects the custodians of these mores. Wise governments not only guard that which we all cherish, they try to polish and hone things into the bargain. This notion, the current government regards as old hat.

John Howard is no respecter of conventions. He was not a principal player in 1975 in the Senate's outrageous conduct, but he did not demur either.

And now, as Prime Minister, he can effect a much more certain influence in matters, he disregards convention to the service of his political convenience.

Let me begin with the Governor General. I said at the time of Dr Hollingworth's appointment that it was in my view an error of judgement to appoint a churchman to the position. I made the point that had I sought to appoint someone like the former and now retired Catholic Archbishop of Sydney, Cardinal Clancy, there would have been an outcry from Howard and the conservatives.

Apart from the issue of principle at stake in mixing church and state, John Howard knows as well as anyone in contemporary politics that it is really only since the end of the 1970s that we have buried sectarianism in this country in any substantial way.

In my lifetime I saw advertisements in the *Sydney Morning Herald* saying 'Catholics need not apply'. We are blessed to be rid of this stuff. All of us. Why would you take a chance on any of it rearing its ugly head, given that these days there are a lot of ugly heads around? Nevertheless, John Howard was prepared to give the cage a rattle.

As far as Dr Hollingworth himself goes, history is perhaps going to be the more important judge of his tenure. But without waiting for the history I think we can say with full confidence that apart from the initial error of judgement in seeking to appoint a churchman to this position, John Howard did not even adequately determine, as he should have, personally, the suitability of Dr Hollingworth for the job.

Dr Hollingworth is not just a victim of his own circumstances, he is a victim of John Howard's judgement.

A Prime Minister must approach major appointments with conscientiousness and much forethought and take responsibility for his decisions.

But the appointment of the Governor General is not where the government's disregard for institutions ends.

We have witnessed the scandalous attacks on the High Court over the Wik judgement. These people say they believe in the rule of law, except the laws they do not like.

And that 'good fellow' Tim Fischer, was not so good a fellow when he was attacking the High Court and the Chief Justice for all he was worth.

Contrast that with the Labor government, which was thrown one of the greatest curve balls in constitutional history when the High Court declared that native title emanated from the common law of Australia but gave no indication of what it was, who had it or how it could be obtained.

But, unlike this government, the Labor government celebrated the essential justice of the Court's judgement and did everything to make the decision work. It didn't leave the Court out in the cold, out on a limb. It devoted two years to building, from the ground up, a massive piece of property and cultural law.

Canberra, above all other cities, understands the wider meaning of the shocking revelations we have heard about the institutional and, in some cases, personal behaviour of the public service and the ADF during the boat-people scandal. And I don't choose the word 'shocking' lightly.

We have seen how far the Australian public service has been cowed. It has been politicised well beyond any point we have known in the past.

I worked for over thirteen years as a Minister and as Prime Minister with men and women in the public service. I liked and admired Australian officials. I admired the integrity of their efforts. Most of what we accomplished in those years could not have been done without their skills and commitment. They served the government loyally but understood that the highest manifestation of that loyalty was their ability to advise fearlessly without recrimination or rebuke.

Michael Keating, for example, or Mike Codd before him, or Chris Higgins, or Bernie Fraser, never did, and never would have, regarded themselves as political strategists for the Prime Minister or the Treasurer. They would not have seen their role as preserving the impression of ignorance among Ministers about a matter at the centre of an election campaign simply because the truth might be politically inconvenient.

The government is to blame for the shameless politicisation of the public service. It fired off the warning shots within days of coming to office with the unprecedented dismissal of six departmental secretaries. It changed the Department of the Prime Minister and Cabinet into a de facto extension of the Prime Minister's political office.

And the government is to blame for the way it has used the armed forces for flag-waving political purposes and seduced senior officers into political service, thereby creating a dangerous void around the ADF.

But the blame does not end with the government and its appointees. It also rests with individual public servants and military officers who did not do their duty in a period of political tension or who found it convenient not to enquire too much.

It is impossible to imagine any reviews of public-service standards and performance being generated from within the government or from central public-service institutions. Such reviews will have to come from self-reflection within the service, from parliamentary oversight and from public and media discussion. And it is essential that that happens.

But the attack on institutions and our conventions is even wider than that.

We have seen a Chairman of the national broadcaster introduce the Head of Government to a political fundraiser.

A Chairman of the Broadcasting Authority campaign with the Prime Minister in an emotive referendum and attack his newspaper critics in public speeches. The same Chairman who is in the press defending the current Governor General in the matters of controversy surrounding him.

The concept that a statutory officeholder owes allegiance to the country and not just the government that appointed him is regarded as simply irrelevant and old-fashioned.

It is not proper and it is not right, but to this government everything is to be chewed up in its determination to win at all costs.

The government lied its way through an election campaign about a matter of central consequence and then sought to stonewall its way out of it. And when Admiral Barrie, the Chief of the Defence Force, finally 'fessed up', the Prime Minister, brazen as brass, said Admiral Barrie enjoyed his full confidence even though Barrie's admission destroyed the integrity of a central factor in the Prime Minister's election campaign.

The Howard government reserves the right to make a hero of a general when it suits them and a fool of an admiral when it suits them. And pawns of the whole Defence Force whenever it fits their convenience.

John Howard does not understand that the moral basis of our politics has to be protected and nurtured. The moral gutting in the way our affairs have been recently run will exact costs down through history. Governments have to be wise enough and decent enough to know that such fraying is hard to stabilise once started, and that such opportunism must be desisted with.

I want to turn now to the reason all this matters. I think the world is changing in ways which will make Australia's environment more dangerous and difficult.

At the end of the Cold War, we found ourselves without a guiding light. We saw the aggregation of great wealth to the liberal capitalist economies and, with it, triumphalism and smugness at their centre.

We let go the remarkable opportunity we had then to remake the institutions of power in the world so they were more representative, to run the international system more cooperatively, to do something about actually getting rid of the world's 31,000 nuclear weapons. It wasn't that these things were too hard, it is that they weren't attempted.

Michael Ignatieff described the post-Cold War period recently as 'a general failure of the historical imagination, an inability to grasp that the emerging crisis of state order in so many overlapping zones of the world would eventually become a security threat', a threat to the contented established order, even to a superpower.

Then came the terrorist attacks of September 11.

I don't believe, as some commentators have claimed, that the world was changed utterly by the terrible events on September 11. On the contrary, I think we got to understand the world better.

It was a reminder to us of JK Galbraith's remarks that the tribulations at the margin of society would eventually upset the contentment at its centre. September 11 made his point compellingly. There were few more contented places than Wall Street.

However, the attacks on the Twin Towers and the Pentagon did profoundly change one very important thing. They gave Americans a new sense of their own vulnerability.

I believe many aspects of the responses to the terrorist attacks were completely necessary. Rigorous efforts to track down the perpetrators of the attacks and those who directed or helped them had to be made.

And I agree with the action taken to prevent such attacks happening in future, including the sort of intervention we saw in Afghanistan.

But I am worried about wider aspects of the United States' response to the September 11 attacks.

Far from tempering the unilateralist instincts of the Bush Administration, the attacks seem to have fuelled them.

The Administration insists that other countries are 'either with us or against us'—and that being 'with us' means saluting smartly whenever the current policy response is announced.

The US conjures up a non-existent 'axis of evil' and demands action to prevent the proliferation of weapons of mass destruction. It's a worthy aim but it ignores the fact that non-proliferation requires de-proliferation.

Yet the Bush Administration has refused to participate in talks on the implementation of the Comprehensive Test Ban Treaty and has announced its withdrawal from the ABM Treaty.

Instead, it will spend billions of dollars on a Missile Defence System that will not do the job it is intended for, but will make the global strategic environment even more dangerous.

All of this works now because of the overwhelming dominance of United States power and its capacity to act on its own in the world at remarkably little risk to its men or its treasure.

But American unilateralism is simply not a sustainable leadership model for the world.

The developed world cannot just take the economic benefits of globalisation—the trade and investment—and ignore the demands from other parts of the globe for a voice and for representation. Such action will simply store up fiery resentment which will eventually manifest itself in ever more dangerous ways.

Australia cannot ignore these dangers.

This is the only nation in the world with a continent of its own. But there are only twenty million of us. Around one-third of the population on the little island of Britain.

Australia will never have the benefit of the unearned weight of size. Unlike China or the United States or India or the EU or Indonesia, we don't have the clout that comes from having a large mass of people.

Australia's national image of itself, and our view of where we are entitled to sit in the international pecking order, was largely set in the nineteenth and early twentieth centuries, at a time when a combination of British imperial power and the Industrial Revolution gave us a privileged international position as commodity producers with secure markets. That world has gone forever.

The way we can best leverage our influence in the world now is through good ideas and the powers of persuasion. And especially and importantly, by remaining good international citizens.

The US Congress cannot make Australian foreign policy, and we would be foolish to want it to. If we are to get this part of an enlarging vision right, we have to stop thinking of ourselves as the 'Orphan in the Pacific', as David Malouf memorably put it, and find ourselves at home here.

I made the point last year at the Labor Party's centenary dinner that the First and Second World Wars meant that for much of the twentieth century, Australia had a British century. I hoped that the twenty-first century would be an Australian century. But John Howard and his conservative supporters are determined to make it an American century by virtually surrendering any real strategic policy independence to the United States and doing it unthinkingly. Surely our sense of nation demands that we have our own role in world affairs, and not allow ourselves to be cast as an extra in the stage play of American unilateralism.

To keep the best notions of Australia bubbling within itself, to keep us from that gated refuge of nothingness, the more we remain members of the great project of humanity the better off we will be, and the happier we will be.

The more we resist arbitrary and parochial distinctions between peoples, the more our security in this great part of the world will be guaranteed and the more our participation in it will be rewarded.

Ours is an age of distraction. The background to our lives is the white noise of inconsequential television programs, pompous pundits, shrill talkback callers, ten-second news grabs, and the cult of celebrity.

In this environment, the need for contemplation and some introspection becomes compelling; a time to stop and think, to make our way, guided by a moral compass, a bearing that divines our best instincts.

Manning understood this. He taught us that the way people think of themselves in the cosmos will affect the way they behave in the physical framework of their lives.

In that last speech I made at the National Library in 1993 I also spoke about Manning. I said that, 'More than any other Australian writer, he elevated Australian history to the point where all of us could say that the story of Australia was part of the universal story—uniquely Australian, but at every stage connected to the world beyond.'

How right Manning has been.

And how vital it is that we understand the importance of that connection now.

3

FILM AND ART IN THE AUSTRALIA OF NATIONALISM AND CYNICISM

Sydney Film School, Palace Academy Twin Cinema,
Paddington,
11 July 2007

Invited to speak at an awards ceremony at the Sydney Film School,
Paul Keating used the occasion to attack John Howard's manipulation
of the term 'elites' and of Howard's identification with the so-called
mainstream as being anti-cosmopolitan. He uses the speech to make
clear the important distinction between patriotism and nationalism—
reminding people that biology, unlike human love, has no charity.

I WAS FLATTERED TO BE asked to speak to such a distinguished group of young film makers.

I should say at the outset that I am not a film goer. That is not to say I do not like films. The films that have made an impression on me were mostly produced during my adolescence and, indeed, some before. Ones which used the medium of film to carry a message.

Too often, these days, the medium is the message, where we are showered with cinemagraphic phantasmagoria, expanded mightily by the boundless development of digital imaging and sound. But we, nevertheless, leave the theatre not that much the wiser for the experience.

Maybe when cinema at large rediscovers the power of writing, performance and direction may we see film return to those deeper messages that were once so much part of its milieu.

There is no question that as a medium, film has the instrumental power to represent a broad range of ideas and opinions.

In the documentary field, let alone in features, film can carry potency which the visual information media lacks. Michael Moore's films on American society and the war in Iraq are cases in point. They provided us important dialogue when demagoguery was firmly afoot.

Art has always been about revelation. And film is an element of the arts. It enjoys a huge ability to reveal things. It may even be true to say that short film, more often than not, carries more truth about it than does its grander cousins.

But it has neither the time nor the budget to indulge in cinema-graphic tricks, relying mostly, as it does, on the poignant delivery of something more recognisable and more real.

Film has become an important part of the arts. The medium for igniting our imagination, of telling us something not only about ourselves, but about the wider world we should otherwise only ponder.

Film is able to bring other cultures to us; indeed, to get inside those cultures so as to present them from their standpoint—from a vantage point we could never ourselves enjoy.

The arts provide a mirror of what we have become and have the ability to let us see ourselves, warts and all, and sometimes, at our finest.

In the modern world, the arts are central to any notion of 'cosmopol-itan-ness' or plurality. The *Oxford Dictionary* describes 'cosmopolitan' as something 'free from national limitations or prejudices; of or from or knowing many parts of the world; consisting of people from many or all parts'.

Art is universal, as film is universal, and that universality informs and educates us while playing to our 'cosmopolitan-ness'.

This is especially true in a country where the antennae or receptors of people are looking for messages, in a country of people 'of or from or knowing many parts of the world.'

It is no secret that the arts are having a very bad time of it in Australia these days: not simply in terms of funding, which is the thing most often discussed, but rather, in terms of the milieu of its growth and prosperity.

One always gets a choice: one can celebrate our cultural diversity and all that enlivens it, or one can lament it, finding comfort in a more monocultural and less cosmopolitan environment.

So, in the current political environment, when the Prime Minister, John Howard, disparages 'elites' over what he celebrates as the mainstream, he is in fact disparaging cosmopolitan attitudes *vis-à-vis* the certainties of the old monoculture, of older-style nationalism.

It has, in a sense, always been thus. A cornerstone of nationalism is a propensity to call into question the motives or to attack the attitudes of other members of the national family.

When John Howard famously advertised his wares in the 2001 election, his advertisements said 'We will decide who comes to this country and the circumstances in which they come'. The 'we', of course, was not meant to be all of us, but only some of us. And the 'some of us' are the people Howard believes are the keepers of the Holy Grail; the sentries at the gates of the true Australia, not the cosmopolitan ones of the so-called elites.

I have long been interested in views George Orwell first promulgated in 1943, when he sought to distinguish between nationalism and patriotism.

In the popular debate, nationalism and patriotism are often regarded as much of the same thing. But, in fact, they are completely different.

Orwell pointed out that nationalism is a notion arising from the myth of a people, whereas patriotism is belief in a particular place and its history. He made the point that nationalism is invariably populist, while patriotism is both traditionalist and inclusive.

The historian, John Lukacs, made the same point. He said 'a patriot will not exclude a person of another nationality from the community where they have lived side by side and whom he has known for many years, but a populist will always remain suspicious of someone who does not seem to belong to his tribe—or, more likely, his kind of thinking'. Shades there of John Howard's discomfort with Australia's multicultural community and his distrust of its Islamic community.

The fact is, nationalism is arguably more exclusionary than racism. It is the generator of those phony and parochial distinctions between the civic and the human community, owing to its propensity and ability to stigmatise cultural, religious and linguistic attributes.

Indeed, Adolf Hitler, perhaps the exemplar populist, wrote explicitly on the subject in his *Mein Kampf*, 'I was a nationalist but not a patriot.' Hitler also said in 1927 in a speech entitled 'Nationalism and Patriotism' that 'we are not national; we are nationalist'. In other words, we are not simply patriotic, we are nationalist, where he distinguished celebration of the state as between cosmopolitanism and the attitudes of the *volk*, the myth arising from the cultural but not cultured mainstream.

The German word '*volksgemeinschaft*' or 'people's' community' identified and defined this primary grouping; in Hitler's terms, his concept of the *volk* as distinct from the German state itself.

In English, the simple translation of the German *volk* is 'people'. But the *volk* were not simply people or *the people*; rather, a community of particular people.

In the reporting of the 'Nationalism and Patriotism' speech, the *Völkischer Beobachter*, the Nazi party's organ, which was edited by Hitler himself, carried the subtitle 'the international cosmopolitanism of the upper ten thousand . . . the dynastic patriotism'. In Hitler's day the term 'elite' had not come into being. Had it had, the nationalist in him would have compelled him to use it, for its easy shorthand, if nothing else.

Margaret Thatcher famously used the phrase 'for all of us' when, at the time, she completely meant for some of us. John Howard's 'all of us' was reduced to the single word 'we' in his infamous 2001 advertisement.

I say this not to suggest or to align, in any way, Margaret Thatcher or John Howard with Adolf Hitler. To do so would be as unreasonable as it would be absurd.

I use Hitler's words in this narrative only to make the distinction between nationalism and patriotism which he himself made. For, importantly, in this context, he was the twentieth century's leading nationalist, its leading anti-patriot.

Lukacs tells us that 'nationalism is atavistically human, deeper and stronger than (merely) class consciousness. The trouble', he says, 'is not only its latent inhumanity, but its proclaimed love of the people'. He makes the point that nationalism is both 'self-centred and selfish' because human love cannot be the love of oneself, it must be the love of another. But not, it seems, for those outside the nationalist tabernacle or 'people's community'.

On the other hand, patriotism encompasses all that is traditional, inclusive and cosmopolitan. It is not biological because the charity of human regard has nothing to do with biology. Nature is biological but nature has and shows no charity.

Let me pull the threads of this short dissertation together.

In political terms, for instance, I am a patriot, I am not a nationalist, for all the reasons I have referred to earlier. John Howard is a nationalist and not a patriot for all the reasons I have also referred to. This is not to say John Howard does not have what we might call patriotic instincts; of course he does, but they all come from his larger carpetbag of nationalism.

For him, Gallipoli was an exercise in nationalism. For me, Kokoda was an exercise in patriotism. The nationalism surrounding the First World War and Gallipoli in particular has fuelled the Australian conservative story for nine decades. The same nationalism that prevented the conservative parties from similarly celebrating Australian heroism in Papua New Guinea and in South East Asia. Those Australians fought for all we had created here and had become, not for some notion of a ruling class or people's community, let alone an empire.

It is no coincidence at all that a predecessor party of the current Liberal Party called itself the Nationalist Party. It was led by another nationalist at the time, Prime Minister Billy Hughes, the Prime Minister most associated with the populism and jingoism of national bravery and sacrifice. The Prime Minister who threw his nationalist cloak and the flag over the long years of the mourning. These days, the conservative rural rump that once called itself the Country Party now calls itself the National Party. Different families of leopards, but always with the same spots.

All this stuff about the swelling chest of a class or group riveted by a superior sense of self is, of itself, nationalist.

Nationalism is, I believe, a dangerous and divisive tendency; its stock and trade is jingoism, populism and exclusion of the most calculating kind.

The catchcry of film in Australia has always been to tell the Australian story. But which story should it tell? The story of Australia's dynamic cosmopolitanism with all its emotional inclusion or the hard-hearted story of a community calibrating others against the smug and self-serving image it has of itself?

The Howard years have been the years of calibration; indeed, years of populist manipulation of Australia's best instincts. The country's moral compass has been recalibrated into the bargain and it is this environment which has been so deadening to the arts.

The arts flourish in times of enlargement and optimism, when the human spirit is off and running and encouraged to do its best. These are not those times in Australia. This does not mean that as individuals you should not do your best. To provide your own narrative on Australian society, but in doing so, resisting the temptation to be part of the arid philosophy that has become part and parcel of John Howard's Australia.

4

4

NEW URBAN DOMAINS
Potsdamer Platz

The Sydney Festival,
Sydney,
23 January 2001

*Paul Keating was invited to open an exhibition on the rebuilding of
Potsdamer Platz in Berlin and the design processes involved. He used
the opportunity to put his perspective on Berlin, a city with which he
had maintained a long interest, from the vantage point of his wider
interest in neo-classicism.*

IN THE RUINS OF BERLIN in 1945, amid the debris, Richard Strauss
mused reflectively on the devastation around him, speaking disconso-
lately of the world he once knew: 'Goethe's house, the world's holiest
place destroyed. My lovely Dresden, Weimar, Munich, all gone!'

Like so many others, he could not understand the fate that had
befallen Germany, the punishment that had been meted out to it.

The world of Germanic spirituality, the reach for new heights, the
revolutionary idiom of Wagner, the science of Einstein and Planck, the
art of Liebermann and Grosz, the writing of Brecht and Zuckmayer,
the architecture of Gropius, the prescience of Mahler, and all that
nurtured it, swept away.

In its majesty and its tragedy, Germany was at once a crucible
of accomplishment and a sink where darker emotions were fed by a
pervasive skittishness and vainglorious ambitions.

4

The German empire, having squandered the legacy of a century of peace in smouldering resentment of its detractors, set about destabilising the very homeland that was Europe.

Few saw the First World War coming, but the artists did. They understood the resonances which the statesmen and the zealots failed to feel. Mahler, who died in 1911, three years before the First World War began, had seen the twentieth century coming. His life's work in composition focused on the titanic struggle between the life force and the death force; premonitions of the gruesome conflicts to come; the carnage and the bestiality and written against one of the most languid backdrops of all history—the century to 1914.

Berlin, the provincial capital of Prussia, seat of Frederick the Great, architectural laboratory of von Knoblesdorf and Schinkel, centre of Bismarck's creation, home of Wilhelmine nationalism, of Weimar's promise and Hitler's Third Reich came to straddle perhaps the most notorious fault line of all humanity.

A small intimate capital nurtured by a generous river and surrounded by lakes, Berlin could have been the subject of a classicist's ideal, of a Caspar David Friedrich or a Turner.

A cluster of baroque and classic buildings huddled around a central tree-lined axis opened by a triumphal gate with canals that gave a hint of Venice, all surrounded by lakes and gentle hills sprinkled with palaces and follies. A fairytale prince's capital. Civil, civilised, structured, full of promise. A place of destiny.

But its destiny was to take some rueful turns.

Bismarck's fastidious statecraft with its balancing treaties and guarantees was to fall prey to crude notions of Junker glory.

The First World War scarified Germany and took away most of its sons.

After the war, the old social order crumbled in an orgy of political fashion and of social debauchery.

The always opportunist right and the old militarists shafted the Weimar Republicans while the country struggled under the yoke of Versailles' reparations and smarted at its humiliation. That was before

Stresemann died and after Rathenau was murdered and before inflation wiped the floor with people's savings.

We all know the next bit. From the chaos came Mr Hitler who, on his first day in office, outlawed legal trade unionism. That story was to end as Russian troops fought a gruesome battle street by street to the Reich Chancery, but only after twenty million of their brothers and sisters had died repelling Hitler's tyranny.

And not before that fateful Saturday in the January of 1942, on a sunny day on the Havel at Wannsee when the Nazis nonchalantly decided to commit the most breathtaking and monstrous crime of all human history: the industrial extermination of a race of people, Europe's Jews.

And where even after the war, at Cecilienhof, the Allies carved Europe in two and consigned two generations to penury behind the Iron Curtain. Only now do they limp into daylight, many too scarred to make anything of it.

Berlin is no ordinary place.

This is not a talk about history but of a grand rebuilding project, part of the rebuilding of Berlin. But I do not believe that one can think about the new Berlin without putting the historic settings into open view.

Its rebuilding cannot simply be the subject of a model urban renewal program or a test bed for the world's architects and city planners; where thinking big or being creative is the only consideration or even giving the Germans back their capital. The new Berlin and its architecture must be set against its turbulent history. Seen in a context wider—and more important—than simply urban renewal.

If you could choose a setting between the two world wars that said much about Europe and its society, I suppose you would have to have the Hotel Adlon in Berlin on the list. Nestled in the corner of Parisier Platz, flanked on its left by the Brandenburg Gate, it was one of the social hubs of the Continent. In the 1920s and early 1930s, over a week, you might have seen political icons like Gustav Stresemann, or Walther Rathenau, or even Max Planck, or Greta Garbo, or Otto Klemperer or Lotte Lenya.

The creative and artistic life of Europe, once hubbed in Paris, had migrated to Berlin. The place was skittish but wired with enormous creative energy. For instance, between the wars the royalty of western music lived and worked there.

Richard Strauss, Ferruccio Busoni, Karl Böhm, Vladimir Horowitz, George Szell, Arturo Toscanini, Arnold Schoenberg, Erich Kleiber, Gregor Piatigorsky, Herbert von Karajan, Rudolf Serkin, Claudio Arrau and Igor Stravinsky lived there. Arthur Nikisch and Wilhelm Furtwängler ran the Philharmonic, Otto Klemperer the Kroll, Erich Kleiber the State Opera and Bruno Walter the Municipal Opera.

Parisier Platz was the elegant forecourt of the Unter den Linden's long axis. Its chic catchment.

Frankly, I doubt it will ever be again. A forecourt, maybe. A place of bustling elegance, I cannot imagine. Today in the new capital, the New Adlon Hotel is about as appealing as an old Hilton. Devoid of originality and the ferment with which it was once invested by Berlin society.

The only concession made in the new plan to Parisier Platz is the pre-war height limitations; the great classic structure of Langhans' Gate now set between two buildings that resemble double stacked mobile homes. Around its perimeter, the architecture has every chance of being pretty ordinary. Dumbed down by those few devices taught in modern architecture schools. Sheer walls, blade walls, windows without architraves, pediments without cornices, etcetera. Raw beams exposed like a good pair of legs at every available opportunity. Mies and Corbu certainly left Berlin, but their spirit still lingers.

Friedrichstrasse, once one of the most elegant and bustling streets in Europe, with its canvas awnings decked out for its summers and pulled together by its variegated architectural homogeneity, is now a cold copy of its old self.

It is a street of architectural brand names. Every architect in the world has been invited to have a go at it. Acres of marble and glass, a canyon to Corning and Carrara, aesthetic flights of fancy curtailed only by height. It is about as inviting and people-friendly as a WalMart after shopping hours. Not even Renzo could strike a note here. But he tried! God bless him.

The French gave back Schinkel's sculptures that adorned his bridge over the Spree—the Schloss Brüche. It has to be one of the most romantic bridges in Europe, but the modernist mausoleum built by the GDR on the site of the Old Palace adjacent to it rains on its parade. And if one turned around quickly, the site of Schinkel's Bauakademie is adorned with another piece of junk also courtesy of the GDR: its Foreign Ministry, obliterating the building which was the model for many from Times Square and Wall Street to Chippendale and Pyrmont.

All along the Unter den Linden the buildings look much as they did in 1838 in Gartner's famous picture which hangs in the nearby National Gallery. Except that their façades were deformed by artillery and pockmarked by shrapnel, many replaced; given a quick makeover in render—their interiors gone. Cavernous spaces given shape by plasterboard or a quick rebuild GDR style, terrazzo abounding. More is the pity but much of it is fake like the interior of Schinkel's Altes Museum. A cost of adventurism and defeat. The patination of one's history suffers.

Today we are to talk about the phoenix at Potsdamer Platz, the gleaming bit of the rebuild.

Let me turn to the exhibition itself, and begin by complimenting the organisers, especially Peter Droege. It is extremely comprehensive and impressive, one of a kind Sydney too rarely sees.

It is an architect's feast and a show for ordinary mortals too.

There are many plans and models and much background provided to the scheme. It is very illuminating.

The scheme itself is ambitious. It tries very hard, and better than most, to establish some of the rhythm of the old precinct, such as keeping to the original street forms, etcetera.

For me, the problem the new Potsdamer Platz has—that is outside the wider problem of Berlin itself—is the classic problem of all large urban renewal programs. They lack that calibrated organic quality that evolutionary architecture and town building brings.

Precincts created in a single stroke—all that is the antithesis of the evolving city.

The old buildings of old cities were scaled to serve a function. Hand-crafted, they were tailored to meet a particular need, each denoting its relative commercial importance. And naturally limited in height by their materials and structure, they lived in genuine harmony with their streetscape despite their undesigned juxtapositioning.

Notwithstanding this scheme's earnest aspirations and, indeed, efforts, it demonstrates how impossible it is to recreate organic human scale precincts at a single stroke, especially when commercial imperatives demand that developments be so grand and so dense.

Architects are constantly confronted with developers' schemes that are too commercially driven for their sites. Potsdamer Platz will stand alone in the historic medium-rise of Berlin, a site where the buildings are too large and too clustered, its periphery not feathered back into anything approaching the old medium rise that surrounds it. Rather than being a part of the whole, it will stand alone.

The precinct is heralded by two commercial high-rise towers which act as a de facto entrance. Potsdamer Platz is going up, when as any aerial photo of Berlin reveals, it doesn't need to. There is much more land around for more medium-height use. Berlin was always generously proportioned.

Piano himself admitted to many of these concerns a couple of years ago when he addressed the Biennial Jerusalem Seminar in Architecture:

Making a scheme for Berlin is an impossible job, although I would never say this in front of my clients. A civilised person is called urbane, even in English, and when we refer to this term, we immediately think about all the beautiful cities that have ever been. We know, however, that they were not designed. They were and still are a product of organic growth. When you walk around these cities, what is beautiful is the very fact that what you are looking at has not been designed. Instead it represents the materialisation of the millions of life stories that have been enacted within their respective walls across centuries.

When you are asked to design a piece of a city, even as little as fifteen buildings, it is really difficult, because you don't have the time to do such a thing. However, being an architect you still accept the challenge to do it . . . Being an architect, especially when you are asked to design a piece of a city, is like being an acrobat. However, if you have grown up in the European humanist atmosphere, you have a net beneath you.

That net had quite a few holes. Le Corbusier's Plan Voisin pour Paris of 1925, fortunately rejected, provides a case in point. It would have utterly changed a large part of central Paris, removing completely any notion of this area remaining part of the organic whole. Cold, dismal and deadening, it provided a lesson in what not to do with a large urban renewal project in an old city.

The new Potsdamer Platz avoids that trap but falls into others by virtue of its scale, density and 'instantness'.

The Potsdamer Platz project gives us the opportunity to ponder whether Berlin, the new capital of the Federal Republic, can become the lively credible place that its champions hope for and that the country, or at least the government, seems to want.

For my part, at one time I thought it might. But I do not believe so anymore, to the extent that I ever thought breathing life back into Berlin was easily capable of accomplishment, or was desirable.

Berlin is now and, I think, will remain a shadow of its former self, in substance and in spirit. A collage of made-over gutted historic sites mixed in with the GDR's greyest and new architecture's finest.

Will the whole add to more than the sum of the parts, creating a flux of its own and a new legitimacy? In short, can Berlin reinvent itself yet again? While much went on in the subsidised and pampered west side of Berlin, you don't get the sense that the whole city, free of its Cold War straitjacket, will—in social terms—come to anything remarkable.

The war and what happened before it not only belted the body of Berlin, it belted the soul out of it. One should not wonder that Berlin has been gasping ever since.

The rebuilding of Berlin is, in a great many respects, a hoax against postwar German history and achievement.

The Bonn republic, in restoring Germany's credibility among the society of nations, garnered its legitimacy through its people's earnest intentions and their profound labours. Bonn in its modest surroundings came to represent all that was real and good about the new Germany, the Federal Republic.

A return to Berlin, to reclaim the capital, is to reclaim it in the name of what? And to reclaim what? The ungainly reunited state, with its great disparities? Its eighteenth or its nineteenth-century romanticism? Prussian intellectualism, Germanic notions of the Second Reich or Weimar's culture? The brief, dark glory of Hitler's '1000 years'? A flicker in the German soul of how much better it might have been, given the chance to start over?

A unified Germany in a uniting Europe can form, as Helmut Kohl saw, the basis for a much more hopeful century on the Continent. But the ghosts in the capital will make the task just that much harder.

Wishful thinking that a reunited Germany embedded in Europe anchored in Berlin can, by its reincarnation, deal with the stain of Wansee or the fact that history's greatest criminal set up shop there? Or that it was the seat of trouble in the two world wars that destroyed Europe, robbing it of the promise and the opportunity of the twentieth century?

The reality is that the new nation of the Federal Republic will begin the twenty-first century in the old capital with its fake buildings and its haunted streets. That dark history. I think it is a pity.

If there was one city in the world that would have been better left in ruin, it is Berlin.

A monument to false notions of glory, to nationalism, to idolatry, to racism, to political criminality. A reminder to all that some places can never be remade. That history cannot be replastered. That a place from where such devastation was wrought and from which such evil sprang should be left to its own haunted spaces.

What people in Australia might call, with reference to Aboriginality, an unsacred site.

A site made sacred by its unsacredness. To be remembered for why it was destroyed rather than the living that went on there in the past. Not that that living was not good. Or that the people were not good. But that some of them were not good and that others were exceptionally bad. That it is fruitless to try and attribute value to particular layers of history and not to others but the sum total of it led to Berlin's destruction in 1945 and attempts to unravel it, to unscramble it, to erase it, by rebuilding it would have best been left untried.

It is, I suppose, a question of weight and meaning and memory rather than utility.

Schinkel's Schauspielhaus with its pediment holed by artillery, its corinthian columns smashed by shrapnel, dangling like stalactites, overgrown with weed, would, I believe, have been more authentic and relevant to its history than it is now with its new cosmetics.

Ditto for ground zero at Potsdamer Platz. It would have better been left uncleared as after 1945.

Piranesian romanticism provides, I believe, relevant instruction when thinking of Berlin. Piranesi scoured ancient buildings seeking to distil their essence, improvising as he went, bringing the buildings to life by reducing their essentials to ruin.

In Berlin in the twentieth century, he would have found a real one. Ruined in pitiless attacks, by an indefatigable enemy seeking an exasperated vengeance.

This exhibition is one about architecture and the city. About a huge rebuilding plan for an old, worn place. It is a discussion of a new vision. But is it the only one? Or the right one?

Let me give another: the Brandenburg Gate pockmarked by shrapnel, twigs growing from its crevices, the Apollonian horses and carriage still forlornly heading skywards.

Down the Unter den Linden, through the rubble of Parisier Platz, the Adlon Hotel squatting in its own decadence. No smart cars, no one in smart dress, just the odd crow providing the banter.

Along the Linden, those young trees planted in the 1930s, now fully grown but deformed.

Tufts of weeds growing from the gutters and between the cobblestones. The craggy presence of the great classic buildings, façades blown away, pediments smashed, columns hanging, nature doing its best to reduce everything further to rubble.

The Arsenal, in its baroque grandeur, stoically holding itself together, its face pockmarked, wearing its classic statuary on its cornice like a crown; all overgrown with moss.

The old Imperial Palace reprieved but still standing; shell-shocked, its grand front to the river shattered beyond recognition. The National Gallery perched high on its rock, intact but burnt back by incendiaries, its doric colonnade sprayed with shrapnel, its egg-and-dart cornices carved away as if by a knife. And across the Spree, Schinkel's Altes Museum, its magnificent frescoed façade charred black by the explosion of that fuel truck. Its Lustgarten obliterated, but its great red granite urn standing proudly unscathed.

When the children looked at such a Berlin they might well have asked: why is the place like this? And they could have been told, without pretence or apology, why. Or they could inquire of another vision, a newer one at Potsdamer Platz, one of spangling buildings and creative invention shooting skyward and the answer would probably be—'This is Potsdamer Platz. It was the subject of an architectural competition where all the world's great architects were invited to contribute and where many of the great corporations are housed.'

And a child replies, 'Oh, I thought Potsdamer Platz was flat, flattened'. And is told, 'It was, but that was long ago.'

5

THE LAUNCH OF
THE HISTORY WARS

Melbourne,
3 September 2003

*The so-called History Wars arose as conservative Australia under
the Prime Ministership of John Howard militantly reacted to and
resisted the philosophies and policies of Paul Keating and his Labor
Government. Eschewing the notions of inclusion, multiculturalism, a
genuine reconciliation, a republic and an integral place for Australia
in Asia, conservative history warriors sought to supplant the Keating
edifice. In this extemporaneous address Paul Keating extols the writing
of* The History Wars *with its interpretive value while taking the
conservative establishment to task.*

THE WRITING OF *THE HISTORY WARS* is very important. The book will
sit on the shelves of libraries as a sort of code stone to help people
understand the motivations of players in today's contemporary debate.
It sheds light on the political battle which is carried on in the pubs
and on the footpaths about who we are and what has become of us.
For the protagonists and antagonists in academe are now surrogates in
a broader political battle about Australia's future.

We should reflect on this: alone, among the peoples of the world, we
have possession of a continent, a continent we laid claim to as part of
an empire, one we expropriated from another race, but a continent that
is no longer an island in a sea of subjugated and colonial places. The

Dutch no longer control Indonesia, the French no longer Indo-China. And the Chinese: well, they now run China for themselves.

We occupy a continent surrounded by ancient societies; nations which have reclaimed their identity and their independence.

The Australian story, for it to be a record of continuing success, must come to terms with our expropriation of the land, our ambivalence as to who we are and our place in the new geopolitical make-up of the region. That is, being part of it, rather than simply being tolerated within it.

History is always our most useful tool and guide. Understanding our past helps us to divine our future.

To see the long strands which denote our character and which have been common in each epoch of our development. And how they might be adapted in our transformation as an integral part of this region, while, at the same time, re-energising our national life.

How do we pick the good strands and the step changes we need to make on the pathway to our security?

Because there are only twenty million of us, the primary matter in our national policy is how we maintain possession of the continent. How we find the pathway to a genuine security, and a naturally reinforcing one. Our security in Asia rather from Asia. Where we are other than a client state perennially searching for a strategic guarantor.

Once, all our faith was in the British Navy. Now it has swung to the American defence establishment.

Those who militantly defend the conservative orthodoxy in Australia see all change as an affront to the past, especially *their* view of the past. Whereas, knowing the past and seeing it for what it is, with all its blemishes, allows us to divine a destiny, for our appointment with reality.

And our appointment with reality is coming around. We are no longer part of some empire. No longer a passenger on the British Lion. No longer protected by their navy, that is, to the extent that we ever were.

While people may say we enjoy protection by the Americans, we have to be clear what this really means.

I have never understood why the Howards and the Blaineys are so defensive. So resistant to novelty and to progress. They are more than conservatives—they are reactionaries.

Conservatives gradually, if somewhat reluctantly, accommodate themselves to change. Reactionaries not only resist change, they seek to reverse it. Understanding and acknowledging the past and moving on to bigger and better things is anathema to them.

They absolutely insist on their view and the lessons *they* see in our history. Yet in their insistence, their 'proprietorialness', their 'derivativeness' and in their rancour, they reduce the flame and energy within the nation to a smouldering incandescence. What they effectively do is crimp and cripple our destiny. Like suffering some sort of anaemia, robbing the political blood of its energy.

The problem for the Howards and the Blaineys is that their story is simply not big enough for Australia.

No great transformation can come from their tiny view of us and their limited faith in us.

Their failure is not simply one of crabbiness; it's a failure of imagination, a failure to read our historical coordinates correctly while moving to a bigger construct, a bigger picture as to who we are and what we might become. That's the real job of political leadership.

Their timidity not only diminishes their own horizon, it is a drag on the rest of us. The country always has to make its progress despite them. Always they have to be dragged along and they will only accept a new norm after someone else has struggled to put it into place.

But the fact is, their view will not prevail. They cannot win because they have no policy framework to win with. And deep in their tiny, timorous hearts they know it.

The undertaking is simply too big for them.

This is why you get all this thrashing about in the press and why we are drenched in the babble of the lickspittles and tintookies who support them. And it's just that: babble. It's babble because at the heart of their wrong-headed campaign is an attempt to contain and censor the human spirit; to muffle, muzzle and vitiate it.

Their exclusiveness, whether we are talking about White Australia in the past or boat people now, relies on constructing arbitrary and parochial distinctions between the civic and the human community. Who is in and who is out. Who is owed possession. Who has rights.

If you ask what is the common policy between the Le Pens, the Terre'Blanches, Hansons and the Howards of this world, in a word, it is 'citizenship'. And it has always been. Who is in and who is out. Who is approved of.

Wolfgang Kasper, writing in *Quadrant*, was brazen enough to instruct us in the 'frictional costs of Australian settlement of Muslims'. An example of the new fascism.

Rather than celebrate the successful multiculturalisation of Australia, they seek to shear people off playing on old prejudices by the use of implicitly negative phrases like 'for all of us', when they really mean 'for some of us'. This is a government that talks in code.

John Howard does not understand that base motivations of these kinds run through a community and a polity like a virus, that these things are poison to a nation's soul. They are part of an anti-enlightenment. John Howard has recalibrated Australia's moral compass, where due north is only for elites, whoever they might be.

A national leader, I think, should always be searching for the threads of gold in a community. Nurturing and bringing them out. Focusing on the best instincts—running with the human spirit and not punishing it.

A growing public morality and probity based on notions of charity and human regard should not be traduced by slurs such as 'political correctness', with implicit support for an official 'incorrectness'. It takes a long time to build institutions and to build new norms of behaviour, new acceptances of protocols in any country. But to build them and then have them traduced is a terrible thing.

Those who want to celebrate only our European past, rejoicing in its prejudices, who want us exclusive and cocooned and who employ division and ridicule, must lose.

Many people are dispirited by this period and they think the Bolts, McGuinnesses, the Devines and the Albrechtsens somehow have the upper hand. In my view they will simply be a smudge in history. What have they put into place which makes any heart skip a beat or which is enduring? Nothing. In the end, there will be no punctuation mark in our annals from their paltry efforts.

The game is too big for them.

This is why those of progressive mind shouldn't despair, arid as this period is. Because in the end, the vapid and heartless messages of the militant conservatives will fail to make headway.

Always confronting them will be these things. Who are we? Can we borrow the monarch of another country perpetually? Can we go to the region and say we've turned a new leaf but, by the way, we never got to a proper basis of reconciliation with our indigenes? How do we find our security in the region rather than from the region? How do we make our multiculturalism work better? How do we make everyone feel as though they belong, that the place, truly is, for all of us?

These questions remain on the agenda; unsatisfied perhaps and unattended. But still sitting there.

I notice people saying this debate hasn't harmed us in Asia. I don't know who they are talking to. The publicity people in foreign affairs departments around the region perhaps, certainly not those who actually run these countries.

The fact is, there are a lot of wise heads in this part of the world, those who see Australia in a longer context and who are waiting for us to recover our equilibrium.

The History Wars rolls out the canvas of this debate. It helps us better understand the battlefield. It provides us with some of the infrared we need to discern the shapes in the current darkness. We owe Stuart Macintyre and Anna Clark for that.

It is with most respect that I launch *The History Wars* and wish it well in its journey to the library catalogues.

6

THE LAUNCH OF
THE LONGEST DECADE

Sydney,
2 June 2006

In co-launching George Megalogenis's book, The Longest Decade,
*a study of the Keating and Howard governments in office, Paul
Keating provides one of his rare written commentaries on the Keating
government and its achievements—its path-breaking reforms—separate
and distinct from those of the Hawke government.*

HISTORY, OF COURSE, IS DIFFICULT to write, if for no other reason, than
that it has so many players and so many authors.

It is hard enough to get any history right, even if one was a principal
player; it is even harder to get it right when one is an observer.

Except with one caveat: the effluxion of time and events presents
epochs as panes or tableaux where the spin, like melting snow, has long
allowed the architecture to speak for itself.

With some time and the context of other events, it becomes possible
to divine a period, especially if one is in the position of knowing some
of the primary facts. And that, of course, is best facilitated by actually
being there.

George Megalogenis's *The Longest Decade* makes this valiant
attempt. And he does so in a detached, stand back-ish and honest way,
seeking to make sense of things for his reader where his pictures are

influenced only by the views he strongly developed during the period about which he is writing.

Some of those views carry the splashed paint of a journalist's quick and imprecise brushwork; impressions that are either over-gilded or shaped by transient myth.

However, the strength of this work is that the writer tries to peel away important leaves of journalistic impressionism, the over-gilding, by seeking to de-myth and demystify some very important developments in our recent national history.

If I had to characterise George Megalogenis's attempts here, I would say his book is about 'myth-busting'. This in itself says something important about him as a writer and about the book as a work.

George came to the Canberra Press Gallery as a young economics journalist in the salad days of my treasurership.

He is a serious fellow who has a good understanding of policy, a keen sense of the macroeconomic imperatives and an eye for the facts at the pointy end of the economic argument.

So naturally, much of the book turns on his interpretation of economic events, though he has attempted to dig deeper and put those economic changes in socioeconomic terms, ascribing certain outcomes to classes of voters and then tracking their movement between the Labor Party and the Coalition.

His observations about trends in such things as property prices, in women joining the workforce, in the changing composition of home and work attest to an inquiring and perceptive mind which is confident enough to step outside the strictly economic terrain.

For my part, I gave George eight or ten hours of time because I thought he was genuinely looking for insight and for truth. And I appreciated the opportunity, to reflect upon the period in my own words.

With a decade beyond my leaving office, George felt confident enough to look back, that far at least, to make some preliminary judgements.

There are some I like and there are some I do not like. There are some I agree with and others I disagree with.

Would I write a better book? Well, of course I would. I write better than George and I know more. But George is not me and he is not John Howard and his third-party view is worth something. Is it worth the world? No. But is it worth something? Indeed, it is.

In a world laced with opinion, sensationalism and dross, George's book is, at once, characterised by its sobriety; its conscientious attempt not to drive the material down his readers' throats. And, its wont to make judgement calls while inviting the reader to consider the supporting arguments.

There is the odd flush of caprice; George took himself out of the Canberra Press Gallery to write this book but he could not quite take the Canberra Press Gallery out of himself.

But let me go to one of the bits I like.

George says at page 183:

*The final year of Keating, and the first year of Howard Mark II . . .
would be the best policy year of Keating's prime ministership; a return
to his Treasury form of the early to mid-1980s. In April, he signed
the competition policy agreement with the states. In May, he turned
the $4.5 billion of tax cuts he still owed voters into superannuation.*

To that George could have added unveiling in the House of Representatives a detailed model for a shift to an Australian republic and later in the year the signing of a security treaty with Indonesia which importantly included ANZUS-like phrases.

George went on to say that my prime ministership had what he called 'five very good policy ideas'. And he listed them in what he thinks is their order of importance.

- *labour-market reform*
- *universal superannuation (those assets should cross a trillion
  dollars any time soon)*
- *engagement with the Asian region*
- *native title, and*
- *competition reform.*

He went on to mention the republic, though he did not mention in this list one of the greatest reforms, and that was the setting into place and the maintaining of, during the recession, the tariff cuts announced in early 1991. Announcing a policy is one thing; sticking with one under stress is entirely another.

Without this change, Australia would never have broken, big time, into the world of internationalism. And our low inflation rate would not have been maintained without the unfettered import competition.

Nor did he mention in his five examples the establishment of the APEC leaders' meeting. An event, at my sole initiative, which built the first and primary piece of political architecture in the Asia Pacific.

To these I could have added the development of Working Nation, the first case-managed, work-obliged, job-subsidised program of any kind in the western world to deal with long-term unemployment. Or reform of the electricity market, creating an interstate grid down the east coast of Australia for the very first time. Or the first standard-gauge railway across the continent, closing the gap between Adelaide and Melbourne.

And all of this happened in four years and three months. Not ten years.

I say I like these points because some of the literature to date characterises me, at that time, as resting on my laurels or being exhausted or running a government which was uncoordinated and unfocused.

Of course, none of that was true. The huge reforms that occurred in the life of the Keating government, as distinct from the Hawke–Keating government, are the ones which have underpinned the fifteen-year expansion:

- the opening up of the labour market with the abandonment of centralised wage fixing
- the complete opening of the product markets with the 2000 'end game' tariff cuts
- the setting up of superannuation as the country's only mandatory and primary savings vehicle, and
- the turbo-charging of Australia's capital market by the lock-in of superannuation with the equities market.

Hopefully, in the end, the facts speak for themselves. The facts that are devoid of spin of the political or journalistic kind.

In these respects at least, George has articulated the facts.

He turns his attention to the recession of 1989–90. He says what made this recession different from all the others is that it carried the name of the Treasurer and not the Prime Minister. But, he said, my taking responsibility for it validated my stewardship of monetary policy because it underwrote the longest decade, extending it by five years to fifteen years; that is, beyond the customary ten-year expansion we seem to have had between recessions.

He says 'wages were held' and we entered a 'golden era of low inflation'.

He is, of course, correct. Entirely correct.

In policy terms, had we not checked demand then we would have been back to where John Howard left us with his recession of 1982. Double-digit wages growth accompanied by double-digit inflation.

There would have been no prosperous 1990s or these, the first five years of the noughties, without the smashing of inflation.

By holding wages with the Accord through 1989 and 1990, while curbing demand, the Labor government, once and for all, broke the dismal legacy of Australia's boom-and-bust history. We de-linked wage blowouts from the expansion and inflation itself from wage booms.

Ian Macfarlane, the current Governor of the Reserve Bank, said as much recently:

> I think that some of the economic interpretations are completely wrong and, even more importantly, the political interpretations are completely wrong. The episode in Australia which returned us to a low-inflation, stable growth economy was regarded as a policy error, whereas in America it is regarded as a policy triumph.

It follows, therefore, that if I am to take the brickbats over the interest rates of 1989, surely then I am entitled to the laurels of the 1990s growth years.

The fact that the Labor Party saw fit not to contest the point in 2004 says more about it than it says about me.

Another bit I like is George's putdown, albeit incidentally, of the Howard and Costello claim that the government I led left the budget in a black hole in 1996.

The fact is, the budget between 1991 and 1996 performed the primary task that was expected of it and should have been expected of it, and that was to support overall demand at a time when private demand had fallen sharply. And to support those people unemployed in the process by appropriate levels of income support.

It is called the natural stabilisers and I told the public that, over time, the budget would 'whirr back into surplus' after 1995–96.

George says, and I quote him, 'the budget behaved as Keating had predicted by swinging dramatically into the black.'

He went on to make clear that, 'the surplus for 1998–1999 was $4.3 billion, not the $1 billion Costello said it would be.

'The following year 1999–2000 it surged to $13.1 billion and would have gone higher had the Howard government not spent the money.'

What George is telling his readers is that there never was a black hole.

Black holes are, of their essence, near irreparable.

What John Howard and Peter Costello did for their political reasons, was to contest the timing as to when the budget should swing back to its natural point of equilibrium. It boiled down to an argument about timing and when the stimulus to the economy from the budget should be withdrawn and at what pace. The proof, though, on the correctness of fiscal policy, was always in the eating and my economy has roared along at just under 4 per cent GDP growth ever since the *One Nation* package kickstarted it back into growth.

The Prime Minister and Treasurer used these hollow arguments to scuttle their own promise to honour my proposed payment of the second round of the LAW tax cuts into superannuation accounts.

There was no shortage of budgetary funds, no macroeconomic reason why savings vested in individuals' superannuation accounts and preserved to age 60 were not qualitatively better than leaving funds on the Cabinet table to be spent opportunistically.

The cost of this paltry decision was to prevent superannuation savings rising from 9 per cent wage equivalent to 15 per cent wage equivalent. That narrow decision lost this country the accumulation on that extra 6 per cent of wages. Had that happened, superannuation assets would now be well on the way to two trillion dollars rather than one trillion, remarkable enough as that figure itself is.

George finishes this episode by posing what he calls a trick question. Who did break the LAW tax cut promise? He concludes, 'it wasn't him [Keating]'. In other words, it was them, Howard and Costello.

There are many, many examples which the book points up.

George reminds people that in February 1992, two months after I took the job, Labor's primary vote stood at 34 per cent and the Coalition at 52 per cent.

He further reminds his readers that I was able to lift that primary vote by eleven percentage points to 44.9 per cent at the election in 1993. In percentage terms, a lift of 33.3 per cent.

He concludes that, 'Fightback! drove the stake through Hawke's leadership', opening up an eighteen-percentage point gap between Labor at 34 per cent and the Coalition at 52 per cent as at February 1992. And he attributes to my One Nation package the lifting of Labor off the floor, getting it back in the game, trailing the Coalition by just one percentage point, 43 to 44 per cent at the end of March 1992, just one month later. This outcome, he says, validated my challenge to Hawke's leadership. I thought it did, too.

George has a few other bons mots I agree with.

He says, 'The 2004 election was the first to be decided by the winners of the open economy.'

I believe that is true.

He then makes a related point.

He says, 'The twist is that the more winners that deregulation creates, the more recruits there are for the Keating agenda.'

By that, he means the socially inclusive, multiculturalist, reconcil-iation-focused, republican-committed, engagement-with-Asia agenda.

He then makes a further and related point. 'After 2004,' he says, 'Keating hoped the penny would drop, that Labor would not return to power without playing to its former strength in the middle and at the top of the income ladder.'

That is precisely what I had hoped.

He is correct in this. For the notion that Labor should play to its base, or more particularly, return to its base—is to return to primary support somewhere in the region of only 37 per cent.

Without recruiting or getting back some of the winners from Labor's new economy, George's middle and top of the income ladder, it is not possible to secure sufficient primary votes to win a national poll.

Perhaps I could finish on this point.

George says, as he nears his concluding thoughts, that 'Paul Keating tried to change Australia; John Howard returned it to what it was.'

That, I believe, is true in the first part but untrue in the second.

I certainly did try to change Australia.

And I hope that at the very core of its economic being, I, in fact, did.

Its economy is among the most open and competitive in the world and it has had the longest continuous phase of low inflationary growth of any other OECD country.

But I also tried to do something else. Something George calls the three Rs.

And this was to re-orient Australia towards its surrounding region; to come to terms with Aboriginal dispossession and reconciliation, and to claim our constitution as our own from the monarch of Great Britain.

On the first of these, the renewed emphasis on Asian engagement, the Prime Minister is only now returning to my policy of a decade ago.

Even John Howard recognises the primary importance of Indonesia to Australia and the need to integrate ourselves further with China and Japan.

Howard walked away from the Aborigines on Wik but he did not destroy my *Native Title Act* because he couldn't. Of that, George

Megalogenis says, 'Keating's contribution is all the more remarkable. He established a system, however complicated, that could not be turned back.'

So, has John Howard returned Australia to what it was? About this, I believe, George is in error. The answer to his question is, I think, 'NO'.

Howard certainly shifted our moral compass. He has bruised our soul. He has played to the basest of human instincts. He has, with his wages policy alone, turned our sense of fairness and egalitarianism on its head.

He has sinned mightily.

But he has not put the stake through the Australian heart that is characterised by its propensity for enlargement. For in time, we will be more integrated with Asia. We will accept reconciliation with all the moral weight it deserves. And we will turn our back on the English monarch, claiming our constitutional arrangements for ourselves.

I commend George Megalogenis and the publisher, Scribe Publications, on this important work and recommend it to any interested person.

I have much pleasure in co-launching the book with the Prime Minister.

7

BALMORAL
Meeting with Her Majesty, the Queen
18 September 1993

*This extract, or 'note for file', was written by Paul Keating in 2001
from handwritten notes he made on the evening of his meeting with
Queen Elizabeth II at Balmoral Castle in September 1993. The notes
were turned into this extract to be part or form part of a comprehensive
history of the Keating government. The extract was supplied to
the prospective author either to be drawn upon or for inclusion as
an addendum. The history never eventuated and the extract went
unpublished. It is included here for its intrinsic historic value. No Prime
Minister of Australia ever told the Queen that the monarchy's service
to Australia had outlived its relevance and that, in its best interests,
Australia should become a republic. Paul Keating did this, in this one
on one meeting with Her Majesty at Balmoral.*

I MET THE QUEEN AT Balmoral at six pm on Saturday, 18 September
1993 in the Victoria and Albert Room, the drawing room of the house,
known to be have been Victoria's favourite.

The Queen told me the room was as Victoria had left it. Furnished
in the manner of William IV, the last remnant of its classicism fallen
prey to its decoration; the looming romanticism that would define itself
by appropriating Victoria's name.

Interestingly, the furniture was not of the age of mahogany, nor the
second age of walnut. It had the colour of a woody lemon reminiscent

of amboyna or Kurelian birchwood, somewhat in the manner of Charles X and faded. Dry, its parched complexion gave the sense the room's earthly moistures had long since vapourised.

The floor was clad in a tartan carpet. Sparse in pattern, its faded blue and green grid resisting being subsumed into its background; a spritely biscuit turned grey by time and wear.

The rather grand desiccation of it all hosting a not-quite-formally-dressed Queen at a most unlikely juncture.

I had come from Australia on the unpleasant errand to tell her, in all her conscientiousness, that we did not need her any more.

I admired the fact she met me alone. Advised but without advisers, she faced what she knew was a conversation about her life's mission: the propagation of the monarchy and its centrality to the states within the realm and to her family. She was to entertain a heretic—delivered to her home by a foreign constituency whose message would call into question all she stood for.

When she looked at me I wondered in the 40 years she had been the monarch how many Prime Ministers she had met. Indeed how many Heads of State, Chief Ministers and Mayors she had had to deal with—this lone woman who had not chosen this role for herself and who very nearly missed it. All that weight and all that time and now the head of the government of the favourite 'dominion' had come to repay the conscientiousness by telling her, as far as Australia was concerned, it was going to come to nought.

I have always had much regard for women in public life as I had for her. In the poignancy of this moment the Queen sat with her dignity and the long history of her family and I with the aspirations and live mandate of a people.

I wanted her to understand how and why Australia had changed, how it was different now than the way she might have found it in 1954 when she first visited.

I reminded her of our former policy of white Australia, how it had come close to marginalising us in a way that South Africa had been marginalised. That we live in the East Asian hemisphere and that for 50 years we had had an ambitious migration program which had changed our character; I told her the monoculture was a thing of the past.

I reminded her of how we had relied on commodities for our national income and how these were now failing us. Our national income had been cut yet we still had to pay our way—and pay it other than by borrowing from the world's savings.

I told her Australia had to engage itself meaningfully with the region around it, which already took 60 per cent of its exports. That our position was not unlike the one Britain found itself in; it had had to make its way with Europe out of economic and strategic necessity. I said Australia had to find its security in Asia not from Asia just as Britain had to find its security in Europe not from Europe.

I reminded her that on our door step stood 200 million Indonesians—the largest Islamic country in the world. Australia had to be relevant in these places. I told the Queen that task was made more difficult when we appeared uncertain as to who we are; when our head of state was not one of us, when we go to the region as the Australian nation with all of our hopes and aspirations yet go with the monarch of another country. With a monarch whom a great number of Australians—especially of non-Anglo descent—feel no association with, nor any affection for.

I told the Queen as politely and gently as I could that I believed the majority of Australians felt the monarchy was now an anachronism; that it had gently drifted into obsolescence. Not for any reason associated with the Queen personally but for the simple reason she was not in a position to represent their aspirations. They were Australian, she was British.

I explained how much people appreciated her efforts down the years and that it was not my wish nor the government's to involve her in any way in the current debate—in a way that would be detrimental to her personally or to her position as Queen of Great Britain. I said I would do all that was possible to conduct the debate along lines that removed her from the fray and that the government would be considering proposals for a constitutional change that could be agreed by the major parties.

I made clear to her that the matter was not about me. Some people may tell her this, or say this, but this was not so. I said I had been given the rump end of a long government which I had managed to extend by winning another term but winning six elections consecutively would be difficult. I told her things had improved from a recent recession but when change seems costless a fickle public may believe change can be made with little risk to themselves or to the country at large. This was not true but many people thought it was. I said you may not be dealing with me but the issue would not go away.

The Queen knew I had come to Balmoral to broach this topic with her and she had sat through what must have been a difficult conversation for her. When I finished my remarks she said, rather plaintively, 'You know my family have always tried to do their best by Australia.' I said, 'Yes, I know that, Ma'am.' She said, 'I will, of course, take the advice of Australian ministers and respect the wishes of the Australian people.'

I said, 'We would expect no less of you and ask no more.'

It really struck me, by her references to her family, how tenuous the hereditary nature of the position was. There was no allusion to a divine right or position of political superiority, any inherent political right. The occasion reminded me of the remark made by John Adams, the American revolutionary and second President, that there were no queen bees in the human hive, that we all arrive the same and are made the same and that it was belittling that any one of us should be 'the subject' of another of us without us having any choice in the matter; the so called consent of the governed. The hereditary nature of the Queen's position, her remoteness from any contemporary mandate, struck me at that moment and at that proximity, as banal; sad even, and what a continuing fantasy she was forced to play out.

Nevertheless, I think, in some way, the Queen felt relieved by the nature and course of the conversation. She had faced up to it and while her Prime Minister might be a republican he was not there to score off her. If it was inevitable, better with someone who had the horsepower to steer it through while keeping her well above it. I had that sense of it.

I said to her that as these conversations go, the norm or protocol was to say nothing publicly about them. On this occasion this would be a mistake. I said it would be much better in the longer term for Her Majesty to let me say that we discussed the issue and that she said she would take the advice of her Australian ministers and respect the wishes of the Australian people. I said to the Queen, once that is said, once that is known, I could elevate her above the battle. But if it is fought out around her and her family as the surrogate for what is good and not good about Australia and its constitutional arrangements, she must be at a disadvantage and maybe not only in Australia.

I said, 'Sir Robert Fellowes (her private secretary) will probably advise you to say nothing and not authorise me to say anything on your behalf. I think this will be wrong advice for you.' She looked at me wanting to believe what I said was correct. In her own way I think she knew I would do my best by her, which subsequently I did.

Later she talked with Fellowes and it was quickly agreed that I should say something.

Things lightened up when I got on to the other business; the 'Waleses' and the timing of their next visit to Australia and for her agreement and an announcement to extend the term of the Governor General Bill Hayden.

The Queen then offered me a whisky—which we were both glad of. Later, dressed down to tweeds, she drove me in a Land Rover to a barbecue in a remote hut that Victoria had built for Albert; lest while hunting for game he was caught unawares in inclement weather. As she steered her way into the night along the rough road and rocky outcrops, I reflected on the singularity of her mission, hoping that she might regard our conversation somewhat philosophically—without otherwise feeling too hurt.

8

THE DECADE OF MORAL EROSION
The Stocktake

Editorials published in the *Sydney Morning Herald* and *The Age*,
November 2007

*On the Friday before the seminal 2007 federal election and on the
Monday after, the* Sydney Morning Herald *and the Melbourne* Age
*invited Paul Keating to contribute pieces for their editorial page. Read
together, they present as an example of the Keating polemic at its
most effective. Paul Keating urges the Australian community to restore
a moral basis to its public life by 'driving a stake through the dark
heart of Howard's reactionary government'. Paul Keating traverses the
structural and institutional inheritances bequeathed to John Howard by
the Hawke and Keating governments and how Howard failed to see the
opportunities and squandered them. The pieces are a reckoning by one
Prime Minister on another; since Howard was Keating's successor. In
this sense the writing is historic.*

22 *November 2007*

THE PRINCIPAL REASON THE PUBLIC should take the opportunity to
kill off the Howard government has less to do with broken promises on
interest rates or even its draconian WorkChoices industrial laws, and
everything to do with restoring a moral basis to our public life.

Without this, the nation has no standard to rely upon, no claim that can be believed, not even when the grave step of going to war is being considered. When truth is up for grabs, everything is up for grabs.

Cynicism and deceitfulness have been the defining characteristics of John Howard and his government. They were even brazen enough to corrupt a United Nations welfare program for the provision of Australian wheat. And when they were found out, not one of them accepted ministerial responsibility. Not Downer, not Vaile and certainly not Howard. What they were doing was letting the cockies get their wheat sold through the Australian Wheat Board (AWB) while turning a blind eye to the AWB's unscrupulous behaviour, illegally funding a regime Howard was arguing was so bad it had to be changed by force—the regime of Saddam Hussein.

John Howard took us into the disastrous Gulf war on the back of two lies. One, that Iraq possessed weapons of mass destruction, capable of threatening the Middle East and Western Europe; the other, that Howard was judiciously weighing whether to commit Australian forces against an evolving situation. We now know he had committed our forces to the Americans all along.

If the Prime Minister cannot be believed, who in the system is to be believed?

When Opposition leader in 1995, Howard told us he would restore trust in government, when trust in government was not in question at that time. He also told us he would make us more 'relaxed and comfortable'. Well, some relaxation and some comfort. These days, there are many parts of the world where Australians dare not go. Something new for us all.

But bad as all this is, how much worse was it for John Howard to begin the fracturing of his own community?

His tacit endorsement of Pauline Hanson's racism during his first government, his WASP-divined jihad against refugees—those wretched individuals who had enough faith in us to try and reach us in old tubs—while his wicked detention policy was presided over by that other psalm singer, Philip Ruddock.

This is the John Howard the press gallery in Canberra went out of its way to sell to the public during 1995. The new-made person on immigration, not the old, suburban, picket-fence racist of the 1980s—no, the enlightened unifier who now accepted Australia's ethnic diversity; the Opposition leader who was going to maintain Keating Labor's social policies on industrial relations, on superannuation at 15 per cent, on reconciliation, on native title, and on the unique labour-market programs for the unemployed. Even on Medicare. And on that, contrary to his commitment, he forced each of us into private health or carry the consequences.

These solemn commitments by Howard which helped him win the 1996 election bit the dust under that breathtaking blanket of hypocrisy he labelled 'non-core promises'.

During the 1996 election campaign, a number of people I regard well said to me, 'Oh, I think Howard will be all right'; meaning, while not progressive, he would not be reactionary or socially divisive, or opportunistically amoral.

Well, Howard wasn't 'all right'. He has turned out to be the most divisive Prime Minister in our history. Not simply a conservative maintaining the status quo, but a militant reactionary bent upon turning the clock back. Turning it back against social inclusion; cooperation at the workplace; the alignment of our foreign policies towards Asia; providing a truthful and honourable basis for our reconciliation; accepting the notion that all Prime Ministers since Menzies had—Holt, Gorton, McMahon, Whitlam, Fraser, Hawke and me—that our ethnic diversity had made us better and stronger; and that the nation's leitmotif was tolerance. Howard has trodden those values into the ground.

He also trod on the reasonable constitutional progression to an Australian republic, even when the proposal I championed had everything about it that the Liberal party could accept. A president appointed by both houses of Parliament, meaning by both major parties, while leaving the reserve powers with the new head of state as the Liberals had always wanted. The price of Howard conniving in its defeat will probably mean we will ultimately end up with an elected head of state, completely changing the representative nature of power and of the Prime Ministership and of the Cabinet.

To compound Howard's transgressions, he has run dead on the continuing obligation of structural economic change, just like he did as Treasurer in the 1970s. He and Costello have simply made hay while the sun has shone from the great structural reforms introduced by the Hawke and Keating governments. Those changes—open financial and product markets, the new decentralised wages system of 1993—were married up with a trillion dollars in superannuation savings to completely underwrite the country's prosperity and renew its economic base.

Howard's sole example of reform is his GST. The one he told us in 1996 he would not give us. A regressive tax on all spending regardless of income.

Nations get a chance to change course every now and then.

When things become errant, a wise country adjusts its direction. It understands that it is being granted an appointment with history. On this coming Saturday, this country should take that opportunity by driving a stake through the dark heart of Howard's reactionary government.

26 November 2007

On Saturday night when it was clear the Howard government had been defeated, many Labor supporters around me said, 'You must be so happy'. But my emotion was not one of happiness, rather, it was of relief.

Relief that the nation had put itself back on course. Relief that the toxicity of the Liberal social agenda, the active disparagement of particular classes and groups, that feeling of alienation in your own country, was over. And, over in the only way that could be final: with a resounding electoral instruction of 'no more'.

In the Sydney *Sun Herald* last Sunday, John Howard nominated the putting asunder of political correctness and the celebration of our Anglo-Celtic past as the pinnacle of his social, indeed national, achievement.

In making the claim, he was nominating as a virtue political incorrectness of a kind which gave some the right to speak and behave towards others in terms disparaging of their colour, religion, class or social standing. In a country of immigrants, such a view emanating from the Prime Minister is social poison.

Saturday night's victory was not just a victory for the Labor party, it was also a victory for those Liberals like Malcolm Fraser, Petro Georgiou and Judi Moylan, who stood against the pernicious erosion of decent standards in our public affairs.

The Liberal party of John Howard, Philip Ruddock, Alexander Downer and Peter Costello is now a party of privilege and punishments. One that lacks that most basic of wellsprings: charity.

The French philosophers had it pretty right with the Enlightenment catch-cry of liberty, fraternity and egality. There was not much liberty for the boat people or fraternity for the Aboriginals or the Moslems or egality for the trade unionist who believed in nothing more revolutionary than the simple right to collectively bargain.

John Howard says that he was the progenitor, the giver, of the last eleven years of economic growth and without him or Peter Costello, the growth would evaporate.

This election result means that the public didn't believe him—otherwise, they would not have repudiated him. They knew it took more than simply being around and spending up big to create the conditions which have underwritten the longest economic expansion in our history.

John Howard's greatest inheritance from the Labor party was low inflation, the factor which above all others provided the golden thread through each of those sixteen years of growth.

When John Howard decided to go after workers with his WorkChoices legislation, he did so not out of any economic necessity, as the economic record for wages and inflation attests. He did it simply to break the back of the unions. His motivations were ideological and spiteful, telling us he had learned nothing from the fact that there had been no wages breakout in Australia since the one he detonated 26 years earlier.

Howard proudly mentions his GST as an example of reform, yet its great harvest of money was not spent on education or health or infrastructure. It was largely spent on giveaways, which means it was not necessary in the first place. So cynical was Howard about it he forbade the Treasury from accounting for it in the Budget papers, even though it is collected as a federal tax and allocated under Commonwealth policies.

When I turned over the Prime Ministership to John Howard in 1996, the opportunities presented to him, as the century closed, were unprecedented.

A new-made economy, with open financial, product and labour markets for the first time in our history. Five years' growth already behind us, at an average inflation rate of 2.5 per cent. A universal and compulsory superannuation system, where the previous Labor government had encouraged workers to save 9 per cent of their wages for their retirement. A framework for the movement to an Australian republic with a model designed for acceptance by the Liberal party.

A set of new international relationships abroad, especially with Indonesia and China, with Australia sitting as the founder of the major piece of political architecture in the Pacific, the APEC Leaders' Meeting.

As we turned into the new century, what did John Howard do with these new opportunities? The short answer is, he squandered them.

He took a knife to the new enterprise-bargaining wages system the moment he got control of the Senate. He left superannuation jammed at 9 per cent of wages after promising to maintain the commitment I had made to take it to 15 per cent. He connived in the defeat of the republic referendum so that now we are more likely than not to have King Charles and Queen Camilla as our heads of state, as ludicrous as that would be. His triumphalism over Timor destroyed the relationship Labor had built with Indonesia which probably can't be rebuilt, or if it can, only after decades. He attended every APEC Leaders' Meeting since 1996, but brought not one new idea to it, not even to his own meeting in Sydney this year.

In the end, John Howard didn't understand how great his opportunity was and how it could not be advanced by regressive and reactionary policies fuelled by social exclusion and division.

Let us hope the Liberal party purges itself of its reactionary majority, for Australia cannot afford another Prime Minister like John Howard.

9

THE LAUNCH OF
CHURCHILL AND AUSTRALIA

Sydney,
30 October 2008

Graham Freudenberg invited Paul Keating to launch his Churchill
and Australia *as they both recognised Churchill's unique relevance to
Australia. Paul Keating had often said that regard for Churchill and his
life was the main reason he himself had taken on a political vocation.
Both men are taken with Churchill's moral clarity and principally his
'rejection of the devil's bargain (with Hitler).'*

GRAHAM HAS DONE ME THE honour of asking me to launch his book,
Churchill and Australia, a request he made of me about a year ago.

He has produced a marvellous and important work about the person
who, more than any other world leader, was central to Australian
fortunes in two world wars: Winston Churchill.

The book, as we might expect, is extensively researched and beauti-
fully written, though its innate beauty arises more from its honest quest
for truth than necessarily its prose.

John Lukacs, the American historian, wrote that 'there can be no
good history that is not told or written well'.

Graham's *Churchill and Australia* qualifies in both respects.

Graham's storylines are long and colourful and crocheted as simply
or as complexly as the events they are describing demand. It is enjoyable

to see a political storyteller turn his hand, so confidently and so persuasively, to so specialised and yet so grand a narrative.

From the period of our Federation through the following half-century, Britain was the country with which we were most engaged and its empire was the structure on we which we so fervently relied and rejoiced at inclusion in.

We did not know and could not have known that the Edwardian period was to be the zenith of Britain's long international history and that the First World War effectively ended its primacy in the world. Nor could we have known that the seeds of the Second World War had been sown in the settlement of the first and that the second conflagration would involve us as comprehensively as had the first. And that one person, above all others, would be common to the events of both epochs and to the fortunes of Australia and Australians. That person, of course, the subject of Graham's book, Winston Churchill.

Graham pretty well sums up Churchill and his view of Australia at the opening of his book, in its prologue, and at its closing, at its last page. In the prologue he says:

Churchill's involvement with Australia, unparalleled by any other British leader, covered and influenced every stage of our transition from a dependent colony of the British Empire to a dependent ally of the United States. From beginning to end his primary interest in Australia lay in its capacity to contribute to Britain's military strength, on which he believed everything else depended.

And at the last page Graham writes:

Incomparably, Winston Churchill thought more about Australia and more about what Australia thought of him than any world leader before or since, or ever will again.

Churchill had spoken of his 'solemn responsibility to the Australian people'. Graham asks 'which foreign president or prime minister will ever write 'my solemn responsibility to the Australian people', with half so good a will as Churchill did?' And he goes on to say that in the disputes with Curtin in 1942 'the essential difference between Churchill and Roosevelt was that Churchill genuinely believed that Australian interests, however waywardly he interpreted them, counted for something in the common cause [whereas] Roosevelt did not'.

Graham approvingly quotes Menzies as saying 'as for all of Churchill's ambivalence and contradictions, none was as great and powerful a friend as he was'. To which Graham adds 'we shall not look upon his like again'.

These are not the words or the sentiment of a snarling nationalist, unable or unwilling to recognise the integrity of a man set against the backdrop of his own times and history.

To say that Graham Freudenberg has been fair to Churchill in this analysis of his relationship with Australia would be to way understate the decency and objectivity with which he has treated him.

Graham's motivation for his early and express invitation to me to launch this important work only became apparent to me as I started to read my way through his book. I think he wanted me to know that, even through the prism of Australia, his ambivalence towards Churchill did not blind him to Churchill's greatness. The same view that I have long held about Churchill myself.

I have said on many occasions, unlikely as it might be for a Labor person to say, that the inspiration for my entry into public life, and into the Labor Party itself, came from Churchill. Nominally, a classic Edwardian and a British conservative. But as we know, more than that.

I was attracted to him for his braveness, sense of adventure, compulsion and moral clarity. That at the most important moment of his political life and probably in Britain's history, upon assuming the prime ministership, he was being prevailed upon by his Conservative Party benefactors to trade with Hitler. More than that, to keep the prime ministership, he would be expected to trade with Hitler. And his resounding 'no' to that demand turned out to be the fatal spike in Hitler's scheme of tyranny, leading, as it did, to the salvation of Western Europe.

As Graham says, 'Churchill's rejection of this devil's bargain is his eternal greatness'. He makes the point, correctly, that 'Hitler wanted to recruit the British Empire as an accomplice in his criminality on a world-wide scale.'

A lesser political figure would have gone along with his party and the establishment he belonged to. Hitler had held out the prospect of Britain retaining sovereignty over its islands and its empire, without military conflict, an outcome appealing to Britain's upper class, including, as we now know, the then Queen.

As Graham notes, Churchill's strategy never varied. It was, that if Britain held control of its island, that if the moat of the English Channel and the North Sea could be reinforced and maintained, then Hitler could never win his war. And that the principal role of Australia in that strategy was to militarily reinforce Britain.

If any one of us were to occupy the prime ministership of Britain in May 1940, with the British Army holed up in Calais and Dunkirk waiting upon Hitler's death blow, with France capitulating and the Dutch queen seeking refuge in London, would it be unreasonable to worry about reinforcements?

By that stage, of course, the matter had became tribal, leaving scant place in Churchill's mind for niceties as to the views of the so-called dominions. We should remember this was more than two years before Japan showed its hand in the Pacific.

For all that, the two most obvious Australian strikes against Churchill remain Gallipoli and his 1942 disagreement with Curtin as to the defence of Australia. To that we may add his promise of protection by strength of the fortress of Singapore.

Graham writes that 'No event in Australian history is more closely associated with Churchill, with praise or blame, than the Gallipoli campaign of 1915'.

On all the evidence since, I think it is reasonable to say that Churchill did overcook the arguments in favour of a naval and infantry campaign against Turkey in the Dardanelles Strait, with the object of control of Constantinople, the modern Istanbul. It is even worth arguing, as Graham argues, that Churchill drove the Turks into the arms of the Germans when he requisitioned and seized control of the two dreadnought battleships which the Turks had ordered from British yards and had already paid for.

Indeed, it may even have been that a phalanx of British battleships both old and new was unable to take out the Turkish forts. It was certainly true that control of the Gallipoli peninsula was not capable of realisation without infantry and that the Turks had been put on red alert when Britain had earlier tried to mine the mouth of the Dardanelles.

But Graham makes this powerful point:

> *Asquith was the cleverest British Prime Minister of the twentieth century. Kitchener was hailed as the greatest British soldier since the Duke of Wellington, and Lord Fisher the greatest British seaman since Lord Nelson. Churchill became the greatest wartime Prime Minister in British history. Between them, they produced Gallipoli.*

They did produce Gallipoli. But with the Western Front in a quagmire and standstill and given Australian loyalties to 'King and country', it was entirely explicable that we would be there to help, including at Gallipoli.

So our motivations were, as Graham notes, divided by nationalism and imperialism; between loyalties to the empire and a desire for a more independent Australia. Importantly, he suggests that 'Churchill's ambivalence about Australia was a mirror image of Australia's ambivalence about itself'.

On the one hand we were out to prove that 'the British race in the antipodes had not degenerated' yet we resented being dragooned into a war which did not threaten our own country or its people.

As Graham says, 'In an almost theological sense, Australian Britons had been born again into the baptism of fire at Anzac Cove', questioning, somewhat tongue in cheek, whether we needed being reborn at all.

The 'reborn' part went to a lack of confidence and ambivalence about ourselves. Who we were and what we had become. If our sons suffered and died valiantly in a European war, such sacrifice was testament to the nation's self-worth.

In some respects we are still at it—not at the suffering and the dying—but still turning up at Gallipoli, the place where Australia was needily redeemed.

The truth is that Gallipoli was shocking for us. Dragged into service by the imperial government in an ill conceived and poorly executed campaign, we were cut to ribbons and dispatched.

And none of it in the defence of Australia. Without seeking to simplify the then bonds of empire and the implicit sense of obligation, or to diminish the bravery of our own men, we still go on as though the nation was born again or, even, was redeemed there. An utter and complete nonsense.

For these reasons I have never been to Gallipoli and I never will.

One of the most powerful parts of the book goes to what Graham calls Churchill's overheated reaction to Curtin's 'looking to America' message of January 1942. Graham contends that this episode distorted Churchill's relationship with Australia for the rest of the war and beyond. He says 'the root of the trouble lay in an irreconcilable outlook'; namely, 'Curtin could never accept that Australia's fate must be completely subordinated to Churchill's grand strategy'. And that he stung Churchill by saying 'we know that Australia can go and Britain can still hold on'. Graham writes that the sting came from the fact that Churchill knew in his heart that 'not only was this true, but that his own policy had made it true'.

In his Second World War history, Churchill wrote that the Australian government had a duty to 'study their own position with concentrated attention' but, he said, 'we had to try to think for all' while 'observing a true sense of proportion in world strategy'. In other words, the grand strategy warranted primacy, notwithstanding the seriousness of the parochial peril.

On 26 January 1942, in a public address on Australia Day, Graham records that Curtin said, among other things, that 'no single nation can afford to risk its future on the infallibility of one man and no nation can afford to submerge its right to speak for itself because of the perceived omniscience of another'. There were no marks for guessing who the one man was.

But what really got Churchill's goat was Curtin writing to him about arrangements being worked out between Roosevelt and Churchill and their military chiefs. Curtin told Churchill that Australia had been left in the cold and that 'our chiefs of staff are unable to see anything in these proposals except the endangering of our safety'.

Curtin communicated to Roosevelt, as Graham records, three seminal paragraphs which changed the course of Australian foreign policy.

Without inhibitions of any kind, I make it quite clear that Australia looks to America, free of any pangs as to our traditional links or kinship with the United Kingdom.

We know the problems that the United Kingdom faces. We know the constant threat of invasion. We know the dangers of dispersal of strength, but we know, too, that Australia can go and Britain can still hold on.

We are, therefore, determined that Australia shall not go and we shall exert all our energies towards shaping of a plan, with the United States as its keystone, which will give our country some confidence of being able to hold out until the tide of battle swings against the enemy.

Graham wrote that, 'The Greatest Living Englishman left no doubt about his own thinking: "I hope there will be no pandering to this," he cabled Attlee, "while at the same time we do all in human power to come to their aid." To Lord Cranborne, he categorised the article as "misbehaviour". He claimed in his memoirs that Curtin's article had been "flaunted round the world by our enemies"'.

Graham's extract on this episode is probably the best of any in the book. He writes:

Curtin's offence was compounded by its timing. Churchill saw it as an impertinent intervention by a colonial politician who did not truly represent his own country. In his eyes, everything was wrong about the message: a gift to German and Japanese propaganda; a challenge to his political position in Britain; yet another Australian attempt to seat itself in the British War Cabinet and now a bid for the Anglo-American high table; an unwarranted assertion of

Australian independence; a weakening of the unity of the Empire; an ill-timed exposure of the bankruptcy of three decades of British Far Eastern strategy; an affront to his honour as the man who had given his pledged word about the rescue of the kith and kin; an insult to the efforts that even now he was making on their behalf; a competitive bid for American aid; a threat to the 'beat Hitler first' strategy; and an infringement of his monopoly with Roosevelt as the voice of the Empire.

For all of Churchill's undertakings, Curtin knew the Singapore guarantees, though conscientiously given and solemnly meant, were either unenforceable or rapidly becoming unenforceable .

Over Christmas 1941, he made the historic turn to the United States, forsaking the covenants of Empire. For the first time, he lifted Australia's interests beyond the general, to their appropriate point of primacy.

A history of these subjects and of this kind needed to be written. Of its essence, Graham Freudenberg's book is a history of Australia's relationship with Britain during the Imperial period.

In some ways, Graham has employed Churchill as a prop to tell a wider story of the two nations.

But Australia's relationship with Winston Churchill, for good or for ill, is one of the defining aspects of Australian history, especially as it related to our involvement in the two world wars.

The Imperial period, covering the first half of the twentieth century was the time when what happened in the British Foreign and Dominions office set the scene for policy in Australia. Those days are now well over.

These days Australia makes its own foreign policy. No longer do we subscribe to the Richard Casey view that 'the foreign policy of Great Britain is the foreign policy of Australia'.

The key point being that it is incumbent upon us to construct a foreign policy in our own interests. And just as the twentieth century was the British century for Australia, we should not allow the twenty-first century to be our American century, notwithstanding the flying start John Howard made for us in respect of the latter.

People may say, well, of course that is now the case. Yet Graham makes a telling point in the book, indeed an exceptional one, when he reminds us that Australia declared war on Japan before Britain declared war on Japan. Where before, according to form, we would have otherwise tagged along. And, as it turned out, upon that declaration, Prime Minister Curtin wrote to the King instructing him that his Australian ministers had declared war on Japan and that acting on the advice of his ministers, the King was also at war with Japan. That was, the King of Great Britain, George VI.

This would be akin to the Australian government of today declaring war on another state and advising the Queen of Australia, also the Queen of Great Britain, that she, too, on the advice of her ministers, was at war with that country. Underlining again, if it needs underlining, that the earlier our head of state has interests entirely coincident with our own, the better it will be for us and Queen Elizabeth II, her heirs and successors.

Churchill was, as the historian John Lukacs said, 'uncharacterisable'. He said most of the political establishment distrusted him because he was the kind of person whom mediocrities instinctively fear.

A biographer, Roy Jenkins, wrote that Churchill's aristocratic background never governed his career. 'Churchill was too many-faceted, idiosyncratic and unpredictable a character to allow himself to be imprisoned by the circumstances of his birth.' In an entirely different setting, I should say 'hear, hear' to that.

But there is another side to Churchill, an important one worth making reference to: his magnanimity.

Churchill could be overbearing, truculent and even petty but never mean. That good mind was also a fair one.

His fight with Curtin was about his management of the war and his priorities; it was in no way about punishing or ostracising Australia.

Indeed, immediately after the war he was advocating the cause of a united Germany. In 1946 he was promoting reconciliation between France and Germany. In the same year at Fulton in Missouri he was decrying the division and the isolation of the East European states.

In the early 1950s, as the Cold War got going in earnest, he was arguing a place for the Soviet Union in the new world order, including a place for it in Europe.

In 1948, in a famous speech given at The Hague, he advocated a European Union Congress to provide political and functional unity to Europe.

He could have been excused for thinking that after six years of punishing conflict with Germany and Britain's chance victory, that he should have been all defensive and recriminatory. But not him. His magnanimity and judgement frogmarched him on to even more expansive campaigns.

As Graham says, we shall not look upon the likes of him again.

Principally, he had the temperament of an artist, from which sprang his boundless imagination.

Leadership, after all, is as I have so often remarked, about two things: imagination and courage. The imagination to see the bigger picture, to make sense of it and to imagine something better; and having the courage to see the changes through. Churchill had these qualities in spades.

As he said, as a young minister, to Asquith's daughter, Violet Bonham Carter, musing over things after a dinner, 'you know Violet, in the end, we are all worms, but I do believe I am a glow worm'. He was a glow worm and he lit up the most miserable epoch of the miserable twentieth century like no one before or after him.

I congratulate Graham on his book, for undertaking such a huge task, 600 pages, and for fulfilling it with such commitment and élan.

Let me also thank the publisher, Macmillan, for encouraging and publishing such an important work.

It is my very great honour to launch *Churchill and Australia*.

10

THE LOWITJA O'DONOGHUE ORATION

Don Dunstan Foundation,
University of Adelaide,
Adelaide,
31 May 2011

*Paul Keating's Lowitja O'Donoghue Oration was his first major speech
on the subject of native title since he introduced the Native Title Bill
eighteen years earlier, in 1993. The Oration presented him with a
number of opportunities: to underline that the development of the Native
Title Bill arose from the first ever full consultation and negotiation
between the Aboriginal community of Australia and the Government of
Australia; that that negotiation was led by Lowitja O'Donoghue; that
notwithstanding that no progress had been made on national legislative
land rights in the then 204-year history of the settled nation, the Native
Title Act received the Governor General's assent just eighteen months
after the High Court's historic decision. Moreover, that the Native
Title Act dealt with the longest continuing problem Australia faced as
a nation: the fundamental colonial grievance, the dispossession of its
indigenous people and the injustices inherent in that dispossession. Paul
Keating made use of the Oration to point out how a more conservative
High Court had treated native title as an ordinary exercise in statutory
interpretation, cutting across the spirit of the Keating government's
legislation, with its fidelity to the Mabo judgment principles. He reminds
his audience that native title is not a creature of the common law, nor a
common law title but an ancient title recognised by the common law.*

I KNEW DON DUNSTAN, THOUGH not well. But I admired him for his ability to see through the conservative social orthodoxy which had developed as part and parcel of Australia.

Don Dunstan used the premiership of South Australia to challenge elements of that orthodoxy, so I am pleased to be associated with his spirit and this foundation in his name. And well may it be the case that Don Dunstan's progressive instincts, reflected in the Foundation's remit, should sponsor an oration in the name of another South Australian progressive, Lowitja O'Donoghue.

I have accepted the opportunity of delivering the Lowitja O'Donoghue Oration for one primary reason: out of respect for Lowitja O'Donoghue as a remarkable Australian leader. A leader whose unfailing instinct for enlargement marks her out as unique.

And unique for this reason: when a great opportunity in history, the history of the Aboriginal people and the largely European population of Australia presented itself, Lowitja O'Donoghue saw that opportunity with great clarity and unilaterally moved to seize it. The opportunity was the willingness of the Labor government I led to legislatively validate and develop the decision of the High Court of Australia in *Queensland v Mabo* (1992), today known as *Mabo (No. 2)*.

Without any position of mandated authority from her people, she caused their mobilisation in what was, the first time, that Aboriginal people were brought fully and in an equal way to the centre of national executive power. In the 204-year history of the formerly colonised Australia, this had never happened. Never before had the Commonwealth government of Australia and its Cabinet nor any earlier colonial government laid out a basis of consultation and negotiation offering full participation to the country's indigenous representatives; and certainly not around such a matter as the country's common law where something as significant as native title rights could arise from a collection of laws which had themselves developed from European custom and tradition.

The High Court of Australia had opened the door to this possibility in *Mabo (No. 2)*, but without a comprehensive, firm and quick legislative response, that door would have just as quickly closed. Most of the states of Australia had adopted a defensive posture to the opportunity of Mabo while Western Australia would have moved to extinguish whatever native title rights were revealed by the High Court's historic judgement, as it, in fact, tried to do.

Lowitja O'Donoghue understood this. She knew that in the dismal history of indigenous relations with European Australia, this was an illuminated breakout, a comet of light in an otherwise darkened landscape.

Many people here tonight will know the history, or some of it. They will know that no one person or group of persons was ever mandated to assume the authority of or to act on behalf of the whole indigenous community. They will know that attempts to so act were often met with reaction and derision. They will know there was no premium for assuming or even attempting to assume such a mantle of leadership. They will also know that in respect of the Keating government's first offers of consultation around the issue of a proposed native title act that many Aboriginal leaders rejected the entreaties of the government out of hand. They will remember the meetings at Eva Valley and Boomanulla Oval in Canberra; they will remember the rancour. They will also remember me saying, as Prime Minister, that 'I doubted whether indigenous leaders would ever psychologically make the change to come into a process, to be part of it, and to take the burden of responsibility which went with it—whether they could ever summon the authority of their own community to negotiate for and on their behalf'.

I like to think those remarks helped galvanise Lowitja O'Donoghue's view as to what needed to be done. But as it turned out—only she could do it. She was the chair of ATSIC. This gave her a pulpit to speak from but no overarching authority, much less power. But this is where leadership matters: she decided, alone decided, that the Aboriginal and Torres Strait Islander peoples of Australia would negotiate, and I emphasise negotiate, with the Commonwealth government of Australia—and that the negotiators would be the leaders of the indigenous land councils. She decided that. And from that moment, for the first time in the 204-year history of the settled country, its indigenous people sat in full concert with the government of it all. This is why I am here tonight: to acknowledge that moment of leadership and to celebrate it.

Of course, Lowitja had helpers. Principal among them was David Ross, a director of the Central Land Council, a leader in his own right and a weighty judge of circumstances. She had Peter Yu from the Kimberley Land Council. She had Rob Reilly from the Legal Service of Western Australia, Noel Pearson from the Cape York Land Council and Gétano Lui from the Island Coordinating Council.

She had, in those important earlier stages, the support and advice of Pat and Mick Dodson, Chair of the Council for Aboriginal Reconciliation and Social Justice Commissioner, respectively. And she had others who came to the process a little later: Darryl Cronin from the Kimberley Land Council, who effectively became secretary to the negotiating group, Darryl Pearce from the Northern Land Council and Marcia Langton, who fulfilled an important general advisory role.

Indeed these people, or most of them, also attended with Lowitja the first Mabo ministerial meeting which I chaired, as Prime Minister, in the Cabinet room Canberra, on Tuesday, 27 April 1993.

Had Aboriginal and Torres Strait Islander leaders not stepped up to the plate, the substance and equity of the subsequent *Native Title Act* may never have materialised. In an instant, I was struck by the opportunity of the High Court decision and was determined to not see it slaked away in legislative neglect. But determined as I was, I needed the partnership with indigenous leaders to get it done and get it done fairly.

We know, sadly, that the history of Aboriginal and Torres Strait Islander land rights had been broadly a shameful one. Not only from earlier High Court decisions implying that all native title rights to land were extinguished at sovereignty, but by unfulfilled promises by a clutch of otherwise well-meaning governments. Save for Gough Whitlam's Northern Territory Land Rights Bill of 1975, passed into law by Malcolm Fraser in 1976, which was, of course, confined to Northern Territory lands, there had been no exercise of the power under the 1967 constitutional amendment in favour of comprehensive land rights.

In 1983, the Hawke government promised a national land rights bill which included an inalienable freehold title and compensation for past acts and alienations. But this promise of uniform national land rights was broken in March 1986 when Bob Hawke buckled to pressure applied by the then Labor premier of Western Australia, Brian Burke, in concert with his federal factional colleague, Senator Graham Richardson. What Burke promised in substitute for Commonwealth national land rights legislation was to provide Aboriginal people with a title to the reserve lands they lived on while providing an unspecified amount of funds to improve local services. The federal cabinet accepted the Burke proposal in lieu of its own act and it did so without any legislative enforcement against Western Australia. This was one of the low points in the campaign for national land rights; it was also one of the rare moral low points of the Hawke government.

From 1986 onwards, I always knew that Aboriginal land rights was unfinished business. And I might say, I had the feeling that in some way I would be called upon to deal with it. It was one of those intractable issues, a bit like endemically high inflation, the kind that tends to follow you around. So when the High Court handed down its decision in *Mabo (No. 2)* on 3 June 1992, saying that there was a concept of native title at common law and that the source of the title was a traditional connection to or occupation of the land by Aboriginal and Islander people, I saw it as an opportunity to deal with the longest continuing problem Australia faced as a nation: the fundamental colonial grievance, the dispossession of the indigenous people and the injustice inherent in that dispossession.

By establishing that Aboriginal and Torres Strait Islanders had a private property right to their own soil, the High Court pointed a way as to how the Parliament could deal with indigenous land rights in a way that marked a turning point in the history between indigenous and non-indigenous Australians. I thought and said at the time, it was 'a once in a lifetime opportunity' to make peace between the first Australians and those who came here later.

I thought this pathway was a superior one to that where land was conferred upon indigenous people by the act of a Parliament. Here we had the High Court saying that title of an ancient kind had survived sovereignty and to the extent that subsequent grants of interest in land were consistent with the title, the nature and content of the title could be determined by the character of the connection to or occupation of the land under traditional laws and customs. In other words, it is not ours to give you but we recognise it as something which has always been yours. A way better approach, I thought, than one where a broadly non-indigenous Parliament gave land back to people who had earlier been dispossessed of it.

But above all that, I saw the approach of using the High Court's native title route as possessing an even greater attribute—and that was truth. There is, especially in public life, no more beautiful a characteristic than truth. Truth is of its essence liberating; it is possessed of no contrivance or conceit—it provides the only genuine basis for progress. By overturning the lie of 'terra nullius', the notion that at sovereignty the continent was possessed by no one, the High Court not only opened a route to indigenous land, it rang a bell which reminded us that our future could only be found in truth. This is the principal reason I found the Mabo pathway to indigenous land rights so compelling. And I said so at the time, in the address to celebrate the launch of the International Year for the World's Indigenous People at Redfern on 10 December 1992: 'Mabo establishes a fundamental truth and lays the basis for justice. It will be much easier to work from that basis than has ever been the case in the past'.

In the event, virtually across all of the year 1993, my cabinet ministers and I negotiated with Lowitja O'Donoghue and her Aboriginal negotiating group to produce the Native Title Act. The Act, while necessarily complex, met two fundamental aims: justice for Aboriginal people and a workable and fair system of land management in Australia. And it did so in accordance with the Racial Discrimination Act. The preamble to the Native Title Act made clear the objective. It said 'the people of Australia intend to rectify the consequences of past injustices by the special measures contained in this Act . . . to ensure that Aboriginal peoples and Torres Strait Islanders receive the full recognition and status within the Australian nation to which history, their prior rights and interests, and their rich and diverse culture, fully entitle them to aspire'. The special measures contained in the *Act* enabled us to determine who has native title and where; it gave native title holders the right to negotiate about actions affecting their land and it bestowed and restored rights without threatening existing rights.

Just eighteen months after the High Court had handed down its decision and one year, almost to the day, after I had extolled the virtue of the common law pathway to truth and justice in the Redfern Park speech, the bill had been built and negotiated and had passed both houses of the Federal Parliament. Receiving assent on 24 December 1993, the *Native Title Act* went a substantial way in settling the funda-mental grievance of indigenous Australia; the brutal dispossession of their lands and the smashing of their ways of life at the hands of an alien imperial power.

I was grateful at Gough Whitlam's kindly exclamation that the unique process of the development of the *Act* 'was a shining example of promptitude in a century old story of procrastination'.

However, in a lecture in the name of someone as significant as Lowitja and around the issues with which much of her public life has been associated, it is opportune to say some other things about the subject of native title and indigenous circumstances in the broad.

At the risk of repeating myself, I saw the opportunity of the native title route as a modality in dealing with and settling unresolved questions of indigenous land justice in this country.

This brings me to an important point and one I wish to dwell on, one made by the majority of the High Court (in *Mabo (No. 2)*) and illuminated in writings by Noel Pearson. And this is that native title is not a creature of the common law or indeed, a common law title, rather it is a title recognised by the common law. Or as the majority said at the time, 'whether the Imperial common law as that existed at the time of sovereignty and first settlement, or the Australian common law as it is today'. In other words, while the common law recognises a native title, native title itself did not evolve nor did it spring from the common law. Here it is worth focusing on a refrain from the *Native Title Act* itself. One of its main objects is to 'provide for the recognition and protection of native title'; that is, those rights and interests finding their origin in indigenous law and custom, not finding those rights and interests arising solely or peculiarly from the *Act* itself.

Indeed, it is worth my taking this opportunity to say that as Prime Minister, I had always intended that native title be determined by the common law principles laid out in *Mabo (No. 2)*. That is, I saw the *Native Title Act* giving expression to native title as native title had evolved, in the same organic and dynamic sense that the common law itself had evolved. The common law, derived from European custom and tradition, was never frozen nor did its development stop with Federation. So, too, native title should not be viewed as some museum-like strain of law which, snap-frozen, requires defrosting around anthropological principles, documentary records that rarely exist, if they ever existed and an onus of proof built within rules of evidence which are calibrated so as never being able to helpfully apply.

Justice Brennan in *Mabo (No. 2)* emphasised the principles of equality in the recognition of native title. The Keating government's *Native Title Act* was built on and around those principles. Yet in two important subsequent cases before the High Court, *Western Australia v Ward* (2002) and *Yorta Yorta v State of Victoria* (2002), the Court treated native title as an ordinary exercise in statutory interpretation instead of recognising that the legislation did not seek to supersede the common law, so much as to give articulation to its recognition of native title. Part and parcel of that recognition is the possibility, according to circumstances, of enlargement and flexibility. But the Court chose instead the black-letter route of statutory interpretation. And it did this knowing there is a body of relevant common law in the United States and in Canada and Britain which had cogently developed over the course of numerous decisions.

In fact, the current Chief Justice, Justice French, said that in Yorta Yorta, 'the High Court again emphasised the statutory definition of native title as defining the criteria that had to be satisfied before a determination could be made'. He said 'to that extent the Court appears to have moved away from the original concept of the Act as a vehicle for the development of the common law of native title'. He went on to say that the Court in so acting 'may have transformed the Act from a vessel for the development of the common law into a cage for its confinement'.

Earlier, I made clear that I regarded common law rights as they were revealed in *Mabo (No. 2)* as being superior to any form of statutory creation. Indeed, s12 of the *Native Title Act 1993* made clear that the characteristics of native title under the *Act* were to be determined in accordance with the developing common law. Section 12, though since removed from the statute, said: 'subject to this Act the common law of Australia in respect of native title has, after 30 June 1993, the force of the law of the Commonwealth'. What it said, or was trying to say, was that the common law, as it had developed in its native title complexion, enjoyed all the force and validity of a law of the Commonwealth. The section provided the guide as to the principles the Keating government endorsed when it constructed the *Act*. Section 12 was removed from the *Act* after the High Court in *Western Australia v Commonwealth (1995)* held it was invalid. But technical objections to the place Section 12 tried to preserve for common law flexibility do not diminish at all the high significance of the legislative attempt to promote the recognition of ownership rather than the gift of rights as the true basis for native title.

It is beyond discussion that the government I led intended native title to be determined by the common law principles laid down in *Mabo (No. 2)*. I raise this issue because of the significance of the derogations from the principles as set down in the *Mabo (No. 2)* judgement and the adoption and incorporation of those principles in the original, 1993, *Act*.

Going hand in hand in this regression is the continuing high onus of proof falling on claimants to native title. These arise from the need to establish continuity of the existence of native title rights and interests on the part of claimants with reference to evidence of an anthropological kind, including archaeological and historic evidence as well as oral evidence as to group customary traditions and evidence and as to how long such traditions have been maintained.

We all know that the rupture of European settlement had an atomising effect upon Aboriginal society as a whole and on particular groups, such that contemporary efforts to reconstitute that society or groups within it, including the resuscitation of traditional ways, is beyond our facilities and probably our imaginations.

This brings me back to *Yorta Yorta v State of Victoria*. In that case the High Court held that a determination under the *Native Title Act* was said to be 'a creation of that Act, not the common law'. This is at the kernel of the problem I just referred to, moving away from the *Native Title Act* as I envisaged it, to the snap-frozen, museum variety the Court subsequently came up with.

Once you are working in the field of literal or statutory interpretation, you are bound to satisfy more precise, or let us call it, stringent characteristics of the kind laid down in the *Act* for the award of title. For instance, the title must:

- be communal, group or of individual rights or interests of Aboriginal and Torres Strait Islanders
- be rights and interests 'in relation to land or waters'
- be possessed under the traditional laws acknowledged and the traditional customs observed by the Aboriginal people or Torres Strait Islanders
- be that relevant people by their law or customs have a connection with the land or waters and that those native title rights and interests must be recognised by the common law of Australia.

In *Yorta Yorta*, the trial judge substantially lifted the bar on the whole issue of continuity. As we know, it was in south-eastern Australia where the effects of European settlement were the most catastrophic and dislocatory to Aboriginal people. Despite this, the trial judge, Justice Olney, made virtually no concession to the claimants on the need to establish proof. Indeed, Justice Olney put the onus on the Yorta Yorta claimants to establish that there was a pre-sovereign society and that each generation of that society had acknowledged and observed the laws and customs of its people—in a material way—and uninterrupted from sovereignty to the present. As an indication of the level of difficulty this involved for the claimants, in the proceedings, Olney would not concede that an Aboriginal person born in the 1840s in the area under claim had any connection with Aboriginal forebears who inhabited the same land in 1788.

Indeed, Olney went out of his way to discount oral evidence by the Aboriginal claimants, preferring to rely on the written records of a squatter in the locality.

In the appeal proceedings before the Federal Court, Chief Justice Black, in dissent, had this to say by way of observation:

For one thing, the use of historical material to answer a claim based substantially upon an orally-transmitted tradition needs to take fully into account the potential richness and strength of orally-based traditions . . . It is necessary too, to bear in mind the particular difficulties and limitations of historical assessments, not least those made by untrained observers, writing from their own cultural viewpoint and with their own cultural preconceptions and for their own purposes.

He went on to observe:

The external and casual viewer of another culture may see very little because the people observed may intend to reveal very little to an outsider, or because the observer may be looking at the wrong time, or because the observer may not know what to look for, or for any one of numerous other reasons. Even a conscientious attempt in past times to provide a complete record would run into difficulties of this nature. The dangers inherent in giving particular authority to the written word, and more authority when it is repeated, need to be borne constantly in mind as well.

But no such caveats stopped the Federal Court and later the High Court in backing in the Olney view—notwithstanding the fact that in a number of jurisdictions abroad, once proof of a pre-sovereign society had been established, courts had accepted or presumed continuity thereafter.

This onerous burden of proof has placed an unjust burden on those native title claimants who have suffered the most severe dispossession and social disruption. It has substantially slowed the right of redress by Aboriginal people to adequate recognition of their rights in respect of land, water and other natural resources.

In fact, after fifteen years' operation of the *Native Title Act 1993*, there have been 1300 claims lodged, arriving at 121 native title determinations, covering just over 10 per cent of the land mass at a cost to the taxpayer of over $900 million.

To ameliorate some of the constraints in the application of the substantive law where applicants are required to prove their continuity with native title rights, the Chief Justice Robert French had some helpful things to say here in Adelaide in July 2008.

In those remarks Justice French highlighted the beneficial purpose which the *Native Title Act* seeks to confer on Aboriginal and Islander people. One of those beneficial purposes is the rectification of the consequences of past injustices wherein, under the main objects of the *Act*, section 3 seeks to 'to provide for the recognition and protection of native title'. Indeed Justice French went on to provide a quotation from the full court in *Northern Territory v Alyawarr* (2005). There the Court said 'the preamble (of the Native Title Act) declares the moral foundation upon which the Act rests'; that is, to recognise, support and protect native title. It went on to say 'that moral foundation and that intention stand despite the inclusion in the Native Title Act of substantive provisions which are adverse to native title rights and interests and provide for their extinguishment, permanent and temporary'.

In other words, the Court reminded people that some substantive provisions within the judicial framework may operate such as to be adverse in their consequences for native title.

To ease the heavy requirements on claimants in respect of those substantive provisions, as they go to proof and matters of continuity, Justice French suggested that some change in the *Act* as it relates to onus of proof could facilitate a presumption of continuity of connection by claimants and continuity since sovereignty. Such a presumption, he said, 'would enable the parties, if it were not to be challenged, to disregard a substantial interruption of continuity of acknowledgment and observance of traditional laws and customs'. He said 'were it desired, the provision could expressly authorise disregard of substantial interruptions in acknowledgment and observance of traditional law and custom unless and until proof of such interruption was established'. In other words, Justice French was suggesting a reverse onus of proof where proof of any interruption would need to be established—to be proved.

In this model, a presumption could be challenged by the respondent party, whether it be a state or a territory, but Justice French went on to say 'it would be important that any presumption be robust enough to withstand the mere introduction of evidence to the contrary'; that is, proof to the contrary being required.

His Honour's other helpful suggestion was also by way of another amendment to the *Native Title Act*. One which would allow extinguishment to be disregarded 'where an agreement was entered into between the states and the applicants that it should be disregarded'. Agreements of this kind, of course, go to certain goodwill and judgement by the states and territories by way of them seeking to advance and protect native title. We know that such a specific objective would require somewhat of a seachange on the part of a number of them.

I realise that amendments encapsulating some of these proposals have been put before the Federal Parliament—and I know the Attorney General has said he will take such proposals into consideration. I can only add my recommendation that the Federal government give legislative effect to such changes so as to enhance the efficiency, effectiveness and equity of the *Native Title Act*.

The other major matter germane to native title I wish to address is the question of pastoral leases and the Wik High Court judgement of 1996.

As Prime Minister, the pastoral lease question was a very vexing and torrid one for me. And for this reason: notwithstanding that the Commonwealth government's legal advice was that the *Mabo (No. 2)* judgement had the effect of extinguishing native title on lands subject to pastoral leases—I did not agree with that advice. That is, I did not personally agree with the logic behind the advice.

Many people will know how much pressure I was under as Prime Minister to clear up the matter once and for all, by having the *Native Title Act* extinguish native title over lands subject to pastoral leases. The argument went, 'if Prime Minister, you say your best advice is that the High Court decision in *Mabo (No. 2)* signalled the extinguishment of native title on pastoral leases, why don't you follow your own legal advice and make it certain in the Native Title Bill?'

I had lots of supposedly good people urging this upon me, like the former leader of the National Party Tim Fischer, who was doing his level best to turn pastoral leases into quasi-freehold titles at the expense of Aboriginal people.

I knew there was a massive potential loss here for Aboriginal people— because in 1993 a very large proportion of the land mass of Australia was subject to pastoral leases. In Western Australia it was 38 per cent of the entire state, in Queensland 54 per cent, South Australia 42 per cent, New South Wales 41 per cent and the Northern Territory 51 per cent.

Given its scale and importance, I was determined not to deny Aboriginal people the chance to test this question before the High Court. So to keep the naysayers at bay and to fend off the opportunists, I decided to record in the preamble of the bill that on the government's view, past leasehold grants extinguished native title. Indeed, in my second reading speech introducing the legislation, I said the following:

I draw attention also to the recording in the preamble of the bill of the government's view that under the common law, past valid freehold and leasehold grants extinguish native title. There is therefore no obstacle or hindrance to renewal of pastoral leases in the future, whether validated or already valid.

I had these words in the second reading speech and in the preamble to the *Act* but I refused to make extinguishment a *fait accompli* under the operating provisions of the *Act*.

I knew that the whole idea of pastoral leases over Crown land arose because squatters decided to move on to land for which they had no title and where their activities, grazing or otherwise, were uncontrolled. The motivation for the legislative regime, first in New South Wales in the late 1820s, was to put some control on squatters without conferring on them a freehold title to vast tracts of the country; country largely occupied by Aboriginal people. So I understood that when the various colonial and state governments came to issuing pastoral leases they did so knowing that the pastoral activity would occur over lands where Aboriginal people were still conducting a traditional way of life. That is, the governments issuing these leasehold titles issued them in the knowledge and acceptance of the fact that grazing could be accommodated concurrently with Aboriginal people maintaining a traditional connection with the land under grant.

So when in *Mabo (No. 2)* the High Court laid down its principles, I could not see those principles being at odds with a coexistence of title as between pastoral activity and a traditional Aboriginal life arising from the latter's native title.

In other words, I had rejected, or at least held under question, the Commonwealth Attorney General's Department advice that the High Court's *Mabo (No. 2)* decision and its principles effectively extinguished native title. I told officers of the Attorney General's Department at the time that I regarded their advice as black-letter property advice, wherein they failed to understand how and in which ways the High Court was peering through the common law to the development of native title rights over the course of Australian history following European settlement.

Putting it in the language of the lawyers, I told them that exclusive possession of land could be an incident of a pastoral lease but in the majority of cases was unlikely to be and need not be.

As it turned out, in the Wik decision of 1996, the High Court by a majority of four to three held that the grant of the relevant leases did not confer on the lessees exclusive possession of the land under lease and correctly, in my view, made clear that, in the case of the Wik and the Thayorre peoples, that a relevant intention to extinguish all native title rights at the time the grants were issued was not present. That is, the grants did not necessarily extinguish *all* incidents of the native title rights that the Wik and Thayorre peoples enjoyed.

Of course, that decision of the High Court was attacked mercilessly by the Howard government. That villain, Tim Fischer, boasted that there would be bucketloads of extinguishment in the Howard government's response to the decision.

Many people here will be familiar with the sorry tale which became part and parcel of the *Native Title (Amendment) Act 1998*. That amendment arose from the Coalition government's so-called Ten Point Plan, a plan facilitated in the Senate with the support of Senator Brian Harradine under the advice of the Jesuit priest, Frank Brennan.

As an aside, let me say, and as a Catholic, let me say, wherever you witness the zealotry of professional Catholics in respect of indigenous issues, invariably you find indigenous interests subordinated to their personal notions of justice and equity: because unlike the rest of us, they enjoy some kind of divine guidance.

And so it was with the Wik amendments. Point two of the amending act declared:

> *States and Territories would be able to confirm that . . . agricultural leases in existence on or before 1 January 1994 could be covered for . . . exclusive tenure . . . to the extent it can reasonably be said that by reason of the grant or the nature of the permitted use of the land, exclusive possession must have been intended . . . thereby extinguishing native title.*

The amendments were entitled 'Confirmation of past extinguishment of native title'. But it was never clear that all freehold grants and leasehold grants permanently extinguished native title.

Mick Dodson said at the time 'by purporting to 'confirm' extinguishment by inconsistent grants, the Commonwealth is purposely pre-empting the development of the common law—not allowing sufficient time to integrate the belated recognition of native title into Australia's land management system'. He said 'this does not require the obliteration of indigenous interests so as to favour non-indigenous interests'. Quite so.

The Keating government's *Native Title Act* of 1993 recognised a right to negotiate given to native title holders and a duty to negotiate vested in government and grantees with respect to grants of mining tenements as well as compulsory acquisition by governments for the giving of interests for a commercial purpose.

The Howard government's 1998 amendments denied the application of the right to negotiate over those great parts of Australia where native title might be established, indeed, to probably half the mainland. The amendments removed many forms of grant from the ambit of the *Act*, seriously diminishing the value of the *Act* while choking off access by native title holders.

The Howard government's 1998 amendments cut across the spirit of the Keating government's 1993 *Act*; the notion that the *Act* was, first and foremost, legislation of a beneficial kind—enacted to redress historic inequities—rather than to compound ones sanctioned by earlier acts.

Finally, I wish to say something about another outcome in that historic negotiation between Lowitja O'Donoghue, her negotiating team and the Keating government. And that is the establishment of the Indigenous Land Corporation and land fund.

In the course of that historic negotiation, I invited ATSIC and the Council for Aboriginal Reconciliation to submit proposals for a wider package of measures to help establish an economic base for Aboriginal and Torres Strait Islander peoples and in establishing such a base to safeguard and further develop Aboriginal and Islander culture.

That invitation and those submissions came together in what was called the Social Justice Package. A substantial element of that package was a land fund—a fund set up to support those indigenous people, dispossessed of their lands, yet unable to assert native title rights and interests. In the second reading speech to the Native Title Bill 1993, I said 'that despite its historic significance, the Mabo decision will give little more than a sense of justice to those Aboriginal communities whose native title has been extinguished or lost . . . their dispossession being total, their loss complete. While these communities remain dispossessed of land, their economic marginalisation and their sense of injury continue'.

The purpose of the fund was to acquire land and to attribute to such land a synthesised native title. In fact, I made clear that I intended that the fund could acquire pastoral leases and convert them to a synthesised native title. That is, where Aboriginal people who own or acquire a pastoral lease and who the Federal Court determines would satisfy the criteria for native title, but for the existence of the pastoral lease and wish to convert their holding to the equivalent of native title, could do so.

The land fund was the centrepiece of the Keating government's social justice measures arising in association with the *Native Title Act*. The fund, which was the subject of its own act in 1994, became the Indigenous Land Corporation, set up with the aim of becoming self-sustaining with over $1 billion of Commonwealth-subscribed capital.

The *Indigenous Land Fund Act* locked in allocations to the fund and the Corporation for ten years. I designed the *Act* to make it extremely difficult for a future government to undo what I had put into place. As it turned out, I succeeded in making it Howard and Costello-proof; vandal-proof. It galled them that the ILC's budgetary appropriations were beyond their executive influence.

By 2010, appropriations to the Aboriginal and Torres Strait Islander Account stood at $1.421 billion. Payments from the Land Account to the Indigenous Land Corporation stood at $650 million. The ILC is now in an advantageous financial position such that it is able to expend funds on assets other than simply the purchase of land. The land fund and land corporation initiative stands as another successful outcome from the 1993 *Native Title Act* negotiations.

Let me, perhaps, finish where I began.

I accepted this invitation to give the Lowitja O'Donoghue Oration out of respect for Lowitja as a remarkable person and a leader of Aboriginal people. As I said earlier, her unfailing instinct for enlargement marks her out as a person of great significance in the Australian political firmament.

I like to think that together, she and I were able to lead our respective political forces towards an historic outcome for a race of people dispossessed and decimated by the process of settlement.

Without having been lobbied or cajoled, I took the opportunity of the Redfern Park speech in 1992 to lay out, openly and truthfully, the history of our inhumanity towards and thoughtless disregard of Australia's indigenous people. For the nation's integrity and moral clarity, I thought it necessary it face up to the truths of our colonial history. Similarly, I saw the Mabo decision and the *Native Title Act* as an opportunity to transcend the history of that dispossession—to put right an historic wrong. An opportunity to restore the age-old link between Aboriginal land and culture, to declare Aboriginal culture a defining element of who we are: to make clear that our spiritual enlargement as a people could best be accomplished when that enlargement included a secure and prosperous place for the first Australians.

Lowitja O'Donoghue has been and remains an important part of this national transformation. This oration in her name is testimony to that reality.

11

NEOCLASSICISM

Cahn Collection, Powerhouse Museum,
Sydney,
17 April 2008

Outside of politics and music, Paul Keating's other great abiding
interest is an aesthetic and historic one—Neoclassicism, the style of the
revolutionary phase that followed the European Enlightenment into the
French Revolution. In this speech he explains how Neoclassicism's 'moral
earnestness' and 'urgent seriousness' supported the values of civicism
and private morals in the paradigm shift that brought the world into the
modern political age. The age of democracy: of man, liberty, reason and
equity. Paul Keating underlines the importance of beauty and harmony
and how art, sculpture and architecture speak to us through the senses
rather than by abstract rationalism. He says poignantly that Neoclassicism
was 'the wallpaper in the salon of revolutionary modernism'.

I HAVE BEEN INVITED TONIGHT to celebrate this important exhibition
of silver by speaking about one of the driving interests of my life—my
lifelong interest in Neoclassicism.

While much of the silver here is Neoclassic, much of it is not. But
I admire things which are good of any period, like some of the early
eighteenth-century Baroque things here, and of course, earlier.

People do not expect a political figure to have an academic interest in
art, much less of a particular period. They may understand one having
the average consumer's interest in the odd picture or *object d'art*, or

visit the latest gallery exhibition, perhaps the odd appearance in arty circles. What they do not expect in a political personality is someone at the apex of international scholarship in a particular movement or style. And with an eye sharpened by decades spent searching for the extraordinary and the exemplary.

Appreciation of the subtleties of art, of the calibrations to greatness, of true subliminal talent, can rarely be learned. There has to be a concomitant artistic impulse to see in a work all that its creator hoped could be represented. Our brains are wired to recognise harmony and composition; this is why we find a consensus of approval around particular and famous works of art. Most people can see it, but fashion directs them to what they should be expected to approve. If they are shown, invariably they will understand it. But not as many understand the greatness or significance of works or of periods of art which have long fallen from the pantheon of fashion, where you have to work it out for yourself: from your own innate idea of what nourishes the sensibilities and what qualifies for the sobriquet of sublime.

Of course, to know is to be liberated from every fashionista peddling a line about art, from gallery directors to auction-house hustlers.

In a sense, one has to have a reasonable idea of the whole panoply of things—works of all periods—before the relevance and satisfaction of specialisation works its compulsion.

I came to Neoclassicism as a young man. I came to it from two directions: the purely aesthetic for its sobriety and heroic elegance, and the historic, for the expression it gave to the birth of the modern political age, the age of democracy.

The art historian Hugh Honour summed up Neoclassicism succinctly when he said:

Neoclassicism is the style of the late-eighteenth century, of the culminating, revolutionary phase in that great outburst of human inquiry known as the Enlightenment. The moral earnestness, the urgent seriousness, the high-minded, sometimes starry-eyed idealism of the free thinkers, the philosophers, was all reflected in it. For Neoclassicism in its most vital expressions sought to bring about— whether by patient scientific advance or by a purgative return, à la Rousseau, to a primate simplicity and purity—a new and better world governed by the immutable laws of reason and equity.

The art of the period witnessed political and social revolutions greater than any since the fall of the Roman Empire, overturning feudal and ecclesiastic power and out of which modern Europe and America came to emerge. Neoclassicism was the wallpaper in the salon of revolutionary modernism.

So radiant was the French revolution it illuminated every other phenomenon. And art, like society, returned its scarifying light. So violent was its transformation, it established a new and universal tense: it determined absolutely what was modern and what was past.

Neoclassicism, which lined its cauldron, was a youthful, fiery, rebellious movement. Critics, theorists and the artists themselves called it simply the 'true style'—the reassertion of timeless truths.

These days, Neoclassicism is regarded as a decorative style. People can be forgiven, 200 years on, for not understanding it as the 'stoic exemplar of unspoilt and uncorrupted simplicity, of noble self-sacrifice and heroic patriotism'.

Jacques Louis David's moralising history pictures instructed contemporaries in the virtues of civicism and private morals, rekindling modern appreciation of republican Rome. In Lebrun's phrase: 'Republic, you are borne to avenge the whole universe'.

Indeed, 'the true style' established an identity, a bridge between ancient and modern republicans, at a time when royal prerogative was as part of ordinary life as oxygen in the air.

The stern republicanism of antiquity played an important role in the development of the Enlightenment. So, too, Neoclassic artists saw in it the germs of a new and purer style—one conveying greater truths and meaning—eschewing superficiality.

The discoveries at Herculaneum in 1738 and Pompeii ten years later provided a cornucopia of detail and emblems which fleshed out the new medium.

Notwithstanding that in modern times the style had become so out of fashion as to barely warrant the adjective of unfashionable, I always found the truth of it—its stoic morality—to be completely compelling. Not only was it part of the code stone of the political movement that changed the world, its other world essence, its abstemious simplicity, has transcended art movements since.

As a broad style, it renders any movement of the nineteenth century romantic by comparison, as it stands sentinel-like against those of the twentieth century, with Art Deco perhaps being the exception. But then, Art Deco is but a variation on Classicism's timeless gospel.

Over many years, I often wondered what drove me on with Neoclassicism, why I maintained such fidelity to it, because in art, there are always distractions.

The essential reason was its latent sensuousness, and seriousness. Art, sculpture and architecture do not speak to us by means of abstract reason; we do not deduce or rationalise them. They speak to us through our senses, through that part of the brain which processes beauty and harmony.

The other reason was the identification—the search for the sweetest spot in 'the one true style'—the point of near perfection; the place where the novelty of the new Classicism picked up the resonances of Egyptian, Greek and Roman antiquity, in an altogether new harmonic of earnest utility. In essence, the end high-point, the flashlight moment in the five-hundred-year development of European classicism since the beginning of the Renaissance.

I believe the sweet spot came after the Revolution and the Terror which defined it, in a manner which savoured the peace and sensibilities of the *ancien régime* while aspiring to a new order based on the immutable values of the ancients.

In a sense, this pinnacle is a transitional style, capturing the last gasp of the early Neoclassicism of Louis XVI, but mixed magically with the literal transition of the antique. It is a style with integrity: one which denied the excesses of the Revolution and the Terror yet would not submit to the betrayal of republican principles under the Empire. It exemplified the uncorrupted early revolutionary ethic.

Many high points of style and decoration arise from periods of transition: *Regence* in France; the later transition between Louis XV and Louis XVI; and the transition between Louis XVI and the blousy official Empire style which followed after 1804. This last transition possessed the same integrity and verve of earlier transitions.

These days, the shorthand description of the style is *Directoire-Consulat* and in stylistic terms it lasted from around 1793 to 1803. Artists took their inspiration from Egyptian, Greek and Roman art and architecture. In the philosophy of the day, that which was the more primitive was more pure; this is why there was a fascination for Egypt and things Egyptian.

Egyptian architecture possesses great clarity of massing. It also possesses other appealing subtleties. The capital of an Egyptian column conveys the tension of a bud yet to flower, whereas in the Greek, the Corinthian and Ionic, it had flowered, the leaf in full bloom. The resolution within Egyptian art and architecture captured the imagination of end-eighteenth-century post-Revolutionary France. The style which emerged became known as *retour d'Egypte*, a return to the most ancient and the most primitive.

In the new republic, the United States, the Neoclassic style went by the title of The Federal Period; yet while Washington's victories and the republic's aspirations gave it a recognisable strength and purity of form, it only ever amounted to a not-quite-certain imitation of the French.

Thomas Jefferson, Benjamin Franklin and Benjamin Latrobe were besotted with French revolutionary art and architecture and carried French Neoclassicism to the United States. Jefferson, who witnessed the Revolution firsthand as American Minister to the French Court in 1789, designed his own house, Monticello, in a Palladian interpretation of the style and went on to design the University of Virginia in the full style. Latrobe co-designed the White House and the Capitol buildings in Washington, along with his masterpiece, the Catholic Cathedral in Baltimore.

Louise XVI's execution and the violence and old angers of the Terror, presided over by Robespierre and his Committee for Public Safety, so traumatised French society that next to nothing was built in Paris between 1793 and 1800. Sadly, as the *Directoire–Consulat* style peaked, few witnessed it. And there was little proliferation. Only officials belonging to or near the Directory and the Consulate built things and were able to enjoy the style as it hit its apogee. Hence, the remnants of the period are rare. I have sometimes come across things which belonged to Mirabeau and Cambacérès and Lebrun, as I have to Jefferson himself. Some important items here tonight give us a hint of the resplendence of the period. Artefacts, like architecture, are part of the conversation between generations; this is why it is important those of the revolutionary and immediate post-revolutionary years are conserved and understood.

As a movement, high Neoclassicism skipped the nineteenth century, but the purity of its forms and ideas pollinated twentieth-century architecture. First with Le Corbusier and the Bauhaus and later with architects like Mies van der Rohe, Philip Johnson and Louis Kahn, who took their inspiration from revolutionary architects like Ledoux and Boullee, as they did from the German Neoclassicists Gilly and Schinkel. The cubic massing and austere volumetric clarity provided them with a central organising idea or template. It is true to say that Neoclassicism informed postwar international modernism—what became the international modern style.

I will finish on this note. I have always had a soft spot for sculpture—for its three-dimensionality, the sensuous material from which it is carved and its plasticity. The greatest sculptors of the Neoclassic age were Antonio Canova, Jean-Antoine Houdon and Augustin Pajou.

Pajou's sculpture possessed emotion and grace, most obviously in his *Psyche Abandoned*, executed in 1785. His work filled out a kind of transition between his remarkable predecessor Jean-Baptiste Pigalle and the heroic work of Canova. Houdon, the archetypal Neoclassicist, sculpted the dominant figures of the age, from Voltaire to George

Washington. His work possessed a subjective presence and sentiment which tied it back to the Baroque.

Which brings me to the Baroque and the mid-eighteenth century.

Even in strictly classical settings, there is a place for naturalism and feeling of the kind you find in the work of the greatest masters, Gian Lorenzo Bernini, and his eighteenth-century kindred spirit, Jean-Baptiste Pigalle. Bernini's *St Theresa* and Pigalle's nude *Voltaire* provide the exclamation marks of an art at its highest expressions. They have always caused my eye to wander, to a style truer perhaps than the one 'true style' itself.

Nonetheless, Neoclassicism's epic sublimity was aimed at the soul. Its goal, 'the ideal', was to arrive by order and restrained sensuality—by images transformed into an idea—but an idea which remains eternally potent.

12

EULOGY
On the death of Bill Bradshaw
Woollahra, NSW,
25 November 2009

*To the extent that Paul Keating had an early mentor in his lifelong
interest in neo-classicism, the Sydney antique dealer Bill Bradshaw was
the one. When Bill Bradshaw died at the age of 87, his friends asked
Paul Keating to give the eulogy. Delivered extemporaneously, the eulogy
provides a rare snapshot of the golden age of antique dealing and a
colourful picture of a remarkably complex and interesting individual.
Perhaps as much as that, it provides another element in the matrix of
Paul Keating's intellectual interests and associations unconnected with
public life. Replete with humorous anecdotes, the eulogy authentically
conveys some of the colour of the period and the characters involved.*

THIS IS A SAD OCCASION for us all. We come to mourn Bill Bradshaw—
a dear friend to everybody here.

With his passing comes the end of an era. An era that was a reflection of another time and another Australia. An era of knowledge and
of connoisseurship, of remarkable erudition and of an empathy with
perhaps a more romantic world, the world of the nineteenth century.

Self-taught, Bill possessed great aesthetic sensibilities. As a sixteen
year old he started business with his mother. Approaching the finish
of primary school, he had asked his mother for a book on Regency
furniture. With his own eyes and his own taste, and without any specific

education in the arts, he developed an acute sense of shape and form both of decoration and of architecture, so much so he was able to make a trade of it for the rest of his life. His perceptions were always insightful and always inspired. They were also inspiring.

I think it's true to say that he had the aesthetic and artistic sensibilities of an artist. Though not an artist himself, the eyes and the senses were artistic, though not artistic in the modern or contemporary sense. But, like anybody with an eye for anything good, he liked anything good of any time and of any period. But his great interest was the nineteenth century, from 1800 right through even to well into the twentieth century, as you could hear from the *Prelude* which he chose for this service today. A kind of fruitiness in the music which paralleled the fruitiness of his interests in things later of the nineteenth century.

In a trade dominated by Australia's Victorian heritage, he fashioned and fostered, more or less on his own, a taste for classicism, a classicism that Australia really never knew. While some of it existed in the first quarter of the nineteenth century in New South Wales and Tasmania, it was overtaken, in general, by what we now call second period rococo or Victoriana, as the colonies grew in wealth and as tastes changed in Europe. But as many of us here understand, the essence of this classicism grew from and belonged to the third quarter of the eighteenth century and this is where Bill's eyes really were, where the essence of his interests really laid. At its apogee in 1800, the style informed some of our early architecture; things in the city by Greenway and other architects, and was the source for some important buildings, notably Elizabeth Bay House here in Sydney and others in Tasmania. And, in the decline of classicism, other more baroque forms of Victoriana.

In English terms, its heyday was of course the Regency, the period Bill loved and admired perhaps above all others. For Bill the Regency kind of had it all. It had the classicism, it had the glitz, clothing Britannia in all her glory at the height of her powers. His proselytising in favour of this style really changed the developed taste of Sydney. And I think it is completely true to say that, more or less alone, and from sheer belief and passion, he informed the taste of a community, away from the prevailing tastes. In Sydney, of course, this was the balloon back chair, the elaborately decorated chiffonier, the ornamented cabriole leg. Bill did his best to do that style in, but of course, it could never be completely defeated. He knew that too. He used to call it 'bordello baroque' or 'whorehouse rococo'. And while on the one hand he despised it, and he did despise it, for its fakery, on the other, he was charmed by its earnest, try hard romanticism. But, to be contrary, he claimed this interest in William IV-cum-early-Victorian furniture. Many of us would say 'Bill, why are you doing that, when you know the real stuff only exists around 1800?' But he kind of wanted you to know you couldn't put him in a box. He was intermittently fascinated with this more fruity style and that then went to such things as American shelf clocks, musical boxes and pianos, where he became the great authority in pianoforte and early pianos. That came from the classic furniture interest; it also came from his off-beat musical interests.

A friend of mine once said that 'there are only two kinds of people, lovers and others, and who wants to be one of the others'. Well, Bill was not one of the others. He was someone who loved the romantic drumbeat and really ran his life by it. In the dichotomy we hear between the 'the punishers' and 'the enlargers', Bill was without a doubt an 'enlarger'. True to his Catholic egalitarianism he hated overbearingness and pomp, he held the monarchy in contempt, and was a committed republican. He was not sure about my *Native Title Act*. He thought I'd taken things a bit far. His enlargement didn't embrace everything but his life was guided by a certain moral compass. A bit skittish on occasions, but mostly true.

The fact is, Bill was a complete original. We will not see the likes of him, perhaps not ever again. Coming from where he did as a young man in the first half of the twentieth century, growing into adulthood through the second half of the twentieth century and in business, his attitudes and interests were often a reflection of the Edwardian 1920s and 1930s period of his mother's epoch. Those interests in that way of life and social norms were part of his background. Of course, it is unlikely to ever appear in this guise again. As I said, it's the end of an era.

That ferocious brain, the laser-like focus, the brilliance, the whimsy, the caprice, all came together to give us something and someone original.

Bill was capable of new perspectives. You could say something to him and he would cut through the detail to its essence in a second. It was such a good mind. He would invariably think outside the paradigm. Sometimes a bit mad but always interesting. Though, of course, while he could often be hard to get along with, and God knows we have all had a tongue-lashing from him, he was consummately generous. Generous in spirit and generous in knowledge; he gave the knowledge away to people. To people in the trade, many a dealer was encouraged by Bill and taught things by him. Some he despised, like Stanley Lipscombe, or 'Stella', as he used to call him. But in the big ledger, Bill was a help rather than a hindrance.

But I suppose the thing most of us loved about him was his zaniness, the surreal behaviour, the unpredictability, the thunderbolts of brilliance. You know, I came one day, at about 3 o'clock in the afternoon, it would have been in the late 1980s or early 1990s and Keith Lehane was holding shop. I could hear the piano going in the upstairs parlour and there he was pumping away at one of these piano players with mechanical fingers, with a piano roll inside. He was up there belting out one of those big Klondike saloon numbers and he said to me as I walked in 'This was Lola Montez's favourite tune'. At three in the afternoon, going for his life, by himself, pumping at the pedals; it was surreal. You said to yourself, 'I'm not going to see this anywhere else.'

He was one of the funniest people ever. The off-beat humour, the ribald conjuring of images, the stiletto observations, the irreverence, the vicious remark, there was really no-one like him. Bill was pure mischief. And no-one was really more amused by him than he himself. I think he was completely amused by his own behaviour. It sort of kept him going, ridiculous as it often was.

But a slab of the old Australia goes with him, including the working-class vernacular. We all know how the jokes have died, how the use of language has declined. He loved words; he loved the play on words, the humour from the roots from which all of us here came. He could have been a gag-writer, or an art historian, or a spinner of stories, or a classical scholar, or a musicologist, or a museum curator or a slapstick comedian. He could have been anyone because he really was a construct of all of them. And that's what we loved about him: the erudition, the zaniness, the brilliance, and the passion, but mostly the irreverent originality. He was always irreverent and always original. And the phrases: 'Never argue with a mug', etcetera.

Of course we had the extended comic phases with him and his mother, Ruby. Paul Kenny used to talk about the 'Big Sister' pudding phase when they discovered Big Sister puddings. Opening the top of the can with a can opener, a pudding would reveal itself and they'd chop right into it. Anyone who'd been invited to the shop, whom he used to often call 'victims'—'another victim'—he'd have the tea out with the Big Sister pudding to hand. Then there was the 'Camp Pie' phase where he and his mother put the Camp Pie on toast; the endless rounds of tea, the diphtheria risk with the crockery. Bill would often say to me, 'Don't wash that cup, it's OK' and I would say, 'No, I'll wash it up, Bill'. You would wash it to prolong your own life. And then, of course, the wedding cake episode from David Jones. Paul Kenny tells the story of Rube telling Bill she's bored. She said, 'I'm bored witless, Bill. For Christ's sake, go down to David Jones and get us a decent cake.' So he comes back in a taxi with a three-tier wedding cake which they then, unceremoniously, proceeded to chop to pieces. Hopped straight into it, and had the remnants ready for anyone who came in that week.

The shop was always amusing. We had the stewardship of 'Matron' Lehane, who was the early carer and janitor. John, the offshore diver who was affectionately called 'The Mermaid' and also known as 'The Princess Kinkara' for his tea-making prowess. Then his theatre-usher friend, Peter Berry, whom he called 'the glow worm', and of course, his daily comic jousts with Pearl Palmer to see who could out-pun whom. What contests they were! The thing to do was to be around when they turned up in form, two great wits going at one another. A kind of intellectual marking taking place.

He loved funny people. I remember being with him with Serge Baillache at Westbourne Grove in London, where Serge ran a shop. Serge said, 'Bill, tell me some of your great retail stories.' Bill told him some and Serge said 'I'll tell you one of mine'. He said that down the road there was a titled noblewoman who turned up in a very drab, light powder blue overcoat and hat, with a bag over her arm as does the Queen. He said she'd walk into the shop and walk right past him, not even acknowledging his presence. She would go up to everything, look at it, hold it and price it. He said that one day when she came in there was a terracotta bust on the far side of the window box. To reach it, she threw down the handbag on the window box ledge and crawled across the window to have a closer look at the figure. The moment she did, someone walked in the shop and said, 'Sir, how much is that bag in the window?' And Serge, quick as a flash, replied 'I'm sorry, madam, it's just been sold'. Bill roared.

He loved that banter. He loved London; he loved Britain, because it was really the home of his interest. He soaked up the places and the trade and the things you could not see here. He went there until his health prevented him from going. But he loved fun, like about Keith Ball who retailed Chinese antiques next door. He used to say to me, 'You know, Keith's the oldest thing in the shop'. He could be wittily savage.

This is one I witnessed myself. This very important lady, with a toffy voice, came in. She was looking around and Bill, I used to say that he'd come out of that door like a black widow spider, with somebody on his web. Some victim had walked through his door. So in the haughty voice she says, 'Good afternoon Mr Bradshaw, what is this?' He said, 'Well, Madam, that's a campaign bed made of blued steel and brass; they were screwed together on the battlefields for the generals.'

'Oh,' she said, 'yes, I've heard of those but I did not realise they were so big'.

He retorted, 'Oh yes, Madam, big enough for a general and two drummer boys.' Rather taken aback, she said 'Oh, oh'.

Then the next thing she lit upon was one of those Directoire clocks with two black male figures leaning on either side of a wool bale, with a diadem in the hair with a pair of paste diamonds for eyes. And she said, 'This is very attractive, Mr Bradshaw.'

He said, 'Madam, this model was a favourite of a number of English queens.' And then with a pause he said, 'Cecil Beaton, Noel Coward, Norman Hartnell' and he went down a list. Then she knew she was in some kind of trouble.

Moving towards the door, the last thing on display was a pair of girandoles, or candlestick lustres, you know, American ones, made in Philadelphia, which featured American Indian scenes in bronze relief.

She said, 'They're very striking, Mr Bradshaw. Do you have any Australian ones?' He said, 'Madam, there may have been one or two examples, and now there is a great demand for them. As a matter of fact, I'm working up a model right now using the same basic shape—indeed, I've just finished modelling up Raelene and Chantelle from Green Valley for the central image.' At that moment she knew that she was in strife and left. He said, 'That'll teach the old bag to put on the dog with me.'

He was a ferocious salesman. I used to say, 'You're like a black widow spider'. He'd sidle out of that narrow door and come upon them. If they were old customers he would know the approach, but if they were new customers he'd go through the patter, slowly reeling them in—it was something to see.

With Bill gone a piece of all of us goes with him. Life will be that much less good because you won't be able to turn into Queen Street and find him there with a cup of tea begging. Or Ken Muggleston ready to greet you at the door.

But, he taught us all something. The passion, the energy, the belief, the inner confidence in his own taste and the styles he favoured and would proselytise for. His originality and the memory of him will, I think, always warm our hearts. People come through your life and they leave. With Bill, we have all lost a mentor and friend, but as a trade, the antique trade has lost its oldest and most important member. This will say something again about the change in Australian life and Australian society. And of the fashions and tastes. It will be a diminished business without him. We come today to remember and to celebrate him and to acknowledge how much we all loved him. He was remarkable and completely unforgettable.

13

AUSTRALIAN LABOR PARTY
GALA FEDERATION DINNER

Melbourne,
8 May 2001

*The Federal Parliamentary Labor Party celebrated the Centenary of
Federation with an address by the then leader, Kim Beazley, followed
by a gala dinner addressed by the three former Labor Prime Ministers:
Gough Whitlam, Bob Hawke and Paul Keating. Paul Keating's speech
was the last, delivered extemporaneously.*

A POLITICAL PARTY REACHING A century is something to celebrate.
Political parties mostly go out of business: the British Liberal Party went
out of business; the DLP went out of business. The Democrats might
go out of business for their support of the GST.

The other thing we celebrate is the usefulness of the Labor Party to
the country after 100 years of its existence. Its great pluralism. Kim today
gave us the quote from Lenin about Labor parties being bourgeois—we
should wear that quote like a badge of honour; that our creed survived
and his didn't. Because we did represent, and always have represented, the
working class. When I grew up about 30 per cent of the community were
Catholics but about 50 to 60 per cent of the working class were Catholics.
So, there was never any way we were going to be Marxist–Leninist.

We were and are a pluralist party; we've given a home to all sorts of
people—Fabians, Marxists, single-taxers; all sorts of characters. I suppose
our boast is we can absorb any culture, and we have.

I do think that one of the great reforms of the 1980s was the reform of the Labor Party itself. While Gough saved the party in the late 1960s and 1970s, it still nurtured the old culture of protection, of preference; it didn't understand what the word competition meant; it didn't know what a new economic structure could or ought be. But it does now. It has changed Australia forever and for the better. And whatever the Liberals say, whatever they might throw at us, the notion that we can't be trusted to run the economy is finished—forever!

A party with depth and ballast means that whenever the wind blows or bad political times arrive, the party has its depth to hold itself together. This is what the other parties in this county do not have. The Labor Party is a party of conviction—the Liberal Party is a party of convenience. And the others have come and gone quickly. But we have that great ballast of belief and it is the Caucus which from time to time articulates and says what that belief might be.

We are steeped in our history and we're proud of it. The Liberals loathe our history. But the paradox is, obsessed with our history as we are, we are still the party which divines the future. We employ that history to shape the future. And well might that be the case. Because, among other things, we are more alone now than we've ever been: no imperial navy to steam to our defence, no imperial preference to guarantee our trade, no unearned weight of size. The message after a century of Federation is that we have to think anew.

You know, when we put our Federation together, there were no Washingtons around, no soldier statesmen, no people like Jefferson talking about blood being the fertiliser of democracy. Our Federation was put together by lawyers and businessmen—mostly old forelock tuggers—people who set us up as a British satellite. They were little nationalists. Safe little nationalists.

But they did make us a nation. And at its core it was decent. Fair and reasonable wages, the Deakin and Higgins legacy—a fair go for all.

Nevertheless, apart from free trade between the States and a limited defence and currency function, the Commonwealth had no remit for a national economy, no economic tools, no uniform taxation, a corporations power that a conservative court had pushed to one side, a deadly second chamber—the Senate—and kingly powers for the intended British representative, the Governor-General. It was all a massive compromise. And, along with the strategic guarantees from the old country, it gave Australia a British century—and ANZAC and all that came as part of it. Yet in the year 2000 we had a Prime Minister campaigning to keep the monarchy and actually prevailing in the exercise.

Menzies said in 1935, 'The fact is, Australia contemplates no future at all outside the British Empire'. And he talked about it lasting 500 years. You might remember the quote. In fact, it lasted only ten years after he made the remark. It died in 1945 at Potsdam when Churchill remarked to Eden, 'we've been relegated to the status of a minor power.'

What Menzies had in his head was not a racist concept, but a racial concept of Australia. And in the twenty-first century the same cringing, the same emotional cowardice, is pushing the Liberals towards America. The Liberals, given half a chance, will turn their back on our geography: their credo 'security from Asia', rather than ours, 'security in Asia'.

The coming election may well decide whether we have an Australian century in this, the twenty-first century, or an American century, as America rejects multilateralism and with it, a multi-polar world trying on an introspective view of its interests and soaking up its allies into its greater self. The conservatives—you can bet on this—will forelock tug their way to Washington, and our future as an independent country, as a republic, in Asia, in our neighbourhood, will be lost to us.

I think the lesson of the Federation should be that the lesson is over. Australia must have a new idea of itself. We have to strike out in a new direction, in a new way, armed with our self-regard, with our own confidence, fully appreciating our uniqueness. Only down this road will we find fulfilment. All other roads lead us into the shadow of great powers and perhaps, ultimately, our displacement. If not in actuality, certainly in prerogative.

Kim's speech at lunch gave me great hope. It contained a focused indignation at Howard and what he has done and, importantly, what he has failed to do. It also possessed a lightly honed and appropriate righteousness, without which Labor loses the current within its conduits. It was altogether reassuring. For Australia's sake I hope we can consign Howard to the scrapheap of history: to that pile of people who never really believed in us, who had no abiding faith in all we have created here and who would deny us our destiny.

I should conclude by saying how much I have enjoyed this centenary celebration of the Labor Party; the fact that we made the 100 years. We exist because we mean what we do. The others go round like a revolving door. That's the way it has always been.

I conclude by wishing Kim and the party well in this election. I hope that election will bode well for the new century. But a century of our own and not someone else's.

14

THE CENTENARY OF FEDERATION
Beyond the Celebrations

The University of Technology,
Sydney,
30 November 2000

*Paul Keating's 'Beyond the Celebrations' address encourages the country
to be ambitious in the twenty-first century as the act of Federation
helped set up Australia's ambitions for the twentieth century. The
speech is a grand tour of the Keating Vision: an Australian republic, a
new flag, a genuine reconciliation, further economic reform, renewed
engagement with Asia and the importance of Indonesia and the
Indonesian relationship to Australia.*

My thanks to the University of Technology Sydney for this invitation to take part in the debate about what the Centenary of Federation means for the Australian people.

When I declined to join the great trek of present and former leaders to London earlier in the year I said I would prefer to make my contribution here in Australia, so I am glad to have this opportunity to do it.

The commemoration of the Centenary of Federation is obviously a time for us to celebrate our history, but I hope it will also be a time to celebrate our historians. Without historians, we stand on a trackless plain, unsure of where we have come from, less sure of where we might go. Helen Irving and the 1901 Centre here at UTS, together with their network of colleagues around the country, have done a wonderful job in helping to give us a better map of our national experience and I congratulate them for it.

Although we seem to have heard more commentary about the Sydney Olympics than about any other single event of my adult life, let me begin this speech by adding some reflections of my own.

The Games gave Australians a chance to look at ourselves, and we liked what we saw.

We saw in the opening and closing ceremonies many reflections of ourselves. Mexican waves and the joy of sharing the sentiments with each other; of being there together, the presentation of Australia as most of us recognise it; the horsemen; our diversity and multiculturalism; rural Australia and its centrality in our affairs; the truly special place of our indigenous people; the hope of the little white girl and the black elder, the trust in which a genuine reconciliation must be rooted; and in short, the greatest arts show we have ever staged.

The Olympics gave expression to how central the arts are and need to be. The medium that draws out the nation's soul, allowing us to know ourselves and better understand what makes us tick. Whether it be the Tin Symphony or the celebration of the land and sea or the Aboriginal heritage in dance and chant or Men at Work—those Olympic themes. Slaked of those resonances we are but a nation of individuals and not the society we have become.

If Australia has learned one lesson from the Olympics, and there are many, it might be that when our arts are vibrant, so too are we.

We went to the Olympics in celebration of sport. For the pageant: to see the world's best; to see our best; to give them our support.

We remember individual medal performances. Cathy Freeman's 400 metres, Grant Hackett's 1500. And not just the icon events, the many others. But perhaps above all else, we remember what the Olympics meant to us as a people. How the themes of those ceremonies rang a chord in us and gave us something that put into context the truly valiant ambitions of our young sportsmen and women. It made their dedication seem more to us than their winning or breaking another record.

By no means all the things we discovered about ourselves during the Olympics were new. They reflected to a large extent our national image of ourselves. But it was good to get the jolt of surprise that said 'It's not just myth but reality'.

But, despite the success of the Games, I left Homebush on the night of the closing ceremony uncertain whether I had just seen the beginning of something new or the concluding fireworks of the period of reform and ambition in Australia in the 1980s and 1990s, from which the Games had sprung.

We'll get an important clue to the answer from the Centenary of Federation. The way we commemorate and celebrate these events over the next twelve months will tell us a great deal about Australia in the first years of the twenty-first century.

I'm not arguing for academic seminars at the expense of celebrations and I'm not arguing against reflections on the past or recognition of the achievements of Australians over this century. We've come a long way over the past hundred years. We have built a strong economy, a vibrant culture and a vigorous democracy.

We are a better country by far after a century of Federation than we were in 1901. We are more tolerant, more diverse, more equitable and more outward looking. More Australians—women, immigrants, indigenous Australians—have the opportunity to participate in our national life, and do so, than was possible even 25 years ago. These are mighty achievements.

But if all we get out of the Centenary of Federation is a community wallow in the national hot tub of nostalgia, it will confirm our entry into a period of national decline. We need to go beyond the celebrations and to use the event to think about where we should be heading over the next hundred years. To use this centenary for the same purpose as the act of Federation was itself used, to imagine something bigger and better; something which points the way, which lays out a roadmap and which lifts our hearts as we go.

If there is one important message I should like people to take tonight it is that Australia has no time to wait. The world won't do us the courtesy of allowing us a national time-out while we pat ourselves on the back and tell ourselves what a wonderful country we have made.

The challenges Australia faces are no less daunting than were those which faced the pioneers of Federation a century ago. More so, in most respects. The end of the bipolar certainties of the Cold War and the transforming changes wrought by the information revolution and economic globalisation have made Australia's external environment more competitive than we have ever known.

Unlike our ancestors we have no patron to look after us.

No imperial preferences to guarantee us markets. No Royal Navy to steam to our rescue in time of trouble. No massive population to give us unearned weight in the international system. No voice to speak up for us in the world unless we do it ourselves. Unlike New Zealand, we have no Australia to buffer us from strategic complexity.

When it comes down to it, the only things we can rely on are our own ingenuity, dexterity, cleverness, and our goodwill towards others. We need to use them for all we are worth.

We've probably overdosed on debates about globalisation recently but that's because it is so central to our understanding of the sort of world we now live in.

Globalisation is the great glacier which is slowly, powerfully but inexorably reshaping the international landscape.

And despite the tremulous cries of those who hope it will halt in its tracks or melt before it reaches us, it will not. At least not short of the calamitous prospect of global war.

I don't mean by this that governments are powerless pawns of economic forces. Any government can resist globalisation by hunkering down and closing up, finding some isolated valley in which to shelter. North Korea has tried it. The only result will be lower growth and poorer living standards.

None of this is to argue that we don't need vigorous debate about how we should deal with globalisation. Any force this big will have all sorts of dangerous and unintended consequences. Some members of the community will lose from the changes and must be helped along.

Impacts like the volatile money flows which scarified Asia have to be managed better.

But the process of globalisation won't stop pushing onwards. This is because the technologies that facilitate globalisation—that is, digital technology and cheap communications—aren't going to slow down. We've only begun to skim the surface of the social and economic changes that optical fibre technology and cheap, fast internet-enabled devices will bring.

The developing countries, especially in Asia, are not going to give up their hard-won efforts to integrate themselves into the global economy. Asia has had problems, but even the worst-affected country, Indonesia, which suffered a 15 per cent decline in its GDP in a single year, is still much better off than it was before it began opening up.

As for Australia, the global terms of trade aren't going to suddenly flow back in the direction of commodity producers. So even if we wanted to, we can never again rely on export wealth generated by our farmers and miners to pay for the preservation of tariff walls to protect our manufacturing and services sectors from competition. We're in the international game for keeps.

In the way we look at the world and the challenges of globalisation, the Australian community seems to divide into four main groups. These divisions cut across traditional political categories.

The first group—the Hansonists at the extreme end—want to isolate both the economy and the society from the outside world. Their economic agenda is to rebuild the tariff walls, their social one to keep out the foreigners and to return to a mythical golden age of Australian values.

The second group—S11 protesters at its extreme end—wants to internationalise social issues but nationalise the economy. They oppose 'globalisation' in its economic manifestation—free international trade, multinational corporations—but are perfectly comfortable supporting extra-territorial claims for human rights or environmental action.

A third group believes the reverse. Parts of the Business Council of Australia and many conservatives would find a home here. They are all in favour of internationalising the economy, giving free rein to the free market, but they are damned if they think foreigners and international bodies like the UN should have anything to say about social policies here in Australia.

A fourth group—and it's obviously the one to which I belong—believes that for a country like Australia, with a small population tucked away in a corner of the Asia Pacific, economic openness, social inclusiveness and engagement with the outside world is the only way in which we can hope to prosper. The only approach that will give us both the economic growth, the social confidence and the physical security to survive over the next century.

I begin with the proposition that nothing is more important to a country than the way it thinks about itself. In other words, the commonly shared model of what its national values and priorities are. Everything else, including economic growth, flows from that.

The act of Federation was an act of imagining by the men and women who fought for it; that the people of this country could be something larger than we were. They changed the way Australians thought about themselves.

I believe that a similar act of imagining is needed again, and it needs again to encompass a vision of enlargement. Inside Australia, we must move further along the road of becoming one country and one economy and, outside it, an integral part of the region around us.

We must become One Nation. One of the many reasons for my distaste for Pauline Hanson is her hijacking and distorting of this excellent phrase. Now that her ragtag operation is falling apart, I want to claim it back.

In July 1993, while Mrs Hanson was still living quietly in Ipswich, I made a speech in Corowa, commemorating the centenary of the conference there which revived the movement to Federation. I said:

For all our disparity, including the great gulf between rural and urban, there is in the end a collective Australian experience which should unite us. Nationally, we have shared in the triumphs—in sport, in the arts, in industry and science. But the greatest by far is the creation over the years of one of the great multicultural societies, and surely the very best place in the world to live. And we have done this substantially because our effort in the last century has generally been towards including all Australians in Australia's wealth.

This is a loose federation on a vast and varied continent whose population is immensely diverse in origin and culture. These factors can encourage division or fragmentation—they can encourage jealousy and rivalry between states, between cities, between the urban population and the people in the country. There is always that tendency, latent or real. But the great majority of Australians understand, as the founders of Federation understood, that we work much better when we work as one nation.

That was, I believe, another reason for our enjoyment of the Olympic Games. We gained enormous satisfaction from seeing ourselves as one people, no matter where we came from originally, no matter where we lived in the country, no matter what we did for a living.

You remember how enthusiastically the crowds sang 'I am, you are, we are Australian'. And they believed it. That itself was a big achievement of a century of Federation. But it also has implications for what we should do in the future.

Any vision of national enlargement has to deal with those things that were described by Mr Howard and his colleagues as 'distractions' when I was raising them. It's amazing how preoccupied he and his colleagues have been by exactly the same 'distractions'. And the reason, of course, is that they were never distractions at all. No matter what your attitude to issues like indigenous rights or national symbols, they are an essential part of the way we think about ourselves.

I could only reflect upon how much more we would have rejoiced in it all if the Olympics had been opened by our own president and our winning athletes had been draped in a flag that was ours. Without the Union Jack advertising its presence like a tattered maker's label.

The republic is the easiest of these issues to deal with in some ways. We all know it's coming and all opinion polls say that most of us want it. We need a head of state who is an unambiguous symbol of ourselves and not of anyone else.

As I've often said, this is not because of what the republic or the flag say to others, important though that is, but of what they say to us, about us.

Kim Beazley's promise of a plebiscite asking the simple question 'Should Australia become a republic?' is the way forward. We can then debate the modalities. When we do, I will be arguing as strongly as possible for the preservation of the Westminster system of a Cabinet headed by a Prime Minister and drawn from the Parliament rather than a popularly elected head of state—but that is an argument to come.

The challenge of reconciliation with indigenous Australians continues to weigh heavily on us. I'm enormously encouraged by the wide acceptance of this challenge across the political spectrum. The issue has been the subject of a long, grinding debate, with the government dragging the chain at every point, whether in the disgraceful decision to legislate away the rights of Aboriginal people given in the Wik decision or in the refusal to make the simple gesture that all state parliaments have made, and say sorry.

Indigenous problems are deep and entrenched. They have many causes. Some of them, as Noel Pearson has been saying, are for indigenous people themselves to address. That is a debate that will take place most effectively within the indigenous community. But it is just crass sloganeering to claim the recognition of wrongs done to Aborigines and Torres Strait Islanders in the past represents a 'black armband' view of history. It's simply to recognise the truth. We can't change it but we can recognise it.

Another looming constitutional problem for the nation is the long-term impact on our democracy of the provisions of section 24 of the Constitution, which provides that the House of Representatives will always be as nearly as possible twice the size of the Senate.

This nexus means that every time the House of Representatives gets new members because of natural growth in the population, the Senate will also grow in numbers. As it does so, the number of votes needed to secure a quota for representation will fall.

The result will be that the balance of power will increasingly fall to ever smaller and more unrepresentative minority and single-issue parties, parties and individuals who will be able to shape national policy powerfully while representing no more than the fringe of national thinking.

This is not a recipe for good government and it is not a good recipe for improving the standing of the political system generally.

The Senate does not operate now in the way the founders of the constitution imagined it would, that is as a body representing the states. Senators vote along party lines, not as representatives of Victoria or Queensland or Western Australia.

We either have to break the constitutional nexus between the two houses, or if that is impossible, move away from elections at large—by establishing regional electorates for Senators within the state, a change that would not require change to the constitution. The aim has to be to make the election of Senators as representative as possible; where a clear majority is needed to secure election.

Senators who secure a primary vote of something like 5 per cent or less, and who wait to be topped up in the distribution, are kidding themselves and us with it.

Constitutional reformers in Australia have often fallen victim to that most insidious and fatuous of slogans: if it ain't broke, don't fix it. That's a highly dangerous approach for Australia to take. Most things don't break. They just wear out, or cease doing what they are meant to do as well as they once did. Our national approach in the twenty-first century ought to be much more 'If it's not performing as effectively as it can, then change it'.

The states are a problem for the country in more ways than one.

If you were drawing up a blueprint for the nation from scratch, you would surely have smaller sub-national divisions operating under the federal level that better reflected natural regional divisions. But we have to work within the framework we've got. I accept the fact that the states are an unchangeable part of Australian constitutional arrangements. I don't think they are the best possible way of organising the nation, but I wouldn't waste much energy trying to change the current structure. We do need, however, to get the three levels of government working more effectively to create an efficient national economy.

We don't have it now, and Mr Howard's government has been more concerned with buttressing the role of the states than looking at the needs of the nation as a whole. In the Tory view of things the states represent a bulwark against national enlargement of a kind the Commonwealth government and the High Court can foster. The Liberals work on the law of averages. With six states they have at least an even chance on six occasions every three or four years to thwart progressive policy outcomes whenever a Labor government may be in office at the Commonwealth level. They see it as six chances for them to throw a spanner in the project of national enlargement. They would rather pay the GST money to the states and watch them blow it than they would pilot the Commonwealth to the point of natural authority and management of our island continent. Funding the states to grow their realm is an express part of modern conservative dogma.

There are only twenty million of us. Is the idea of running a national economy really such anathema? Doing things nationally?

It's a question to which we need a fast answer. On 14 May 1986, when I warned that Australia was in danger of becoming a banana republic the dollar stood at 71.24 cents to the US dollar. That was twenty cents higher than its recent levels.

It is now at an all-time low. Why does the world think we are worth less than we used to be? Why are our national economy and our personal wealth being both qualitatively and quantitatively valued down in world terms?

There is a strange complacency about the predicament of the dollar now. The general view seems to be, first, that the foolish money markets have got it all wrong and that recovery will come when they realise that the Australian economy is fundamentally strong; secondly, that it's really the strength of the US dollar rather than the weakness of the Australian dollar that we are seeing; and third, in any case, a low dollar is good for our exporters.

There is some truth in all these arguments. Money markets are certainly not always wise. The great strength of the US economy in recent years is whipping the US dollar to new highs at the expense of most other currencies. And the whole point of a floating exchange rate is to let the currency move so that the economy may adjust. We saw the danger of the other approach during the Asian economic crisis, when pegged exchange rates caused Asian countries such problems.

But the dilemma for us is that the Australian dollar has not just sunk against the US dollar. It is doing badly against almost everyone else.

With Australia growing faster than the United States throughout the 1990s, Australia, along with the United States, should have been marked up. Instead we have been marked down with a gaggle of other countries whose macroeconomic performance doesn't get near to ours.

We have had a great decade of growth. Not only have we on average grown more strongly than the US, which has been doing exceptionally well, we have also been growing in a different way. For the first time in several decades, we have been able to sustain low inflation. And for the first time in several decades, we have been able to sustain high productivity growth—higher, on average, than the US has been able to achieve over the same period. Now I don't want to be partisan about this, but this miracle performance did not start in 1996. It started at the beginning of the decade, it has continued ever since, and in my view it is undoubtedly due to the great and difficult reforms we made to the Australian economy in the 1980s and the early 1990s. By these I mean the float of the currency, deregulation of finance, tariff cuts, the use of the Accord to reduce inflation and increase employment, the switch to enterprise bargaining at the beginning of the 1990s and inflation targeting by the Reserve Bank from 1994. They were all reforms designed, as I said at the time, to open the place up, and they worked. I recall speaking to the then EPAC forum as Treasurer in early 1991, and saying then that we had designed our policies to produce a long upswing which would be characterised by low inflation and high productivity growth, and that is exactly what happened. We had low inflation from 1991, and we had the beginning of our high productivity growth in the same year, and both have continued ever since.

So we addressed two of the big problems in our economic perform-ance. But there was one great issue which remained from the 1980s and continued to be problem for us in the 1990s, and is, I think, still a problem for us today. It is a problem that results directly from globalisation, because it is a problem which can only exist in a world of free capital flows. This is the current account deficit, which looked at from the other side is the same thing as the gap between what we invest in Australia, and what we save.

Year by year we have been investing more than we save, and as a result, year by year, we have been adding to our foreign liabilities. I think we have been investing wisely over the last decade, and we have increased our ability to handle foreign debt. But I think we can see in the very cheap Australian dollar some of the consequences of this growing weight of foreign liabilities.

In recent years we have been relying on foreign borrowing by Australian banks to sustain our capital inflow, and I think we have begun to see a fading appetite for Australian-dollar debt in offshore markets. This is one big reason the Australian dollar is cheap, and it is telling us that we should be mindful of the need to sharply slow the growth of Australian-dollar debt offshore.

These are circumstances in which Australia should be aiming for a substantial trade surplus. If we can achieve a trade surplus of just 1 per cent of GDP, for example, we can cut our current account deficit to 3 per cent of GDP. This is a very significant number, because with a current account deficit of 3 per cent of GDP our foreign liabilities would not be growing faster than our national product, and the capital inflow required to sustain the deficit would be almost entirely met by equity investment rather than debt.

So this is a very important and desirable goal, but I want to ask you this. Have you heard anything from the Treasurer or the Prime Minister or any other member of the Cabinet which suggests it *is* an important or desirable goal? Even a reference to it? Have you seen any hint of national leadership on this issue? Have you seen any suggestion that we have here a government which has the imagination, the courage and the vision to build on the gains of the 1980s and 1990s? To do something in its own right to arrest the growth of our foreign liabilities in the new decade?

It's true that the last four years the federal government has run a general government underlying surplus which over the four years accumulates to 2 per cent of GDP. The underlying cash surplus is roughly equivalent to the government's contribution to national saving, and as I said the current account deficit measures the shortfall in our national saving compared to our national investment. With a current account deficit which is still well over 4 per cent of GDP we ought to be running a large Commonwealth fiscal surplus. But we should certainly not be taken in by this surplus. After all, we are now in the tenth year of an economic expansion. A government has to try hard, very hard in fact, not to have a surplus after nine-and-a-half years of uninterrupted economic growth. And while 2 per cent is a useful contribution to national saving, it is less than half the accumulated surplus of 4.2 per cent of GDP Labor built up in successive budgets over the four years to 1990–1991, when we were also fighting a blowout in the current account deficit.

And while the government has achieved a very moderate surplus, it has set us a long way back in national saving in other important ways. When I left office we had a plan in place to take superannuation contributions to 15 per cent of all wages and salaries. Half of the increase over 9 per cent was to come from the government, and half from employees. Another 6 per cent of total wages and salaries into super is equal to something like 3 per cent of GDP—a good deal of which would be a net increase to national saving.

One of the most ideological and reckless things the Howard government did on coming to office was to scrap Labor's 6 per cent addition to the 9 per cent Superannuation Guarantee Charge. In various transmutations the money which was earmarked for the government's contribution to the super of every employee in this country ended up as net income tax cuts designed to sweeten the pill of the GST. In other words, it was blown in order to help a change in the tax mix which I confidently predict will have no discernible impact on our economic performance at all. The GST was always a second-order economic issue.

But if national saving was 3 per cent higher today, we would have a current account deficit at half of the level we had last year, and we would not need to be issuing new debt overseas to finance it. We would have addressed and met the great remaining problem which looms over the economic future of Australia. The last of Australia's great economic vulnerabilities.

This is effectively the Treasurer's only major task. In May 1986 I used the banana republic episode to warn the electorate of our longer-term vulnerabilities. The then government used that community authority to make the most sweeping economic changes since the war. This government now has to do the same thing. To draw down the authority flowing from the exchange rate warnings and use it to deal with national savings and the current account.

If it does not, if it does the electorally 'smart' thing and turns a blind eye, and if perchance it were to stay in office, the debt and liabilities may well go supercritical. The nation will be left in an enormous hole from which it will have great trouble emerging. It would then be left to another government to deal with, similar to the macroeconomic and structural shambles that was left to Labor to deal with in 1983.

I should like to also say a few things about social policy. This is important in a discussion about Federation. For at the time, the one thing that Labor and the Deakinites had in common was a commitment to the social contract—a private enterprise economy with imaginative and compassionate social underpinnings.

Over the last four-and-a-half years, the conservatives have kept all the things which were handed to business by Labor as part of a balanced society. A high profit share, a low corporate tax rate, dividend imputation etcetera. Yet on the other hand, the balancing social aspects of Labor's policies are being gradually whittled away.

The scuttling of *Working Nation*, the windbacks in education and the collapse of R&D represent a massive disinvestment in the country's future.

A fully employed inclusive society invested with education, opportunity and creativity is the only model we can have faith in. A model that promotes division and unequal opportunity or where we have an untrained or poorly trained workforce focused on old economy pursuits cannot give us the future that the new age holds.

We cannot afford Thatcherism by stealth. Where the benefits of a prolonged period of growth are turned over to half the people, consolidating inequity and inopportunity. Two nations, no society. This would be a dreadful betrayal of the Federation past and future. A golden age for some, something of a bronze age for the remainder.

Britain and New Zealand give the example and Australians should take note!

As I said earlier, it will be harder for Australia to make its way in today's globalised, inter-dependent world than it was for us in 1901.

Back then, we knew where we fitted into the international scheme. Imperial policy was our policy. To the cheers of the crowd during the first Commonwealth election campaign Edmund Barton said 'there could be no foreign policy of the Commonwealth. The foreign policy belonged to the Empire. Australians could not affect that policy except by such representations as they could make to the Imperial Government'.

Now, we are alone. The alliance with the United States is important to us, but it is no life-raft. Australia has to have its own foreign policy. We either want to be an organic part of the region around us or stand from it—behind someone else's strength. In reality, the codes to our safety are in our own command—within our own heads. The determining thing is to know this. Our future lies in this area; in East Asia and the Asia Pacific. That's where our economic growth will come from, and where our security must be found.

The Second World War made that clear to us. And although we have taken some detours recently, engagement with Asia remains the grandest undertaking we face in the first decades of this century.

We are already one of the region's natural integrators, providing the raw materials, agricultural products and increasingly the services which drive economic growth in East Asia. But we also need to be a regional integrator in a foreign policy sense as well. In the recent past we were. We must be again. Our future depends on helping to construct the region's institutions. The grim reality is that unless we are a policy maker, we end up a policy taker.

We just cannot afford to have ten years on with Asia and then ten years off.

APEC, as we saw again in Brunei, is drifting. We have lost management of the large economic and strategic issues inherent in the APEC agenda. And Australia is *not* a member of the ASEAN plus three grouping which brings Southeast Asia, Japan, China and South Korea together. Pointedly, we have been left out.

In the area of regional security, the ASEAN Regional Forum has not lived up to early hopes for it, but Australia will *not* be part of the new security architecture being pushed by the United States in Northeast Asia.

We have *not* been invited to join the proposed new Asian Monetary Fund.

The government's hopes for closer relations between the ASEAN Free Trade Area and Australia and New Zealand were embarrassingly dashed and a new free trade link between the ASEANs, China, Japan and South Korea is being floated. But *not* with us.

In other words, we are being turned away from the region's decision-making structures, and the strategic consequences for us will be profound.

Let me say something about Indonesia, because that may be the relationship on which we need to work hardest.

The disintegration of the Australian relationship with Indonesia has been the most disastrous piece of Australian diplomacy since Robert Menzies backed the wrong argument in Vietnam.

At what should have been a defining new moment for Australia–Indonesia relations, with the advent of a new democratic government, we've managed to plunge into a thirty-year low.

This did not need to happen. It was *not* the inevitable result of a choice for Australia between helping to stop violence in East Timor and good relations with the new forces in Jakarta. John Howard has claimed that 'it was quite impossible to avoid a period of tension—especially at the government level—with Indonesia'.

I say that it was not. That it came because of this government's constant preference for perceived domestic advantage over national interest, and the manner in which the policy was implemented—the triumphalism, the lack of any government counter to the wilder effluxes of jingoism coming through the Australian media, the wilful failure to expend any political capital in defence of the relationship. By no means all the fault for the deterioration of the relationship lies on the side of the Australian government, but that is the only part of it we can do anything about.

There has been an unspoken change in Australia's policy towards Indonesia recently. You won't find it in any speech by the government, but it will be found by the historians in 30 years' time when the classified policy papers of this government are available. It is the view that Indonesia can be put on hold. That we can let it all blow by, that there is nothing to be done, that the doing of it doesn't matter so much, and that in any case the Australian people are suspicious of Indonesia and don't want anything done.

I disagree with this assessment fundamentally.

On West Papua the government has to be prepared to articulate clearly what the Indonesia relationship means to us and why it is important. Why it is in *Australia's* national interest that Indonesia remain a unified state. It has to shape the opinion and not leave it to correspondents with a bad case of mission creep.

The challenge of engagement with the region is not just, or even primarily, a matter for governments, however. As with Federation, it begins with a change in the way we think about ourselves.

The change will take place primarily in people-to-people contact, in schools and universities, in growing business contacts, in closer sporting ties, in endless different contacts that will each leave its own thin layer of greater familiarity to build the relationship between Australia and the region more strongly.

But engagement does require government support. Alexander Downer tried to draw a distinction earlier in the year between what he termed 'practical regionalism', which he favoured and which seemed to mean making a buck out of the place, and 'emotional' regionalism which, by implication, was what colleagues like Gareth Evans and I had been after, and which well-bred South Australians found discomfiting. Like their approval of 'practical reconciliation' with our indigenes.

You've always got to be worried when you hear the world 'practical' from this government. It's like an anti-matter particle which obliterates the noun it's meant to describe.

In my experience, practical goals on this scale, whether they involve reconciliation with Aborigines or engagement with the region, cannot be reached without a commitment of the emotions—of the heart as well as the head.

But there is one issue to which the current government has returned to the position of the founding fathers and that is immigration. Immigration was a large part of the Federation argument. Deakin said nothing was more important to Australia than keeping other people out and he was the most liberal of the founders. The government's hysterical tone towards refugees and asylum-seekers returns to this theme.

This important subject requires a change of policy.

It's not that I believe Australia should be fair game for anyone who manages to turn up here. We need to keep control. But there has long been an inbuilt tension in Australian approaches, between the idea that the policy is basically about patrolling the perimeter to keep people out and the recognition that we need to attract good immigrants who are doing us a service by helping to develop the country.

Immigration will continue to be a vital ingredient in Australia's national development and while televised pictures of asylum-seekers in camps in the middle of the desert might deter a few queue jumpers from setting out by boat from southern China or the Middle East, such images do us much more damage in sending a message to skilled young people the world over, that this is a country which is suspicious of foreigners. Like everything else in a globalised world, the competition for immigrants is becoming more intense. We are now competing with many other countries, including traditional sources of immigration like Ireland, to attract the best people.

Let me say finally that if I had to pick one thing that I would most like to come from the celebrations of the Centenary of Federation, it would be that we finally stop regarding ourselves as a young country. The image of youth is persistent in our culture. It stems from those allegorical nineteenth-century illustrations of Australian children clustering around the skirts of Britannia, but it continues to shape our view of Australia today.

The national anthem has it quite wrong, however. Far from being 'young and free', we are old and free.

An old country, obviously. The oldest continent on earth and one whose ancient landscape has shaped our economy and our national character. One that taught us not to take too much for granted, to look to each other, to value space and the sense of personal freedom that comes with it. And an old democracy which is the basis of the Australian contract to which we are all party.

The only sense in which we are young is that white people came to this country just four of my own lifetimes ago. But we then quickly made ourselves one of the oldest democracies in the world. This country had secret ballots, universal male suffrage (apart from indigenous Australians), and votes for women well before most of the rest of the world. We've been governing ourselves for a long time, and we do it well.

It is important that we understand this. So long as we persist in hiding behind the imagery of national adolescence we provide ourselves with excuses for not taking full responsibility for our national life.

The great fear of isolation and abandonment which has shaped so much of Australian history fades when you regard yourself as fully grown.

At the age of a hundred, we can surely permit ourselves confidence in our judgement about ourselves and in our capacity to do what must be done.

If the Centenary of Federation helps us to do that, we will truly have had much to celebrate.

15

FOR THE NEW AUSTRALIA

The University of New South Wales,
Sydney,
11 November 1996

The address 'For the New Australia' made by Paul Keating after his
retirement from elected public life is the first speech that outlined his
holistic view as to how Australia's economy and society had developed; the
rationale for the reforms he undertook; and how he saw the country being
positioned in future. In the address Paul Keating casts the monoculture of
the old Australia as myth and argues it is a role of government to protect
the nation from prejudice. These wider observations roll into a full-blooded
case for an Australian republic, replete with the need for a generous and
necessary reconciliation with Australia's indigenes.

WHEN I LAST SPOKE IN this auditorium in June, I talked about the
growing interdependence between our domestic and foreign policy
concerns. I said that the old divisions between what we do internally
and what we do externally no longer substantially exist.

I also spoke of the need for governments and others involved in
foreign policy in Australia to confront growing fears in our society about
the future and our engagement with the rest of the world.

I said these fears were linked to a yearning for an Australia which
no longer exists.

Tonight I want to reflect on these problems from the other direction,
from the inside. And to discuss Australia itself and what being an

Australian means in the last decade of the twentieth century. And what perhaps it should mean in the twenty-first century.

Public debate in Australia over the past few months has been heavily concentrated on issues like immigration and Aboriginal affairs, on what the parameters of public debate should be and the issue of so-called political correctness.

It does seem a remarkable thing to me: here we are in the last half-decade of our first century as a nation, eighteen million of us on a continent almost the size of the United States, one of the oldest and most stable democracies in the world, sitting adjacent to the most extraordinary economic revolution in the history of the world, and what appears to concern some of us most is the colour of people's skins.

It seems an eternity since we were talking about parallels between our own constitutional ambitions and those of Federation's founding fathers. We who favour a republic drew some inspiration from the achievement of Federation and nationhood. We concerned ourselves with native title, education in civics, a modified multiculturalism, a new relationship with the countries of Asia. Suddenly the strongest parallel with the period in which our nation was created seems to be a preoccupation with racially based immigration.

It has been one of the saddest developments in our recent history. But we can learn from it and it may not be too late to arrest the process.

One result of the debate must surely be an improved understanding on the part of our politicians of this simple reality—there is no escaping the broad view.

Events and policies in different areas are all related. For example, what we say and do about our immigration policy has economic effects far beyond any spurious case that may be made about the effect of migrants on the availability of jobs. It affects the level of investment in Australia, the success of our business abroad—and these things by contrast have consequences for jobs which are anything but spurious. The links are not always direct but, as the business community has been making clear to the government, they exist and they are powerful.

Culture and identity, the structures and symbols of our government and the way we define ourselves as a nation are not distractions from the concerns of ordinary people, their income, their security, their mortgage payments and their children's education and health. Rather, they are an intrinsic part of the way we secure these things.

Two years ago, some people were calling these matters diversions. They were not then, and they are not now.

In truth I think the pity is that at this mature stage of our national life we are still arguing about the most basic issues of our identity. By rights the argument should have been settled years ago. I would be glad if I never heard the word 'identity' again.

That is one of many reasons why I am utterly convinced that we should be a republic. It seems to me that the republic should be and can be the most natural and necessary step. We should be able to take it in our stride. And really we must.

And if Paul Keating saying these things sounds all too familiar or arouses suspicion in some hearts, here is the *Australian Financial Review*—hardly a republican organ or one easily diverted from the economic main game—in an editorial a month ago. We are going through 'Throwback', they said:

> *Australia cannot retreat behind a white picket fence . . . rather Australians must embrace the future and the Government must take the lead. This means adopting a positive outward-looking attitude to all parts of the world, including Asia, and encouraging an understanding of the benefits of immigration so that fear does not drive discussion of it. It means coming to terms with the various, and sometimes painful, histories of Australians and working towards creating a tolerant and inclusive society.*
>
> *It means pursuing a republican constitution and a new distinctively Australian flag in time for the centenary of federation and the Sydney 2000 Olympics.*

How doubly reassuring it would have been to have had such an expression of interest from the *Financial Review* during our days in office! Perhaps only now do they feel free to say what has been on their minds.

All this is by way of introduction.

I want to begin by saying something about the creation of the new Australia—and for all the recent signs of regression, I think the term still applies. And I want to talk about the role of government in nurturing that creation.

I feel obliged to make a few remarks about immigration and multi-culturalism, including Asian migration and to touch on the issues facing indigenous Australians, their place in the new Australia and the implications of their treatment for the rest of us.

And I want to talk about the consequences of these things for the structures of Australian institutions, including the republic.

One of the strangest myths spread recently has been the one that under the Labor government debate in Australia was somehow strangled and the people cowered under a stupefying pall of 'political correctness'. I know I have sometimes been held responsible for terrifying into silence those who disagreed with me.

Well, I obviously wasn't much good at it. Timid little creatures like Bruce Ruxton and Alan Jones and Graeme Campbell seemed to me remarkably undeterred. Newspaper columns, letter pages and talkback radio shows were notably not unforthcoming in their criticism. During the native title debate, Aborigines, graziers and miners did not shirk from saying what they thought. Loggers and greens had their go. The monarchists were not overcome by their natural decorum.

In fact, we have to ask if we are not seeing here a classic case of the oppressors parading as victims.

To my mind, the infelicities and exaggerations of those who are trying to avoid harm and insult, or to make others feel better about their condition, is a relatively trivial sin compared with those whose aim, or effect, is to harm and to affront.

On the other hand, I don't think I can be accused of being politically correct myself—unless expelling Graeme Campbell was politically correct, which I happen to think it was.

Over-zealousness can be an ugly thing, and I have no doubt it has done some harm here and there, but 'political correctness' is not the quasi-totalitarian evil some people are making it out to be.

On the other hand, it has provided a useful smoke-screen for some crude turnings in the national debate. A very ugly, resentful and xenophobic cat has been let out of the bag.

But I think it would be unwise to simply attempt to stuff the beast back and tie it up as best we can without attempting to understand why it escaped in the first place.

Or, more importantly, without developing the sophisticated political responses needed to ensure that a sense of national unity and purpose is restored and strengthened by the experience.

At least the current debate has more sharply focused the choices as we attempt to chart a course into the next century.

In *The End of Certainty*, Paul Kelly wrote that the Australia brought into being through Federation was:

> *founded on faith in government authority; belief in egalitarianism; a method of judicial determination in centralised wage fixation; protection of its industry and its jobs; dependence upon a great power (first Britain, then America), for its security and its finance; and, above all, hostility to its geographical location, exhibited in fear of external domination and internal contamination from the peoples of the Asia/Pacific. Its bedrock ideology was protection; its solution, a Fortress Australia, guaranteed as part of an impregnable Empire spanning the globe.*

Almost a century later, as Kelly says, this introspective, defensive, dependent framework is a crumbling legacy. The major battleground of ideas in Australian politics has become one between what he calls the internationalist rationalists and the sentimentalist traditionalists— between those who know that the Australian Settlement is unsustainable and those who fight to retain it.

I am inclined to agree almost entirely with Kelly. I differ only in that I believe that fundamental philosophical differences between the two major sides of politics, in particular the approach to industrial relations and the role of government in social and economic policy, remain distinct.

But there is no doubt that his analysis is basically correct. And he is just as correct when he writes about the profound and pernicious impact of the White Australia policy—the death throes of which we are apparently still experiencing.

It is worth remembering that it was only 30 years ago that both the major parties abandoned White Australia as official policy; only twenty-odd since Whitlam gave us our first non-discriminatory immigration policy; and only fifteen since the term *multiculturalism* arrived in the official political lexicon under Malcolm Fraser.

The past fifteen years have been so full of rapid and profound change and, with the change, so much uncertainty, it is not so surprising that the Australia of Deakin and Hughes, Menzies and Calwell—that somewhat mythical place of cultural homogeneity and imperial benevolence—should have become an object of nostalgia.

But I think that beneath the nostalgia lies a deeper malaise which is more universal, more complex in its genesis, and altogether more difficult to grapple with. It is a condition which all modern western democracies are experiencing.

At its core is the loss of identity and spiritual frameworks wrought by the rolling tide of forces we wrap up in convenient catch-alls like 'globalisation': the feeling many of us have that our lives are increasingly beyond our individual control, that our cultural signposts are changing without our consent; that old definitions and boundaries are blurring; that the world is becoming an alarmingly small place, but also, paradoxically, moving beyond a human scale.

Essentially, the old certainties are passing. There is a feeling that community and nation-building are not cooperative efforts; that goals are not shared; that there is no guiding light; that modern life is leading to a greater sense of isolation; that, for all their promise, our technologies are often asocial; that modern economies spin wealth to the peripheries and away from the middle; that employment is insecure;

that structural change leaves uncompensated losers in its wake; that the absence of widely shared and binding social and national values leaves people feeling disconnected and searching for some greater meaning in their lives.

The greater affluence, choices and mobility which most have is not leading to the fulfilment they had hoped for, and which they believe they had been promised.

Cynicism with the political process is one inevitable consequence of this: television hosts replace the politicians, talkback shows replace the parliaments—just about anything is seen to be more 'empowering' than the traditional institutions and processes of democracy.

You will not be surprised to hear me say that I find this a worrying development: nor if I tell you that I think Australian democratic institutions are no less democratic now than they have ever been and that Australian governments in recent times have never been more conscientious.

That is not to say that the traditional institutions and processes represent the limits of democracy, or that the politicians in the parliaments have not sometimes failed to deliver all that the people are entitled to expect.

But I do believe that the source of the present discontent is not the same as the target of its expression.

I think there is equally no question that what we are witnessing reflects in part a natural cycle in public affairs.

The prevailing orthodoxy is discharged for the new—only to find that the new is beginning another familiar cycle.

Writing in 1988, Arthur Schlesinger said:

The cycle turns and turns again. Each phase turning its natural course. The season of idealism and reform, where strong governments call for active public interest in national affairs and invoke government as a means of promoting the general welfare, eventually leaves the electorate exhausted by the process and disenchanted by the results. People are ready to respond to leaders who tell them they needn't worry unduly about public affairs, that left to promote action and self-interest in an unregulated market, problems will solve themselves. This mood too, eventually runs its course. Problems neglected become acute, threaten to become unmanageable and demand remedy. People grow increasingly bored with selfish motives and vistas, increasingly weary of materialism and demand some larger meaning beyond themselves.

But what is *new* about the current cycle is that there is a feeling of frustration and resentment which goes beyond a rejection of the former orthodoxy.

The passing of the old certainties, the social maladies I have just mentioned, tell people that their diminished sense of fulfilment and esteem, and the disconnection they feel, has its cause in the preferences they see meted out by government.

In the effort to make sense of the frustrations they feel, they seek to stigmatise groups whom they see as a cause of their problems. Invariably, they are the weaker groups in society.

The danger, as JK Galbraith has pointed out in another context, is that 'the tribulations of the margins will sooner or later begin to erode the contentment of the middle'. The growing number of stigmatised and disaffected will before long upset the value system of the many.

For, in the end, a society does exist as a whole and not in parts—something the Hanson devotees are finding out in another context.

If all this is a consequence of this change, we had better ask how and why we got to this point and whether there were really any alternatives.

Our starting point should be to remind ourselves just what a narrow escape from self-imposed marginalisation we have had.

In the immediate postwar decades we floated in the South Pacific as a sort of message in a bottle—a time capsule of what used to be.

We should not forget that up until the *Australian Citizenship Act* came into effect in 1949—less than 50 years ago—there were no Australian citizens as such. We were all simply British subjects. And it took a long time after that for many of us to stop feeling—or wishing—that we still were.

We felt secure in the assumption that the British and then the Americans stood steadfastly between us and the threat of the yellow peril. Our economy chugged along on the broad shoulders of the miners and farmers whose output more than made up for a sclerotic secondary industry camped behind a wall of protection.

Yet we may well have felt more certain of who we were and where we were headed.

We had built on the Gallipoli legend in both major theatres in the Second World War. We had stopped the Japanese on our doorstep (with a little help from our friends) and in so doing felt that we had finally earned a place in the world.

We enjoyed full employment; the first Holdens rolled off the production line and the world lined up to buy our unprocessed commodities. The 1956 Olympics and the Snowy Mountains Scheme seemed to confirm our assessment that we were finally a nation to be reckoned with.

Our sense of national identity was built on legends born of the struggle to subdue a difficult and alien landscape, on our deeds in war and sports, on a great soprano and a horse.

And, of course, we were white, and determined to stay that way.

What we didn't realise until it was almost too late was that the paradise we thought we had exclusive possession of—bar the original inhabitants and they didn't count—was a fool's one.

The warning signs were all there, but no-one was really looking.

So what had happened?

To quote Paul Kelly again:

> In 1870 Australia's average income was about 40 per cent higher than any other nation. Over the next century Australia's GDP growth per head was worse than any industrial country. World Bank statistics show that from the late nineteenth century to 1980, Australia fell from first place to fourteenth in terms of GDP per head. During the nineteenth century the Australian economy was relatively open; in the twentieth century it was relatively closed. The transition from success to failure ran parallel to a rise in protection.

He points out that:

Australia's share of world exports fell from 1.7 per cent in 1960 to 1.1 per cent in 1987, a measure of its closed economy and declining competitiveness. Australia was the only industrialised nation that failed to increase its proportion of exports to GDP over the thirty years from 1960. Australia's ratio stayed at 13.5 per cent when the expected growth should have taken this ratio to about 19 per cent.

In fact, since the mid-1980s Australia's exports to GDP rose from 14.8 per cent to 19.2 per cent. But up until then, our performance was woeful. The rest of the world was experiencing a massive surge in trade and Australia was just not an effective participant.

By the beginning of the 1970s we were well on the way to becoming an economic museum. And most of our political leaders were doing little more than wandering about the place looking uncomprehendingly at the exhibits; the rusty old factories built on tariffs with marketing objectives extending not much further than the surrounding suburbs; a primary industry still doing all right but feeling the pinch from competition in traditional markets; no service industries to speak of.

The growing trade relationship with Japan apart, our relationship with the region in which we lived was governed mostly by ignorance and not a little fear—by prejudice. The White Australia policy was not the only expression of this, but it was the most striking. And why anybody should pretend otherwise, or suggest that we pretend otherwise to our children, I simply cannot understand.

The difficult economic and social recasting of the past couple of decades was an inevitable legacy of these misguided years and our refusal to recognise the profound changes that were occurring in a world to which our backs were largely turned.

These changes were the foundations of a modern, competitive economy. Labor was the government which made them, but it can be truly said that they were made by all Australians. Unions and business were active participants. And everyone lived with the effects. They did so because it was accepted that these changes were the only means of giving us a chance: a chance of a prosperous future in an unsentimental world which is waiting for no-one and owes no-one a living—at least not a country with our endowments.

If we are now experiencing the ripple effects of these changes, as we are, and if they have brought with them uncertainties, which they have, then it has to be said that the consequences of the alternative—to muddle along in progressive decline—are unthinkable.

And of course layered over the economic changes were others which were just as critical.

Postwar immigration, the demise of the unifying ethos of White Australia, the introduction of a non-discriminatory immigration policy, the influx of new migrants from the region, the transformation of the Asia Pacific from a region of military threat to one of economic dynamism, the belated realisation that self-reliance rather than fading historical allegiances is the key to our security, the irresistible struggle of our indigenous people for recognition and rights—all these things have rendered much of the old Australia—the one established by the Australian Settlement and still deeply embedded in the psyche of many of us—no longer relevant or useful.

Nor is it real. The great tragedy of the shamelessly regressive politics of Pauline Hanson is not so much that it is rooted in ignorance, prejudice and fear, though it is; not so much that it projects the ugly face of racism, though it does; not so much that it is dangerously divisive and deeply hurtful to many of her fellow Australians, though it is; not even that it will cripple our efforts to enmesh ourselves in a region wherein lie the jobs and prosperity of future generations of young Australians, though it will—the great tragedy is that it perpetrates a myth, a fantasy, a lie.

The myth of the monoculture. The lie that we can retreat to it.

The changes are permanent and, while we may be going through a consequent period of general uncertainty and unease, they are, in my view, almost universally for the better.

It is not going to seem this way to everyone of course, but Australia simply is a richer place these days: a far more open, creative, dynamic, diverse and worldly place.

And I'm not just talking about Double Bay and Paddington.

Our integration with the rest of the world has made more than the streets and the arts and the food more interesting: it has created new opportunities in agriculture and horticulture, tourism and hospitality, education, manufacturing, retailing, science, arts and entertainment. It has changed the nature of work and workplaces—and if there is a general hankering to go back to the old ones it can only be because a lot of people have forgotten what they were like.

This is to say nothing more than that we have joined the modern world but we could not have joined it without the changes.

Now, we can embrace this new Australia or we can reject it. That, fundamentally, is the choice I mentioned at the beginning. We can engage with it, recognise its potential and accept the fact that nothing in this world comes easy. We can work to sustain the momentum and expand the opportunities for our kids.

Or we can regress. We can retreat. We can stop to have a scratch— amuse ourselves with sectional interests. We can say this is too hard for Australians. It's not us. *They* are not us. In the best traditions of the old Australia we can call a national smoko. We can relax—and be comfortable.

The latter is folly, but it *is* an option. We can retreat to a past that never was, and create a future that never can be anything but third-rate. But if we do, we can be sure that the world will not be in a hurry to forgive us or bail us out. Even if they forgave our prejudice they could never forget our stupidity.

In the last ten years 77 per cent of all export growth has been to East Asia. More than three-quarters of our future is there. And some Australian politicians are talking about a discriminatory immigration policy again.

Pauline Hanson or her sympathisers might say, who cares? But future generations will care—and they won't readily understand why we were more persuaded by our prejudices or by perceived political advantage than by their needs.

In the current debate it is easy for people who do not share Pauline Hanson's philosophy to throw up their hands and lament. You hear it around now—what has happened to the Australian people that they will listen to such prejudice and do themselves and their country such an injury?

But I don't believe the responsibility lies principally with Pauline Hanson's supporters or even, in the final analysis, with Pauline Hanson. You can find a Pauline Hanson anywhere and anytime. You can find substantial discontent with our immigration policy and multiculturalism anywhere and anytime. Had a referendum been held—or a people's convention—to consider changing the White Australia policy in, say 1970, I don't think there's much doubt it would *not* have been changed. And had it not been changed, Australia would today be—deservedly—an international pariah, and in every way a much poorer country.

The fact is that it is the responsibility of *governments* to protect the national interest against the tide of prejudice. In all circumstances, including the present ones, the best protection is to maintain the momentum. We have to educate certainly, and you might recall that in office we were in the process of developing a national curriculum and community education program for just this purpose. But above all it is up to governments to maintain momentum. To keep the national eye on the national interest—not on the polling, at least not on crucial matters like this. If this immigration business has done nothing else, I hope it has persuaded a few more people of what an insidious caper polling can be.

If multicultural Australia, and with it our hard won good name for tolerance and fair play, falls over—the good name *our* generation has done more than any other to win—if that falls over, it will be because the government has stopped pedalling. And on the government's head, not the people's or Pauline Hanson's, will the responsibility rest.

Australia's postwar immigration policy was one of the greatest strategic decisions this country has made.

It transformed our country and strengthened our economy.

It has made Australia a culturally richer, more varied and much more interesting place to live. It has given us weight.

For half a century, when asked whether they supported the immigration program, most Australians would tell the pollsters, no.

But these responses—and we still see them—reflect in my view a shallow dissatisfaction, a feeling of apprehension about future competition for jobs, rather than a commentary on what has already been done.

Throughout these five decades successive governments persisted with the immigration program because it was in the national interest.

The level of the program rose and fell in reaction to economic activity.

And its composition changed too, in response to different national needs and to developments in the world.

It is important to be clear about the figures.

Forty two per cent of Australia's population was born outside this country or have one parent who was born overseas.

The immigration program this year, including the refugee component, is about 83,000. Around one quarter are the spouses and fiances of Australian residents. This means not just recently arrived immigrants, but young Australians who work or study overseas and want to marry—as I did—someone from another country.

The size of the program is hardly unreasonable in a population of 18 million. It is certainly not the cause of the unemployment problems in Australia.

The reasons we favour or oppose migration have more to do with the sort of country we want this to be than with any concern about migration's impact on unemployment, or any expectation that it will provide an immediate boost to economic growth.

There is a perfectly reasonable debate to be had about immigration numbers in Australia. But that debate has hardly been absent from Australian politics over the years.

Some very sensible people worry on environmental grounds about whether Australia can sustain a much larger population.

I say that the environmental problems facing Australia, especially the quality of our soils and water, are indeed serious issues for us. And they need to be addressed. But the way to address them is not to slam down the shutters and put up a 'house full' sign at our borders.

My view on immigration is shaped by a belief that this country has extraordinary potential and that we will be better able to survive and prosper in the world if we have a young and growing population.

But this recent debate is not really about immigration *per se*—it is about *Asian* immigration, as most of the best known participants know full well.

The same codewords and subtext are seen in the debate about multiculturalism. It is a multiculturalism of the dark imagination which is on trial here, not the reality.

Multiculturalism is an inelegant word which has almost as many meanings as it has users. And I would be as happy as anyone to drop it from my vocabulary as soon as something better turns up.

But I wholeheartedly support its meaning and purpose.

In his book *The Culture of Complaint*, the critic Robert Hughes describes multiculturalism like this:

> *Multiculturalism asserts that people with different roots can co-exist, that they can learn to read the image-banks of others, that they can and should look across the frontiers of race, language, gender and age without prejudice or illusion.*

Like everything else in our society, multicultural policy reflects a balance of rights and responsibilities. It proclaims the right to express and share our individual cultural heritage, and the right of every Australian to equality of treatment and opportunity.

But it imposes responsibilities too. These are that the first loyalty of all Australians must be to Australia, that all must accept the basic principles of Australian society. These include the Constitution and the rule of law, parliamentary democracy, freedom of speech and religion, English as the national language, equality of the sexes, tolerance.

These descriptions of multicultural policy are not new. They are part and parcel of what multiculturalism in Australia has always been about, and few Australians would disagree with them.

In any case it is difficult to imagine the monocultural alternative in the late twentieth century. How could there be one model of Australianness with which we could all identify? Who would decide it? Would it ever change? How? Would it be an urban, suburban or rural Australianness? Male or female?

From the earliest times of European settlement, Australia has been a work in progress, redefining itself, shifting its image of what it means to be Australian in response to the changing world.

Yet these recent events have done considerable and utterly unnecessary harm to Australia's reputation and to the principle of tolerance which had become a definitive part of the new Australia—*and* which made this country something of a model for others.

I have seen how the manifestations of the debate have played out in the region around us. I have seen the impact it has had on Asian Australians and on others in our community.

Damage has been done to our interests: our economic interests and to our international standing.

And just as important has been the effect on our confidence, and the pride we take in the society we have created here.

Ignorance and fear need to be confronted with knowledge and reassurance: not fanned by those who implicitly agree with the sentiments expressed, or who, even more culpably, seek to attach themselves for reasons of self-interest to whatever they think might be a passing current of public opinion.

There is so much more we need to do than have this futile and damaging exercise. Above all, we need to keep the momentum of our economic and social progress. This debate is a stick in our spokes—an almost incredible self-inflicted stumble.

Almost incredible not because the conditions are not ripe for grievances to be aired, but because there is so little justification for this one and so much for every one of us to lose.

Just as surely, the way we deal with the indigenous Australians will also determine how we are judged abroad and by future generations. It will always be a measure of our success as a country and the esteem in which we hold ourselves.

In 1992 I made a speech to a group of people gathered in Redfern for the launch of the International Year for the World's Indigenous People. I said then that the way we manage to extend opportunity and care and dignity and hope to the indigenous people of Australia would be a fundamental test of our social goals and our national will: our ability to say to ourselves and the rest of the world that Australia is a first-rate social democracy, that we are what we should be—truly the land of the fair go and the better chance.

I also said, and I think it bears repeating in the current climate, that the process of reconciliation had to start with an act of recognition. Recognition that it was we non-Aboriginal Australians who did the dispossessing; and yet we had always failed to ask ourselves how we would feel if it had been done to us.

When I said these things, it was not my intention to impress guilt upon present generations of Australians for the actions of the past, but rather to acknowledge that we now share a responsibility to put an end to the suffering. I said explicitly that guilt is generally not a useful emotion and, in any case, the recommended treatment is confronting the past, not evading it.

It was the treatment we recommended to Germany and Japan after the Second World War. There are many people in this country who call the study of injustices done to Aboriginal Australians in our own past a 'black armband' version of history, or a 'guilt industry', yet who are among the first to decry any sign that Japan is hiding the facts of history from young Japanese.

It is not to inflict guilt on this and future generations of Australians that we should face the realities of Aboriginal dispossession, it is to acknowledge our responsibility and their right to know.

In fact, in recent years we have made great progress: through the Native Title legislation, the Indigenous Land Fund, the work of the

Council for Aboriginal Reconciliation and various social programs. It has been a more than useful start to solving our most intractable problem.

Along the way we have made the extraordinary, if belated, discovery of an indigenous culture so rich, such a unique and integral part of the fabric of this continent, that its elements have become, over a very short time, the most internationally recognisable symbols of us all. It has become part of the world's mental image of Australia, just as it has changed the way we see ourselves.

It will be a tragedy if we now squander all this—because there is so much more which has to be done.

Yet our policy in government revolved around one central premise: that this should be the moment in our history when we made a concerted effort to break the cycle of despair and disillusion that had engulfed successive generations of Aborigines and cast them on society's scrap heap.

We believed that such a process would nevertheless represent a sound national investment. That a real and mutual sense of reconciliation would bring immense national dividends.

Reconciliation will not solve the material problems—the health, housing, education and other problems—but it is an essential part of the process. Goodwill and honesty will be needed on both sides. And I might say that representing the forcible removal of a generation of children from their parents as being little different from sending kids to boarding school is not an expression of goodwill and honesty.

Whatever the bean counters or the paternalists might say, the challenge is psychological and spiritual as well as material. This fact seems to have been lost somewhere along the way.

It seems to me that we will be able to debate these issues and to resolve them as a community much more successfully when the structures of our government and the symbols of our nation reflect better the underlying realities of who we are, where we live, and what we must yet do together.

One of the most important of these structural shifts is the move to a republic.

Last June I set out the then government's preferred approach to what I continue to regard as one of the most critical steps we must take as a nation.

This is much more than shallow symbolism. Those who still argue that our continuing links with the British monarchy do not handicap our international efforts, and those who think we should go on waiting until every last one of us is in total agreement, simply do not understand the stakes we are playing for.

The overwhelming logic of the argument is not difficult to follow. Australia at the end of the millennium occupies a unique place in the world and makes a unique contribution to it.

An Australian head of state can embody and represent our values and traditions, our experience and contemporary aspirations, our cultural diversity and social complexity in a way that a British monarch who is also head of state of fifteen other member countries of the United Nations can no longer adequately hope to do.

One of the impediments to the nation at large in accepting a design for the shift to a republic is the question of what powers the Head of State might have and how that person ought be appointed. Is he or she to be elected at large or appointed upon election by both Houses of Parliament?

Let me take this opportunity, on November 11, to say a few further things about this.

In the model propounded by me when Prime Minister, I proposed that the so-called reserve powers should remain with the Head of State but that the source of the Head of State's authority should be the two democratically elected chambers of the Parliament.

Some have argued the Head of State's power should be defined down to remove the reserve function, making it explicit that such persons may act only upon the authority of ministers via the Executive Council. Such people argue that if the powers are less, and largely ceremonial, it is then safe to have the Head of State popularly elected.

The problem with this argument is that no one will agree as to what explicit powers should remain with the Head of State, how a deadlock between the House of Representatives and the Senate should be resolved, and whether the powers of the Head of State to deal with such a deadlock ought to be removed.

There is no agreement about this—none between the political parties or even within political parties.

Yet even if agreement was likely on the general principles, writing it down explicitly and succinctly for the purposes of a referendum for a change to the Constitution would, in my opinion, be nigh on impossible. The proposals would fall under the arguments about the detail.

Yet to leave the powers as they are with the Head of State, and see that person elected at large, would be to change our system of government absolutely.

In such circumstances, and in a very quick time, the premier person of power in the political system would be the Head of State and not the Prime Minister. The whole notion of power in a Cabinet headed by a Prime Minister would change, and the greater powers in the land would be vested in one popularly elected person—the Head of State.

On November 11 each year we reflect on the events of 1975, and on the powers that Sir John Kerr used and on his use of them.

It is particularly instructive now that we are debating what powers a Head of State ought have under a republican model and now that we are more aware of the power of the Senate to frustrate or block the will of the House of Representatives.

In my view Sir John Kerr did not abuse the reserve powers *per se* by using them to dissolve the House of Representatives for an election.

His abuse occurred in not taking the elected Prime Minister into his confidence, and appointing as Prime Minister the leader of the party who lost the previous election. And in persisting with this appointment after the House of Representatives expressed no confidence in his appointee.

The other abuse of the powers was his failure to wait within the timeframe governed by the appropriation to see if the Opposition Senate tactic would hold—that the appropriation bills would actually be blocked. To wait for an impasse to actually occur.

But if in fact a full deadlock had occurred, if an impasse had truly been reached and he had advised the elected Prime Minister that he believed advice from the Prime Minister to him recommending an election was the best course of action, it would be difficult to argue that the use of the powers in these circumstances would have been irresponsible or abusive.

These issues are still with us. With the nexus between the House of Representatives and the Senate, the Senate is bound to grow in size as population growth expands the numbers in the House of Representatives.

And as it grows, under its system of proportional election, the quotas for the election at large of a Senator for each State will gradually get smaller. They are small now.

Many more independents and single-issue representatives will be there over time. This will diminish the stabilising influences of the major parties, perhaps leading to more institutionalised instability.

In the event of an impasse or a deadlock, how should the nation secure a resolution of a problem? Does the maintenance of a reserve power in the hands of a Head of State provide a proper device to resolve an impasse or force a resolution of a dispute? Or would it amount to an anachronistic use of a residual and old power in a contemporary political setting?

If the source of the Head of State's power is *not* popular election and *is* the delegated authority of the House of Representatives and the Senate, if the source of the power is diffuse and, in the case of the House of Representatives, fully representative of the community, then the source—as distinct from the instrument—derives from a contemporary and representative political authority. In these terms, the use of the powers would simply allow the country to avail itself of a device that could be useful in certain circumstances.

And given that the power has been used once, and only once, in 96 years and given that its operator subsequently suffered the broad admonition of the country for what was seen as his capricious use of the power—it is unlikely that any incumbent as Head of State would want to visit the same contumely on himself or herself.

And if it was used once and only once in 96 years, and given that the Senate is becoming more inherently unstable yet enjoys a wide panoply of powers given to it under the Constitution, and given that no agreement is likely about a delineation of the reserve powers or the power of the Senate itself—I do not see a grave threat to our polity by leaving the powers with the Head of State provided that the source of his or her power derives from the House and the Senate. Any such constitutional change should also be complemented with appropriate provisions for recall for improper or dubious behaviour by the Head of State.

I believe this approach is preferable to an unpredictable, unsolvable situation between the Houses and where a collection of members in the Senate may bail up the House of Representatives and the political system with it.

And if a collection of anti-migration candidates, a collection of Pauline Hansons, or Greens, or such-like were to bail the system up, in whose hands and judgement are we best left for a measured course of action to resolve an impasse: a Bill Deane sitting above the system? Or Senate independents or a major party behaving opportunistically, given that the likely path through such an impasse would be an election?

Such a system would ensure that whoever was elected was, as far as is humanly possible, 'above politics.'

It is surely one of the great oddities of this debate that so many people have been both *against* a politician becoming head of state and yet *for* a popular election.

It was also extraordinary that while I was advocating the minimalist position—and that to be achieved only by referendum—my opponents succeeded in convincing people that something sinister was afoot—even to the point of claiming that I wanted to be the President of 'Keating's Republic'—when I was advocating an approach which guaranteed that it could never be.

On this day also, Remembrance Day, many Australians who fought in war will feel a huge attachment to the ethos and symbols of their period and their youth. But they fought for the right of younger generations to make their own stamp on Australia, to make their own way in the world.

Just as younger generations of Australians have appreciated and recognised the role of those who served in these great conflicts, they must now be afforded their own rights to their time in our history.

There is no better place to argue these issues than here at one of Australia's great universities.

Because our campuses show us more clearly than almost anywhere else in the nation how far Australia has changed in the past 30 years and, more importantly, what the next 30 years will be like.

And because what I have been talking about tonight is a debate about the future, in which our young people hold the strongest stakes.

I want to end, therefore, by saying to the students here this evening and to those at other universities and schools and workplaces—this is your debate, about *your* country's future, and its resolution will be yours.

I tried in my public life to say what I thought and how I felt about these matters, and to set in train processes which would help set Australia up for the twenty-first century.

But it will be for you and your generation to provide the good ideas and see that they don't just stay that way: good ideas never acted upon. Never made reality.

It will be for you to decide how Australia preserves its place in a globalised world; how we cement our engagement with Asia; how well we are regarded and how well we regard ourselves. You will decide how, in the information age, we construct a society in which the wealth and knowledge and the opportunity and influence flow to the many and not the few. You will decide how much the idea of the fair go—the oldest Australian idea—is a reality of Australian life in the twenty-first century.

You will decide whether we can continue to persuade ourselves and the rest of the world that we are earning our privileges or simply enjoying them; making the most of our advantages or squandering them; facing up to the realities of Australian life—past, present and future—or pretending something else about them.

As you go—if you go wholeheartedly—I can assure you of two things. You will make mistakes—you will go too far in one direction, and not far enough in another; you will bring on consequences unforseen—and you will have to wear the blame.

That's the first thing, but it's not the most important.

The most important thing is not to be frightened off. It's useful to put an ear to the ground, but there's nothing more debilitating than trying to put both of them there. Think and do. Do even the things that don't have to be done.

Better to wear some criticism than to never take responsibility for what should be done.

After all, what does a democracy mean if not the right, the privilege, the chance to take responsibility?

And when you've got a democracy like we have, why settle for anything less than taking it?

For remember this—if we lose momentum, if we drift or retreat, if we begin to let fear, ignorance or prejudice govern us—it won't be me or my generation who pays the greatest price. We'll drop off the back of the cart. It will be young Australians who will have to ride it into the twenty-first century—and just now I reckon they should be seriously planning the means by which they can get hold of the reins.

16

OBSESSION
Australia and the Challenge of Asia

Asia Lecture to the Asia-Australia Institute,
University of New South Wales,
Sydney,
12 June 1996

*Paul Keating's address to the Asia-Australia Institute of the University of
New South Wales was the first summation of the foreign policy he had
adopted for Australia since assuming the Prime Ministership in December
1991. Delivered only three months after leaving office the address provides
all the codes and directions of his subsequent writings and approaches
to foreign policy. It is the story of the major re-orientation of Australia's
foreign policy towards Asia and the Pacific—where he says all of
Australia's interests; political, economic, security and cultural converged—
and for the first time. The address repeats two major Keating formulations:
that Australia must find its security in Asia, rather than from Asia and
that no country is more important to Australia than Indonesia. These two
formulations rankled conservative elements in Australia. The address also
repeats another element of the Keating mantra, also not comprehensively
accepted in 1996, that the integration of China is central to the peace and
growth of Asia; that containment of China is counterproductive and will
not work; that the policy must be one of engagement. The address also
predicts the coming nostalgia and reactionism of Hansonism which Paul
Keating urges the nation to counter and resist.*

IT IS A GREAT HONOUR to be speaking for the first time as a member of the University of New South Wales—and to so many people.

In some important ways, Australia's international position has been transformed during the past few years. Some of this was our own work; some of it was the effect of global changes.

What I want to do in this speech is to give an account of those changes and why they happened.

But I also want to look forward—to say something about the issues which will next concern Australia and the region, and what we can do about them.

A great deal of what we did over the past four or five years lies outside the ambit of this address, and I will spare you a comprehensive history.

Throughout the Labor government's thirteen years in office we put sustained effort into our external policies. Gareth Evans, for example, will surely rate as one of this country's finest Foreign Ministers. But I won't be covering his work on the Chemical Weapons Convention or United Nations reform.

I won't be speaking about the establishment of the Canberra Commission on the Elimination of Nuclear Weapons, or Peter Cook's and Bob McMullan's work through the Australian-originated Cairns Group to help secure a successful outcome to the Uruguay Round of trade negotiations, or Gordon Bilney's reforming work on sustainable development in the South Pacific.

My focus is more narrowly on what happened in relation to the Asia Pacific, the geographic area of most immediate concern to Australia— where our economic and security interests are most intense and where we have the greatest opportunity to influence and shape the future.

This must be the key foreign policy issue for any Australian government: the degree to which Australia can influence for the better the region which will affect us most directly; how we can ensure that our voice is heard and that it is effective.

In this, as in other aspects of public policy, the role of the Australian Prime Minister is not laid down in any formal way. The extent of that role, and its focus, is set essentially by the incumbent.

For my part, I was determined that the focus I would give to it would be more heavily than ever before on the region around us.

I am regularly accused of claiming to have invented Australia's relationship with Asia, so before I go on, let me repeat for the record what I have said in every major speech I have made about Australian foreign policy.

Australia has a long history of engagement with Asia—the role of Australian forces in the Second World War, our contribution to Indonesia's independence struggle, the creation of the Colombo Plan, our early support for ASEAN, our great partnership in the economic development of Japan and South Korea.

All this is a record of which we can be proud. But it is not the whole story.

The other part of the story is that during the 1950s and 1960s, Australia came perilously close to marginalising itself in the region and the world.

The White Australia policy was an affront to those who were excluded by it as it was to morality and commonsense. It clouded our view of the world. It was also a serious impediment to the pursuit of Australia's best interests which depended upon finding an effective voice in the region and the world.

My own party must bear a good deal of blame for it, although it was also my party, under Gough Whitlam, which finally gave Australia a completely non-discriminatory immigration policy in 1972. We could not go into the modern world—we certainly could not deal confidently with the modern region—wearing this badge of prejudice and fear.

The same can be said of the appalling anomaly in our Constitution which excluded Aboriginal Australians from legislative inclusion and protection. It brought no good to us as a people, and it brought discredit internationally. The 1967 referendum and the Mabo legislation, and some initiatives between those two milestones, set us at least on a more promising path.

But this is also unfinished business, which must not now be neglected.

But in part, Australia's encroaching marginalisation also had an economic base. Our efficient and innovative farmers and miners generated sufficient resources to enable governments to protect with a ring-fence of tariffs a secondary industry which was, with few exceptions, sluggish, timid and inward-looking. Convinced it could never compete internationally, for the most part it did not even try. We were at the bottom of the OECD table on manufacturing exports and we had no serious services exports.

Cultural marginalisation was also a threat. By the 1970s, Australians were beginning to see themselves as more than a branch office of Britain, but so long as many of our most important companies were in fact no more than this they could hardly be expected to share the view. And Australian governments of the time were not always of a mind to adopt a more independent standpoint. Until as late as the early 1970s, for example, formal responsibility for Australia's relations with the United Kingdom lay not with the Department of External Affairs but with the Prime Minister's Department, on the grounds that Britain was not really a foreign country.

From the election of Gough Whitlam in 1972—which brought with it recognition of China, withdrawal from the Vietnam War and a new focus on cooperation with Asia—Australian foreign policy changed markedly. And once that shift had been made, foreign policy developed on the basis of a new bipartisanship.

This continued in most ways under the Fraser government, although the area of the world where Malcolm Fraser had his deepest interest and made his most important contribution was probably southern Africa.

Following Labor's return to power in the early 1980s, two particular developments—one of our own doing, one to which we responded— again worked to reshape Australia's relations with the region around us.

The first was the series of decisions we made to open Australia up to the world.

Even for someone who was engaged in all those changes—the floating of the dollar, the removal of exchange controls, the deregulation of the financial markets and the dismantling of the tariff barriers—it is hard to recall how insulated Australia was before those walls came down. And not just economically insulated, socially and psychologically as well.

As it turned out these reforms were introduced not a moment too soon, as by the middle to late 1980s we could clearly see the sweeping consequences of the emerging global economy. Had they not been introduced when they were, the economic tsunami would have wiped us out.

The second change, to which we reacted, was the collapse of another wall—this time real as well as symbolic.

The end of the Cold War from the breaching of the Berlin Wall to the disintegration of the Soviet Union was an almost totally unanticipated development.

It was an unexpected bonus at the end of a century which had not experienced many of them.

From the end of the 1980s, most of the commentary about the end of the Cold War focused on its impact on Europe. And understandably so. That was where the confrontation between East and West had been most immediate and most dangerous.

What was not fully absorbed at the time, however, was the impact of these changes on the Asia Pacific.

Indeed, the conventional wisdom was that there would be few consequences at all—that Asia's strategic divisions and political tensions were little affected by the East–West divide of the central balance.

In one way that was true. But what the conventional wisdom failed to take adequately into account was the dynamic effects of the changes to the global system.

Because the end of the Cold War unfroze the international structure, with the development of a truly global economy, it made possible the most significant changes to the international system this century. Indeed, it made them inevitable.

As I have argued elsewhere, the end of the Cold War permitted a new focus on regionalism and regional approaches. The very shape of the history of international relations over the past two centuries—imperialism first, then Marxism's claims for global revolution, two world wars and a global cold war—all taught us to think about the world and its problems in essentially global terms.

Regional approaches were in place as well, of course—in Europe most prominently. But even there, regionalism's aims were basically global—to tie Germany into Europe so that it could never again threaten world peace and to strengthen Western Europe and the Western alliance against the threat of the Soviet Union in the emerging Cold War.

But with the end of the Cold War, regionalism was no longer constrained by global priorities. Opportunities for cooperation opened up; opportunities we could never contemplate earlier.

I am not saying that global multilateral solutions were no longer relevant, or are no longer relevant. In important ways—in economics and communications, for example—they have never been more central. And negotiations like those now underway for a Comprehensive Test Ban Treaty are critical for our future.

But regional approaches, I am convinced, are where we can make most progress in the immediate future; where the ideas are most fertile, and the prospects for quick action are greatest.

And of all the world's regions, the opportunities and requirements for change are greatest in the Asia Pacific.

For one thing, this is where the wealth is being created—and at a rate and volume never seen before in the history of the world.

The increasingly wealthy, increasingly self-confident countries in the region were well placed to take advantage of the opportunities opened up when the constraints imposed by the bipolarity of the post-war years disappeared.

For example, with the direct threat from the Soviet Union removed, Japan has been forced to address more directly an issue from which it—and its neighbours—had tended discreetly to avert their gaze—that is, how and to what extent it should exercise a role in international leadership commensurate with its economic strength.

It has been encouraged to look again at this question by a United States more conscious of the burden that it has been carrying as the world's remaining superpower, and less convinced that the American people will continue to bear this burden willingly in the absence of an obvious adversary like the Soviet Union.

Economic disputes between the United States and its friends have gained a much harder edge as the political considerations which softened them during the Cold War disappeared. The diplomats can no longer be relied on to hold the trade negotiators in check.

China found itself growing rapidly as a result of Deng Xiaoping's economic reforms and at the same time more dependent on the rest of the world for continued growth than it had ever been. Its per capita GDP has quadrupled since 1978, and its foreign trade has grown annually by more than 16 per cent over the same period.

Its strategic importance and room for action grew as the immediate tensions with the Soviet Union diminished. China was no longer a card to be played in the game of international relations but an important dealer at the table.

The most dangerous of all the regional flashpoints—the Korean peninsula—changed as well. After the Cold War, a miscalculation by the North no longer had the potential to bring about a global nuclear confrontation between the superpowers. But at the same time the chances of a miscalculation increased as the regime in Pyongyang became more isolated from its Chinese and Soviet patrons and more unsure of its own survival.

In Southeast Asia, Vietnam, too, found itself without its principal economic and military backer, the Soviet Union. Partly in response, Hanoi instituted major economic reforms which, together with the Cambodian settlement, made it possible for Vietnam to join ASEAN, ending Southeast Asia's major political divide.

So when I became Prime Minister at the end of 1991, these two great changes—the opening up of the Australian economy and the end of the Cold War—had already begun to make their mark on Australia. But the business was unfinished.

As I said earlier, Australia had a long history of engagement with Asia. But never before the 1990s had all our interests—political, economic, social and cultural—converged so intensely there.

To me, good public policy always depends on understanding the structure of things—because it is only when you have comprehended the underlying structures that you can see where the weaknesses are and put the building blocks of lasting change into place.

I was sure that the structures supporting Australian policy in the region, and the broader regional structures themselves, needed to change. My aim was to address both the form and the intensity of Australia's engagement with the region and, in doing that, to help change the region itself.

The problem which confronted us in the early 1990s was two-fold. How could Australia encourage the institutional changes in this part of the world which were increasingly necessary in the post-Cold War environment? How could we ensure that Australia was part of the conversation?

The institutional changes depended first on the question of how the region was defined.

The key issue for us was to ensure that we were dealing with a trans-Pacific region—with the Asia Pacific, not just East Asia.

This was not because we were a stalking horse for the United States, or felt Australia needed to have Washington around in order to feel comfortable. And it was not because we were hostile to any cooperation between the countries on this side of the Pacific.

It was because we were convinced—I was convinced—that one of the great dangers to a post-Cold War world was for a new divide to emerge down the Pacific, encouraging the development of a world effectively split into three contending blocs in Europe, the Americas and Asia.

I also believed that the strategic support the United States provided its allies in this part of the world—Japan and South Korea as well as the Philippines and Australia and New Zealand—had an enduring relevance to the strategic outlook in East Asia.

Given the region's rapid economic growth and the extensive modernisation of military forces, given China's growing military potential, given the growing likelihood of Korea's reunification, but under circumstances no-one can predict, a real danger existed that a serious loss of faith in the United States' staying power and commitment would generate a competitive bout of rearmament, including by Japan.

This would have the most dangerous and unpredictable consequences for Australia and for the region.

We were also concerned that, with the end of the Cold War, the United States administration needed to justify its external commitments to a people and a Congress for whom East Asia increasingly meant economic competition and complaints about job losses. A new, firmer underpinning was needed for Washington's trans-Pacific security commitments. Compared with the dense network of contacts and institutions which joined the United States to its Atlantic allies, the ties across the Pacific were fragile, limited and essentially bilateral.

The definition of the region also had an important economic dimension. The United States remained the largest or second largest market for every East Asian member of APEC except Brunei. It was a critical source of investment and the transfer of technology. It was clear that if a central aim of regional institutions was to maintain the economic growth rates in this part of the world, the United States was an essential element.

If I may divert for a moment, it was these quite deep issues about the future of the region, rather than any personal animosity, which lay behind my disagreements with the Malaysian Prime Minister Dr Mahathir over APEC and the EAEC.

Dr Mahathir is a formidable leader who has transformed Malaysia in ways I greatly admire, but we had different visions of the region into the twenty-first century.

The driving force in his vision was a strong pan-Asian nationalism which asserted that the time had come after centuries of colonial rule for Asia to take control of its own future.

Mine has been shaped by the conviction I set out earlier—that Australia's interests and the region's are best served by making the Asia Pacific the focus of our institution building efforts because the dangers—economic, social and strategic—of creating a divide between the two sides of the Pacific were overwhelmingly greater than the advantages of an East Asia-only approach.

And, of course, Australia's exclusion from significant regional bodies like that proposed was quite contrary to the government's view of Australian interests.

It was also contrary to our view of the region's interests. I am convinced that Australia's active engagement in the region—our energy, our creativity, our economic resources—are an asset for the region as a whole.

At the time I became Prime Minister, regionalism was already beginning to make its mark in this part of the world, especially through the development of APEC, the ministerial body that my predecessor, Bob Hawke, had launched in 1989.

APEC was developing slowly but consistently. It was presided over by an annual meeting of Ministers of Trade and Foreign Affairs, but its aims were modest.

I concluded that the APEC template was the right one to build on—right in its economic focus, right in the scope of its membership, and right because Australia had a prominent role in it and the capacity to get things done.

But I doubted whether it could deliver what the region needed—especially confidence in continuing economic growth—at a speed faster than its most cautious officials wanted.

There was also a striking institutional problem in the Asia Pacific; namely, this most rapidly growing region in the world had no forum which engaged the attention of Heads of Government.

This meant that regional leaders were often strangers to each other. The institutional links which facilitated early warning of problems or the development of informal solutions to them simply did not exist here.

And direct relationships between political leaders, unmediated by officials, can change things in ways in which decades of meetings between officials cannot.

Now, much of what has been best about Australian public policy over the past decades has had its origins in the creative approach of our public service. But officials cannot—and are not entitled to—take risks as politicians are able.

Australia badly needed such a forum. Most of my predecessors like Malcolm Fraser and Bob Hawke, for example, knew the Prime Minister of Jamaica or the President of Zimbabwe or the Prime Minister of the Cook Islands better than they knew the Presidents of Indonesia or South Korea, simply because the biennial Commonwealth Heads of Government meetings and the annual meetings of the South Pacific Forum were the only international forums in which they were engaged— the only ones they ever attended.

This had a distorting effect on Australian foreign policy, not least by engaging the attention of Australian Prime Ministers on parts of the world which were very distant from our immediate interests, indeed parts of the world that were remote from Australia's interests.

Within days of taking over from Bob Hawke in December 1991, I had to welcome President George Herbert Bush to Australia. This was the first time in more than a quarter of a century that a United States President had visited Australia and I made sure that I should address some of these vital structural questions.

So I raised first with President Bush in Australia, and then in correspondence with the leaders of other APEC states, the idea that we should introduce a series of regular meetings at APEC leadership level.

I launched the idea publicly at the first speech I gave to the Asia-Australia Institute here at this university in April 1992.

The official responses were mostly positive but cautious. The US Administration wanted to keep a low profile, ostensibly out of concern that their endorsement would frighten others away; in reality, I suspect, because American officials feared that the idea would not run.

This turned out to be a blessing in disguise, however, because it meant that when the incoming Clinton Administration was looking around for some ideas early in the following year it found a new one, ready made. There is no doubt that without President Clinton's support and his invitation for APEC leaders to meet in Seattle, the idea would have had a much longer gestation. By his boldness, he did the region—and I believe the United States itself—a great and, I hope, enduring service.

One of the most important things to come from that first Seattle meeting was quite intangible. The leaders met alone, without a firm agenda and without officials present. For many of them—and for many nervous officials—this was a very new type of forum. But sitting in that log hut on an island in Puget Sound all of us gained, I think, a new sense of the way in which our own economic and political ambitions for our countries related directly, and in many senses *depended* directly, on what the others were doing.

It was inter-dependence at its clearest.

Seattle was a useful meeting, but if we had gone away from it deciding that it had been no more than a pleasant get-together, it would have had no lasting impact. I wanted to ensure that it became the first of a regular pattern of meetings.

Upon inquiry, President Soeharto had already told me that he would be prepared to host another follow-up meeting if our colleagues agreed. So Prime Minister Goh Chok Tong of Singapore, who has been an unshakeable source of support for an APEC structure, proposed a follow-up meeting in Indonesia the following year; President Soeharto nodded assent and it was agreed.

The next problem was to ensure that when the leaders met next in Indonesia they had something of substance to talk about, and something which would address the real needs of the region.

That was why I was convinced that our aim should be to push out APEC's ambitions; to give it bold free-trade goals; to give it objectives. Nothing short of this was likely to have the impetus to keep the region moving in the direction I wanted.

So the Bogor Declaration was developed, with its commitment to free trade in the region by 2010 for developed countries and 2020 for developing countries, and the means of its implementation was fleshed out at the following meeting in Osaka in November 1995.

I will not rehearse again the implications of APEC's free-trade agenda, except to say that it provides a new model of trade negotiations to the world. Unlike previous GATT trade rounds, APEC's goal has been set in advance: it has targets, and our negotiations are about how to get there, not where to go. It represents the best practical cooperation we have yet seen on this scale between developed and developing countries. It gives meaning to the expression North–South cooperation.

The other fragility in the structures of Australia's external relationships was bilateral. From the beginning of my political life I believed that Australia's one great underdeveloped relationship was that with our largest neighbour, Indonesia.

It was a relationship which held such promise at the time of Indonesia's independence when Australia helped marshal critical international support for the new Sukarno regime. But it had run adrift.

The reasons were complex. Confrontation, of course, and later the takeover of East Timor, had been important elements.

But the main problem was, again, structural. Our relationship had become the prisoner of politics. It swung between extremes and neither country seemed fully able to come to grips with it. In recent years it had been dominated by the single issue of East Timor, an issue of great importance but not properly the sole determinant of how everything else in the relationship was handled.

Indonesia tended to look north to ASEAN and to ignore its southern neighbour. Australians failed to understand Indonesia in all its complexity.

We needed to recast the relationship, to get people in both countries to look afresh at what it meant to have the world's fourth most populous nation with its great cultural traditions living next door to the resources, both natural and human, of the only country in the world with a continent to itself.

Gareth Evans had already been working hard with Ali Alatas to put ballast, as he put it, into the relationship. And Robert Ray and the leadership of the ADF, especially General Peter Gration, had been very effectively building links in the defence area.

But what was badly needed was a signal from the top. That was why I made Indonesia my first overseas visit as Prime Minister. And why I made another four visits while in office.

It was why I said publicly on that first visit what had been said only privately by our political leaders before—that the coming to power of the New Order Government in Indonesia was the regional event of greatest strategic benefit to Australia since the end of the Second World War.

Australia has been able to develop this country at the rate we want, and to maintain an appropriate defence force for a relatively modest percentage of our GDP, largely because the Indonesian archipelago, from or through which any direct threat to Australia would have to come, has been stable, united and increasingly prosperous. And because the Indonesian government has been spreading the gains of 8 per cent average annual rates of growth widely throughout the population.

Another point I wanted Australians to understand was, as I put it later, that there was no country more important to Australia than Indonesia. This formulation put Indonesia where it should be—in a triumvirate of Australia's most important bilateral relationships alongside the United States, our major ally, and Japan, our largest economic partner.

To try to shift the structure of the relationship and not just the rhetoric, President Soeharto and I agreed during my first visit to establish a ministerial forum—an annual meeting of ministers from across the range of government, including the major economic portfolios. The next of those meetings will be held later this year. Our aim was to increase the number of stakeholders in the relationship in both countries.

We also sought to do this by encouraging the growth of non-government links—embracing everything from the private sector to youth and cultural links. That strategy is already bearing fruit. On the trade front alone, more than 300 Australian companies are now represented in Indonesia and Australian investment in Indonesia is probably around $300 million. Two-way trade has been growing rapidly and has reached $3.3 billion.

But I had also felt for a long time that the relationship needed to be underpinned by a more public declaration of trust on both sides. And I saw that as requiring us to address our security relationship.

It was not just that Australia and Indonesia do not threaten each other, but also that we have significant common interests in the peace and stability of the region around us. And even beyond that, what we do together can help preserve and enhance that peace and stability. I thought this should be set out in a formal document.

This was new territory for both of us, but we saw that the region itself was entering a new era and that we needed to think about our approach to security in new ways. In Australia's case that means seeking our security in Asia rather than from Asia.

I discussed the proposal with my colleagues on the Security Committee of Cabinet in February 1994. What I had in mind was consistent with all we were saying publicly and privately in the Defence White Paper and elsewhere about our desire for closer defence relations with Indonesia.

I outlined the proposal to President Soeharto in June 1994 and, as you know, it was finalised following a discussion between us at Osaka in November 1995—another practical advantage, I should note, of the opportunities provided by APEC Leaders' Meetings.

I believe the Agreement on Maintaining Security will help transform the way in which Australia and Indonesia regard each other and work together. And I believe it will make a very positive contribution to the security of the wider region.

It will become part of a growing network of contacts and relationships, economic and political as well as security-related, which will inject greater confidence and resilience into the whole East Asian security framework.

But the question which matters most for Australia is not what happened last, but what happens next. What are the emerging problems for the region and how should Australia react?

For regional governments, including ours, all the complex policy questions about the future of the region reduce down to this fundamental one: what do we have to do to ensure that East Asia continues to develop economically and socially, and that it does so in peace?

A very large number of very difficult questions hang from that of course. But it is the goal we need always to keep in mind.

I believe we need to do four things in particular:

- press ahead with the APEC free-trade agenda, because on that rests Australia's continued prosperity and the economic integration of the region as a whole
- work harder and more effectively to include China in the affairs of the region
- begin to address the question of encouraging a region-wide political and security dialogue, and at the right level, and
- find an effective Asia Pacific way of incorporating more social and environmental issues onto the regional agenda.

APEC, as I commented often to colleagues in the past twelve months, is not like the G7 or the General Assembly of the United Nations. It is not at a stage where it can stand a failure. Unless each Leaders' Meeting produces a worthwhile outcome, the tendency always will be for leaders to start delegating representation to their deputies and the whole process could easily slip away.

For that reason it is critical that the next Leaders' Meeting later this year in Subic Bay delivers individual country programs, as they are called, which show real commitment to reaching the Bogor free-trade goals. Which provide credible down-payments towards the targets.

This is important not just for the sake of a successful meeting, it is important because the region's continuing prosperity and security, and therefore Australia's prosperity and security, depends to a very high degree on ensuring that the trade and investment arteries in this region keep flowing.

The alternative model—closed markets—has been tried before this century. It is no way to begin the next millennium.

The second thing we must do is to work as effectively as we can to integrate China fully into the world economy and global and regional institutions. China's sheer size—both the number of its people and its land mass—make the question of whether and how this can be done the most important question for international policy-makers in the last years of this century.

The shape and health of the international system in the next century depends on our getting it right.

A large part of the answer is beyond the capacity of the rest of the world to deliver. It lies in how China itself manages the political consequences of the succession to Deng Xiaoping, whether it can successfully manage the political and economic consequences of soaring economic growth and different regional growth rates, how it copes with Hong Kong's return to Chinese sovereignty.

But what we do will also be important and will help shape China's responses.

The choice which is often put between engagement and containment is too simple, but it has the advantage of clarifying the two broad paths we can go along.

I am unambiguously in favour of engagement. Whatever the other reasons against a policy of containment, it is not appropriate, it will be counter-productive, and it will not work.

China is not the old Soviet Union. No-one believes China is engaged in fomenting world-wide revolution of a sort American containment policy against the Soviet Union was designed to counter. And China's neighbours in this region have long centuries of experience in dealing with it. They also believe that we will all be better off by working to engage China.

As so often in international relations—or in life for that matter—the issue is more complex than it looks on the surface.

Of course, as the United States argues, if China is to enter the World Trade Organization, we need to get the terms right, because this may already be the world's second largest economy, and will almost certainly be its biggest early next century.

And of course countries like Australia need, among other things, to fight for protection of intellectual property rights.

But China has the size and economic weight of a superpower. Like the United States, it will hear the siren song of unilateralism because it is big enough to make unilateralism stick. Already there are voices in China asking why China should join the WTO, asking what is in it for them. And those voices are not the voices of reform and openness.

But for those countries whose position in the global trading scene is smaller and weaker, the advantages of getting China as soon as possible into an agreed international framework on proper terms are overwhelming. This should be the guiding aim behind our policy towards China.

It should certainly be one of the main preoccupations of APEC leaders before and during their meeting in Subic Bay, which takes place immediately before the first WTO ministerial meeting in Singapore.

China and its future direction also lies at the heart of the debate about regional security.

Frankly, some of the recent commentary about the Asia Pacific security environment sounds ominously like potential threats rushing to fill a post-Cold War vacuum.

In a lot of this commentary the unspoken sub-text is China—the whispered suggestion that China is the next global threat, that we are seeing the return of the yellow peril.

The areas usually mentioned are the Korean peninsula, tension between China and Taiwan, and sovereignty disputes in the South China Sea.

These issues are of real concern, of course. But I believe each of them can and will be managed in a way which avoids general conflict.

It is true, however, that China's very size allows it to overshadow its neighbours. A strong, united China will sometimes be uncomfortable for its neighbours to deal with—but not as uncomfortable as the alternative of a weak, divided China.

There is no doubt that this will be a happier and more peaceful part of the world next century if China's neighbours are self-confident, if our own relationships are in good repair and if all the countries of the region feel that they can help shape its future by their participation in active and healthy regional institutions.

So while I do not see China as a threat, I agree that the other main dimension to the problem of engaging China in the world is the unfinished business of regional security.

I believe there is a need for an effective region-wide security forum. However sanguine our outlook, we have to plan on things going wrong, because it is to cope with the worst case that regional institutions must be constructed. We will be in no position to build them once the worst case arrives.

This was one of the motivations behind the creation of the ASEAN Regional Forum.

But although the ARF is a good place to begin this conversation about regional security, I am not at all sure that it is where we shall end up.

When you look at the potential for the further development of the institutional structures of the region, it is clear that the only body which provides the coverage and the high-level participation necessary to provide a forum for such discussions is APEC.

Not least, this is because the security issues facing the region are essentially North Asian issues and because there is a need to engage the attention of the very leaders who attend the APEC Leaders' Meetings.

The next step has to be for APEC to take on more openly the strategic and political colourings which shade it already, not least in the corridor discussions between leaders at their meetings.

There are obvious difficulties, some of which I have expressed myself in the past. Among other things, APEC is by name and design a group of economies. It was only in this way that the three Chinese economies of China, Taiwan and Hong Kong could be included. And that is a critically important element in APEC's future.

But other more intractable issues have been resolved by APEC in the past. It should be a high priority for APEC participants over the next couple of years.

The final area of change for the region should be in the broadening of the regional debate to incorporate social and environmental issues.

It is imperative for all regional governments to understand that environmental and social issues have to be addressed if they are not to become an impediment to economic growth.

This is happening already. A recent East West Centre study estimates, for example, that the annual cost of China's environmental pollution and degradation is probably at least 10 per cent of its GDP and may be as high as 15 per cent. The head of China's National Environmental Protection Agency recently described the state of China's ecosystem as grave.

And Asia's rapid economic development is bringing with it social transformation to an unprecedented degree. Throughout the region, essentially rural populations are becoming in a matter of decades the most urbanised on earth. Cities like Manila and Bangkok are likely to double their populations by 2010.

Entirely new issues will arise for our neighbours—the breakdown of traditional family social-support mechanisms, the need for education systems to be reformed, massive new health challenges like AIDS and drugs, complex new urban planning problems. The list is long.

And the problem is not just one for individual countries. Failure to cope with these tensions will generate political unrest and economic strains which will affect all of us.

As I said earlier, I am convinced that many of these issues can be dealt with more easily in regional than global forums at present.

This conversation is already beginning to happen. The Asia–Australia Institute, for example, is doing some very innovative intra-regional work on social issues.

The solutions which are identified will no doubt be very different from the models of the past. But their resolution will be easier and more effective if we can draw on the experiences of others. In these environmental and social areas, Australia has a great deal to offer the region.

The new government has promised to prepare a White Paper on Australian foreign policy later this year. It is always useful to reflect on our national direction and I hope the White Paper will contribute to a better understanding among Australians of the way in which it is now impossible to disentangle our domestic aspirations from our international ones. We can no longer see what we do overseas as disconnected from whatever else we do.

I have to say—if I can offer some well-meant advice to my successor—that I would be surprised and disappointed if the White Paper does not end up supporting most of the following propositions which I believe are the core of Australia's foreign-policy interests.

These are that:

- while Australia has interests all over the world, the focus of our foreign policy must be the Asia Pacific
- that Australia's interests are served by the continuing engagement in this region of our major ally, the United States, among other reasons because that is the best way of ensuring that the region continues to develop in security and stability; and
- that Australia's relationship with important countries outside the Asia Pacific will be better, stronger, and more mutually rewarding if we have our relationships with our neighbours in the right shape. In other words, for Australia, it is not a matter of choosing between Europe and Asia.

One of the complaints sometimes made by my opponents when I was Prime Minister was that I ignored our 'traditional relations' with Europe. I was always startled to realise that this was me they were talking about. The same person accused of an un-Australian liking for things like French art and nineteenth century German architecture.

But the reality always was that the centre of our effort has to be Asia and the Pacific. Australia is in no position to do more than influence developments in Europe or the Middle East around the periphery. We have views and we should put them. We have economic interests and we should pursue them. On many important matters we can and do make a contribution beyond our weight. But the area where Australia can most make a difference, where our ideas can be most effective—where they *need* to be most effective—is in the Asia Pacific.

Australia's history and our interests lead us quite clearly to certain conclusions about our foreign policy. In that regard we have national interests which transcend the party political.

I happen to think, as you might expect, that Labor's approach is more creative, and its implementation more adept, than on the other side.

There are particular policy areas where I disagree. I think the government underestimates the long-term regional importance of Vietnam, for example. And I am certain that the issue of an Australian republic is something which is important to our foreign-policy interests, as well as—and more importantly—for its value to us.

But I am quite happy to acknowledge that there is now broad bipartisan agreement between the parties on the major foreign-policy questions we face—the importance of Asia, the maintenance of our security arrangements with the United States, the APEC agenda and so on.

I endorse and welcome the priority which the government has given to our regional relationships and I will do all I can to support them in this.

I am glad there has been no talk since the election about redressing the 'obsession' with Asia for which I was criticised and less talk about restoring the balance with our so-called 'traditional friends'.

I said during the election campaign that I believed that while Asian leaders would speak to a Coalition government, they would not deal with it. If I am wrong about this—if the deals *are* made, if the spark of creativity and commitment is there, I will be happy to applaud.

But Australia's interests send us in the direction of Asia so forcibly and so comprehensively that it is not possible short of perversity—and real pain—to reverse the trend. And I don't believe the new government wants to do that.

I do want to sound a note of warning, however, because we have seen recently some signs of a backlash against the foreign-policy consensus of the major parties.

A backlash from people who are frightened by the changes in the world, frightened by Australia's openness, frightened by the need to compete in a global economy. People who see Asia and Australia's relations with the countries of the region as a threat—to security, jobs or culture.

And we saw in the last elections successful candidates in some places appealing to such fears as if to satisfy a yearning for a cosier, more predictable Australia.

It is not surprising that, in a time of rapid change, people become apprehensive and seek solace in the past. And I do not for a moment suggest there is no room for debate about Australia's foreign economic and security policy.

But the information revolution alone will ensure that, whatever happens in human history from now on, rapid change will be its permanent feature. Nostalgia or xenophobia or a return to protectionist policy approaches will not bring back the past.

Those who hold views like these are in a minority, and they are likely to remain so. There is no evidence in opinion polls that their numbers are growing.

But we should not wait for such evidence before responding.

And reassurance has to be at the core of that response. Because this is an historic opportunity for Australia. Eighteen million of us have the bounty of a continent in the middle of the fastest growing region in human history.

Australia's opening to the world does not cost us security, culture or jobs. If we are willing to think and act with vigour and confidence, it guarantees them. It is the only possible way of ensuring that our children have the number of jobs—and the interesting jobs—which we want for them.

Part of this reassurance must come from government.

But more importantly, over the long run will be debate at a deeper cultural level.

And the people who will have the greatest impact over the long term will not be our political leaders. They will be teachers and business people, journalists and artists and writers—people who can interpret Asia to us, and Australia to our neighbours.

In short, we wish to see the creation of a community between East Asia and Australia.

Whatever form this takes—and there is a big debate to be had about that—it is one of the largest and most exciting enterprises Australia has been involved in. The reason it will continue to interest me is that everything we still hope to achieve in this country depends upon it in one way or the other.

In whatever I do next with my life, I will want to contribute to it.

If it is an obsession, I'm inclined to think of it as a magnificent one.

17

INTRODUCTION TO MAHLER'S *SYMPHONY NO. 2*

West Australian Symphony Orchestra,
Perth Concert Hall,
12 March 2003

Invited by the West Australian Symphony Orchestra to introduce
Mahler's Symphony No. 2 *to the audience, Paul Keating went to*
his well of information on Gustav Mahler and to his deep emotional
connection with the work. His profound and reverent regard for Mahler
is evident in his description of the symphony and the processes of its
creation. Paul Keating has always believed that music is the highest
form of the arts; a metaphysical voice which, unlike other forms of art,
is not representational. He subscribes to the Mahlerian view that music
is the art of the inner senses. Gustav Mahler's Symphony No. 2, *his*
'Resurrection Symphony', had a visceral impact on Paul Keating when
he first heard it as a young man and his appreciation to Mahler for its
creative genesis has never diminished.

GUSTAV MAHLER'S SYMPHONY NO. 2 is a great outburst of what he called the affirmation of the soul. It goes beyond any music of its kind ever written.

At the end of its first performance in 1895 under his own baton, Mahler said, 'The whole thing sounds as though it came to us from some other world. One is battered to the ground and then raised on angels' wings to the highest heights'. He told Richard Strauss in a letter: 'One can create only once or twice in a lifetime works on such a great subject. Never again will I attain such depths and heights'.

Mahler's second symphony was in reality his first symphony. What is now famously his first symphony was originally written as a tone poem. He began the first movement of the Second when he was 27, while conducting in Leipzig. The first movement, the Totenfeier or requiem, is an epic funeral rite proclaiming the rites of the dead and provides the emotional core of the work. In a sense, Mahler put what one might expect to have been his last movement, first. Having 'buried the hero', he took six years to inspire himself to top it.

Mahler loved voices. He always had the idea of the human voice for the last movement of this symphony, a chorus. But he said he feared people might think it 'in servile imitation of Beethoven's Ninth'—until then the only symphony with a sung movement.

As I said, he had to wait to find inspiration for the other four movements. And it turned out he found that inspiration at the funeral of the great conductor, Hans Von Bülow, in March 1894, where a children's choir sang the resurrection chorale from Klopstock's religious epic, The Messiah: Arise, arise, my dust, after your brief repose.

'It flashed to me like lightning' Mahler told a friend an hour after the service, 'the flash that all creative artists wait for'.

Having lit upon the musical inspiration, Mahler then went searching, scouring all the likely literature and the Bible to find his narrative. And find it he did. His fifth movement, the finale, his 'lifesaving affirmation of the soul' materialised in his head.

Beginning with the trumpets remote and high in the gods, comes 'the great call'. As the trumpets cease, the choir comes in, in what is the softest choral entrance in all music—it ends in a triumphant crossing from the subliminal to something, that is probably for most of us, a glimpse into the purpose of life, into the supernatural, into infinity.

The symphony is written to represent the triumph of hope over despair, of belief over doubt, of resurrection—of life over death.

What is amazing is that another being is able to let the rest of us into such a transformation. As Kant said, 'Only artistic genius discloses a new path to us'.

The symphony has a big beginning and a big end; the burial at the beginning—the resurrection at the end. In the middle are three intermezzi. The first, the happy memory from the life of the deceased and the sad remembrance of his lost innocence; the second, themes built upon the Wunderhorn poem songs where the hero despairs of himself; and the third, the song 'Urlicht, The Primordial Light', sung by the contralto—the song of simple faith: 'I am from God and will return to God . . . He will give me a life of eternity'.

That movement, from the folk poem, Urlicht, returns a tone of seriousness and gravity to the symphony which ends very softly and dies away as the tumultuous fifth movement begins with the whispered entry of the choir.

Then we experience Mahler's 'Auferstehen', the rising, with its haunting resurrection tune, which you will recognise instantly— 'O glaube, mein Herz, O glaube', 'O believe, my heart'—sung by the soprano. The symphony then moves to its majestic close.

Mahler worked on a big canvas with a big orchestra; 115 players in all. Four of each woodwinds, ten horns, eight trumpets, five tubas, two solo voices and the choir. His tonal imagination and poetic structures enabled him to paint vast musical pictures.

In the last movement the end of life has come. God is beckoning . . . the ground moves, the graves open and in a mighty procession, the dead arise—free of condemnation or preference, or punishment or judgement, into God's loving embrace.

18

THE LAUNCH OF 'IN DENIAL
The Stolen Generations and the Right'
Melbourne,
6 April 2001

Paul Keating was invited to launch the first edition of Quarterly Essay
*and within the edition, Robert Manne's essay, 'In Denial: The Stolen
Generations and the Right'. In this address Paul Keating mocks the
Howard government and its media apologists for their stigmatisation
of 'elites' and of alleged political correctness while controlling all the
agencies of government with virtual free rein in the media. He also
underlines the important message in Robert Manne's essay: that the
Australian Right was willing to condone the racism inherent in the
Stolen Generation policies rather than confront the basic ethical issues
and the terrible things done to indigenous people.*

A COUPLE OF IMPORTANT THINGS are happening here today.

First, any time a new forum for public debate in this country opens
up—rather than closes down—it is a cause for celebration.

So I'm happy to be in a position to congratulate the publisher, Morry
Schwartz, the editor Peter Craven and all the other people associated
with the *Quarterly Essay* on this, the launch of its first edition.

Out here, on the edge of Asia, a long way from major markets and
natural groupings, ideas are all that Australia has to garner a position in the
scheme of things and to shield it from the harsher winds of globalisation.

Not military might, or a large population, or unique resources; simply ideas.

Ideas are what will sustain our democracy and drive our economy into new areas as we cope with the transforming impact of economic globalisation and the information revolution.

In these circumstances you should think we would want to search out ideas and nurture them carefully. But instead we have a government which is hollowing out the education system, cutting back on R&D and trying to close down our national debate.

You might remember that John Howard used to claim that the election of his government would release the nation from the thrall of intellectual terror in which he claimed it had been held by me and the Labor government. The years when free speech was suppressed by squads of ALP Thought Police and terrified conservatives whimpered in darkened corners. That was the reason, you will recall, that Mr Howard found it necessary to let Pauline Hanson spout her bile unchallenged in the national Parliament.

But apparently—as it turns out—it can't have been me at all.

Because, according to the government and its allies on the Right, now five years on, the nation remains bound down by these powerful and mysterious fetters.

Is there anything in contemporary Australian life more outrageous than the sight of the most powerful figures of Australian conservatism cloaking their well-nourished frames in the rags of the powerless? The men who control the national government, who declaim from the opinion columns of every newspaper, who stack each government-controlled board in the land, who draw their funding from the largest corporations in the country, claiming to be the victims of a conspiracy to silence them?

Is there anything more absurd than the Minister for Workplace Relations whining about the power of the 'elites', when what he is really complaining about is that some people disagree with his brand of politics?

If new ideas are to grow, they need topsoil packed with nutrients, and there's precious little of it around in Australia at the moment.

The radio shock jocks set the political agenda. Television news trivialises itself with its ten-second grabs. The ABC exhausts itself in a frenzy of pre-emptive self-censorship at the behest of the most partisan administration we've ever seen. Magazines wallow in the shallows of celebrity obsession. Even the serious print media seldom allows opinion articles to go longer than 800 words.

In this environment, the creation of a forum for the expansive and unhurried expression of ideas, which can then be debated, also at length, is one the Australian public badly needs and deserves. I hope the *Quarterly Essay* will be embraced by readers of all political beliefs and that it will explain, provoke and inspire for a long time to come. It's a bold thing to take on a new publishing venture of this sort and we owe a debt of gratitude to Morry Schwartz for his courage.

The magazine has made a very good start with the second of the important things we are celebrating today: Robert Manne's essay 'In Denial: The Stolen Generations and the Right'.

I have admired Robert's writing, but I've never read him with the familiar comfort of the reader who knows that he will always agree with the author. Robert doesn't deliver identikit responses. That is one of the things about him that infuriated his former *Quadrant* colleagues. He couldn't be relied on to buy the full package.

But his readers have always known that, whether you agree with him or not, he will be addressing the largest issues facing our society, and always with clarity and rigour.

All these qualities are evident in this important essay. It is a work of both the head and the heart. It is carefully researched and powerfully expressed. It needs to be widely read. It addresses the way in which members of a powerful network on the Right of Australian political life combined to undermine with distortion, omission, overstatement and lies, the history and experience of indigenous Australians first set out in *Bringing Them Home*, the report by Sir Ronald Wilson and Mick Dodson into the removal of thousands of Aboriginal children from their families over the course of the twentieth century.

But the essay ranges beyond the questions of the Stolen Generations. It looks at the roots and consequences of what Robert correctly sees as a wider cultural war over the meaning of Aboriginal dispossession.

One of the most depressing things to emerge from this work is Robert's account of how the Right in Australia—or at least this tightly networked part of it—when forced to choose between their ingrained philosophical hostility to a strong and intrusive role for the state and the defence of overtly racist policies, chose the latter.

Characters like McGuinness, Akerman, Devine and Bolt who can usually be relied on to recycle tedious British Tory clichés about the 'Nanny State' or homilies about the sanctity of the family, find themselves preferring to defend a terrible example of government-instituted social engineering designed to change the genetic make-up of Australia rather than acknowledge the extent of suffering caused by racist policies.

It's important to understand this: this is ground on which they themselves have chosen to fight their cultural battle.

What is it about this part of the Australian Right? What drives this secret terror, this fear of difference? This willingness to condone racism rather than acknowledge that, whatever the variety of motivations involved, a terrible thing was done to large numbers of our fellow Australians, not in the distant past but in a way that still affects many of them now?

When the Labor government in the early 1990s began to address issues like reconciliation, the need for an Australian republic and cultural issues, the Liberals in opposition thundered that these were 'distractions'. Sideshows. Not part of the *real* challenges facing Australia.

These challenges, we belatedly discovered, turned out in the Coalition's mind to have been a ham-fisted effort to implement a 1970s-style consumption tax that John Howard heard about 25 years ago and never forgot.

Once the Howard Government realised that, inconveniently for them, issues like reconciliation between indigenous and non-indigenous Australians would not simply disappear, it set about redefining the problem. Ministers began to claim that what was wrong was that Labor and the bleeding hearts had focused on the wrong things—questions of confronting historical wrongs. Instead of these irrelevant, emotional issues, we should have been talking about *practical* matters. It was all about economics and could be fixed with a bit of money and a few tough administrators.

The Howard government's use of this favoured word 'practical' repays careful study.

We've had John Howard's 'practical reconciliation'—which means marginalising any version of history acknowledging past injustice as 'black armband' and therefore 'impractical' and doing everything possible to avoid confronting moral issues of indigenous dispossession.

And Alexander Downer's 'practical regionalism', which suggested that while it was OK to make a buck out of Asia, we should avoid 'emotional' regionalism—in other words, coming to grips with the deeper issues of Australia's relations with the region around us.

Then recently we had the Parliamentary Secretary for Immigration adding her own helpful proposal for 'practical multiculturalism', which she defined in culinary terms as the rest of us enjoying the occasional plate of Chinese take-away.

As I said on another occasion, the Howard government uses the word 'practical' like an anti-matter particle designed to obliterate the noun it's meant to describe.

But, of course, questions about how we define ourselves as a community and how we confront basic ethical issues are not, and never were, distractions. Mr Howard and his colleagues have been reminded of the fact every day.

The distraction comes when we fail to address them, when we avert our eyes from these core moral issues of national responsibility and pretend we can shuffle towards the future without acknowledging the truth of our past. That is what impedes our ability to move forward as a nation.

And none of these issues is more central than addressing the place in our society of indigenous Australians.

No-one denies that physical problems—health, housing, education, employment—are important to reconciliation. Certainly not me. It was the theme of the first speech I made as Prime Minister about Aboriginal issues, just a few weeks after taking over the job.

In February 1992 I told the inaugural meeting of the Council for Aboriginal Reconciliation that one of the big changes I wanted to see as Prime Minister was change in the status of Aboriginal people and Torres Strait Islanders:

> *I believe—in fact I'm quite certain—that the best way to improve rela-tions between Aboriginal Australians and non-Aboriginal Australians and the best way to provide a basis for reconciliation is to close the gap in living conditions.*
>
> *At present the gap is huge. It has to be closed—in the end it has to be diminished to the point where no-one can point to someone and say the reason for that person's poverty, or illness, or alcoholism is that he or she is Aboriginal.*

That remains true. But reconciliation must be about more than living standards. It has to begin, as I said later in 1992 at Redfern, with an act of recognition.

Recognition that the European settlement of this continent, from which we have all drawn huge benefits, came at a terrible cost to Aboriginal Australians. Acknowledgement that we failed to adequately recognise what was done and, with some noble exceptions, to make the most basic human response and enter into the hearts and minds of indigenous Australians. We failed to ask—how would I feel if this were done to me?

That 'failure to imagine' is what pervades each page of Robert Manne's account. He points out that probably the most important issue that *Bringing Them Home* has to teach is how 'almost no-one was able to see through the kind of racism which could make it seem that tearing Aboriginal children from their mothers and communities was a natural, even noble, act.'

The question of why that was continues to haunt us today.

It began with the lie of *terra nullius*.

When the High Court made its great and just decision in the Mabo case in June 1992 my government decided that we had to face the issue and to develop what became the native title legislation. I often think there was nothing better we did as a government.

I certainly never did anything more difficult. But the important things are always the hardest. And until we confronted the original lie that this was a continent of no-one, I don't think we had any chance of coming to terms with the history that followed.

There's nothing I regret more about losing office than losing responsibility for reconciliation and native title and other Aboriginal issues. We would have made such a difference.

For indigenous Australians, the lies have continued. The denial of the frontier massacres. The denial of the experiences of the stolen generations, supported by the government's submission to the Senate enquiry. And all pumped out into the public debate by the network of right-wing polemicists that Robert describes.

You could see John Howard at it again during the week on Paul Kelly's *Centenary of Federation* documentary on the ABC, refusing all invitations to apologise because 'I don't believe in apologising for something for which I was not personally responsible'.

As if that was ever the question. Or the issue.

John Howard says: I will not take responsibility for something I did not actually do. But I will bask in the reflected glory of things I didn't do; I will be a grateful heir to things I didn't do. I will, in other words, be very selective about my history.

But despite the past—and aspects of the present—I'm optimistic about the future.

One reason for this is an important point Robert makes in his essay.

He describes *Bringing Them Home* as a process, not just a conclusion. The same thing was true of the native title legislation and of the struggle over the Howard government's disgraceful decision to legislate away the rights of Aboriginal people recognised by the High Court in the Wik case.

No meaner thing was done by a Commonwealth government to a dependent and vulnerable constituency.

But one reason why Aboriginal people can assert their interests more confidently and look with greater hope to the future is that these processes have strengthened the indigenous community and have led to the emergence of a quite remarkable group of indigenous leaders in this country, including, of course, Lowitja O'Donoghue.

These different processes have given a new energy to debate inside the indigenous community. And that is where much of it has to take place.

But not all of it.

At the end of my speech in Redfern in 1992 I emphasised that it wasn't my intention to impress guilt upon present generations of Australians for the actions of the past, but rather to acknowledge that we now share a responsibility to put an end to the suffering.

I said that:

Down the years, there has been no shortage of guilt, but it has not produced the responses we need. Guilt is not a very constructive emotion. I think what we need to do is open our hearts a bit.

And that's the second reason for my optimism. I think hearts *are* opening. We see it in the powerful, spontaneous support for reconciliation right across the Australian community.

We see it, too, in the determination of writers like Robert Manne never again to let the distortions and untruths stand unchallenged.

I'm proud to launch the *Quarterly Essay* and Robert Manne's 'In Denial: The Stolen Generations and the Right'.

THE LABOR GOVERNMENT, 1983–96

University of New South Wales,
Sydney,
19 March 1999

*Paul Keating's 'The Labor Government 1983–96' was delivered in
his role as visiting Professor in Public Policy at the University of New
South Wales. It constitutes his first formal summation of the Labor
government and to the time of this publication, his only one. The
address sketches out the manner in which the Hawke and Keating
governments differed from their predecessors and how they approached
the modernising of Australia's economy and society.*

I THOUGHT QUITE HARD BEFORE deciding to speak about the Labor
government from 1983 to 1996. I was an active participant in that government, not a dispassionate observer, and I'm no more dispassionate now.
To the inevitable charge, 'He would say that, wouldn't he?' the only
response can be that I probably would.

And no single individual can speak comprehensively about those
years in government. Bob Hawke was Prime Minister for nine of the
thirteen years. And through five governments, the original policy work
of people like Neal Blewett, Don Grimes, Brian Howe, Susan Ryan on
social policy, John Button, John Dawkins, Peter Walsh and Ralph Willis
in the economic portfolios and Kim Beazley, Gareth Evans and Bill
Hayden in defence and foreign policy made their own contributions.
Each of them would have a different story to tell.

Thirteen years is a long time. A lot happens in thirteen years—kids are born, grow up and enter secondary school, new technologies are invented, social attitudes alter, new industries emerge and, during our particular thirteen years in government, empires fall. And in our case it involved five election victories. It was more than the British Tory Party managed during all the long Thatcher and Major years. I was especially proud to have led Labor to a fifth consecutive victory. I was not able to manage number six. But had I had, Labor would have clocked up sixteen consecutive years—four American Presidential terms back to back—a difficult thing to do in this day and age.

On the other hand, I was one of the few who were there at the beginning and the end. I was involved in most of the decisions. And I strongly believe that the Labor government between 1983 and 1996 changed Australia for the better in ways that it would not otherwise have changed.

In a single address you cannot attempt a chronological account of what happened and why over thirteen years, and I am not going to try. But the passage of time has given some perspective to our views of those years and I thought there could be value in setting out my own belief about what happened in Australia during that period and why it mattered.

I have to say that it never felt like anything less than an adventure. It felt like a big story then, and it feels like it now. It felt like we were making of Australia what we felt it could and should be. That we'd been granted this fantastic opportunity and privilege. In those thirteen years Australia was refashioned—not in every detail, and not always to the point of completion. No such point exists in my experience.

There were a couple of moments of drift and some policy mistakes and certainly some political ones. There was a lacerating recession which bore down heavily on people who deserved better, many of whom had accommodated the economic changes, seized the new economic opportunities, who had put their faith in us.

Golden Ages only exist in the minds of the melancholy, or political parties drifting on the outer edge of darkness. But it was an unprecedented period of deliberate and often brave reform in which the government and the people strived to make Australia a first-rate country—a place with a powerful economic engine and a soul to match. Sprawling and strange to outside eyes—but savvy and subtle and worldly. Sometimes you could feel the charge of energy that came from this sense of common purpose. It was palpable.

Institutions which can so easily be moribund or aimless—the Parliament, the public service, the Labor Party—suddenly revealed their purpose and their utility. Perhaps not a golden age, but there were times when you felt like yelling, 'Eureka, it works'.

The fact that Australia has come through this first phase of the economic crisis in Asia so well has been heavily due, mostly due, as almost everyone except the current Prime Minister and Treasurer has acknowledged, to decisions taken by the Labor government. On their side, they like to pretend that the fundamental reforms of the Australian economy in the 1980s simply popped into existence one day while no-one was paying attention. A genie that popped out of some Treasury laser printer.

But try to imagine the Australian economy today with an uncompetitive exchange rate. Or the situation we would face if we had to try to maintain a peg or some other arrangement against speculative attack by financial markets. Instead, the floating currency has acted as a shock absorber within the system by providing a *real* devaluation of 20 per cent. Or imagine where we would be if we still had the jurassic economy of the late 1970s, and we were still trying to protect jobs in decaying manufacturing structures behind high tariff walls, with current commodity prices.

Central to the story of the Labor government from 1983 to 1996 are these points.

First, the Labor government found—and had to find—a new way of delivering growth to the Australian economy. It did this by embracing openness rather than the protectionism of the past. It saw competition as the best way of ensuring that in a more open economy the interests of ordinary working men and women were better secured.

194

Second, the Labor government found—and had to find—new ways of delivering social justice—that is, cushioning change and supporting the weak—in a community that was changing rapidly. In the past, the centralised wage fixation system had been the principal means of achieving equity in Australia. But the economy, the nature and composition of the work force and the broader society were all changing. More women were working and the nuclear family structure was no longer the norm. The wages system could no longer perform the same task.

Third, for a similar range of reasons connected with changes to the economy and society, the Labor government had to begin the transition from a welfare state system whose model was directive, top-down, universal and passive, to a welfare model which was focused on the needs of each individual and which maximised choice: an active one.

Fourth, the decision to open Australia economically brought with it—and had to bring—consequences for other areas of social and external policy, including our relations with our own indigenous people and with our neighbours in the region.

What this added up to was the construction in Australia over these years of a socio-economic model which was unique in the world and which subsequently helped shape the thinking of other social reform governments. This model placed a strong weight on markets, but accepted that there were circumstances in which markets alone could not adequately serve and support communities, and which saw an active, though different, role for government in shaping social outcomes.

Life was difficult for a social reform government in the late 1980s and early 1990s. The prevailing political winds from the northern hemisphere were alien and cold. In Reagan's America and Thatcher's Britain, great society and welfare state solutions were being abandoned and dismantled. It was hard, under the constant gaze of markets, to make the case for a more efficient Australian economy moulded with a Labor heart. But we did it.

And it was a highly collegial effort. A former official who observed much of the debate in the Cabinet over those years told me recently that the impressive thing about it was how those in Cabinet—whether from the economic portfolios or the social portfolios—all had a coherent view of where Australia needed to move. I think that is true. It was one of the strengths of Labor and the government during that period.

We didn't call what we were doing the Third Way. For Australia, we saw it as the only way.

The reasons had been becoming clearer for two decades.

When the salad days of Australia's postwar growth were coming to an obvious close, it was apparent to anyone in Australian public life that a succession of governments following Menzies' resignation lacked a coherent framework to guide Australia through to its next economic age.

Beginning with the development of agriculture and the Gold Rush of the nineteenth century and moving through the other phases—lead and zinc, iron ore—Australia's economic story, and very much its social story, had been the exploitation of the country's bounty.

Coupled with this was the obvious comfort the country had from our economic ties with Britain through imperial preference. Imperial preference inculcated in Australia the notion that we were entitled to some preferential treatment in the world order and that we could pay for it by resort to our natural wealth.

New expression had been given to this approach in the Menzies years under the policies of John McEwen. A whole generation of Australian industrialists grew up believing we could live and grow in a featherbedded system.

The rot set in when the terms of trade began their long-term decline about the time Robert Menzies retired. Through a succession of governments and treasurers it seemed there was no understanding that a fundamental shift was taking place away from commodity producers and towards the products of the open and large manufacturing and services markets of the United States, Japan, Germany, etc.

Then came the OPEC-induced oil price rises beginning in 1973 which unleashed the first big shift in inflation.

The combination of the surge in oil prices and wages being bid up led to rising inflation which was quickly becoming entrenched by the time the Whitlam government left office in 1975. High inflation underpinned high interest rates. Profits collapsed, dislocating private investment and, with it, employment.

The Fraser government was elected with majorities in both Houses of Parliament. Many people hoped it could develop a framework to deal with our economic malaise, then called stagflation: stagnant growth and high inflation.

In those years of the mid- to late 1970s the terms of trade really shifted for the worse for Australia, denying us the increments to national income that had allowed the blowsy policy of protectionism to remain affordable. But the Fraser government and Treasurer John Howard did nothing about it. The structural issues were left unattended. Even the Fraser government's own Committee of Economic Inquiry, the Campbell Inquiry, which had set out proposals for regeneration, was ignored.

In the three years leading up to the 1983 election, the leading figures of the opposition knew that Labor not only had to do better but could do better. Others, including the trade unions and the public service knew it too. In many respects, it was the last throw all of us had to make the Australian economy and society, in any controlled way, modern and competitive. Perhaps the last chance to throw off the cargo cult mentality and the belief that nature would bestow its beneficence on us by periodically dropping a new bag of money in our lap.

This was the time people like the then secretary to the Treasury, John Stone, were contending that an efficient, competitive manufacturing sector was inconsistent with Australia's burgeoning primary export sector. The argument went that minerals and the mineral boom would make the exchange rate more valuable, allowing competitively priced imports to knock down the industries that lived under the umbrella of protection. A somewhat determinist view that we were bound to be a quarry forever, but not much more than a quarry.

There was no orthodoxy in existence at the advent of the Hawke government about how to address the national problems and bring the country along with us. The Cabinet had to develop this by itself.

Nobody, but nobody, comes to office with a flawless schematic for change. But some of us in the Labor government came to office with a greater belief in markets than our conservative counterparts. A belief that in the long run, the social contract would only hold if it was underpinned by growth and wealth and that the only way this could be procured and enjoyed was by making Australia internationally competitive and promoting a more cohesive and inclusive society.

The economic summit of March 1983 was in many respects a summit of desperation. All the participants knew that, despite its natural wealth, the fundamentals of the Australian economy were all wrong and that we needed a paradigm shift in the way we conducted ourselves economically.

When I look back on those thirteen years of Labor government I think of the period after that summit as the intensive care ward.

First, we sought to restart growth and employment after the Fraser/Howard 1980–82 recession, and to adjust the factor shares between wages and profits. We knew that the profit share was too low to get employment growing strongly again. Employment had to expand quickly and that meant aggregate wage restraint. But we did not want to achieve this simply by screwing down wages. The Accord with the trade unions was the device we used to see that the burden was shared. We got cooperative agreement on wage restraint but used rising employment and the social wage to maintain household income and to protect equity.

We reduced the Commonwealth's public-sector outlays by five percentage points of GDP. This was a huge amount, but we believed it could be done without adverse impact if we created a more focused, better targeted and more efficient public sector. With a smaller public sector we obviously needed less tax revenue, and we took the revenue share in GDP for the whole country down to one of the lowest among the OECD industrialised countries.

We wanted a public sector large enough to sustain the social contract but not so big that it crowded out employment-creating private invest-ment. Unlike some people on the left of politics we believed that if the call by the government sector on national resources was too high it would squeeze private-sector activity and initiative. We reduced the top personal tax rate from the 60 per cent rate under Malcolm Fraser and John Howard to 49 per cent—a big and meaningful shift. We reduced the company tax rate from 46 per cent to 33 per cent, and we removed the double taxation of dividends with the imputation system (which also strengthened Australian companies and investment in Australia). This greatly favoured investment in equities, improved the stability of our stockmarket and presented the biggest break ever for private companies and public-company shareholders. These were things Labor governments—in the old Labor paradigm—did not do.

Later in the period of the government, once the shares between wages and profits had been adjusted, we began to move away from broad wage adjustments through the national wage cases to the new enterprise-bargaining framework. The Keating government made the historic 100-year shift away from centralised wage fixing. The objective was to lift enterprise productivity and share it by agreement between employers (profits) and employees (wages).

This was part of an intense effort to lift productivity from an abysmal trend rate of 1.25 per cent in the ten years to 1985 to 2.25 per cent in the decade to 1995. Indeed productivity from those changes touched on 3 per cent this year.

But just as important as labour-market reforms to this process was our comprehensive microeconomic reform agenda. This included telecommunications reform, the national road system, national rail freight, electricity and gas reforms, a national TAFE system and the national training agenda.

Second, we tried to address the core components of Australia's international competitiveness (then badly out of line). We did this by floating the exchange rate and freeing the financial system so interest rates could be set in the market where banks could become creators, not rationers, of credit, and by dismantling the tariff wall which had insulated Australian industry against the world and kept it from improving its performance. Tariffs had kept the cost of goods to

Australian working men and women well above what they should have been; they cut into their standard of living.

One result is that Australians can now buy a Commodore as good as an Opel, and at the same price, not twice the price as before.

Third, we put a long overdue focus on remedies for the decline in national savings. We pulled the budget into surplus and augmented private savings through the introduction of award-based superannuation, which later became the Superannuation Guarantee Charge.

In the early 1980s only 40 per cent of employees—and less than a quarter of female workers—were covered by superannuation. This left many people relying only on the old age pension to live through their retirement. The cost to the budget—and to future taxpayers like many of the young people in this audience tonight—was set to grow substantially as demographics increased the number of retirees in relation to working age people. The risk will be that the budget will not be able to afford a healthy retirement income for them. In the long run the aged are better off with their own bucket of savings, largely independent of the public pension. The Labor government will have given it to them, and in doing so laid down the most fundamental of changes.

Labor's national superannuation scheme delivered Australia a net increase in national savings of about 2.5 per cent by 2005, and 4 per cent over the long term. The present government took the employee and government contributions off the agenda in the 1997–98 budget. The thought of unions having influence on large amounts of national savings horrified John Howard. As a result, compulsory contributions will reach only 9 per cent of earnings rather than 15 per cent by 2003, and Australia's improvement in national savings will be reduced by about 1 per cent of GDP. You never expect much of conservative governments but you would have thought thrift was one policy they would applaud and support.

Considering what we had in place with the agreement of the trade unions, and the high level of acceptance we had achieved in the community generally, this decision by the Howard government is a savage blow to Australia's economic security.

Faced with the recession of the early 1990s, while doing everything possible to alleviate its worst effects, the government was duty bound to ensure that the pain was not for nothing. So against the understandable tide of popular opinion, the Keating government stuck with policies like the tariff cuts, which we knew were in the country's long-term interests. Announced in two tranches, in 1988 and 1991, the foreshadowed tariff cuts only mattered if they were stuck to—implemented.

This was the period in which Australia decisively broke with inflation. The wage–tax trade-offs from 1986–87 onwards had helped us to retain the advantages of the 27 per cent competitive depreciation of the dollar during 1985–86 without unleashing a new surge of prices. The aggressive, then steady, monetary policy we pursued bore down on inflation. Australia went into the recession with inflation at 5 per cent and came out of it at 2 per cent. I believe it will maintain this into the next decade.

I recently came across one left-wing critique of our term in office which said: 'The Labor Government embraced [rationalist policies] out of insecurity with its past, lack of clarity and uncertainty and hesitation in a rapidly changing environment.' The only response you can make—this being a university address—is 'Nonsense'.

The Labor government embraced rational economic solutions and market-oriented policies because they were the best way of getting growth and therefore the best way of ensuring the future of ordinary Australians. We could see clearly that in a rapidly changing global environment this was the only choice we had that did not leave us condemned to slump into irrelevance and decline, that increasingly seemed our lot.

Economic rationalism has been turned into a fashionable bogey man. But as ogres go, it really doesn't cut the mustard. If the claim is that Labor believed that markets can be an efficient mechanism for all sorts of economic and social purposes, then it is true, but isn't saying much. If it is suggesting that Labor was in some sort of ideological, Thatcherite thrall to markets, then it is demonstrably false. In policies ranging from the Accord to Medicare to *Better Cities* to industry policies like the *Car Plan* to *Creative Nation* to *Working Nation*, Labor consistently believed in an active role for government in Australia. But a more focused role. Using the government to steer the boat, not row it.

I want to say something specifically about the public service. Almost all the best work we were able to do in government depended on the cooperation of a creative, hard-working and independent public service, which included people of the highest calibre and commitment to good government. Labor acted to make the public service more responsive. We amalgamated departments and worked to shift the emphasis of their work from inputs to outcomes. But this was a far cry from the move towards an American system which the incoming government made in 1996 by purging—without explanation—six departmental secretaries. The problem for Australia at present is that we now have the worst of both worlds—a cowed public service, but without America's flexibility. The next Labor government needs to find ways of addressing this issue and restoring the essential values of the Westminster system to the Australian public service.

This brings me from the first of the points I began with—the Labor government's emphasis on growth by opening the economy—to the second point, the need Labor had to find new ways of delivering social justice.

The incomes of ordinary Australians were once guaranteed almost entirely by the wages system. But by the beginning of the 1980s Labor knew that wages policy could no longer be used to achieve social equity because we no longer had a society in which a male breadwinner supported a wife and children through a lifetime spent in one job.

We needed another way of dealing with these equity issues and we found it in the 'social wage' element of the Accord—that is, the combination of disposable income plus non-cash government transfers for education, health, housing, etc.—which enabled us to compensate low income wage and salary earners and their families for wage restraint by providing government programs and payments to those who needed them.

The steady but determined implementation of Labor's social priorities in those thirteen years is a roll of honour, doubly worthy in my view when you accept that it was achieved against a background of that declining share of Commonwealth expenditure as a percentage of GDP. From Medicare to Working Nation I believe the Labor government had an outstanding record of social reform.

To take one proud example, at the end of Labor's period in government the most needy families in our community had seen an 80 per cent improvement in real terms in their income support.

The list of Labor's social reforms can sound almost pedestrian when you read it out—Medicare, pharmaceutical benefits, repair of the social safety net, a 200 per cent increase in childcare places, housing assistance, rent assistance, a system of geriatric assessment, introduction of the Home and Community Care Program to help the elderly and disabled, major improvements in the education and training systems to give young people, particularly the disadvantaged, a better chance in life, a 250 per cent increase in Year 12 retention rates. Not to mention the extension of superannuation coverage across the workforce, sex discrimination legislation, and the reshaping of higher education. But each of those reforms and all the others changed the lives and social outlooks of millions of people.

And just as importantly, I think, one of our achievements was to help change the aspirations of the Australian community—to alter the sense of what this society ought to be like and what equity in it really meant.

The policy enshrined in the Accord worked both as a means of facilitating employment creation and as an instrument of social justice. Over the thirteen years of the Labor government, employment rose at an annual rate of 2.2 per cent, more than double the rate of under 1 per cent during the preceding seven years of Coalition government.

It is easy to understate this achievement. But if Labor had only managed the 1.5 per cent growth rate we have seen under the Coalition government during the past three years, 700,000 fewer Australians would have been in work. During the 1980s Australia had the highest rate of job growth in the OECD. Thirty-three per cent more people were in work when Labor ended office than when it began. In all Western

Europe, in comparison, net employment did not increase by a single job between 1973 and 1994.

I want to specifically address a claim which is often made about equity in Australia over those years, particularly the distribution of income. Excuse these detailed figures, but they are important. According to the most comprehensive study of the entire period 1981–82 to 1993–94, Australian households were, on average, better off by the end of the period than at the beginning. Taken together, all household types benefited from the increase in average total household income—that is, private income, government cash benefits and the value of government non-cash benefits—of 9.1 per cent over the period.

And at the end of the period Australia was a society with a more equal distribution of income than in the early 1980s. Households in the lower income ranges received a greater share of total income over the period, whereas the top 20 per cent of income earners received relatively less.

The non-cash social wage played an increasingly important part in this redistributive process. The disposable income of the lowest 40 per cent of households increased from 20.2 per cent in 1981–82 to 21.1 per cent in 1993–94. Social income for the same lowest 40 per cent of households increased from 24 per cent to 26.1 per cent. Most of the increase was at the expense of the top 20 per cent of households.

This was against a global background in which almost every industrialised society saw before-tax income ranges widen because of the relentless pressures of globalisation and technological change.

The data, for those interested, are in the December 1995 report *Trends in the Distribution of Cash Income and Non-Cash Benefits* by David Johnson from the University of Melbourne and Ian Manning and Otto Hellwig from the National Institute of Economic and Industry Research.

The third theme I wanted to talk about is the transformation of the idea of welfare which emerged with increasing strength towards the end of the Labor period.

It was becoming clear by the end of the 1980s that the sort of society which was now emerging in Australia and throughout the developed world—better educated, more atomised, more diverse in its social structures—was one in which the traditional downwards, passive and universal model of welfare was becoming less appropriate. A new welfare model was needed which imposed greater responsibility on the individual but which was also more responsive to the individual's needs.

We began to place greater stress on finding ways of assisting people to help themselves, and to focus much more on individual responsibility and personal choice. The Child Support Agency's role in ensuring non-custodial parents met their responsibilities to support their children, and the introduction of the Higher Education Contribution Scheme, designed to help fund the expansion of tertiary places, were early examples of this.

The fullest example of the new approach to social policy came in the suite of programs covered by the government's 1994 White Paper, Working Nation.

Although the proportion of Australians fifteen and over engaged in active employment rose during the period of the Labor government from 63 per cent to 65.5 per cent, unemployment remained high. The problem was that too many Australians did not have the skills and training to fill the jobs being created. A modern, sophisticated open economy was essential and it has brought untold advantages. But there were victims, and how well a government looks after them, how well it opens the way back to opportunity and a share in the general prosperity, is the ultimate measure of success.

The Keating government's *Working Nation* took a comprehensive approach to the question of unemployment. Economic growth is far and away the most effective creator of jobs, so *Working Nation* contained programs for a more efficient economy—quickening the pace of microeconomic reform.

But while growth is fundamental to job creation, it is not the answer for the long-term unemployed, for the unskilled and poorly educated, for those trapped in a cycle of poverty, or for those in the regions of

Australia whose economies are in long-term decline and in need of fundamental—and socially painful—restructuring. To these people *Working Nation* offered an entirely new way—a set of education and labour-market programs to provide training, work or individual case management for all who needed it.

Working Nation also introduced the notion of reciprocal obligations. This has become widely fashionable since. But our reciprocity was of a particular sort. The reciprocal obligation did not lie on the government's side, as the present government seems to believe, simply in the payment of unemployment benefits but in the provision of individual training and skill development in return for work and study by the unemployed.

I won't go into the details. *Working Nation* was the first comprehensive program of its sort in the world and elements of it have since been adopted by the Blair and Clinton governments. When so many of its programs were scrapped by the incoming government, not only the unemployed, but all Australians were the losers—and in the long run I think we will all pay.

My final point is that once Australia had begun to open its economy, other forms of openness imposed themselves on government policy.

Through the Labor years the share of exports in the economy rose from 16 per cent to 20 per cent. Services and elaborately transformed manufactures grew much faster than our traditional primary exports. And Asia was becoming increasingly important to our economy. The developing countries of Asia took 20 per cent of our exports at the beginning of Labor's period, 36 per cent at the end of it.

As I have said in this auditorium before, the distinctive thing about Australia's relationship with Asia during the Labor years was that for the first time all our interests—not just political and strategic interests which we had long had, but economic as well—started to come together in Asia. We did not, as the current easy government lie has it, have an Asia Only policy, but we did have an approach to our national interests which went beyond the idea of great and powerful friends. Our foreign policy and our defence policy of self-reliance gave us a larger role in the Pacific. I have spoken here several times before about the changes

Labor brought to Australian foreign policy, and I don't want to cover that ground in any detail now.

Except to say that the changing structure of our economy had some quite specific consequences. Once the dollar had been floated, and the tariff barriers started to come down, it became less important for Australia to fight to protect our privileged access to other markets in the way we had done when Britain joined the Common Market than to fight to get others to open their markets with us. That was part of the rationale for APEC and the development of the Cairns Group.

Once our economy began to depend more heavily on the export of services rather than bulk commodities, the way we presented ourselves to the world became more important. Decisions about where you educate your children or seek health care or look for legal assistance or buy your entertainment are quite different from decisions about where to source steaming coal.

We could not, in my view, represent ourselves to the countries of the Asia Pacific in the way we needed to, but more importantly, we could not be at ease with ourselves until we had acknowledged the reality of our relationship with indigenous Australians. Well before Mabo came along as a decision of the High Court of Australia, Labor had begun addressing the questions of Aboriginal reconciliation. The native title legislation gave us the opportunity to redress a great wrong. The Labor government did not hang the High Court out to dry when it presented the difficult challenge of Mabo. You don't need to be a political scientist to know that the Coalition did just that when the High Court presented its Wik decision not many years thereafter.

Much of Labor's agenda was about preparing Australia for the world we knew was to come.

We wanted to strengthen Australia's intellectual infrastructure. In addition to the resources we put into expanding the higher education system—nearly doubling the number of university places in the eight years to 1996—we tried to strengthen the links between our fine pure research base and its industrial application by creating the Cooperative

Research Centres which have made an important contribution to the Australian economy.

In our 1995 cultural policy *Creative Nation*, we set a world first in efforts to forge bonds between the creative element in Australia and the emerging digital economy. Some of the media depicted *Creative Nation* as an indulgence in my affection for the arts, and I still see it referred to in the press as an arts policy. It was much more than this—so much more, that quite a few in the arts community expressed disapproval of its broadness.

Creative Nation was of a piece with *Working Nation* and other government labour market and industry policies. It was a policy for the arts, but it was also a far-reaching cultural policy that picked up on the developments in new media and opened conduits between that burgeoning technology and the creative spirit in the community. It was very much a jobs policy and an industry policy.

There was nothing precious about it—it was carefully thought out policy which the British, American and other governments have since used as a reference point in developing their own cultural policies. The central premise was that the most successful modern economies and the best modern societies were, above all, creative ones. Fostering the arts is always a good idea *per se* and a basic responsibility, but in an era dominated by these new technologies, commonsense tells us there are irresistible benefits to reap of an economic and social kind. Art overlaps with design, design with media and landscape and the environments in which we and future generations will live; literature overlaps with literacy and self-knowledge and these things overlap with ambition and achievement.

The renewed interest in our sense of ourselves was inculcating in many of us a new awareness of what it meant to be Australian. To know that this meant not being British or North American or Asian or anything else but ourselves.

Labor knew what sort of Australia it wanted. It knew we had to be in the world. It knew how we ought to be seen. It knew what role we ought to play. It knew what sort of society we wanted at home. It knew that breadth of mind and inclusion was the way to a cohesive country.

The internationalisation that came with the changes Labor wrought, and that globalisation fostered, played to our sense of individuality and diversity. The multicultural society eschewed by some was seen by most as the very way in which our new international role could best be performed.

The same was true of the republic. How could—how can—Australia go into the second century of our existence as a Commonwealth, borrowing the Head of State of another country? And in circumstances in which, however you do the polling, more than half of all Australians don't think this situation adequately represents our country? We don't need the republic because we want to change Australia's institutions, but because we want to strengthen them.

One of the great structural reforms over the period was reform of the Labor Party itself. Generally, political parties wear out, particularly if they can lay claim to being 100 years old or older. They simply fade away; they become irrelevant and the nation loses them.

Gough Whitlam gave the Labor Party mouth-to-mouth resuscitation almost at the point of expiry but, given the split and its aftermath, he and his colleagues had great difficulty trying to refocus it in a policy sense.

The achievement of the last Labor government was to know and understand the Party's innate altruism and to take the time to guide it towards the world Australia had to belong to. To include it in the deliberations of the government. To bring its constituent unions into the policy milieu. To give it a sense of mission. To convince it that Labor had power at an entirely critical juncture in Australia's history and that although the party had faced all sorts of challenges in the past, including war and depression, we had never had to change by root and by branch—to fundamentally remake—a peacetime economy.

The Labor Party is a very hard outfit to manage at the best of times. But going against the grain of ingrained beliefs and philosophy is especially difficult. But we did this in spades in areas like abandoning control over the exchange rate for the long-term good; giving banks the power to create credit at the expense of building societies and credit unions; letting foreign banks take market share from our own banking system; cutting the top personal rate of tax; putting an assets test on the age pension; setting up competition to Telstra; selling the Commonwealth Bank and Qantas; reforming the waterfront.

This was hard work. But it was done willingly, cheerfully and persuasively by a Cabinet with an amazing degree of policy unity and purpose.

In these things belief always matters. Urgency matters. Inclusion matters and courtesy matters. Time and effort and patience matter.

Surely no government spent more time on consultation, meetings, consensus—more meetings, more consultations, more consensus—than this one.

And it was an uplifting process. When people truly understand the problems, comprehend the framework and then see the light, it is, for anyone deeply involved in such a process, like winning the lottery.

There were many inconclusive meetings but plenty of beaming ones, where we would all go off to some little café for a hamburger and a Coke at midnight, happy we had made another step for Australia.

I also believe the public understood this too. They watched this creative tension knowing that most of the time there was something in it for them and the country. A word of high commendation here for Bill Kelty and the Australian trade unions is appropriate: for their clear-headedness, their preparedness to change and their fidelity to the interests of working people.

But we could not have done what we did without the Australian community. They knew things were not right and had to be put right. They were prepared to trust us in the process. They took the step into the dark with us, but as they saw the adjustments come and the outlook improving, they gave us another chance: in 1984 after the big financial reforms, in 1987 after the dollar collapse, in 1990 as the economy was growing and in 1993 after the recession, rejecting what they saw as the extreme alternative. What we might call today the Elliott view of life.

We finished with a more healthy and robust country and a Labor Party that would never be the same again. One that had broken out of the yolk sac of central planning, of policy dogmatism, of insularity, to enjoy the great range of opportunities it had created for itself.

I am the last person to argue that the work of the last Labor government should be holy writ for the next one. Australian social democracy is lucky to have in public life at present some highly creative men and women who are already setting out new approaches to public policy. Politics is a battle of ideas. The twenty-second grabs and the photo opportunities are what you have to put up with to convince people about the ideas, but they are not what it is all about.

The world changes and the challenges change. The 1991 edition of the *Macquarie Dictionary*, published in the year I became Prime Minister, doesn't have an entry for the word 'Internet'. Yet it is hard now to think of any area of public policy that is not in some way influenced by it.

The things governments need to do change at different periods of history. Part of the art of government lies in knowing what should be on the agenda now. Australian governments once needed to build telecommunications infrastructure, to run airlines and banks. Now the need is different: it is to prepare the country for an exciting but uneasy existence as an open, service-oriented, knowledge-dominated economy engaged as a centre of the Asia Pacific. To help equip Australians to participate in a knowledge-based society, and to deal with the consequences of those changes for equity in our community.

I believe the essential message from the period of thirteen years of the Labor government is this: Australians should have no fear.

The country and the community showed an astonishing capacity to remake itself, to reform and to adjust. Far from constraining or limiting us, globalisation, for all its problems and complexities, gave Australia the ability to free ourselves from a fate as a commodity price-taker, at the mercy of markets far away. It helped make us phobia-free—most of us anyway.

The same will be true of the future. If you were asked to imagine a society with the capacity to succeed in the twenty-first century, you could hardly go past what we have here—a robust democracy, a vibrant, well-educated and creative community, with people drawn from all over the world, situated in the region of the world which will continue to be the fastest growing over the next century. And having been granted the inestimable gift of a continent for ourselves.

The Labor government between 1983 and 1996 saw that reality and pointed the way forward. But others now must get us there. I hope some who will do so are in this auditorium tonight.

20

THE COMPACT CITY
Urban Design and Architecture

Urban Development Institute of Australia National Congress,
Sydney,
9 March 2010

*This address articulates many of Paul Keating's long-held views about
cities, architecture and design. It lays out how and why he developed
certain rules or protocols about city development and how such thoughts
might apply, with particular reference to Sydney. Paul Keating's
continuing interest in Sydney Harbour is also evident, including the
mammoth Barangaroo development of which he is progenitor.*

MY PARENTS WERE RAISED AND grew up in the inner suburbs of
Sydney. Every Sunday late afternoon and evening my family drove from
Bankstown, where we lived, to my father's family house in Annandale.
And I will always remember, during the summer twilight, the many
young people congregating along the footpaths, while in the street the
sodality of their parents was apparent.

We would drive away from that density and those points of congregation back to the suburban grid of fibro-built Bankstown with its
quarter-acres blocks, unmade roads and footpaths. Bankstown had a
sense of community about it but it lacked that tightness and compactness
which the community of Annandale possessed.

Those streets of inner city semi-detached houses lacked the backyard
and side driveways and, more often than not, the Hills hoists of their

suburban peers, but what they lacked in space and idle amenity, they made up for in community and proximity to the things of interest: in the main, the city.

As we drove home I was always aware of the stark change as we crossed from the older, more architecturally uniform, denser places to the more uneven, spread landscape of the western suburbs.

I did not quite understand it at the time, but I was in the process of developing my own ideas about how a city should be. And whichever way I looked at it, I always came to the same conclusion: that the best, most interesting city was the compact one. That the suburban sprawl atomised and derogated from that intensity, an intensity which made the organism of the city both enjoyable and sustainable.

All the great cities have compactness and a geometry that facilitates the movement of people through them. And generally a geometry that has arisen over time through habit and convenience.

When, as Treasurer in the mid-1990s, I made some remarks on radio about the nature of the cities and the lack of housing choice, including the primacy of the Hills hoist, I suffered brickbats for months. Indeed, before the deregulation of saving and trading banks, which I presided over, including the deregulation of housing financing, it was virtually impossible for any private developer to build attached housing or apartment block-type development. They simply could not marshal the required levels of debt and individual buyers could never be sure that finance was available to settle a contract. There was no off-the-plan buying. Those days, the days of the so-called free-enterprise banks, were the days of credit rationing. Credit rationing achieved through Commonwealth regulation.

So the suburban sprawl with its quarter-acre block was not only the creation of urban planning, or the lack of it, it was also a product of the then financial system.

Today we can do more, our financial leverage has been vastly improved and in terms of planning, we know better. Or I hope we know better. But the truth is, our cities are not working well. And they are not growing well.

That said, the future will be more about redressing failures than it will be about moving forward with some notion of a blank slate.

Our transport arteries will have to work and if they do not, we will have to invest in them. Our densities will have to increase but they will have to increase with built forms that garner popular acceptance by enriching the landscapes people live in and traverse daily. And places where public spaces are good, where people go and will want to go. Places where communities can prosper, where people share a common ambience and when issues arise, some common cause.

It seems to me that improving densities has to be the main way we accommodate larger populations in our cities and especially here in Sydney.

Melbourne and Adelaide have a flat canvas to work on, with very particular grid structures of long streets availing both cities of future development and redevelopment options. Sydney is completely different; the harbour bifurcates the city, leaving it much more compromised in development. This is also true but less true of Brisbane and Perth.

But let me say that generally, we are not doing higher density well. In Sydney, for instance, there are many examples of good medium-density redevelopment but there are hundreds of shockers. And it is not that we have not done it well in the past. In the last half of the nineteenth century and first half of the twentieth we did it exceedingly well.

If you take areas like Potts Point and Kings Cross, you find the highest densities in Australia but densities accomplished in a very pleasing way. Five to seven storeys, similar heights and scale, uniform setbacks off roadways, often similar materials, like the use of liver brick in the 1920s and 1930s. These characteristics make aesthetic sense and people will pay to live in them.

The great architect Leon Battista Alberti said 'potential for awareness of harmony and beauty is innate in the mind'. He said 'with beauty it is not opinion which matters but rather a kind of reason which centres on divine gifts which the human intellect enjoys'. I have always believed that. That's why people know that when they walk into a well-formed street or precinct or indeed, an attractive room, something in their

DNA is telling them this is harmonious and harmonious with them. It makes sense to the intellectual goings-on in their mind, even if they have no formal training or formalised appreciation of what their eye should and should not like.

For instance, the Potts Point apartments stand mostly as individual but related sentinel blocks; slightly detached from each other but with resolution over the façades. The older apartment buildings, the ones that people like, have an 'all façade' fenestration which the eye can make sense of. The façades do not present as a grid of verandas and sliding glass doors with no overarching composition. People are more interested in the aesthetic composition of the façade than they are in the mostly unused, quasi-amenity of a veranda that offers some free floor space by virtue of a gaping concession in the planning system. And those verandas inevitably give rise to those charmless ice tray façades. All cubes and no composition.

And a lot of this failure is not public policy, though, of course, some of it is. It arises, more often than not, from an absence of civic conscientiousness on the part of developers and their architects. Or, if not that, a kind of urban incoherence.

This kind of development not only dumbs down those in the community interested in buying the product, it cuts right across the idea of the city as a composite project. The notion that our pride and pleasure can be best found in the composition of the whole rather than in the quest for the singular.

The great cities and more particularly the attractive, compact ones have always been a composition of the whole that has taken precedence over the particular. Paris and New York are perhaps the obvious examples where common setbacks and the common use of materials have been the key variables in their success.

In putting architectural ideas together in my own head, now for over 50 years, I have come up with what I believe is a rule and a truth. And it is that 'variety is the antithesis of grandeur'. The buildings of the great Paris boulevards are each different to the other but they obey common rules as to materials and form such that they present a variegated uniformity which invests those boulevards with grandeur. And by grandeur, I mean a larger, simple massed greatness. A whole greater than the sum of the parts.

These days of course, we live in the age of the steel-frame building. Buildings are, more often than not, not clad in stone. We celebrate the new material use—glass and steel, concrete and natural stones—and we know we can do wonderful things with these materials. And there are many truly great modern buildings, especially commercial ones. But inevitably they are greater when they relate one to another in civic compositions, ones by which the human eye can detect a rhythm and pattern.

We cannot continue to do higher density the way we are doing it. This will produce more and more resistance even though the policy of doing it is utterly rational. The resistance comes from the truly gormless nature of much that is being produced. Our community is walking around with that DNA Alberti spoke of; they do not need instruction in architecture or design to know what is mediocre or bad. But they are depressed by what they see and are forced to inhabit and they resent it.

Which brings me back to Sydney in the main, a subject I was asked to expressly address in this talk.

Let me approach it this way. All the great cities have clear definition at their core and the communities of those cities have done all in their power to maintain the clarity of that definition. Whether we are speaking of New York or Paris or Copenhagen, their municipal governments and their people have kept faith with the central motif of their place.

In Sydney's case, the defining and central motif is its harbour, but the harbour is an abstract work of headlands and inlets providing definition to a larger water body. It seems to me that at all costs, we should brook as little derogation from that conception as is possible. This is not to be judgemental as to what has taken place to date; it is all about attaching a premium to the natural defining characteristics, especially and particularly the public places. The places that belong to us all.

You see a city which has good public places and good public spaces and you see a city with a soul and a sense of itself. As the architect Richard Rogers said last Friday in the *Sydney Morning Herald*, 'cities are the grandest physical expressions of our humanity and are at the heart of our culture'.

Our city on the water does not come from a built form as did, say, Venice, which is entirely built. Nor does it come from a great and single river like the Neva through St Petersburg, with its complementary geometry of man-made canals. Ours, rather, comes from a truly ancient gift which only nature could divine. We would be recreant in our civic obligations not to do all in our power to keep as much of its natural form as we could, or if not all that, to make certain that the lost bits of the jigsaw are returned or mostly returned to their rightful place. Like the stone in the pond, we should follow the ripples out such that the rings of development relate to one another, taking their strength, reason and inspiration from the natural fantasy at their epicentre.

Of course, some distance from the harbour, that imperative wanes. As we get further away, the character of the harbour and its impact on its surroundings weakens. But generally the topography remains synonymous with the drama at the foreshore and it is not till we approach the reaches of the western and southern suburbs that that relevance peters out.

But of course, along the coast, the idea of Sydney as a water place remains: along the beaches and book-ended by those powerful marks: the Hawkesbury River and Port Hacking.

But unique as it is, the harbour has no *one* aesthetic authority. The harbour foreshore has been beaten up by government authorities and by various municipal councils. Some councils understand it well, others seemingly couldn't care less. For instance, Manly Council gave us all those indifferent apartments blocks perched either side of the Manly wharf, as it gave us that most horrible strip of harbourside residential development along that escarpment at Seaforth immediately to the west of the Spit Bridge.

Canada Bay Council had the opportunity to sympathetically plan the post-industrial period of the inner Parramatta River and made a botch of it. Or, let me say, it and departments of the state government made a botch of it.

There is a reasonable case to be made that the actual perimeter of the harbour should be deemed an area of state significance to be administered by a single authority. The rolling membership of councils and the confused municipal-planning processes can never and will never do the harbour justice. Accordingly, our great inheritance, the great natural gift, is either defaced or expunged by studied indifference, benign contempt or incompetence.

What has saved Sydney Harbour for most of its history has been the lack of development monies. Most developments were limited to single dwellings or modest apartment buildings, yet no such sensitive and vulnerable place can survive the onslaught of an open financial system where anything that is bankable is fundable. Places like the harbour can only be protected by standards and by regulation because the market will abuse it for all it is worth. This leaves its protection to under-resourced, single-action community groups who, in the collective, must fail.

As in all things, what is needed here is leadership and as we know, there are only ever two ingredients in that: imagination and courage. And, mostly imagination. Because it is imagination that sketches the wider perspective, providing patterns and frameworks to encompass myriad elements that would otherwise remain unwoven.

Some of you might know that I have had a long interest in cities and civic projects. I was the first among those who, for over seven years, wrote the design requirements for the new and permanent federal Parliament House and I had a hand in selecting the design of Aldo Giurgola. At an earlier time I had joined Tom Uren, then minister for urban and regional development in saving the Glebe Estate from mortal damage.

In government myself, I funded the *Better Cities* program and took a particular interest in specific projects. The redevelopment of East Perth from a collection of warehouses and smash-repair yards to one of that city's most desirable residential precincts. The redevelopment of the railway yards in Launceston; the establishment of light rail in Sydney out through Glebe and, more famously, buying down seven storeys off East Circular Quay, while building beneath it a colonnade reminiscent of the Rue du Rivoli in Paris, a space which is now enjoyed in a unique Sydney way. And of course, more recently, helping to save Ballast Point here in Sydney from inappropriate development. But even more immediately, throwing thunderbolts at the Huns and Visigoths who would have preferred to concrete in East Darling Harbour, robbing us of that last great piece of Sydney's western waterside perimeter. But I should also say that, at the same East Darling Harbour, now Barangaroo, I am supporting a grand-scale development which represents a paradigm change in the way our CBDs normally approach the water.

So I maintain what, for me, has been a long interest in these matters.

Indeed, I came to the conclusion years ago that many of the larger-scale development and infrastructure projects could only be suitably executed with the interest and assistance of the Commonwealth government. Notwithstanding good intentions on the part of the state governments, their relative financial incapacity limits the kind of progress they should make.

When I became Treasurer in 1983, most of the key economic variables were on the Cabinet table: the exchange rate, interest rates, wages, tariffs and of course, the Budget. The reforms of the 1980s and 1990s put most of these variables into the market and removed some altogether, like tariffs. Broadly, only the Budget remains for the Commonwealth to fashion.

In the economy of today, what happens in the states and in the cities is now, in reform terms, more important than that which happens routinely at Commonwealth level: health, education, transport, infra-structure; those things which go to the efficiency and productivity of the non-traded side of the economy. Hence, the Prime Minister's current quest to reform the national state health systems.

But what is true of health and education is just as true of urban development, transport and infrastructure and here there are great lags; here we have lost much time. I think I can say that without the Commonwealth's ambitious and direct involvement we will not see the reforms that have to be made.

In this city, the primary building of the radial suburban railway system occurred now, just on a hundred years ago. When we were dirt poor we did so much more. In the century since, we have seen but incremental additions to the rail system.

Here in Sydney, with our demonstrated inability to bring the housing stock into better balance with demand, the real price of housing is rising such that our children cannot afford to house themselves. Whichever way you cut housing affordability, it is now beyond the reach of almost all, other than relatively high-income earners. But, more than that, the city is growing towards the mountains, displacing more and more open space. The answer, I believe, is better and more acceptable higher densities in the inner Sydney basin, with a valve to Newcastle, the Hunter and the North Coast. This can only be put in place with a very fast train.

Fast-train proposals die on the drawing board in sparsely settled countries. This is why a fast train from Sydney to Melbourne or Sydney to Brisbane runs foul of the marginal cost of a wet-leased aircraft seat. Incremental air-seat capacity is massively cheaper than the sunk cost of a train seat. But this is not true over shorter distances where wide-bodied aircraft cannot be an alternative. This is the case with Newcastle, where wide-bodied aircraft travel into Sydney is not an option.

In terms of key infrastructure in this city, there remains the need for a second and complementary airport to Kingsford Smith. There is only one possible site and that is Badgerys Creek. As Treasurer, I bought the Badgerys Creek land with the then transport minister Peter Morris in 1986 to give the city that reserve option. That was just on 25 years ago. Longer-term thinking like this should be rewarded with the kind of development I had Laurie Brereton legislate, as federal minister for transport, in 1995.

The Howard government revoked the Badgerys Creek appropriations in its first budget and did nothing over twelve years to reinstate them.

And now, the Rudd government has announced that it intends, with the state of New South Wales, to cancel the option and sell off the land. This is a diabolical decision which will cap Sydney's future air-traffic growth and, with it, Sydney's progress as an international place. This is a decision that has to be reversed. And quickly.

Sydney is getting away from us, Melbourne less so. Brisbane's whole-of-city administration is improving its relative development. And we could probably be more sanguine about Adelaide and Perth. From here on out, there can only be one approach that can make a real difference and that is Commonwealth–State cooperation, but it has to happen earnestly and quickly.

21

BANKSTOWN CITY
Silver Jubilee
Bankstown Town Hall,
Sydney,
27 May 2005

*Paul Keating was invited to give the keynote address to commemorate
the Silver Jubilee of the City of Bankstown. He accepted the invitation
as the former Federal Member of Parliament for the area for 27 years
and as a resident of Bankstown for 39 years. In the address he canvasses
the cultural changes in Western Sydney while commenting on wider
development issues within the Sydney Basin.*

I AM EXCEPTIONALLY PLEASED TO be back in Bankstown on this, the twenty-fifth anniversary of its becoming a city. I remember that occasion 25 years ago, when many of us interested in the civic affairs of Bankstown regarded its new city status as some kind of compliment invested in all of us who lived here.

And if you had lived here a long time, as I had, and many before me, you understood what a compliment it was.

When I grew up in Bankstown in the 1950s, every amenity was basic. With the singular exception of the Bankstown Olympic Swimming Pool, which a later council filled in, most of the roads were without kerb and gutter and the homes without sewer.

The municipal sanitary cart was the brunt of hundreds of jokes which one could reel off like leaves from a ream of paper. And the sports ovals, save for one or two, were open patches of clay which increased one's incentive not to fall over or be tackled.

But for all that, Bankstown had something about it which marked it out from the urban sprawl. It was as if it had a ring around it and within this ring was a group of people with a very enhanced sense of community and an equally shared sense of obligation. A camaraderie or *esprit de corps* of a kind that all too few communities are blessed with.

And while there were many remarkable people, the most interesting thing about Bankstown was the importance and value of the many who went unremarked upon. The mums and dads, the teachers, the helpers, the communitarians, the volunteer ambulance, the volunteer first-aid, the youth sports administrators, the coaches. The list goes on.

Of course, we've had more than our share of those who've hit the high spots. Not just in Bankstown terms, but in national terms. Some in international terms.

The Waugh twins, as I said in an earlier speech, at cricket, simply the best in the world. Another set of twins, the Konrads, who came here from Latvia, and broke every Olympic record they contested. And latterly, Ian Thorpe, who carries on this high tradition. To them we can add Kevin Berry and Sandra Morgan and great coaches like Don Talbot and Forbes Carlisle and Frank Jordan.

Or great administrators like Nobby Clark who built the modern National Australia Bank. Or Ken Cowley who built News Limited over a couple of decades. And Bert Evans who fashioned the Metal Trades Industry Association into one of the most progressive organisations in the country.

Not to mention the long-serving mayors like Ron Lockwood and Doug Carruthers, along with more contemporary successors.

Bankstown had a Premier too, in Jim McGirr and, of course, a Prime Minister in me.

I lived in Bankstown until I went to Canberra as Treasurer of the Commonwealth at the age of 39. When I was living in The Lodge, John Howard, as Opposition Leader, was cheeky enough to say I needed a *Gregory's* to find my way home. A bit of poor man's hyperbole which was struck down by a journalist who made the observation, 'You can take the boy out of Bankstown, but you can't take Bankstown out of the boy', which was, of course, true.

Unlike John Howard, I came from a community who had nothing to sell but its labour and its people's time. As far as I was concerned, the shysters and the spivs could be represented by somebody else, but not by me. I always regarded my role in public life as being tested by what measure I advanced the common cause of ordinary people's lives. The people who lived here. Whether it was access and equity in health or access and equity in education or the right to a living wage and employment opportunities or superannuation, these were the coordinates that governed my political imperatives.

To whatever extent Australia flowered in the blush of its multiculturalism under the postwar migration program, in Bankstown it was a harvest. As a member of the Anglo-Irish community who settled Bankstown in the first half of the twentieth century I grew up with kids who were born in Holland, Italy, Malta, Germany, the Baltic States, as well as the newcomers from the British Isles. By the time I entered the House of Representatives, you could add Vietnam and Lebanon and some other places to that august roll-call.

I can recall South Terrace Bankstown, on the southern side of the railway line, where businesses bearing the names of HG Palmer, Nock and Kirby's, Woolworth's, Centreway Cakes, Adler's Hardware, City Price Radio and Hackett's Haberdashery, had given away to stores which carried business names only in Vietnamese. Such was the cultural transformation. And great places of congregation like the Bankstown Sports Club and the Bankstown RSL Club and the many such clubs in the satellite suburbs of Bankstown reflected the area's social and cultural milieu. The kind of milieu, I might say, to this day, John Howard does not understand. Or, might I add, accept.

Bankstown saw the monoculture come and it saw it go. And the place was the richer and the stronger for it.

These days, of course, Bankstown is relatively inner city; in my day, it was on the periphery of the sprawl. From Bankstown I used to bike it, every weekend, to all manner of places. West to Warragamba, south-east to Cronulla, and south to Bulli. A mate and I would often attach ourselves to the back of a truck going up the Bulli Pass, cadging a free ride to the top, cigarette in hand. You could not do that today and live to tell the story. Life was more simple then.

Now, the places I used to ride to and through are covered by McMansions and tartaned by expressways. Now in western Sydney, you do need your *Gregory's*; John Howard would need a pocket GPS device. Of course, there is no cultural equivalent of those geographic diviners for him, save for some back edition of the *Boys' Own Annual* or the Baden-Powell Guide to the Outdoors.

Western Sydney now provides one of the greatest challenges to the country. To our great Commonwealth. Forty per cent of Australia's GDP is created in the greater metropolis of Sydney, that which lies between Newcastle and Wollongong. But we know that Sydney is landlocked between the Pacific and the Blue Mountains and that we have a choice about whether we keep the great green spaces yet house more people or whether we carpet-lay it with endless permutations on the McMansion model. Rewarding all those dairy farmers who have lived long enough to see their rezoned land blast them to the top of Australia's rich list.

An architect friend of mine, Peter Myers, calls this opportunity 'the Third City'. The First City was the place lived in and frequented by Aboriginal people, distinguished by shell-midden mounds of the scale and of the kind which existed at Bennelong Point.

In Myers' concept, the Second City is the one we created between European settlement and now. Victorian, Edwardian, modern, postmodern.

And the Third City is the new city: the emerald jewel which holds out the promise of a more sympathetic settlement with nature, giving those to the west and northwest of the city a sense of community and lifestyle choices of a kind many in the outer Second City never had.

These days, Sydney grows at a rate of about a thousand people a week. Families are getting smaller and the change in household composition has meant that about 100,000 homes have been built in the last twenty years to accommodate roughly the same number of people. For each of the next ten years, Sydney will need roughly twenty to twenty-five thousand new homes. We need to give these people not just accommodation, but choice and affordability without blotting out our landscape with mindless, massive brick-skinned vaults of a kind which many project builders provide with both pride and alacrity.

You might have gathered from the few references so far that I have an exceedingly low opinion of McMansions. And their block-straddling, vacuous ordinariness.

Encouragingly, the NSW Government of Bob Carr is turning its attention to this huge issue. Its Planning Minister Craig Knowles's proposed Metropolitan Strategy holds out the promise of doing things differently: weaving in a requirement on infrastructure agencies, such as the RTA and the rail authorities, to coordinate their rollouts in the context of land-release programs, sustainability targets and the provision of social infrastructure.

I believe what we need is more attractive medium-density housing, in the context of more open space, serviced by adequate transport and social infrastructure, with points of congregation that give people some more adequate feelings of belonging. If not in every place, a village concept, something nearer to the High Street, where access is less dependent on motor vehicles. Including and especially those four-wheel drives.

Where the government goes with its transport and social infrastructure, so goes increased value of land holdings and property. And in the context of property being rezoned, the enhanced development value has to be siphoned down such that the necessary infrastructure can be provided. Other than seeing people marooned in extensive housing estates with little to bind them and even less to service them.

Without some greater metropolitan plan, the city's future will fall prey to cameo property rezonings and extraordinary development applications designed mostly to make their proponents rich. God knows, Sydney has had enough of that.

Something better, I might also say, includes revitalising some of our older suburbs, which the government is attempting to do, with proposals which include improved residential building and design, and which recognises the importance of corridors for linking communities within the suburban matrix.

The natural boundary of the Sydney Basin, circumscribed as it is by its geography, means that over time, in terms of population pressure, Sydney will have to make a more effective throw to Newcastle and to the south.

Newcastle and its attractive environs, the great valley to its hinterland, provides an enormous opportunity to ease settlement pressures within the Sydney Basin. This can only effectively be undertaken with a new piece of infrastructure. That is, a very fast train connecting the central business districts of the two cities. In this way, Novocastrians can find quick and easy access to the city of Sydney, while Sydneysiders can view Newcastle and the Hunter as a place of options that can be enjoyed other than by a three-hour car trip or a ride in the historic rail corridor.

Some quite important person said to me, 'But it's all sandstone in between' to which I replied, sympathetically, 'That's right, but it's not going to go away, so the earlier we hop into it the better'.

Bear in mind that Sydney's suburban development was built around the hub-and-spokes network of our rail system, a system built mostly in the 1920s when we were as poor as church mice. And we have been living on it ever since.

In this day and age, in this period of such great wealth, is it really inconceivable that we cannot build a rapid line to Newcastle? Or even do it on the balance sheet of the State's public accounts?

Public policy choices should be made without reference to the marauding gangs of investment bankers and fund managers who glare, King Kong-like, over the most propitious bits of the city's landscape.

I hope we are not forever condemned to have things which are only of interest to organisations like the Macquarie Banks of this world or avian extractors of value like Max Moore-Mascot and his new private monopoly.

The internationalisation of the economy in the 1980s and 1990s by the Labor government that I had the privilege to both serve and lead opened up vistas of opportunities like no other in the twentieth century. The diminished expectations and means of the past, even that which obtained in 1980, the year of Bankstown's city-bestowed status, seems, in the new world now, like aeons ago.

Our children now come to a world with education and opportunity, such a cry away from the relative poverty which attended frontier communities like Bankstown, when social binding and interdependence were almost the only thing upon which people could reliably depend and trust.

Bankstown's twenty-fifth anniversary, is in many respects, a very big story. A story of the new Australia: the Australia of tolerance and diversity, the Australia of growth, wealth and opportunity. But it is even more than that. It is a story of what we have become and what, with some imagination, courage and forbearance, we might aspire to.

On behalf of the community of Bankstown and its environs, I congratulate the Mayor, Helen Westwood, her fellow councillors and officers and the many out there in the streets who ask for little but believe in so much.

22

ALP LIFE MEMBERSHIP
ACCEPTANCE SPEECH

Australian Labor Party—NSW Conference,
Sydney,
3 October 1999

*For anyone seeking an understanding of what Paul Keating's public
life was all about, his acceptance speech on the occasion of his
life membership of the Labor Party is required reading. Delivered
extemporaneously to the 1000-strong NSW ALP Conference, an assembly
which had met continuously at the Sydney Town Hall for over 100 years,
Paul Keating outlined his credo and some of his many achievements with
an earthiness demonstrably rooted in his Bankstown working-class origins.
He talks of the philosophical and ideological renovation of Labor coming
from his policy construct: the golden circle of high growth, productivity
and low inflation; of superannuation; of Australia coming to terms with
its geography; its identity and the relevance of the republic; Australia
finding its security in Asia but going there as 'us'. The speech is also a
reminder of his often bruising parliamentary performances, replete with
attacks on John Howard, the Packers and assorted party identities.*

THANK YOU, ONE AND ALL, delegates, friends. It's my very great honour
to thank you on behalf of the group assembled here—those of us who
have received life membership. All of us have had much from the
Labor Party. All of us have had the joy of contributing to it. But all of
us have had more from it than we have given to it. There are some

of my former federal colleagues here today: Vince Martin, who was the member for Banks and Michael Maher, who was the member for Lowe. Three of my branch members with whom I went to meetings over the years and, of course, many other distinguished people. And on behalf of them, as for myself, I thank you. We all owe the Labor Party—I owe it especially because I was given the singular honour of leading it and of leading it in office. That's a privilege reserved to very few Australians.

I was always grateful for everything that was done for me by branch members, and I kept going to monthly branch meetings until I became Treasurer. That was from age 25, when I was elected, and 39 when I became Treasurer. I was still doing regular branch meetings for a few years after that, thirteen or fourteen a month. I always appreciated everyone who handed out literature for me, those who did duty on the polling booths. You know, getting to the right spot at the booth at 7:30 in the morning, putting up the regalia, the pictures, etcetera. And taking some others down occasionally! Putting things in letterboxes and taking someone else's out. For all those things. For those people who stood in the rain and in the sun and came back in the night for our celebration or our commiseration. Burnt to a crisp. I appreciated every one of them. And I used to often say to colleagues, 'We have these battles in the Labor Party, philosophical battles on the right and the left, but you know who's on your side on polling day. There's us and there's them: all of us and them, the Tories.'

So I owe a special debt of thanks to a very loyal group of people in Bankstown and in the electorate of Blaxland. I owe a special debt of gratitude to my family. My mother, who is here today, and my father, who is not, but who had the founding interest in the Labor Party. My sister and my children are here. We all love the Labor Party and the things it is able to do.

There are a lot of other people in my life who were important: Charlie Oliver, who was the State President, John Ducker, John Armitage and many friends, like Barney French. Many friends who were in the machinery at the time and mates I grew up with: Leo McLeay, Laurie

Brereton and Ron Dyer among them, many of whom went to the House of Representatives, mates for life.

You know, most political parties decline over time. Most parties run out of puff or run out of energy, but the Labor Party has always been able to remake itself. Even great parties like the British Liberal Party expire. We are now 110 years old. In world terms we are an old party, because we have always been able to remake ourselves. In this vein, one of the great reforms of the 1980s and 1990s was the philosophical and ideological renovation of the Labor Party itself. We gave the country back its one true mass party, and we gave it back renovated and modernised—able to pick up the cudgels on behalf of Australia. Always useful to the country.

The strike against us by the Tories was that we could not manage the money. This was the cry through the Menzies years: 'You can't trust Labor with the money'. Malcolm Fraser was still saying it in 1983: 'You have to put your money under your bed'. But, in the end, who gave Australia the new open market competitive economy? Who gave Australia 1.5 per cent inflation and 4 per cent growth a year? Who doubled the rate of the Australian economy's capacity to grow, and with it, employment? The Australian Labor Party.

And with the Accord—the enormous cooperative effort we had over the thirteen years, with Bill Kelty leading it—the greatest leader of labour this century. We gave Australia this beautiful set of numbers: 4 per cent for wages, 2.5 per cent for productivity, and 1.5 per cent for inflation. Let me do the sum for you: $4 - 2.5 = 1.5$. That's the magic circle we left to Mr Costello and Mr Howard. The golden circle: four, two and a half, and one and a half. And that's why when Mr Costello picks up the monthly statistician's release on inflation he finds, guess what? Inflation's 1.5 per cent again. I'm sure he thinks being Treasurer is a whiz of a job. A whiz. When I got the job the inflation rate was 11 per cent. *Eleven!*

And of course, productivity was 1.25 per cent in the ten years to 1985. A miserable 1.25 per cent! We doubled that trend productivity by taking the Accord; taking a little piece of it and putting it in every factory in the country with enterprise bargaining. As a result, by doubling trend productivity and paying five rounds of tax cuts, keeping wages growth to 4 per cent, we ended up with 1.5 per cent naturally restraining inflation. Productivity coming through the pores of the skin of the economy. That's what we gave to Australia and that's what we left to the Liberal Party. And, as well as that, getting the budget back to surplus. And that could only happen because we cut spending by about 5 or 6 per cent of GDP. The largest reduction in recurrent spending in the OECD area.

You know, whether you add the last brick to the top of the building is immaterial. There is only one relevant question: who built the structure? The answer: Labor built the structure. Essentially, growth through a cooperative model. And think about this. Four per cent for wages and 1.5 per cent for inflation means a 2.5 per cent real wage increase for everyone, every year. Over ten years, this is a 25 per cent real increase in wages. Not an inflationary increase, a 25 per cent increase in real purchasing power. Now that's what Labor governments are about. That's what it's all about here at the Town Hall. It's what it has always been about. Lifting the real living standards of working people.

We brought a new word to the Labor lexicon—competition. Competition is our word, not their word. Not the Tories' word. We set up the Competition Commission because we were tired of paying twice as much as we should be paying for cars, for telephones, for clothing, for electricity. By cutting tariffs and by lifting domestic competition, we created a low price structure, thereby allowing people's wages to go further.

Bill Kelty always knew, I always knew, that the great evil in Australia was inflation. The great evil of working Australians was inflation. This was not as true of the business community. They always did well from inflation because they were always geared and able to pass on costs. But for ordinary people, inflation ripped away their savings and put enormous mortgages on their backs. And so competition became a goal and a new idea. Part of Australia's renovation—indeed, our renovation.

In Britain, Tony Blair calls our philosophy the 'Third Way'. I said to Tony one day, 'Why would you call it the Third Way? That is to concede that there is a first and a second'. And what is the first? Unrestrained capitalism? Private initiative and private reward being everything? The sort of thing that obtained before the Depression? Well, I don't concede that that can be the first way. In that case, what, then, is the second way? State intervention? State planning? State ownership of assets? That has never worked. Didn't work in Western Europe. Didn't work in Eastern Europe. Wouldn't work in Australia. Didn't work in Britain. I said to him, 'Our way was not the Third Way, it was the *only* way'.

And that way was a good and open market economy grafted to a kindly social wage. With access and equity in health, in education, in aged care, in retirement incomes. Putting the two concepts together. A low inflation, high productivity, high growth economy, married to a good social wage. The thing that every party like us always sought but which we did, in fact, conceptualise fifteen years before the British Labour Party came to it. We were more interested in doing it than finding a label for it. We wanted to get the numbers on the board and to strike out for equity.

Let me just say something about superannuation. One of the things that I am most proud of is superannuation. Because next year, the ninth percentage point of the Superannuation Guarantee Charge drops into the slot. Nine per cent of everyone's wages. Everyone in the country. This is going to build $1000 billion, a trillion, in savings by 2007 or 2008. But we had a further scheme in place that I announced in 1995; a further 6 per cent of wages into superannuation, taking the 9 to fifteen. It was 3 per cent paid as tax cuts, but paid as savings and not cash. Paid into people's individual superannuation accounts and preserved to age 55 so that there was no decline in national savings. It went off the budget, straight to private savings, where it could not be touched. So it was 1 per cent, 1 per cent and 1 per cent of wages for each of three years: 1998, 1999 and 2000. And Bill Kelty and the ACTU agreed to match those tax cuts with a co-payment out of workers' pockets of 1 per cent, 1 per cent and 1 per cent. So, in each of those three years it became two, two and two. That is, 6 per cent over the three years. Six on the existing 9 per cent became fifteen. Fifteen per cent for everyone and vested in their own name—a world first.

But then John Howard scrapped it. In one of the first things he did, he cost the average Australian, in today's dollars, $250,000 at the end of their working life. Just imagine what would have happened to us if we had knocked a quarter of a million off the average working person in retirement. But that's what Howard and Costello did. They preached the cause of national savings, but the first time they had a chance to put the sword through the only genuine national savings scheme we ever had, they did it because they did not want workers managing money. They just hate the fact that the industry unions have got hundreds of millions and some, billions, in their charge with the employer organisations in the industry funds. They cannot stand it. They think you have to be in a pinstripe suit and have a Liberal Party ticket in your pocket before you are entitled to manage money.

These people that go on about savings. Here we had not just 3 per cent of wage equivalents coming off the budget, we also had 3 per cent coming from people's pockets. All now gone. Yet the Libs put some rinky-dink scheme in place about deductions for bank deposits. And took it away twelve months later. Our scheme would have built $2 trillion in savings by 2015 and given everybody, at least, average weekly earnings in retirement for the rest of their life. For the rest of their life. Now about $40,000 a year, for the rest of our life.

Another of our contributions in office was to develop the country's philosophy, its sense of itself. Its identity, and coming to terms with its geography. The fact that we are not simply a European nation sitting in the bottom of Asia, as Mr Howard thinks, but that we are part of the whole. A country that will find its security *in* Asia, not a country that has to find security *from* Asia. We went honestly to the region saying we'll approach the region's indigenes by first dealing fairly with our own. We say, 'The Australian nation has turned over a new leaf—but by the way, we still have the concept of *terra nullius*, the great lie that no one was here before us'. We tried to right some of that wrong with

Mabo, by recognising the prior ownership of the land by Australia's indigenes. And not by celebrating our independence, our innovation and our culture, and all we've created here by borrowing the monarch of another country. Instead, believing we should go to the region as ourselves, with our own head of state—as an Australian republic.

Lifting the sense of ourselves, celebrating our identity, going to the region as us. Enjoying the diversity of Asia, not being frightened of it. Of all the bequests one could imagine, the one given us, just the twenty million of us, alone in the world, was a continent of our own. All we have to do is steer it properly and understand where we live. To get that right. That's all we have to do. Understand where we live, and get it right. But first, you've got to know who you are. You can't be ambivalent as to who you are. Now, in this year 1999 there are still people who doubt that our head of state should be one of us. We are in this surreal debate headed by a Prime Minister who believes in a foreign monarchy. The monarchist who never mentions the Queen. The love that dare not speak its name.

Of course, I liked the Queen, and let me tell you, I think she liked me. She sat me next to her on the *Britannia*, among other places. When things got a little boring, she and I would have a competition as to who made the silver on the table. At one point she said to her Private Secretary, 'I think the Prime Minister's trying to get away with my silver'.

I remember a story Dan Minogue, the former Irish Member for West Sydney, once told. His sister was a nun at Sale in Victoria and Arthur Calwell was the leader. And every year Dan used to go to the convent in Victoria to spend two weeks with his sister. After one of these sojourns in January, he came back to the first Caucus meeting of the year, Arthur greeting him. Arthur, who knew everyone's relatives by name, said, 'Dan, how's Evelyn? How are the nuns going down there?' He said, 'They're going well, Arthur.' He said, 'Tell me Dan, what are they saying about me?' Dan looked at him and said, rather confidentially, 'Well, Arthur, they're praying for you—but they ain't voting for you.' Now this is a bit like me with the Queen: I'm praying for her, but I ain't voting for her.

But John Howard is. Can you believe this? In this day and age, with all we've come to represent, the national leader can believe we should be represented by the Queen of Great Britain. What sort of fossilisation gets you thinking in those terms? The fact is we need the republic and we need it now. Not because of what it says to others about us, but what it says to us about ourselves. That's why we need it.

Howard is now appearing in his true colours, the colours that the truant press gallery pretended he didn't have. We saw it this week with taxation. I made the taxation of income the same as or in equal terms to the taxation of capital. By introducing dividend imputation and capital gains tax, I wanted equity taxed once, not twice, and capital gains fully taxed. Again it takes the Labor Party to encourage the dynamic production of income. That's why businesses are now encouraged to make more income. That's why the stockmarket has been re-rated at over 3000 now for the All Ordinaries Index. The day I became Treasurer, the All Ordinaries Index stood at 451. When I left it was 2600, a five-fold increase in value. It is now 3000. That came from a better economy while supporting the production of income—as opposed to lazy capital profits.

What did the Libs do? Quick as a flash, they're back to lurks again: back to getting people to turn income into capital. No thought about building companies. They want to make sure that the local doctor who bought a private hospital gets his capital gains at half taxed rates in fifteen years' time. That's what they're about: no vision.

Again, the regional deputy point. You know why it took a week for Howard to deny the regional deputy claim? Because he actually believes it, that's why. It took him a week to get out of it because that is what he did in fact say to the journalist. The journalist followed the words. This is Howard's view. The disappearing Howard doctrine. The unbearable tension between Howard's view of the world and the world as it really is. He keeps getting mugged by reality.

We're about to discover the cost of a defence policy that tries to find our security from Asia. From Asia. As if we hadn't learnt. So many of us have had and lost members of families in our first major engagement in Asia in the Second World War, 50 years ago. We must know that our security can only be found *in* Asia, not *from* Asia, as Mr Howard would have us believe.

At the beginning of the new century, we have a Prime Minister who believes in things that obtained at the beginning of this century. Security from Asia, the monarchy, powerful friends, except now it's not the British Navy, it's the United States Navy. Now the deputy. The charge against us by Howard was that we let the United States relationship rot. Did you notice just a month or two ago when Howard when to see Bill Clinton, he got only twenty minutes with him? Twenty minutes and no photo. No photo. Now, if I'd got only twenty minutes, the foreign-policy writers would have been wringing their hands. It would have been, you know, he only got twenty minutes. You might remember, as Prime Minister, I was ensconced in Blair House with Annita, with all the relics of American history around me for a week (that's the President's guesthouse opposite the White House). You almost expected Dolly Madison to pop out of the cupboard. The only one that popped out of Howard's cupboard was the guy checking the mini-bar at his hotel. No Blair House for him.

This is supposed to be the fellow with the special relationship. And who were the two people he sent to manage it? Andrew Peacock in Washington and Michael Baume in New York. Now, get that! Andrew only knows Republicans and Shirley MacLaine! The problem with this is there's a Democrat administration in office.

But to compound everything, Howard is now presenting himself as the champion of human rights. Not human rights for Australia's indigenes or an apology for the stolen generation. Not human rights— extinguishing native title under pastoral leases given our indigenes by the High Court. Not those kinds of human rights. The man who was critical of us over our anti-apartheid policy; who called policies like the elimination of nuclear weapons 'a stunt', who played fast and loose with Pauline Hanson's racism? Now he is offering himself as our human rights champion in Asia. That's what he would have us believe. If we were silly enough to believe it. The persuasive one who went to

President Habibie of Indonesia over Timor. The transitional President who couldn't deliver the country or the army. The one who was not able to pull the country and the army into the decision.

Let me say a few things about Timor. It was never that the Timorese were not entitled to autonomy or independence. The matter was how you would slip the card out without the pack falling in. That was all it was ever about.

In this country, the nation preceded the state. We were a nation before we became the Commonwealth of Australia. In Indonesia the state preceded the nation. When the Dutch left they became the Republic of Indonesia before they became a nation. Soeharto's concern was always how the nation should hold together. He believed that if one bit let go, the whole lot would start to fall away. And that's why as an old soldier he was adamant about East Timor. It is not that Whitlam, Fraser, Hawke and I didn't press him. We did. It was just that he believed his state would disintegrate before the sense of nation was able to hold it together.

The fact of the matter is, the only reason there was ever an opportunity to do something about East Timor was not because John Howard discovered human rights, but because Soeharto left. And another President came—one who thought he could play with the issue and do something with it. Howard claims to be battling in the name of principle, not interest, but his policy has as its genesis the lowest interest of all—rank domestic opportunism. He thought he would come at the Australian Labor Party from the left. He thought he would tie up the Catholic church and the East Timor lobby by coming at Labor from that quarter. That's what it has been all about.

The big impact on the Liberals was the French testing in Mururoa. They couldn't believe their good fortune when they tapped a chord over the French tests, when people believed we were too tardy in making objections to the French. And rutted into the Howard and Downer minds is that inside the Australian body politic are foreign policy issues that strike a domestic chord. Howard didn't play the human rights card in Timor; he played the Mururoa card. He played the opportunist card to come at Labor with political angling from the left. This is the reason he made the move.

Is Australian policy now one of unqualified support for ethnic self-determination *à la* Timor? This is one of the questions he should be asked. Is our policy now one of unqualified support for ethnic self-determination anywhere? And if so, what principles apply? What are the principles that will govern Australian foreign policy? Australia does not have the capacity or the power to impose its preference or its values on the rest of Asia.

When Soeharto used to say, of Timor under pressure, 'No' to me and 'No' to Bob Hawke, what did people want us to do? Invade the place? Commonsense dictates, as Gareth Evans said during the week, 'There must be a balance between realism and moralism'. Knowing where to steer. Knowing where we must go and where we can go. The problem is that the Howard government does not know where Australia's vital interests lie.

To our immediate north are 200 million people. Indonesia, the fourth-largest country on Earth. The biggest Islamic country in the world. We are locked together for eternity. Our vital interests are about managing that relationship among others, but Howard doesn't understand where those vital interests lie. He does not pursue a policy which supports them.

In three years, Howard now has our largest, nearest neighbour at our throats. Yet he promised to make us relaxed and comfortable. I wonder how many Australians now feel relaxed or comfortable with John Howard's policies as the regional deputy, as the sabre rattler. We are having a debate now in the newspapers about how we should pump defence spending so we can go around as the US deputy, putting our values on the rest of Asia. Of course, Australia will always stand for its democracy, its liberty, its human rights, its heart, its compassion. But not all societies are like we are and we have to approach them in a way that gets the maximum result. This does mean steering between the issues of realism and moralism—what can be achieved. Reasonably achieved.

Let me now say a few harder things about the next few years: about who is with us and who isn't. Who are friends and who are not. And we should be beware of a few malevolent interests out there, especially those tied up with Channel Nine and associated with the Packer family.

Now, the Packers are sniffing the breeze. They are not silly at Park Street. They've watched Beazley get more than half the votes in 1998, they've watched Carr win, they've seen Beattie win, they've watched Bacon win and they've watched Kennett hang on by a gossamer thread.

So what have we seen this week? An article in the *Sydney Morning Herald* by Graham Richardson, little Richo. A full article. Not a comment, an article telling us Kerry's just a working-class hero. That Kerry is offside only with Keating, not the Labor Party. That he's basically not a bad bloke. Well, let me tell you this: don't believe him. In this Victorian election a couple of weeks ago, this working-class hero and his network did everything possible to stop Labor in Victoria. Nothing to do with me or anything about me. The first thing they had was a special anti-Labor piece on the *Sunday* program on branch-stacking in Victoria. Then they had Jeff Kennett going for a ramble in his garden on *Burke's Backyard*. A nice little humanising piece. And then another puff piece about Jeffrey on *60 Minutes*. Guess what? All timed to do maximum damage to Bracks and the Victorian Labor Party.

I will tell you this, if we let one editorial opinion manage the biggest television network, manage the biggest clutch of magazines, manage the biggest website, *ninemsn* and the *Sydney Morning Herald* and *The Age* and the *Financial Review*, we would have rocks in our head. Rocks in our head.

I stood up to Packer (in office), and I'll stand up to him again. His network had those toadies at *60 Minutes*, the Paul Lynehams of this world, prostitute their journalism chasing after me without even asking me a question on the record. But the thing is—they'll be snivelling back to Beazley's office the moment he becomes Prime Minister. Now, I like little Richo. But I don't want him anywhere near Kim Beazley's office, and Kim shouldn't either.

When the chips are down you can see who is with you and who isn't. In 1995, when it mattered, people like Richardson had smart little pieces in *The Bulletin* while hopping into us on the television networks. There were really no institutional forces on our side, only the unions. It's only ever the unions and ordinary working people.

Kim Beazley Snr used to say, 'The party of social attack has to be exemplary'. There is a much higher bar for Labor; we have always got to pass a bigger test. They expect the others to be not up to much. To be not about much. But us, they expect us to be better and we have been better.

We have remade Australia; remade its economy, while giving it a sense of egalitarianism and fifteen years ahead of the Third Way in Britain. An economy that grows twice as fast as it used to grow under the Liberals. They averaged 1.8 per cent in the ten years to 1985. We average 4 per cent. But we do it with the universality of Medicare. Look at schools: when we started, three kids in ten completed Year Twelve. Now it is eight in ten. And we trebled the number of places in universities from 200,000 places to just on 600,000.

We have done these social things, but we have to get it right in Asia as well. We must understand where these economic things are. We must go to Asia as an Australian republic. If we stand for real values and real policies, we'll win

I don't have to say, here, 'Keep the faith'. Because this is the home of faith—of the true believers. Everyone here believes in Labor. But we need good candidates out there who can win seats. We can beat the Liberals. We can win next time. We can give Australia the direction it deserves in the twenty-first century, rather than being led by a throwback from the beginning of the twentieth century.

Thank you very much for the life membership: it is a compliment I will cherish.

23

EULOGY
On the Death of Geoffrey Tozer
St Patrick's Cathedral,
Melbourne,
1 October 2009

Geoffrey Tozer told the executor of his will that in the event of his death only Paul Keating should deliver the eulogy. Paul Keating's funeral oration is a story of Geoffrey Tozer's life, emotionally mixed with admiration, artistic acknowledgement and indignation at his ultimate treatment by Australia's music establishment. Paul Keating ranks Geoffrey Tozer as Australia's greatest pianist. He puts him in a class of accomplishment with Nellie Melba, Percy Grainger and Joan Sutherland. The eulogy underlines Paul Keating's profound respect for truly subliminal artistic ability and his obvious grief at its sudden loss with Tozer's passing.

GEOFFREY TOZER'S DEATH IS A national tragedy.

For the Australian arts and Australian music, losing Tozer is like Canada having lost Glenn Gould or France, Ginette Neveu. It is a massive cultural loss.

The national run rate for artists of Tozer's accomplishment is about one in every hundred years. In fact, if you think of our greatest artists, those who are so regarded in world terms, three come to mind: Nellie Melba, Percy Grainger and Joan Sutherland. In terms of sheer artistry and musical power, Geoffrey Tozer could well be the credible addition to that triumvirate.

Tozer belonged to a small and rarefied stratum of world pianists. He was certainly of a calibre of greats like Emil Gilels, Arthur Rubenstein, Sviatoslav Richter, Ferruccio Busoni and Artur Schnabel, the latter two whose music he championed.

In terms of musical comprehension, intellectualism and facility, Geoffrey's talent was simply off the scale. He could read an orchestral score, hear the entire work in his head and then play a piano transcription of it at sight. He could transpose anything put in front of him into any key and give a perfect performance of it. He could arrange, orchestrate, compose and improvise; indeed, improvisation was one of his specialties, weaving other melodies through the larger works of composers like Liszt.

The remarkable thing about Geoffrey Tozer was that in these last 25 years we were witnessing an artist with a level of musical understanding and repertoire you would have expected to witness in the last 25 years of the nineteenth century or the first 25 years of the twentieth, when classicism and scholarship in music was at its zenith.

Geoffrey would not have been out of place in 1920s Weimar Berlin in the company of people like Erich Kleiber or Otto Klemperer or Igor Stravinsky. Or with pianists like Rudolf Serkin or Claudio Arrau, who were playing there then.

Geoffrey made his international musical debut at the age of fifteen, playing Mozart's *Concerto No. 15* with the BBC Symphony Orchestra under Sir Colin Davis at the Royal Albert Hall. *The Daily Telegraph* critic wrote that 'Geoffrey Tozer played Mozart's Concerto in B Flat with agreeably crystalline touch, faultless technique and good sense'. *The Times* critic considered that Geoffrey 'played in a way that many an artist twice his age might envy'.

Following his debut, in Belgium in November 1970 in which Geoffrey played an enormous program of Bach, Beethoven, Haydn and Chopin, the *Antwerp-Stadt* reported that Geoffrey Tozer 'has become one of the great revelations to astound the musical world . . . he showed that his technical skill is merely a means to clarify the complete and often celestial way he plays, feeling the deeper meaning of everything he performs. Geoffrey Tozer will become one of the great pianists of the world'.

The following year, in 1971, the great composer Benjamin Britten invited Geoffrey to stay with him for several weeks, inviting him to also perform at the Aldeburgh Festival, where he accompanied the master Russian cellist, Mstislav Rostropovich.

Geoffrey could play anything written for piano from any period in history right up until now. He had virtually played and mostly knew anything of any substance written for the piano. His repertoire included over 200 concertos; for instance, it included 24 of the 27 Mozart concertos. Geoffrey had the ability not just to put himself into the head of a composer, he also had the ability to understand the milieu within which a composer worked, the musical influences at the time, the tastes, the comprehension of the whole.

When the pianist Tatiana Nikolayeva, a mistress of Shostakovich, came to Australia in the 1990s, she said to her tour promoter, 'I want to hear the one who plays like a Russian'. And, of course, she meant Geoffrey. But if Geoffrey was playing Purcell he would bring an English feeling to the work or Liszt a more obviously Hungarian or middle European one.

He was unbelievable.

Born in the foothills of the Himalayas, Geoffrey's infant years were filled with music. His earliest memory of the piano was when, as a three-year-old, he began to play Beethoven's *Appassionata Sonata*, music he had just heard his mother teaching to a pupil.

Musical genius flowed through Veronica Tozer's family and she realised at once that her son was possessed of vast musical ability. Just how rare it was became clear when she began to teach him music of Bach, Bartok and Beethoven.

By 1958, when Mrs Tozer brought her two sons to Australia to settle in Melbourne, Geoffrey was already immersed in music, playing, singing, reading and listening to music on a wind-up gramophone.

It was here, in Melbourne, that the world first discovered the young boy who was quickly dubbed a 'musical genius' by Australia's foremost musicians. Within five years of his arrival in Australia, Geoffrey's life as a professional musician began in earnest. This was an extraordinary period of his life, one during which he began to receive the patronage and recognition that would enable him to develop the full range of his virtuosic abilities, and become a concert pianist of the highest standard.

In 1963 when Geoffrey was eight, Dr Clive Douglas auditioned him for a concerto performance for ABC television. The performance, with Geoffrey playing Bach's *Concerto in F Minor* was filmed in February 1964 with Dr Douglas conducting the Victorian Symphony Orchestra. On April 11 of that year, Geoffrey made his public debut in the Nicholas Hall playing the same concerto, this time under George Logie-Smith. Later the same year he gave at least eight more performances, playing concertos of Bach and Mozart with the orchestra in Melbourne and Ballarat. The phrase 'musical genius' was applied to him right from the beginning.

Geoffrey's introduction to Eileen Ralf was the most important event in his musical development. She lived in Hobart. So, in order to foster Geoffrey's prodigious talents, TAA announced that it would fly the young musician every week to Hobart and back free of charge, so that Geoffrey could have lessons with Eileen. Let's hear what Geoffrey himself had to say about her influence and his lessons in Hobart during those early years. I am quoting from the text of Geoffrey's lecture on the great pianist Artur Schnabel which Geoffrey delivered at the Berlin Festival in September 2001 in the presence of the entire Schnabel family:

> By the greatest of good fortune I found a teacher who was the living, breathing embodiment of all the vitality I was getting from the recordings of Schnabel. This was the Australian pianist Eileen Ralf. She opened up for me a world of serious, probing musical thought I knew must exist but I had never experienced. Her teaching was the greatest musical gift given me.

For the next five years Geoffrey performed a vast amount of music in public performances, both in recitals and concerts. By the age of thirteen his concerto repertoire included all five of the Beethoven and nine of the Mozart as well as concertos by Bach and Haydn, and he later added more than 200 pieces to his solo repertoire. Geoffrey also recorded the first movement of the Brahms *Second Concerto* with the Sydney Symphony Orchestra in a studio performance arranged by Reuben Fineberg, the man who would manage Geoffrey's career until his own death in 1997.

How was Australia to develop such a rare and prodigious talent, one that was already nationally recognised? The solution came when the committee of the Churchill Fellowship decided to lower the minimum age by five years and award Geoffrey a Churchill, extending it to two years instead of the usual one. Four years later the committee awarded Geoffrey a second Churchill as he began to make the difficult and, for many gifted teenagers, usually impossible transition from child prodigy to fully mature artist.

In 1969, the first of Geoffrey's Churchill Fellowships enabled him to travel to England with his mother. That year he entered the Leeds Piano Competition and became the youngest semi-finalist. The same year he won the prestigious Alex de Vries Prize, making his debut with the English Chamber Orchestra soon afterwards. In May 1970 he won First Prize out of 157 contestants in the Royal Overseas League competition and was presented to the Queen.

And as I said earlier, on 17 August 1970 Geoffrey made his debut at the Royal Albert Hall playing Mozart's *Concerto No. 15* with the BBC Symphony Orchestra under Sir Colin Davis.

In 1971 Geoffrey returned to Australia to begin the next phase of his career; the difficult years of transition when the musical world had to decide whether he was just another prodigy, albeit one of seemingly superhuman ability, or whether, like Mozart, he was in fact a great musician whose artistry would continue to develop and improve as he gained maturity.

At least once a year throughout the 1970s he toured Australia playing concertos with all the major orchestras around the country, while frequently travelling to America, Britain and Europe for concert appearances.

During this period he hugely expanded his repertoire and toured Japan and New Zealand, also giving recitals in Israel, America and England where he resumed lessons with Maria Curcio, a pupil of Schnabel. In Israel, in 1977, Geoffrey won the first of his two Rubenstein medals, being awarded the prize personally by Arthur Rubenstein who described him as 'an extraordinary pianist'. Many of his performances during this period were recorded and broadcast by the ABC as had been done in the 1960s. They included numerous concertos and recital performances and, sometimes, vocal performances. In 1978, for the ABC, Geoffrey gave the Australian premiere of the Medtner *Vocalise* with the soprano Loris Synan. This reflected his deep love of the vocal–piano repertoire as well as his ongoing relationship with the music of Medtner.

Geoffrey was already breaking convention by not fading from view like many prodigies before him and by his preparedness to explore new musical territory. He also knew that the vocal repertoire was a vitally important part of his future. The last recording he made for Chandos, released in 2004, the fortieth anniversary year of his career, was of the Medtner *Vocalise* sung by soprano Susan Gritton. It was a recording which earned Geoffrey one of the best reviews of his career in *Gramophone* magazine.

In 1980 he travelled to Israel to compete once more in the Rubenstein competition. This time he won the Gold Medal, returning to Australia for a celebratory tour. There, among several superlative reviews, he received what he considered to be one of the greatest compliments of all from the critic Ron Hanoch: 'Geoffrey Tozer . . . is not only a great pianist, but also a great musician'.

The 1980s were halcyon days for Geoffrey. In 1983 he decided to base himself in Canberra. He was briefly on the staff of the Canberra School of Music until it became clear that his national and international touring engagements were as incompatible with such a position as some other aspects of institutional life. By now Geoffrey had become immersed in the music of Liszt. He toured Australia and New Zealand at least twice a year playing concertos and recitals, while constantly expanding his international career. He made debuts in many parts of the world, including Hungary, Germany, Finland, Ireland, Switzerland, Canada, Holland, Denmark and Austria, returning also to Russia for his debut with the Moscow Symphony Orchestra and also touring in Japan.

During the 1980s he began his commercial recording career. Although Geoffrey had made numerous recordings since as early as 1964, none had been commercially released. In 1986 he made his first commercial recording, the John Ireland *Piano Concerto in E Flat* with the Melbourne Symphony Orchestra, a recording that is still ranked by most critics as the best recording available of that music.

The same year, in recognition of his ability, Geoffrey was one of a handful of musicians around the world to receive the Liszt Centenary Medallion awarded by the Hungarian government. The following year he made his second commercial recording, an LP entitled *Geoffrey Tozer in Concert*, on which he played the music of Liszt, Brahms, Haydn, Weber and Chopin. In 1989 he joined Peter Sculthorpe to record *Landscapes*, a disc of Sculthorpe's compositions for piano and strings.

Geoffrey had spent the 1980s performing around the world while based in Australia. He loved Australia and believed that the time had come when an Australian of international standing could build and sustain an international career from here. This involved substantial costs and, while he could generate a living from his touring engagements, once he had covered the costs, there was very little left. So it was then that he accepted a job at St Edmund's College, Canberra to help him pay the rent. To its credit, the school allowed him great flexibility so that Geoffrey could continue to perform in many parts of the world while remaining on the staff.

It was owing to his decision to work at St Edmund's that I first heard Geoffrey play. He was playing two works, one by Scriabin and the other by Liszt, for the school's end-of-year pre-Christmas break-up. The playing was breathtaking. When the formalities ended I made my way over to him to inquire of his playing and career. It was then that I understood the under-realisation of Geoffrey's international standing and of his straitened circumstances; earning $9000 a year at St Edmund's, relying on a bicycle for his transport.

It was Geoffrey's power and poverty that caused me to realise how little Australia valued artists of accomplishment, especially those in mid-career: in his case, the explosive power of his playing, yet his meagre capacity to afford the basics of life.

This sharp reality caused me to study the circumstances of other Australian artists who, while accomplished, found themselves marooned in mid-career. The novelty of their earlier work having faded, being left to fend for themselves, doing things that had naught to do with their art.

This was the inspiration for the Australian Artists Creative Fellowships, a Commonwealth-funded program paid to artists at about one-and-a-half to two times the average weekly earnings and paid for periods of one to five years. The inspiration for them came from Geoffrey's greatness and his circumstances. It is not that many other artists were not also great but Geoffrey was one so obviously so and the one I actually ran into.

A country's indifference to such accomplishment says something about it. When there is no obvious premium on this level of accomplishment, one has to ask, where and when does such a premium apply?

As it transpired, 63 other artists were awarded fellowships under the program and most did something substantial and valuable with their term awards.

In Geoffrey's case it gave him a chance to develop works in parts of the piano repertoire beyond his great staples like Mozart, Beethoven, Bach, Liszt and Brahms. The musician in Geoffrey Tozer fell in love with beguiling compositions that had either rarely or never seen the light of day. One such composer was the Russian Nikolai Medtner, who composed three dramatic and complex piano concertos, only one of which had ever been recorded, and then, during the 1940s in London. Geoffrey began working up these concertos as he did the formerly unrecorded piano concerto of Ottorino Respighi and other compositional works by composers like Rimsky-Korsakov and Busoni. But he had nowhere to perform them; certainly no program to perform them.

So, in 1988, as Treasurer, I made my way down from London to Colchester in Britain in the High Commissioner's car to engage the founder and managing director of Britain's foremost recording company, Chandos Records. That person, Mr Brian Couzens, said, 'why on earth would someone like you be making an appointment with someone like me?'

I said, 'I have come to introduce to you one of the greatest pianists of world' and he said, 'Who is that?' and I said, 'The Australian, Geoffrey Tozer'. He said, 'Yes, I have heard of him but not recently. Has he done anything I can listen to?'

I immediately brought forth a number of audio tapes for his listening. But Couzens said, 'Audio tapes are often compositions themselves, many artists break down and can't complete a full work across the dynamic range of the composition'.

I said to Couzens, 'Well, I will get him over here. He will astound you'.

Well, Geoffrey did get over there. Couzens rang me to say he was unbelievable. He said not only can he play anything; he actually prepares the orchestra and individual players for you. The first thing he recorded for Chandos were the three Medtner piano concertos with the London Philharmonic Orchestra conducted by Neeme Jarvi. They hit the world of recorded classical music like a thunderclap and that year won for Chandos the world's highest prize for classical music, the French Diapason D'Or. In the same year, the recordings were nominated for a US Grammy Award for Best Classical Performance—Instrumental Soloist with Orchestra. Geoffrey and Chandos missed winning the Grammy by one place, to the American cellist Yo-Yo Ma.

France's top classical music critic, Alain Cochard, wrote of the Medtner recordings, 'All that Medtner demands, Tozer possesses. This is the playing of a grand master; there is no doubt about it. This is a landmark in recording history'.

Geoffrey went on to make 36 recordings with Chandos, which for any pianist is a major recorded legacy. Indeed, he left behind more recordings of modern listening quality than were capable of execution by the pianists he most admired: Busoni, Schnabel and Rachmaninoff.

But Geoffrey's great international success with orchestras like the London Philharmonic, the Swiss Romande, the Scottish National Orchestra and the Bergen Philharmonic was not replicated in Australia. Geoffrey gave his last performance with the Melbourne Symphony Orchestra fifteen years ago, on 5 June 1994, with the *Emperor Concerto* in a sold-out performance at the Town Hall. About fourteen months later, he played his last concert with the Sydney Symphony Orchestra.

From those performances, and for the rest of his life, he received nothing further from any major symphony orchestra in Australia. Indeed, in 1996, in one of the most stupendous performances of his career, he played Brahms' *Second Concerto* with the Newcastle Symphony Orchestra under Roland Peelman. In the impossibly difficult passages towards the end of the first movement, we hear Geoffrey Tozer outdo Vladimir Horowitz.

But for all that, he could not make the cut with the latter-day Melbourne and Sydney Symphony Orchestras. Their indifference and contempt towards him left him to moulder away, largely playing to himself in a rented suburban Melbourne house. The people who chose repertoire for those two orchestras and who had charge in the selection of artists during this period should hang their heads in shame at their neglect of him. If anyone needs a case example of the bitchiness and preference within the Australian arts, here you have it.

Geoffrey was not just a musical genius; he was also an explosive performer. Some of these people felt this put an onus on them to engage him, which then, out of some kind of inverted snobbery, they resisted, choosing lesser artists they felt more comfortable with. Or agents they could do deals with.

This malevolence more or less broke Geoffrey's heart. After all, all he wished to do was to give out. In a famous interview for a Melbourne newspaper, he said, 'it's a waste to have someone like me here, not being used'. Artists like Tozer secured the psychic income through sparkling performances and by mesmerising audiences. It was never about money. He only ever wanted enough to keep going.

The last time I saw him play was at the Australian Institute of Music in Sydney in 2005 in the company of Miriam Hyde and her daughter to an audience of about fifteen people. He played Miriam Hyde's massive piano concerto, a concerto she told me needed someone of Geoffrey's power to play. She had always made a good fist of it herself but Geoffrey ate the piece. On his program, he also had pieces by Sibelius and Scriabin, played with such fantasy and facility you knew you were in the presence of someone extraordinary. In reality, he was simply mucking around with our heads, and he knew he was. But in his humility he threw off these works, self-effacingly, like a stroll in the park.

But he did get to do other things outside of Australia. In 2001, with the support of close personal friends in Melbourne, Mr and Mrs Wu, he undertook a concert tour of China at the invitation of the Ministry of Culture, playing the *Yellow River Concerto* to a massive television audience. That was the year he performed the Schnabel *Sonata* for the Schnabel family at the Bergin Festival and then at the Festival En Blanco y Negro in Mexico City. Also, in 2001, on the anniversary of Medtner's death, he gave the most transcendental recital of his career in the assembly hall here in Collins Street. Though the program was a sell-out and the playing was for the gods, there was not one review of the performance in the media, print or broadcast. This cut Geoffrey to the core.

His last grand tour of Australia in 2004 was a privately promoted one, where he gave over twenty performances around the country, including to a sold-out recital at the Sydney Opera House. The tour was promoted by Jim McPherson, who did Geoffrey the honour and the country the favour that the established orchestras had long denied him and it.

Peter McCallum, the *Sydney Morning Herald*'s music critic, had this to say about the performance:

Tozer plays as though he is trying things out, playing for himself with everything being imaginative and free. Then suddenly . . . something quite extraordinary emerges—a moment of special inspiration, special because it was unplanned, perhaps not fully even noticed or comprehended.

McCallum went on to remind his readers that Liszt first devised the piano recital. He went on to say 'Tozer here revived something of its original spirit: a great Australian musician and a true original'.

His early death at age 54 reminds us of the death of Maria Callas at the age of 53. Performing all their lives, both artists finally reached the stage of wondering what it is all about. After operating constantly at a level of high achievement they needed the spiritual sustenance of audiences and friends. They needed the acclamation to stir the genius in them. When the acclaim stopped, both of these people turned towards an inner, more human life, with a lower premium on the art and on longevity. Geoffrey had had a bout of hepatitis. He lived by himself, didn't look after himself and his health suffered accordingly. In the end, his liver failed.

But I have to say we all let him down. Franco Zeffirelli, Callas's great collaborator, said much the same thing following her death. He said 'we thought she was all right in Paris, that she had the intellectual resources to hang on, if even in semi-seclusion'. But as it turned out, she didn't. We should have cared more and done more. He could have been speaking for us about Geoffrey Tozer.

That said, it's also worth saying that Geoffrey had many who cared deeply for him. Most of all, his mother and teacher, who put pressure on him but also loved everything about him, Reuben Fineberg, his mentor and manager, whom he lost in 1997 and Peter-Wyllie Johnston, the executor of Geoffrey's estate, who took up where Reuben Fineberg left off and gave Geoffrey succour and support at important periods over the last decade.

Geoffrey is survived by his brother Peter and members of his extended family.

Geoffrey Tozer's last public performance was here in Victoria with David Pereira in Bendigo, an artist whom he held in the highest esteem and finally, more privately, for the nuns and brothers at the Presentation Convent Chapel in Windsor.

When one has been touched by the stellar power and ethereal playing of a sublime musician, one is lifted, if only briefly, to a place beyond the realm of the temporal. Geoffrey Tozer did this for many people. His remembrance is the small recompense we give him in return.

24

THE PRIVACY IMPERATIVE IN THE INFORMATION AGE 'FREE-FOR-ALL'

The Centre for Advanced Journalism,
University of Melbourne,
Melbourne,
4 August 2010

The Centre for Advanced Journalism at the University of Melbourne
invited Paul Keating to give an address about public policy as
it related to journalism. The subject Paul Keating chose was not
political journalism or issues relating to the media generally but rather
something he felt strongly and urgently about; namely, the right of
an individual not to have their privacy shredded in what he calls the
information age free-for-all. In what was his magnum opus address of
2010, Paul Keating repudiates the view that privacy in modern times is
dead, asserting that individuals have a right to be left alone and in the
event they are not, to enjoy a right of remedy at law—a right of action
rather than merely a right to complain. Paul Keating argues in favour of
the recommendations of the Australian Law Reform Commission urging
the government to move beyond piecemeal common-law case exploration
to a statutory cause of action for breaches of privacy arising from media
excesses and runaway technological capability.

The press is overstepping in every direction the obvious bounds of
propriety and of decency. Gossip is no longer the resource of the idle

and of the vicious, but has become a trade, which is pursued with industry as well as effrontery. To satisfy a prurient taste, the details of sexual relations are spread broadcast in the columns of the daily papers. To occupy the indolent, column upon column is filled with idle gossip, which can only be procured by intrusion upon the domestic circle . . . In this, as in other branches of commerce, the supply creates the demand. Each crop of unseemly gossip, thus harvested, becomes the seed of more, and, in direct proportion to its circulation, results in the lowering of social standards and of morality. Even gossip apparently harmless, when widely and persistently circulated, is potent for evil. It both belittles and perverts. It belittles by inverting the relative importance of things, thus dwarfing the thoughts and aspirations of a people. When personal gossip attains the dignity of print, and crowds the space available for matters of real interest to the community, what wonder that the ignorant and thoughtless mistake its relative importance.

SOME OF THAT LANGUAGE IS a give-away—that it wasn't written by me, or written yesterday. But the content is highly relevant to a discussion about privacy and the media, as a trip to the local newsagent, or time spent in front of the television, or online will quickly affirm.

The quote is from *The Right to Privacy* by Boston lawyers Samuel Warren and Louis Brandeis, published in the *Harvard Law Review* in 1890, perhaps the most famous attempt at a definition of privacy.

Warren and Brandeis wrote about the 'right of the individual to be let alone', a right they put alongside 'the right not be assaulted or beaten, the right not be imprisoned, the right not to be maliciously prosecuted, the right not to be defamed'. They of course acknowledged that the right to be let alone was not absolute, and must on occasion give way to a higher or general public interest.

However, they said:

The design of the law must be to protect those persons with whose affairs the community has no legitimate concern, from being dragged into an undesirable and undesired publicity and to protect all persons, whatsoever; their position or station, from having matters which they

may properly prefer to keep private, made public against their will. It is
the unwarranted invasion of individual privacy which is reprehended,
and to be, so far as possible, prevented.

Warren was said to have been prompted to write after a newspaper published the guest list of an 'A'-list dinner party he hosted in Boston. Brandeis went on to become a justice of the Supreme Court.

Both writers would turn in their respective graves at developments in the 120 years since. Whole industries now revolve around so-called celebrity, fame, rumour and gossip; often more correctly straight fiction which is published these days, often by media organisations. These organisations proclaim the importance of free speech in the dissemination of news, but clearly are more at home in the entertainment business.

The Warren and Brandeis concept of privacy strongly influenced the development of the law in the US and elsewhere, although as others have pointed out, 'the right to be let alone' as a bald statement is meaningless (a person engaged in criminal activities has no such right), and is difficult to distinguish from other legal concepts, such as assault, nuisance and interference with bodily integrity.

Privacy has been enshrined as an internationally recognised human right in the *Universal Declaration of Human Rights,* and the *International Covenant on Civil and Political Rights.* And Australia is a party to both. Article 17 of the *Covenant* states:

1. *No one shall be subjected to arbitrary or unlawful interference with his privacy, family, home or correspondence, nor to unlawful attacks on his honour and reputation.*
2. *Everyone has the right to the protection of the law against such interference or attacks.*

Freedom of expression is also an internationally recognised human right in Article 19 of the *Covenant.*

These rights are not absolute, sometimes conflict, and often need to be balanced and reconciled. 'Importantly, free speech means freedom governed by Law.'

Privacy in a broad sense is under attack these days on a range of fronts. Electronic surveillance, terrorism laws, growing police powers, business practices associated with information mining and marketing, and new technologies.

And the battle Warren and Brandeis fought against the evil of gossip has been well and truly lost with the passage of time.

However, the right to what I might call privacy remains an issue, particularly where to draw the line between freedom of expression and any remaining right an individual has to have some control over the gathering and publication of information about personal aspects of their life. And what can or should be done when that line is crossed.

I take issue with and repudiate those who assert that privacy in modern times is dead and, that we should get over it. And with those who claim the current framework within which the media deals with privacy issues and concerns is effective and works well. It is, of course, ineffective and works, in the main, to the benefit of media organisations.

I also want to lend support to the case made strongly and convincingly in two Law Reform Commission reports that you won't see widely reported or subject to objective analysis in the media: that 'the law should provide recourse, in the event of an unwarranted serious breach of an individual's privacy by the media'—or anyone else for that matter.

These issues are topical, owing to obvious examples of questionable calls about balancing privacy and freedom of expression. They are there for all to see. Some leaders of the industry and the profession dismiss errors as unfortunate, inevitable and rare, and claim a strong and continuing commitment to ethics and values that include respect for privacy. I know many good editors and journalists struggle with these issues, conscious of their responsibility to get it right, and the harmful effect of getting it wrong.

But many like me have the impression that 'the tone at the top' and the practice of journalism in many media organisations is driven by other more pressing values. Of course it's hard to generalise, but Margaret Simons, who authors *The Content Makers* suggests, and research by Denis Muller for his PhD at this university in 2005 and with 27 years' experience in the profession confirmed, ethics does not enjoy a high profile in the newsroom. Indeed, many of those involved apparently have little more than a passing knowledge of the issues. Ethical considerations can complicate life for those keen to get the story. Muller described it as a 'sorry picture'.

Or, as Professor Mark Pearson puts it:

> *The reality is that editors and news directors are motivated as much by circulation and ratings as by a public duty to deliver the news . . . There may be a range of profits or costs resulting from a story involving a privacy intrusion, including gained or lost circulation or ratings, advertising, syndication rights, corporate reputations, legal damages and court or regulator costs . . . there is little doubt journalists go through such a process, either formally or informally, when deciding to run with a story that pushes the privacy margins.*

Often questionable calls involve people in the news for other reasons: photographs claimed to be of a red-headed woman engaged in politics, scantily clad in a motel room with someone else 30 years ago; of an apparently happily married government minister leaving a gay men's haunt; or of a so-called celebrity in the shower. The rights and wrongs of these calls tend to become topics of public discussion themselves.

Probably much more frequently—although no-one seems to keep tabs—individuals going about their daily life or momentarily caught in the spotlight then become subject of a questionable call: those leaving court, particularly where they react angrily to being filmed, always seems to have news value; as did a full-frontal front-page photo of a family that heard the news of the death of a family member for the first time in Victoria's bushfires last year.

Then there was the photo in the Sydney papers last year of two small children (faces not visible) of a murderer just convicted, one wearing a school uniform on the way to school.

And in another, a badly injured and distressed son whose parents had been killed in a boating accident, angrily seeking to avoid a camera recording his stretcher-borne arrival at hospital.

Just about any day in the tabloids and any night on *A Current Affair* or *Today Tonight* you will see examples, including foot-in-the-door interviews claimed to be necessary and justified by the media's right to know, and to publish just about anything they like.

The issue of the media and privacy is also topical, owing to proposals in a 2008 report by the Australian Law Reform Commission on Australia's privacy laws. The report, the result of two years' research, consultation and analysis, runs to 2700 pages in three volumes. It put forward 295 recommendations for change with the general aim of modernising, simplifying and streamlining laws that are generally seen to be dated, complex, confusing, fragmented and full of gaps and inconsistencies.

Four recommendations are of direct relevance to the media. None have yet received a response from the government. They propose changes to, but continuation of, the largely self-regulatory arrangements that are a condition for *the exemption* media organisations enjoy from privacy law. The ALRC argued changes were necessary because of 'ongoing concerns about the capacity of a self-regulatory system to preserve the tenuous balance between the public interest in freedom of expression and the public interest in adequately safeguarding the handling of personal information'.

This important report also recommended legislation 'to establish a general statutory cause of action for breach of privacy' subject to a number of qualifiers to ensure the protection of other public interests. One of the reasons given was to create more certainty for everyone—the media included—as to legal rights, rather than leave the issue entirely to case law with judges developing the common law.

The Commission (supported in argument by a separate report by the NSW Law Reform Commission in 2008) made clear that the proposal for a statutory cause of action is not aimed specifically or solely at the media. The proposal is for a right to seek redress for a serious interference to privacy including interference with an individual's home or family life; unauthorised surveillance; or where an individual's correspondence or private written, oral or electronic communication has been interfered with, misused or disclosed. Of special interest to the media, of course, is that it would also extend to an interference with privacy involving disclosure of sensitive facts relating to an individual's private life, subject to a rider concerning the public interest in people being informed about matters of public concern, and the public interest in freedom of expression.

Reaction to the ALRC report—not limited to the proposed cause of action—took on an 'end of the world as we know it' tone in some media circles. The report and the recommendations were dismissed by industry leaders such as John Hartigan of News Limited, and the Australia's Right to Know coalition on the basis that 'the current media privacy framework is effective and working well'.

Hartigan asserted 'there are very few complaints, investigations and breach findings against the media for breaches of privacy'.

The Australian's Legal Affairs Editor Chris Merritt labelled the report 'outrageous'.

On the cause of action, an editorial in *The Australian* set up a marvellous straw man:

> *Privacy is important. But it would be a serious mistake to remake the rules governing the operation of the media by enshrining privacy as an inalienable right which, at all times and in all circumstances, trumps all other considerations.*

This, despite the fact that the ALRC specifically stated the cause of action should only be available for a serious breach, and 'privacy interests are not to be privileged over other rights and interests'.

There were confident predictions from some that the proposal, if acted upon, would put an immediate end to investigative journalism, notwithstanding that the ALRC concluded that the proposal 'should not hinder legitimate investigative journalism as described by media groups to this Inquiry. For example, allegations of misconduct or corruption in public life would not fall within the (proposed) zone of protection'.

Some media voices called for calm consideration, suggesting a need to get the house in order before jumping to the barricades.

Jack Waterford, Editor at Large at the *Canberra Times*, while mindful of the need to protect freedom of the press and freedom of speech, commented about the wave of criticism of the ALRC report, particularly in News Limited publications. With an eye for self-interest when he saw it running, Waterford said:

> *The public ought to be quite cynical (of) the fact that some sections of the commercial media thrive and profit from invading the privacy of celebrities, starlets, models and sometimes ordinary non-consenting members of the public who have stumbled into a public spotlight. Trivial gossip has become bigger and bigger business in most cases with the implicit consent of most of the 'victims' but has very little to do with the public interest, or with reasons why the media can, or ought to be able to, claim that in respect of its monitoring of the exercise of public power it is acting in the public interest.*

Matthew Ricketson in *The Age* thought some of the claims for free speech for the media celebrity industry were simply laughable:

> *In the weeks leading up to the release of the Australian Law Reform Commission's massive report on privacy, the Right to Know coalition has been sounding the alarm at the prospect of a new law against invasion of privacy. 'Privacy threat to celebrity coverage' was the headline in the Media supplement of* The Australian *on July 31 2008 for its lead story, which began: 'the celebrity media industry could be thrown into turmoil by moves to restrict reporting on public figures'. Am I the only person who thinks this reads rather like an item in the satirical American newspaper* The Onion *or an out-take from the* Chaser?

Well, no, Matthew you're not.

Another prominent industry leader, Mark Scott of the ABC, also broke ranks in suggesting that the media should seek to *negotiate* a suitable outcome on the proposed statutory cause of action rather than leave the development of the law in the hands of the courts.

But let me return to those questionable calls for a moment.

News Limited's Sydney *Daily Telegraph* conceded that the redhead alleged to be in those photos published last year in the lead-up to the Queensland election—the 'other redhead', Pauline Hanson—wasn't her, and according to reports settled a legal action she commenced soon thereafter. The Deputy Editor's first go at defending the publication of what at the time the *Telegraph* insisted were photos of Hanson was the 'public interest'. When questioned about the precise public interest involved, she said, 'That's for our readers to tell. That will be determined by the number of people that buy the paper'. A bit similar to the line by the then editor of the same paper who at the time defended the publication online of a photo taken by a phone camera of Sonny Bill Williams and actress Candice Falzon *in flagrante* in a toilet cubicle with the door closed at a Sydney hotel. He told Monica Attard: 'it is currently the second highest read story of the year so far. The readers clearly loved it.' There we have it then.

Hanson would not have succeeded under the proposed cause of action because she claimed, and News publications eventually conceded, it was not her in the photos, so there was no serious breach of *her* privacy. Whoever was in them has not stepped forward—perhaps with an eye to maintaining privacy concerning happenings 30 years ago. The public apology by the *Telegraph* Editor to Hanson was that the photos were of someone else, suggesting that had they been of Hanson, the public interest lay in their publication, despite the passage of time and the irrelevance of the event to her campaign for office.

Peter Meakin of the 7 Network initially defended the outing of NSW Transport Minister David Campbell through footage taken from the street of Campbell leaving Ken's of Kensington as in the public interest, because of the government car Campbell used to drive there. This was quickly dropped when it turned out there had been no breach of any rules or guidelines for use of vehicles, so other claims about the public interest in knowing the details of the private life of a minister of the Crown were quickly rolled out.

The incident of course raises the issue of whether anything done in public—leaving a gay haunt through the front door, visible from the street, for example, can be regarded as private. Mark Day, for example, argues that everything done in public is open slather to the media. Expectations of complete privacy in a public space for any of us have to be lower than ten years ago and those of someone in public life even lower, but all of us should have a right to go about entirely personal business in the public domain.

On privacy in the shower, the AFL cleared Brendan Fevola in March over his part in the publication of a nude photo of Lara Bingle in *Women's Day* and elsewhere, on the ground there was 'insufficient evidence' to show he had distributed the photograph, taken while the pair were having an affair in 2006. It was reported in March that Bingle was suing Fevola for breach of privacy, defamation and misuse of her image, prompting News Limited lawyer Justin Quill to almost chortle while offering his free legal advice in an op-ed published in the *Herald Sun*.

'There is no right to privacy in Australia', Quill said.

> *I can write that a few different ways if you'd like, but it won't change the position. You hear a lot of people talking about their right to privacy. But unless they're talking about some moral right to privacy, they're talking about something that doesn't exist in this country . . . Taking a photo of a woman in the shower and distributing it is unquestionably reprehensible. On any view. But we shouldn't feel so sorry for Bingle that we demand a privacy law.*

Quill acknowledged she might possibly have a claim for breach of a confidence, but on privacy rights, nothing—and right from the relevant authority in the land, the News Limited lawyer.

The framework of media self-regulation

Managing privacy is part of a broader framework concerning ethics and values in journalism; an essential framework given the media's exercise of significant public power, privilege and the potential to cause harm. This framework is, in fact, key to 'the conditional exemption' media organisations enjoy from the *Privacy Act*.

The *Privacy Act* was introduced by the Hawke government in 1988. It initially applied only to the federal public sector and to credit reporting. In 2000 the Howard government extended the *Act* to cover big business. Media organisations were granted a conditional exemption for acts and practices in the course of journalism. The fact that an exemption was given reflected the importance attached to the public interest in freedom of expression and the free flow of information in our democratic society. The imposition of conditions was an attempt to balance the public interest in freedom of expression and the public interest in adequately safeguarding the handling of personal information. Significantly, all that is required to enjoy the exemptions is 'for a public commitment by a media organisation to observe standards of privacy' in the course of journalism, and that those standards be published in writing. That's it.

Most print and all broadcast media seek to satisfy these conditions through codes or principles that apply to the conduct of their functions, under the auspices of an industry group. In the case of broadcast media, there are a number of industry bodies that operate in a co-regulated system under the *Broadcast Services Act* administered by the Australian Communications and Media Authority (ACMA). Seven separate codes apply to commercial television and other forms of broadcasting. Non-compliance with a registered code may give rise to issues concerning the continuation of the licence, or the imposition of licence conditions. The ABC and SBS have their own codes.

The print media is self-regulating, with most of the industry members of the Australian Press Council subject to its *Statement of Principles and Standards*.

Members of the Media Entertainment and Arts Alliance, but not other journalists, are bound by its Code of Ethics. Estimates of MEAA coverage vary from the Alliance's claim of 80 per cent, to estimates of 50 per cent by others. Some large media organisations have their own code and train to a standard that may differ from the MEAA Code.

Commercial television stations through Free TV Australia undertake to comply with the *2010 Code of Practice*, registered as a code under the *Broadcasting Services Act*:

In broadcasting news and current affairs programs, licensees: must not use material relating to a person's personal or private affairs, or which invades an individual's privacy, other than where there is an identifiable public interest reason for the material to be broadcast (4.3.5). The broadcast of material relating to a person's personal or private affairs may be warranted where the broader public interest is served by the disclosure of the material. When making this judgment stations need to consider the public interest in the broadcast of the particular material. Public interest in a story as a whole, may not justify use of particular material that intrudes on the privacy of an individual.

Weaknesses in the system

Commentators point to gaps (few address specific issues concerning the privacy of children), lack of transparency and independence in the investigation of complaints; overlap and differences between codes and weak enforcement mechanisms, although ACMA can seek enforceable undertakings. 'The Australian Press Council complaints process, for example, has no power to penalise or make an order against a publication. No one has ever been expelled from the MEAA for a breach of standards.'

Media organisations defend the arrangements arguing that any change is unwarranted and unnecessary.

Australia's 'Right to Know', for example, stated:

Media privacy issues are best managed by industry specific codes of practice.

The existing media privacy framework provides all the appropriate mechanisms for dealing with privacy in the media.

The current media privacy framework is effective and working well. This is evidenced by low numbers of complaints, investigations and breach findings. In addition to existing codes of practice that deal specifically with privacy, media in Australia are subject to a wide range of Federal and State laws, which protect private rights and interests.

Any proposal to enhance the rigours of existing media privacy regulation must be limited to addressing specific identified public interest concerns regarding the media's treatment of privacy issues.

The fact is the system of self-regulation set up under the general exemption from the *Privacy Act* is, more or less, a set of hometown arrangements for the media companies. With print media it is established around an organisation that lacks any power of coercion or penalty and which operates, in the main, to excuse the transgressions of its members. Even the funding of the Press Council is dodgy, because it is funded by publishers on a formula based on circulation. News Limited is the major contributor. That is, the body which is adjudicating on complaints is funded by the largest newspaper group, where obviously many of the complaints must arise from its own publications. Denis Muller tells us that 'the Press Council's own research shows newspaper executives are much more likely to be satisfied with the outcome than complainants'. Quite so.

The former Chairman of the Press Council, Professor Ken McKinnon, said, on the occasion of his departure, that the media failed to 'live up to its own rhetoric on ethics, privacy and independence'. A pretty damning indictment, I should have thought.

David Salter in his *The Media We Deserve* said about self-regulation:

It is the most astonishing yet unremarked hypocrisy of the Australian media. An industry that devotes so much of its energy to questioning the motives and morality of others, nevertheless believes it can—and should—be trusted to regulate itself. Our media wish the full force of the law to bear down without fear or favour on everyone except themselves. The faintest suggestion that the output of our print, radio and television empires might benefit from some legislative attention is invariably met with the rolling thunder of outraged editorials all protesting the evil of any such assault on the sacred freedom of the press.

Salter went on to remark that 'the philosophical justification for self-regulation stretches no further than that most over-quoted principle, the "freedom of the press" in "the public interest"'. He went on to say 'Freedom of the press cannot also be freedom to lie, to deceive, to unlawfully incite or alarm, or to pursue a criminal purpose. The only real regulatory power is the law and the law is usually at its best when journalism is at its worst.'

The fact is, it is naïve in the extreme to believe that a clutch of large companies—in this case, media companies—will or can conduct their affairs on some sort of trustee basis, having permanent regard for the public interest—leaving these companies to actually determine what that public interest is.

We do not do this with other large companies in respect of such issues as trade practices or competition policy.

But we do do it with media companies. They get exemption from the *Privacy Act* provisions which every other large company is subject to. And there is only one reason: one, 'Freedom of the Press'. Yet when the Law Reform Commission recommended that the media exemptions should be maintained but with some tweaking for accountability, the media companies moved immediately into high dudgeon. 'Everything is working well' is the constant and only public refrain.

The intellectual case for adoption of the Commission's modest recommendations is barely assailable. It's laid out in detail in Chapter 42 of the report.

The ALRC recommended two new limitations to the exemption for acts and practices in the course of journalism: that a definition of '*journalism*' should be introduced for the purposes of the *Privacy Act* and a small change made to the definition of media organisation. The more significant recommendation was that media organisations should not be left entirely to themselves in setting standards, with the introduction of measures that 'would continue the exemption only where a media organisation was committed to adequate privacy standards developed in conjunction with the Privacy Commission and the ACMA'.

In light of the obvious shortcomings in the current system, this seems highly sensible to me.

The specific recommendation of the Commission is as follows:

Recommendation 42–3 The Privacy Act should be amended to provide that media privacy standards must deal adequately with privacy in the context of the activities of a media organisation (whether or not the standards also deal with other matters).

Recommendation 42–4 The Office of the Privacy Commissioner, in consultation with the Australian Communications and Media Authority and peak media representative bodies, should develop and publish:
(a) criteria for adequate media privacy standards; and
(b) a template for media privacy standards that may be adopted by media organisations.

Few complaints

Hartigan and others in defending media standards claim there are only a small number of complaints and breach findings. This is true of formal complaints—the APC published 30 decisions on formal complaints between July last year and the end of May. Six concerned privacy. Two were upheld. But importantly, we don't have figures on 'how many complaints are made directly to the media organisation concerned and their resolution or the ones people feel aggrieved about but then desist from making'. Factors other than the efficacy of the system may explain the low reported numbers, if in fact it is the case.

One limitation on existing schemes is that complaints can usually only by made by the person directly affected by an alleged breach of privacy, although the Australian Communications and Media Authority has 'own motion' powers and according to reports is investigating Channel 7 regarding the David Campbell matter.

Another factor is that people don't complain because they run the risk of attracting more attention to an issue, thus compounding the problem they are dealing with in the first place. Or they believe the Press Council, despite the involvement of public members undertaking an investigation of a complaint, lacks true independence. In other words, they expose themselves, devote a tonne of time and energy, only to get the brush off.

Perhaps there are few complaints because most people wouldn't know what to do or where to go. Again, Denis Muller from his research tells us, 3 per cent of the public know of the MEAA, while only 4 per cent know of the Press Council.

The Australian Privacy Foundation wasn't far off the mark in stating that the whole system is ineffectual, and that there are relatively few complaints because there is a widely held public perception that when it comes to privacy, the media are effectively above the law.

Media Watch the most effective

Who is surprised that the one mechanism of accountability that stands out for excellence among journalists is not the industry's self-regulatory bodies but *Media Watch*? As Denis Muller told the ABC *Media Report*, in his survey of journalists:

> Media Watch *scored 9.3 on an 11-point scale, and it was far and away the most admired of all the accountability mechanisms, and it's a television program, it's not a properly instituted accountability mechanism at all.*

Scope for improvement

So, moving forward, as the Prime Minister might say, what could be done to improve underlying conduct in journalism while improving the framework?

First, industry leaders and the profession should acknowledge that improvements are needed. Instead of standing aggressively behind the status quo, dressed in the cloak of the Fourth Estate, they need to talk more about responsibility, more about the importance of ethics, more about improvement in the standards of journalism in all respects. We might not be able to do much about some online players but those in the mainstream need to provide real leadership in managing themselves and any self-regulatory system. On the issue of promoting high standards and transparency, there aren't many Australian publications or broadcasters that appear to have followed the example elsewhere of appointing an internal ombudsman or public editor with a role to champion best practice, investigate complaints generally, and with a public platform to explain or attempt to explain news judgements and questionable calls on privacy and other standards.

On enforcement of decisions arising from the investigation of complaints, those involved in self-regulation should be aware that public and private-sector organisations covered by the *Privacy Act* are on notice of a significant proposed step-up in enforcing compliance with the law. Minister Ludwig has announced that the government will amend the *Privacy Act* to introduce civil penalties—to be imposed by the Federal Court or the Federal Magistrates Court—for 'serious breaches when other enforcement measures are not sufficient'. The Minister said, 'They will be serious sanctions. It is essential we have a robust system in place to protect the privacy of individuals.'

The existing Press Council scheme, already criticised over the lack of enforcement powers, may look even weaker in comparison.

This is a separate issue from the proposed statutory cause of action, and relates to an appropriate sanction following investigation by the Privacy Commissioner of compliance with the law. An example might be the Commissioner's recent finding that Google had breached the *Privacy Act* by collecting unsecured WiFi payload data using Street View vehicles. Sanctions available to the Privacy Commissioner were limited to a requirement for an apology and acceptance of an under-taking to do better in future. Under what is now proposed every business with a turnover of more than $3 million a year will potentially be subject to such financial penalties, imposed by a court. This is likely to concentrate minds on the importance of compliance with privacy principles a little more than hitherto. Media organisations outside the scope of the *Act* need to consider whether thrashing serious breaches of privacy with a warm lettuce should continue to be all that their self-regulatory systems can deliver.

Second, media organisations would be sending an important message about where they stand on these issues if they indicated they are prepared to work with, not against, the modest reforms proposed by the ALRC for continuation of the media exemption from the *Privacy Act*.

Third, industry and profession leaders should get back to an issue which has defied reformers for years: the idea that with regard to ethics and standards, the media would benefit from *unified arrangements*, consistent principles and uniform enforcement mechanisms applying to all sides: newspaper companies, journalists, broadcasting companies and Internet service providers.

There are some reported indications of interest at the Press Council in broadening its scope, with new president Julian Disney. Don McKinnon seems to have given it a good but unsuccessful shot during his term. And I'd like to be a fly on the wall at the Melbourne Writers' Festival on 2 and 3 September at the first occasion on which the people with most to do in setting and policing journalism standards are speaking on the same platform—the session, 'The Ethical Journalist Online', with Julian Disney, Australian Communications and Media Authority head Chris Chapman and the Director of Editorial Policies for the ABC, Paul Chadwick.

Fourth, more attention to guidance, education and training will continue to be an issue, especially while some senior journalists and those to whom they report claim that the public interest is anything the public might find interesting. The public interest means publication or non-publication guided by what is in the interest of the public as a whole, not what readers or an audience might find interesting or titillating. It's not always straightforward or easy to apply. But as mentioned previously, it's claimed to be at the centre of media's claimed right to publish generally and said to be a central determinant in deciding that publication of sensitive material is justified.

However, when it suits the argument, media interests seem prepared to jettison the public interest concept, and the important balancing of interests that they claim to manage and get correct every day and most of the time. It's apparently too hard, even for judges. The afore-mentioned News Limited lawyer, Justin Quill, writing in last Friday's *Australian*, argued the dangers to open justice from a proposed change to the law regarding suppression of court proceedings that would give judges power to impose an order where the public interest requires it.

'How could including a power that can only be exercised "in the public interest" be a bad thing?' he asked. And answered his own question: 'the main problem is "public interest" is a nebulous concept that is difficult to define and even more difficult to weigh against the circumstances of a case. It's the practical application that will cause the problems'.

Rather than abandoning the public interest, the media needs to put more time and effort into fostering a better practical understanding of the term, including the notion of a right to privacy within its own ranks.

The last suggestion for change is for the media to get on board in a sensible discussion about a cause of action for serious breaches.

A cause of action for a serious breach of privacy

The case for legislation to better define legal rights in this area is that the threats to privacy are escalating dramatically, driven largely by technological change. That the common law, case-by-case exploration of whether there is a recourse for breach of privacy is a slow, piecemeal and fragmented process likely to lead to different approaches in different jurisdictions. That legislation would give effect to our international obligations under Article 17 of the *International Covenant*; and that the need for better protection of privacy is being recognised in comparable countries including traditional 'peer law' countries for Australia such as the UK and New Zealand, as well as Canada and parts of the US.

The door to the development of such a cause of action at common law was opened by the High Court in 2001 in *Australian Broadcasting Corporation v Lenah Game Meats Pty Ltd*. A majority of the Court accepted that a tort of privacy might be developed in the future, but the nature of privacy protection and its relationship with existing causes of action was not made clear.

To date, two lower courts have held that such a cause of action is part of the common law of Australia; one in Queensland where the defendant incessantly stalked a local council mayor, the other in Victoria where the ABC published in radio news bulletins information that identified the plaintiff—a victim of a sexual assault. This breached the *Judicial Proceedings Reports Act 1958* (Vic), which makes it an offence in certain circumstances to publish information identifying the victim of a sexual offence. Judge Hampel in the County Court of Victoria held that, in addition to breaching a statutory duty owed to the plaintiff by virtue of the *Judicial Proceedings Reports Act*, the ABC and two of its employees were liable to the plaintiff in equity for breach of confidence, and in tort for invasion of privacy. In a few cases the courts have ruled there is no cause of action for breach of privacy.

The ALRC proposal is that the present uncertainty at law should be addressed through legislation to create a general cause of action for an unwarranted serious breach of privacy.

The ALRC recommended that a legal action should be available to remedy a serious invasion of personal privacy, where the individual:

(a) had a reasonable expectation of privacy; and
(b) the conduct complained about would be regarded as highly offensive to a reasonable person.

Further, the plaintiff would have to satisfy the court in each case that:

(c) the public interest in privacy outweighs other matters of public interest—including the interests in informing the public about matters of public concern and in allowing freedom of expression.

As then President of the ALRC Professor David Weisbrot and Deputy President Professor Les McCrimmon, who conducted the review, said at the time, the proposal sets a high hurdle for success when a media organisation is involved:

By including the public interest test, covering only highly offensive conduct, and placing the onus of proof squarely on the person complaining of the breach, the commission has set a very high bar—taking into account the concerns of artists and media organisations about respecting freedom of the press and freedom of expression. Indeed, some privacy advocates and civil libertarians argue that we have set the bar much too high.

This is a sensible proposal. While some media voices shout 'outrage' at the suggestion that there should be a law blocking a cause for action for breach of privacy, others including Mark Scott think differently. Scott told the Australia's 'Right to Know' conference in Sydney in March last year:

With digital surveillance, location tracking and genetic tracing becoming commonplace, there is a very firm case for the law to allow people to protect their privacy. It is a fundamental human right . . . the Australian Law Reform Commission proposal for a new statutory right of privacy, properly worded, is a sophisticated idea worthy of serious debate. To dismiss even the need to address the issue—the need to have a thoughtful and comprehensive debate—doesn't seem to be in keeping with the openness and plurality of perspectives that media freedom should be about.

Mr Scott's colleagues in the industry should pick up the point.

Conclusion

In conclusion, we know in this, the age of knowledge, the age of truly mass communications, with the ubiquity of digital tools, that the occasions for incursions into the privacy of people will continue to rise exponentially. We can take the determinist view which concedes that the privacy of all of us is now effectively gone or we can assert that an innate right of humanity, of, indeed, the human condition, is the right to individual privacy. Or as Warren and Brandeis put it over a century ago, 'the right to be let alone'.

I believe we are stronger as a society when each of us is stronger. And by stronger I mean not having important liberties shorn from us in some revelatory information 'free for all'. The social contract we are subject of involves the surrender of certain rights in exchange for other societal benefits and protections. But at the core of that contract there cannot be, and must never be, derogations such that the notion of individuality is materially or permanently compromised. The essence of the dignity of each of us goes to our individuality and our primary need to be ourselves. Not ourselves shared with billions of others, not ourselves X-rayed by the new intrusive technologies, not ourselves ground to an amorphous mass of human sameness.

For these reasons, privacy will always matter. It will matter because the right to it represents a core and inalienable human liberty. This is why it will still matter in the face of the otherwise overwhelmingly invasive technologies; in the face of the attempts by the image and news wholesalers to have us believe that we live in the age of a new normal, a normal where these astringent and corrosive facilitations are not simply to be tolerated but accepted within a framework of powerless resignation.

What the Australian Law Reform Commission has put on offer is a proposal to remove uncertain and possibly haphazard and fragmented development of the law in favour of a unitary approach flowing from national legislation; legislation to create a general cause of action for unwarranted and serious breaches of privacy.

If, in certain circumstances, people had, or believed they had, a reasonable right to privacy and that privacy was breached, people should have a right of action in law by way of remedy. Not simply a right to complain but a right of action. Not a right to complain to a media-run-and-funded industry mechanism—a right of action at law—for as David Salter reminds us, 'the only real regulatory power *is the law*'.

As I said, Minister Ludwig has already announced that the government will amend the *Privacy Act* to introduce civil penalties with serious sanctions. This will be the new standard for corporations. The notion therefore, that media corporations should continue to enjoy different self-developed and self-regulated standards instead of regulation by exemption, is simply opportunist. Every day the media is out there insisting on ever higher performance standards in the community, urging the full force of the law be applied to transgressions, but not to itself. The hypocrisy, to use a John Hartigan phrase, is 'stomach-churning'.

Industry leaders and the profession itself should acknowledge that the current 'free for all' cannot go on. That 'invading the privacy of celebrities, starlets, models and sometimes ordinary non-consenting members of the public', as Jack Waterford put it, has naught to do with the public interest and everything to do with the profit flowing from the implicit consent of 'victims' who are suborned to the revenue task.

Industry leaders and media organisations should indicate they are prepared to work with and not against the modest reforms proposed by the Australian Law Reform Commission for the continuation of the media exemption from the *Privacy Act* and to acknowledge that the media in general would benefit from legal clarity, consistent principles and uniform national enforcement when it comes to respect for privacy. The media's alternative is to do what the media normally does; use its muscle to bully the government into shredding the community's right to privacy or, more particularly, to turn a blind eye while the media shreds the community's right to privacy.

To date, governments have been pretty wary about meddling with the media. But even wary ones will pick up the public disquiet. And in this, the age of poll-driven policy, it is likely that governments will be encouraged to act and when they do, the remedies will be sharper and more punitive. Far better for media organisations to negotiate now around the Commission's sensible and moderate proposals than to wait for the counter-punch, which has to come.

INTERNATIONAL RELATIONS AND FOREIGN POLICY

1

PEACE AND PROSPERITY
The Spiritual Challenge
Melbourne Writers' Festival,
Melbourne,
23 August 2008

Paul Keating's Melbourne Writers' Festival tour d'horizon stands as one
of the most expansive addresses on international issues ever given by a
Prime Minister of Australia, in or out of office. The address underlines the
breadth and cogency of Paul Keating's world view and the corroboration of
it to principles founded in truth, justice and magnanimity.
He builds the address around a single question: can the well-off bulk of
humanity assimilate a constancy of peace and prosperity or will a spiritless
contentment hollow it out? The address marks the shift in world power
from West to East, of Russia's marginalisation, of China's coming out,
the need for a representative structure of world governance, the threat of
nuclear warfare and a final question: will a universal peace be achieved
and will it come about by human insight or catastrophe?

A PRESTIGIOUS AMERICAN THINK TANK told us recently that 66 per cent of humanity lives in high-income or high-growth countries; up from 25 per cent 30 years ago. A powerful statistic.

Since 1982, the world has experienced a 25-year-long wave of economic growth, overlaid by only two cyclical investment recessions: 1989–90 and 2000–03.

This extended period of high growth and low inflation has brought prosperity on an unprecedented scale. Growth has risen the world over in a long linear trajectory.

This period of macroeconomic consensus and stability has been called 'the great moderation'. A moderation in all the factors that go to the production of goods and services and their overall management in conducive monetary and fiscal frameworks.

And coinciding with this long period of growth and stability was the strategic epiphany at the end of the 1980s—the end of the Cold War—the bipolar rivalry that characterised and threatened the peace of the world in the second-half of the twentieth century. A bipolarity that, nonetheless, evaporated in an instant.

What replaced it was the unipolar moment of the West, with the American eagle perched victorious on its mountain lair.

That victory, by some coincidence, also came with the full onset of globalisation. The opening of borders to goods and flows of funds with its concomitant intensification of trade and financial interdependence. As it turned out, a globalisation of economic growth annealed by a globalisation of peace. The first of a kind since that which followed the Napoleonic Wars.

The key question now and the central one of this address is, can that two-thirds of humanity in those high-income and high-growth countries assimilate that growth and prosperity, or will the condition corrode or hollow humanity out, slaking us of those earnest values and high convictions that have stood by us down through time?

More than that, will the seduction of secularity and self-absorption lure us into a bubble of spiritless contentment, sustained only the inability of others to organise themselves effectively to disrupt or appropriate it?

Is it a case, as Pope Benedict recently remarked, that the Western world is a world 'weary of its own culture', a world 'weary of greed, exploitation and division, of the tedium of false idols and the pain of false promises'? That is, a world without a guiding light, one without absolute truths by which to navigate.

John Stuart Mill made much the same point, seeing the great struggle of life as being between creativity and the 'despotism of custom' or perhaps, we could say, between originality and tradition, of authenticity trying to breach those tedious moulds of contemporary culture, replete with their false idols and chimeras of an idealised happiness.

Benedict told us recently in Sydney that 'life is a search for the true, the good and the beautiful' and we know that whenever those objectives become subordinated, we become lost in a morass of preferences and experiences uninformed by truth or ethics. Experiences, he went on to say, which detached from what is good or true, 'lead to moral and intellectual confusion and ultimately to despair'.

So, are we—those of us in that opportune two-thirds of humanity—capable of forging a second Enlightenment? One not solely dependent on science but one leavened by understanding and virtue, making the most of science? One that goes to the profound and innate dignity of every human life, transcending the old barriers of ethnicity and creed, and of course, geography.

In a world shrunk by transport and communications, vulnerable to shifts in climate and natural disasters and subject to devastating weapons and armouries, can a higher framework of co-existence obtain other than one governed by self-interest or nationalism or, indeed, by a misplaced sense of superiority?

Benedict also told us in Sydney that the State cannot be 'the source of truth and morality'. That that source can only be a set of truths and values which devolve to what it means to be human, one to each other, society to society, state to state. In Benedict's terms, one of God's creatures.

We are currently living through one of those rare yet transforming events in history, a shift in the power in the world from West to East. For five hundred years Europe dominated the world, now, for all its wealth and population, it is drifting into relative decline.

Will our understanding of this transformation and our acceptance of its equity for the greater reaches of mankind lead us to a position of general preparedness of its inevitability, or will we cavil at it in much the same way as Europe resisted the rise of Bismarck's creation at the end of the nineteenth century?

We can see with this the twenty-ninth Olympiad, the questioning of China and the resentment at its pretensions about being one of us. Even becoming one of us! The Western liberal press featured, generally in critical terms, the world-long torch relay, juxtaposing all that it represents and is good about it, with what it sees as China's democratic defects, viewing it almost exclusively through the prism of Tibet. Saying, almost, that the aspirations of this massive nation, a quarter of humanity, a legatee of a century of misery, dragging itself from poverty, is somehow of questionable legitimacy, because its current government's attitude to political freedoms and, in specific instances, human rights, are not up to scratch. Ignoring the massive leaps in progress, of income growth, of shelter, of the alleviation of poverty, of dwindling infant mortality, of education, of, by any measure, the much better life now being experienced by the great majority of Chinese.

In a Western and elitist way, we have viewed China's right to its Olympic Games, to its coming out, its moment of glory, with condescension and concessional tolerance.

The Western critic feeling the epicentre of the world changing but not at all liking it seeks to put down these vast societies on the basis that their political and value systems don't match up to theirs.

Henry Kissinger made the point recently, when he said 'we cannot do in China in the twenty-first century, what others sought to do in the nineteenth, prescribe their institutions for them and seek to organise Asia'. And he went on to pose the question: do we split the world into a union of democracies and non-democracies, or must there be another approach to regional and historic circumstance?

How workable would the world be if it were divided into democracies and non-democracies, along a demarcation line set up by self-approving, Jeffersonian-style liberals?

There is a view that should China become a democracy, a real one, many tensions in the global system would go; that democracies find peace with other democracies; that the former political–military state first turns itself into a trading state and as wealth and opportunity rise, so, too, do democratic values.

But what we must remember is that even if all the states of the world became democratic, the structure of the international system would remain anarchic.

India and Pakistan are democracies but this fact has not lowered tensions between them. Democratic Germany took on the rest of democratic Europe in 1914. Some would say that Wilhelmine Germany was not a pristine democracy but can we divine our way to peace in the international system by a beauty contest as to whose democratic fabric is finest or better than another?

The propagation of democracy is a fraught business but with the end of the Cold War, the liberal interventionists got right into their stride and, Iraq was one of the outcomes.

RH Tawney, the British historian and sociologist, once remarked that war is either a crusade or a crime. Woe betide the rest of us if the crusaders enjoy an open writ to underwrite military adventurism in the name of democracy in states which have not even developed organic domestic political structures to take it, much less grow it. Perhaps we should also consider John Stuart Mill's preference for progress before liberty. Or liberty at least in tandem with progress.

The fact is that for the first time in human history, we now live in a global system. Aviation and telecommunications have underwritten a connectedness that past generations could only have dreamt of. Television news and the digital age mark the events of day-to-day life in real time. No longer do we concentrate our affairs in our own parts of the world, rather we calibrate all we do against the rest of the world as a whole. Our mindset is now global.

From here on, we have to synchronise whatever we do within an overarching global strategy. A strategy which has to have as its basis the progress of human existence and not simply the propagation of democracy.

And it is not as if we have been denied a new canvas to paint out a better picture.

For the first time since before the First World War, the dissolution of the Soviet Union opened the potential for a new era of peace and cooperation.

Russia, humiliated but intact, let the bits fall away from its former Union of Soviet States. Wise men like George Herbert Bush, Helmut Kohl, Brent Scowcroft and James Baker saw to it that the bits came away other than in an outburst of triumphalism: that the bits were strategically parked in the quietest and least celebratory way to underwrite an orderly transition from Gorbachev to Yeltsin. And an orderly transition to the independent functioning of those Warsaw Treaty states outside Russia itself. Gorbachev even agreed to a reunited Germany within NATO, after 26 million of his countrymen and women had died releasing the grip of Nazism on their homeland.

George Herbert Bush talked about a New World Order, then lost to Bill Clinton. And what happened then? Well, nothing happened then! The Americans cried victory and walked off the field.

The greatest challenge we face, whether for managing incidents or easing the new economic tectonic plates into place, will be to construct a truly representative structure of world governance which reflects global realities but which is also equitable and fair.

For two Clinton presidential terms and two George W Bush terms, the world has been left without such a structure. Certainly one able to accommodate Russia and the great states like China and India.

Instead President Clinton and President George W Bush left us with the template of 1947; the template cut by the victorious powers of World War Two, the one where Germany and Japan were left on the outside, and still are 60 years later, and in which China and India are tolerated and palely humoured.

Sixteen critical years have already been lost. And it is not as if we are dealing with a world where things are the same now as they were sixteen years ago. The world is dynamic: sixteen years ago China was not a world power; today it is. Sixteen years ago, Russia was collapsing; today it is growing and strongly.

The fact is, we are now sitting through, witnessing, the eclipse of American power. Yet for those sixteen critical years, two American

Presidents did nothing to better shape the institutions of world govern-ance. To shape it for the day, for that moment in history when the United States becomes another power among equals, or near equals.

And there has been no help from the old powers, Tony Blair's Britain and Jacques Chirac's France. After all, they had box seats to the event, courtesy of being on top in 1947. But Blair's contribution was not anything new or free-thinking, rather he thought being an American acolyte was all that was required. Chirac was simply incapable of adding any strategic value to the equation.

The fact is we are again heading towards a bipolar world. Not one shaped by a balance of terror like the old one, but certainly not a multipolar one. In fact, one heavily influenced by two countries, the United States and China.

This will face us up to a number of major decisions and soon.

For a start, will we regard China as a force for stability and good, a partner in the world, or will we continue to treat China as an upstart economic adversary to be strategically watched?

Some will say, but what about Europe? Don't forget Europe; Europe is a pole.

I do not think it is.

Europe, in settlement of its twentieth-century conflicts, has opted for a cooperative regionalism where the prerogatives of each of the former sovereign states have been blended or subsumed to a homogenous whole. But a whole lacking that most crucial of all strategic ingredients—the political ability to conscript and direct a population; to respond militarily and do it decisively. To do it in its own terms and the terms of its population. In the long history of Europe this homogenisation is actually a welcome change but the challenge for Europe is to extend that supranationalism to others.

States like China and Russia still enjoy a power of galvanic action, politically and strategically, of the kind Europe had and used in the nineteenth and twentieth centuries. There may come a time when the young people of these countries refuse to be conscripted for military service by their respective polities. But that time is not now.

As Chinese military power grows in lockstep with its economy, it is reasonable to assume that the only other major economic and strategic force on the landscape will be the United States. Just the two of them.

But let us not leave out the Russians.

Russia's economy, while growing in strength from the burnt out wreck it was in 1990, will not be in the league of that of the United States or of China. But Russia will still be wealthy; wealthy enough to continue to field its massive arsenal of nuclear weapons. So whether you attribute to Russia full *pole* status or not, you can certainly attribute to it huge strategic standing.

It is more the pity then, that after that unexpected epiphany in 1989, the Clinton administration rashly decided to ring-fence Russia by inviting the former Warsaw Treaty states of Poland, Hungary and the Czech Republic to join NATO.

By doing so, the United States failed to learn one of the lessons of history; that the victor should be magnanimous with the vanquished. In this case, the victor and its agent, NATO, gave those former Soviet-bloc countries an invitation to actually jump camp. And in doing so, strategically occupying the territory that formerly belonged to the Soviet Union which came within the control of Russia.

At some time the United States will be obliged to treat Russia as a great sovereign power replete with a range of national interests of the kind other major powers possess.

In the meantime, the great risk of this sort of adventurism is that with NATO's border now right up to the western Ukraine, the Russians will take the less costly military option of counter-weighing NATO's power by keeping their nuclear arsenal on full operational alert.

This posture automatically carries with it the possibility of a Russian nuclear attack by mistake. The years of Russia's economic poverty, certainly since the collapse of its economy in the first half of the 1990s, has meant the Russians have allowed their surveillance and early warning systems to ossify. To compensate, they are keeping their nuclear arsenal on full operational alert. No need to stand by if you are not, in fact, standing by.

This leaves the rest of the world relying more on generals, battlefield commanders and intelligence assessors to restrain a nuclear response than it does the Russian President or his government. This means that while the Cold War is over, the risk of a mistaken pre-emptory response has increased.

Russia is the only country in the world with the capacity to massively damage the United States to the point of seriously maiming it. And ditto for Western Europe. Wouldn't you think that when the Russians surrendered their empire in 1990, US policy would have been adept enough to find an intelligent place for them in the overall strategic fabric?

That is, to have Russia as part of an enlightened framework of intelligent co-existence, thinking back beyond the Cold War to when we partnered with them to defeat Hitler. But even more than that, in people terms, to invite their 160 million, battered by the twentieth century, into the comity and wealth of nations.

Instead, the United States has conducted itself as unrivalled powers have done throughout time; unchecked, it exploited its position.

It has ring-fenced Russia, treating it as a virtual enemy with its west European and central European clients egging it on.

This week the United States signed Poland up to build a missile intercept system on Russia's border. Nominally, the system is designed to protect Europe and the Middle East from Iran. But even the Poles are now talking about having it to deter Russian aggression. NATO, an organisation rendered moribund by the collapse of the Soviet Union, has been refashioned by the United States as an organisation to extend American power and policy to the security order of Europe.

You could be excused for thinking that when the Wall came down the major states of Europe, Germany and France, along with Britain, would have developed their own security order to respond to their own national interests and culture. Certainly with reference to the United States but not mandated by it. But however likely that might have been, the end result is that the key decisions about European defence and security are made in Washington. Hence Europe's strategic impotence.

One of the negative aspects of these developments is that they play into the hands of Russian nationalists while making the hand of those Russians prepared to give liberal democratic principles a go much weaker.

The old West then complains about Vladimir Putin being a poorly disguised Russian autocrat and nationalist when the West has played a large role in creating him.

All of this serves to underline the most pressing problem of all and that is the continuing existence of nuclear weapons.

Nuclear-weapon proliferation is the single, most immediate threat hanging over the world today.

The Nuclear Non-Proliferation Treaty entered by compliant states in 1970 is on the verge of collapse.

The Treaty represents perhaps the most egregious example of international double-dealing of any international regime.

In a nutshell, the nuclear-weapon states signed up to the elimination of their nuclear weapons while, in the meantime, other signatory states undertook to forgo their development.

But now, most of the nuclear-weapon states are developing new nuclear weapons. Not only have they not rid themselves of their old ones, they are actually making new ones.

Tony Blair announced the New Trident Submarine Program in 2006 while the Bush administration has turned its hand to new bunker-busting nuclear weapons designed to attack underground facilities. The Russians, quick on the uptake, are also refining their arsenal.

The old nukes had the dubious advantage of existing solely for self-defence. This new variety of US weapons is actually being designed for use, for intended wartime deployment and operation. And ditto for the Russians.

What sort of future compliance can we expect from states already signatories to the NPT, let alone non-signatories, when the promoters of the Treaty reserve the right to ignore their obligations as to elimination, while designing and building new devices?

In that strategic quiet after the thunderclap that ended the Cold War, as Prime Minister of Australia, a non-weapon NPT signatory, I established the Canberra Commission on the Elimination of Nuclear Weapons in 1995. I did it taking the opportunity of the strategic vacuum to move weapon states down the path of lengthening the fuse or time on their warheads while proposing to completely dismantle and destroy weapons no longer operationally deployed.

Robert O'Neill, the Australian professor of war and strategic policy who was on that Commission, recently wrote of his experience in approaching the five weapon states upon the report's publication. He said of the five, only the Chinese 'seemed willing to talk seriously about the changes recommended by the Commission'.

He said the reaction of the other four weapon states—the United States, Russia, Britain and France—was completely defensive. The Americans and the Russians made clear they were prepared to talk to each other but Britain and France, O'Neill said, saw nuclear weapons as desirable levers of political influence, devoid of which their governments would forfeit leverage in Washington and Moscow and within the corridors of NATO.

The then Prime Minister, John Howard, and his foreign minister Alexander Downer, who received the Report which I had commissioned, dropped it like a hot cake. The then foreign minister labelled it a stunt by the previous government. They did not want to be in the business of taking the issue to the United States, as I certainly would have.

All the more pleasing therefore, for those of us who know that the have and have not policy of the NPT is not sustainable, to see in January 2007 the former US Secretaries of State, Henry Kissinger and George Shultz, along with former Defense Secretary Bill Perry and Senator Sam Nunn, publish a joint call for the elimination of all nuclear weapons.

In October 2007, those four statesmen led a conference at Stanford University on ways of taking their proposal forward. Robert O'Neill believes momentum is building, and he said on rereading the Canberra Commission's report today, he believed it makes more sense than it did in 1996.

The plain fact is, there can be no non-proliferation without de-proliferation. If the weapon states are not prepared to rid themselves of nuclear weapons, why would other states continue to deny themselves the kind of leverage that these weapons bring?

Look at India and Pakistan or even North Korea. None of these states are NPT signatories, yet India, by having these weapons, is now pulling a deal from the United States for nuclear technology. Pakistan's possession of them saw the regime of General Musharraf treated very favourably by the United States while North Korea continues to be handled with kid gloves.

And what a dicey proposition Pakistan is. Another one of those trustworthy democracies. Bhutto has been murdered, like her father, while Musharraf himself is now gone. Who is to contain and manage Pakistan's nuclear weapons for the long-term benefit of the rest of us—another flimsy coalition of political parties, another General?

It seems if you have nuclear weapons and flaunt them, you are more likely to be noticed and treated concessionally. North Korea is the exemplar in this respect.

Many people will think and some will say that with communications and the globalisation of economic wealth being what it is, an outbreak of major conflict seems more and more remote. That global interdependence and the shrinking of the world makes war a decidedly unproductive way of resolving foreign-policy differences.

People should be reminded that that was said at the time of the last great intensification of trade between Britain, France and Germany along with the growing US economy before 1914.

The lesson is that when the strategic bits go wrong, the economic bits soon follow. Certainly not the obverse: when trade goes well, the strategic wrinkles get ironed out.

As I remarked earlier, the structure of the international system is anarchic. Was anarchic; remains anarchic.

This condition cannot be remedied but structures to mitigate its most violent manifestations can be put into place.

Against this backdrop remains the open question about the West and its fibre. The question which was resoundingly answered by that generation who suffered the Depression and the Second World War and who delivered us into a new era of peace and prosperity.

Is our culture a culture made compliant by too much coming too easily, producing a state of intellectual and spiritual lassitude which can only be shaken by the gravest threats, be they economic, environmental or indeed strategic?

As that pendulum swings from West to East, are the motivations for the West's former primacy swinging with it? Has the bounty of science and industrialisation with its cornucopia of production and wealth encouraged us too far away from simpler requirements and concern for the needs of all?

Was the twentieth century a psychological age, as Roger Smith in his *History of the Human Sciences* pointed out, in which the self became privatised, while the public realm—the realm critical to political action for the public good—was left relatively vacant?

As societies, have we taken our eye off public affairs for way too long?

Let me return to the theme I touched at the beginning of my remarks.

Can we, all of us, assimilate, adjust ourselves to a constancy of peace and prosperity without lessening our regard for those enlivening impulses of truth and goodness? The search, as Benedict said, for what is good, beautiful and true.

A new international order based on truth and justice founded in the recognition of the rights of each of us to live out our lives in peace and harmony can, I believe, provide the only plausible long-term template.

The old order of victorious powers, of a compromised UN, a moribund G8 with major powers hanging on to weapons of mass destruction, is a remnant of the violent twentieth century. It cannot provide the basis for an equitable and effective system of world governance.

Just as world community concern has been ahead of the political system on issues such as global warming, so too world community concern needs to galvanise international action to find a new template for a lasting peace. One embracing all the major powers and regions.

This can be done but it requires leadership and imagination. It cannot be done without understanding and virtue.

The philosopher Immanuel Kant said some day there will be a universal peace; the only question is, will this come about by human insight or by catastrophe, leaving no other outcome possible?

Humankind demands that that proposition be settled in the former and not the latter.

AUSTRALIA AND ASIA
The New Order after the Financial Crisis

John Curtin Prime Ministerial Library Anniversary Lecture,
Curtin University of Technology,
Perth,
2 July 2009

Paul Keating's second John Curtin anniversary lecture offers an important snapshot of the world after the two great discontinuities of the preceding twenty years: the end of the Cold War and the Global Financial Crisis. The lecture tracks Paul Keating's long advocacy of a more representative world structure of power—one that includes the great states of China and India, folding them into a rules-based system. The lecture underlines both the prospect and legitimacy of China's rising power in the context of a relative decline in the United States' economic and strategic circumstances. The lecture points to the importance of an Australian foreign policy for divining Australia's way in the evolving region and is critical of the strategic assumptions central to the Rudd government's 2009 Defence White Paper.

I LAST GAVE THE JOHN Curtin Prime Ministerial Library Anniversary Lecture at this university on 5 July 2002, seven years ago almost to the day.

And, as a former Labor Prime Minister of Australia, I am returning to speak about Australia and the world again.

While this event it not exceptional, it is somewhat unusual. There have not been too many Labor Prime Ministers of Australia, so for one to address national and international issues in a Labor context and then readdress those same issues seven years later and to the same gathering, is somewhat out of the ordinary.

Out of the ordinary, not simply because I am appearing here twice, but rather that I am viewing the very same issues through the same prism: a model I developed in my own mind as to how the world might better work. Any lecture at the Curtin Library is given with reference to John Curtin's own life and experiences as Prime Minister. As we know, he only held one ministry during his lifetime and that was that of Prime Minister. And we know that his service in that ministry was had entirely during a war. Curtin was a wartime Prime Minister and the dominant issue of his prime ministership was the salvation of his country. Something which he accomplished by adapting himself and the country rapidly to changing events and circumstances.

We know at the time Curtin's urgent task was to find Australia's security from Asia; principally, then, from Japan. But we also know that Curtin believed that our long-term security could only be found in Asia. That Australia had been dragged to Asia by war when it had thought that the strategic guarantee of Great Britain was sufficient to insulate it from peril. And while he rapidly put together a new strategic partnership with the United States, his government and that of Ben Chifley's which followed was working towards a new rules-based, multilateral world order to better guarantee long-term peace and security. That world order, with Bert Evatt's help, became the United Nations and the order included the magnanimous reconstructions of Europe and Japan by the United States. It also included the lifting of the colonial yoke from over half the world's population.

The enlightened view at the time was that security in the future was only to be had through partnerships and by the congregation of societies within multilateral institutions. That is, it could not be secured by resort to isolation and defensiveness or, in the case of smaller states, by the quest for yet another strategic guarantor.

You would have thought this lesson was a fairly obvious one, but not so obvious as to deter people in this country, even today, from still thinking in terms of our exceptionalism: finding our security from Asia, by dint either of our own resources, both economic and military, or by way of association with great and powerful friends.

The seven years since I was last here offers two important snapshots of the world then and the world now. The world then was coloured by the attacks on New York City in September 2001 and by the forces of unilateralism which that event unleashed within the United States, with international consequences like the unilateral attack upon and war with Iraq. July 2002 was also eight months before the American economy burst back into life in the biggest growth and wealth phase in world history. Between that time and April 2008, we witnessed these events as the world then began its steep slide into recession and near depression.

And we saw during that same period the United States transform itself from the largest creditor country to the largest debtor country, fuelling its economy with consumption and rising living standards that were had by resort to borrowings, including from the largest of the world's poorer countries, China.

That binge of debt and spending brought havoc to the central and largest Western financial centre, New York City and Wall Street, such that the knock-on effects towards a depression of international capitalism has only been avoided by a rapid and timely swing back to multilateralism.

President George W Bush was obliged to convene a meeting of the Group of Twenty countries in late 2008, a meeting which reconvened in April this year, with the attendance of President Barack Obama. Those meetings were held to garner urgent coordinated international fiscal and monetary action to save the world from another depression. And time will show that that timely action did save the world from the horrendous effects of a second depression.

But before the convening of the Group of Twenty countries at head of government level, the world had been run in a completely unrepresentative way, by the Group of Seven countries, which with the exception of Japan, hailed from the Atlantic. And that group, save for Germany and Japan, was collectively a group of debtor states.

Yet, despite all that had happened in the postcolonial history of the world following the Second World War, in places like India and China, continental Africa and South America, the conceit prevailed that the world could be run without reference to these places or to their interests. And run essentially, by the victors of the Second World War, with outrider roles for Germany and Japan.

The Group of Twenty meeting in London last April finally nailed that conceit. Now the great surplus states like China sit at the head table, as do the large demographically young states like India and Brazil. So finally, the world is being remade, to replace the uncooperative and unrepresentative structure I spoke of in this forum seven years ago.

From the time of Japan's accelerating reconstruction in the 1960s, along with similar developments in South Korea and Southeast Asia and following Deng Xiaoping's economic revolution in China from the late 1970s, we have been speaking of world power shifting from the West to the East. Indeed, in so much of the commentary over the last fifteen years, the weighty point has been that power is moving inexorably to the East.

Well, the fact is, it has now arrived. No longer just moving there, it has actually turned up.

China's economy is now the other powerhouse economy outside the United States. Growing on average at around 8 per cent and contributing roughly $400 billion of new wealth annually, it outstrips new wealth creation in the United States, an economy nearly three times its size, by a factor of two to one. The United States at $13 trillion of GDP will be battling to sustain a 2 per cent GDP growth rate into the near future, producing roughly $250 billion of new growth. Meanwhile, Europe as a zone will be struggling to average 1 per cent growth or slightly better.

Population is a principal driver of GDP. India has a population slightly smaller than China's but it has no ageing. More Indians are born than are dying and India is yet to experience its great wealth spurt. Together, India and China represent over a third of the world's population.

I think we can safely say that the pendulum point of world economic activity has shifted and settled upon East Asia. It has settled, not with any particular comfort, but it has settled.

That being the case, how should the world adjust to this transformation?

Power is alighting in an altogether new world; a new place. But a place riven by deep and unanswered questions: structural, political and strategic.

Let me mention a few.

For instance, can China, on which so much now depends, manage and balance its economic growth within the rigidities of its one-party autocracy? Can Japan, China's wealthy near neighbour, cope with its rapid ageing in a political system that is fundamentally broken? And the Korean peninsula throws up a unique set of issues. Unification with the North is an unspoken anathema in the South, as the South fears the crushing economic and social burden of the kind Germany experienced in its reunification with the East. North Korea seeks to preserve its remote wayward status by garnering economic support and sustenance through a combination of illegal international commercial activities and threats against neighbours, with China fearing a North Korean exodus across its borders in the event it fails to keep the North Korean regime socially solvent. And all the while, with Japan worrying, and not unreasonably, that an eventual reunification will see a united Korea in possession of nuclear weapons.

These are issues of concern which arise among the states where the new economic weight has settled.

And then we have the great uncertainty of the United States itself: a country undergoing a fundamental shift in its global status—its financial mendicancy, its economic structure and its social and demographic problems.

During my last speech here, I mentioned the then great discontinuity that affected the international system and that was the end of the Cold War. Now, seven years later, there exists a second great international discontinuity: the Global Financial Crisis.

These two events and their aftermath have changed the way the world works. The first saw the dissolution of that fracturing bipolarity that had set the world into two competing camps, ushering in a new era of cooperative regionalism and integration. The extension of the European Union into the countries of the former Soviet Union is perhaps the most obvious manifestation of that change. But so, too, in our part of the world, the development of the APEC Leaders' Meeting, was a similar manifestation of that change. A body which as Prime Minister, I helped design to take advantage of that great détente, by instituting a structure which, at a time of Chinese weakness, gave it inclusion with the United States and Japan and other Pacific powers such as Indonesia and ourselves. Remember, this happened seventeen years ago, at a time when thoughts of China's strengths and importance were remote to most people's minds, including to many in the United States.

The second discontinuity, the Global Financial Crisis, has forced changes in international cooperation flowing from economic and financial necessity. Earlier I mentioned the fiscal and monetary coordination that has arisen from the Group of Twenty countries. But this recent discontinuity is going have more profound effects than that. It will give rise to a fundamental repair of the international trade and savings imbalance: the imbalance between the savings-rich, trade-surplus countries and the savings-poor, trade-deficit countries. A change which will have huge effects on the way these countries develop, both domestically and internationally into the future. For instance, surplus countries like China, Russia and the oil states will have to save less and consume more, while deficit countries like the United States, Britain and Australia will have to save more and consume less.

China will have to change the focus of its industrial development away from exports and import replacement to an altogether better mix of growing domestic consumption with a focus on housing and services. On the other hand, the industrial structure of the United States will have to adapt to lower consumption and lower household expenditure with a greater emphasis on net exports. That is, import replacement and exports. Manufacturing in American cities will have to come to life again, as American ingenuity is turned back to productivity, away from the mindless fizz of ever more consumption with its attendant depletion of savings.

These effects will promote profound changes in the character of employment and social development in these countries.

And the same will be true of Australia. In the aftermath of this crisis we too will also have to save more and consume less. This will mean also returning to the well of net exports: earning our way out of our current-account deficit imbalance by replacing imports at home while growing exports abroad. It will also mean, as we grow our savings away from dependency on overseas savings and overseas debt, that household balance sheets will need to adjust as debt is reduced and spending curtailed. It will also mean that in things like our great savings scheme, national superannuation, that mandatory contributions will need to grow, including rising above the current static nine percentage points of wages.

It is obvious that these two great discontinuities, the end of the Cold War and the Global Financial Crisis, will change the way our own country functions as it must change the way we look at the world around us.

And that world will be changing as we change, which will force us to view it dynamically.

With all that has happened and is happening, it will make absolutely no sense for us to think of our security in isolationist and defensive terms. The notion of Australia's security being found from Asia is as absurd now as it has always been since we were dragged to Asia during John Curtin's time.

Yet, obvious as this may seem, it is still not obvious to all.

When I became Prime Minister at the end of 1991, I knew I had come to the head of a government in a rare period of strategic still, one of the kind which follows a storm.

That storm was, of course, the pervasive uncertainty and contingent threat of annihilation which hung over the world during the Cold War.

But having some sense of opportunity arising from the fact that the great powers had been taken aback and stunned by that epiphany, I moved as quickly as I could to propose a new piece of political architecture in the Asia Pacific. One to include regional powers in a new regionalism of a kind rendered impossible during the Cold War.

That piece of architecture was and is the APEC Leaders' Meeting. And in proposing it and pulling all those states into it, I always had in my mind that by thought and cooperation, we could make the East Asian hemisphere a better, safer and more cooperative place altogether. And by we, I mean Australia.

In other words, I took to doing that which I had always believed: that Australia's security was best found when it was searching for it and seeking to divine it in the region in which we live—the East Asian hemisphere.

And more than that, doing it at a time when China, still emerging, was registering its first blip on the international radar, following the post-Mao revolution initiated by Deng Xiaoping.

I possessed then, and possess still, the overwhelming conviction that the future prosperity, peace and security of the Asia Pacific would best be realised if China were included in any new strategic construct following the Cold War and encouraged to play an active role in world affairs, including a multilateral one subject to rules and disciplines.

In the popular commentary during my time as both Treasurer and Prime Minister, my frame of reference was referred to almost daily as 'the big picture'. That big events and long timelines always provided the longitude and latitude from which contemporary circumstances might be best assessed. That commentary was true then and it remains true for me today.

It was from that standpoint that I saw the inevitability of China's rise and the renewal of its power.

Until the early nineteenth century China was the world's largest economy and had been since the Middle Ages. It was knocked off that perch by a much smaller country, Britain, with its Industrial Revolution and the innovations that that had brought: a cornucopia of wealth, with the productivity of Britons exploding as they were taken from manual labours and put in front of machines. And the same thing happened in Germany and then in the United States with an even larger population.

This had to happen in China. Only Mao's primitive view of Chinese society had stopped it happening earlier. But once Deng Xiaoping opened the gate to the freer rein of Chinese industriousness, China was able to leapfrog the old legacy systems of western production. Almost in an instant, the basis of Chinese production became cutting edge, while in the same instant, hundreds of millions of workers left their farms to operate the new capital-intensive technologies.

In the aggregate, China was slated to win the big economic race because China had five times the population of the largest economy, the United States. And more than five times the pent-up demand. It was also putting into place new infrastructure and new productive capacity.

That was apparent to me in 1992, as I encouraged President Clinton and Prime Minister Miyazawa of Japan to join with Australia in giving China a seat at a major leaders' table. The first it had enjoyed since 1949.

As I said earlier, at that time, seventeen years ago, China was weak and barely on the world's radar. An Australian Prime Minister could have done what most other Australian Prime Ministers had done and head to Washington to discuss in familiar terms our mutual interests, with reference to the otherwise complicated world around us.

But the big picture told me that the rise of China was inevitable and that China's unity, while defined by Mao's nation state and disciplined by its Communist Party, owed as much to its own sense of civilisation as it did to its modern statehood.

Two decades on, that discipline notwithstanding, I still believe that observation to be true.

So, this great state, with its profound sense of self and the wherewithal to make a better life for its citizens, has eased itself into a major role in world affairs.

A role which, I believe, will be an altogether positive one for the world at large and for the world immediately around it.

But China's advent will cause adjustments. It will change the relative position of the United States, most particularly, in an economic sense. And as we know, the greatest strategic powers have invariably been the greatest economic powers. So this development will not be without strategic consequences. But this does not mean that at some singular moment there will be a bare transfer of the preponderant power of the United States to China. But we do know China will be a power in its own right and a big player.

I have often made a point as to the unusual position of Japan. The second economic power in the world, it has, for 65 years, remained a strategic client of the first economic power in the world. China will not cast itself in this way.

So, we will live in a world of big powers, including one big new one. And in time, that big new one may eclipse American power in our region. The issue will be how that eclipse will materialise. Will it be gradual, will the United States graciously cede the space or will it be taken up by a multiplicity of rising states?

In the meantime, that other great state, India, will also be on the rise with its huge youthful population. So, in all probability, we will be looking at some concert of powers in the Pacific and Indian Oceans, rather than a balance of power which has often been the device of an uneasy peace.

All of this should tell us that while developments of this kind are as uncertain as they are incapable of prediction, for a country like Australia, they nevertheless hold out huge opportunity.

This is why, I believe, we must always be outgoing. We must be alert, dextrous and positive: never defensive.

For these reasons, I found myself at odds with some of the text of the government's 2009 Defence White Paper. Much of it is unexceptional, saying such things as our 'primary operational environment' more or less ends at the Equator and recognising that 'China will be the strongest Asian military power'. Nothing much wrong with that. But it goes on to discuss what it describes as 'the remote but plausible potential of confrontation' between us and 'a major power adversary', not suggesting who that power might be. Obviously it will not be the United States. You are then left to take your pick of China, Japan, India or Indonesia. And the Paper goes on to outline the kind of military capabilities Australia might need to respond to this contingent risk; foreshadowing an increase in our submarine fleet from six to twelve vessels, quadrupling the number of our bigger warships while acquiring cruise-missile-type offensive capabilities.

Taken as a whole, the Paper struck an ambivalent tone about our likely new strategic circumstances and what we should do about them. Including, for instance, failing to give us an indication as to whether it foresaw the growth of China's military capabilities as a natural and legitimate thing for a rising economic power or whether, to the contrary, it was something we should regard as a threat and for which we should plan.

The fact is, Australia does not know and cannot divine what sort of new order might obtain as Chinese economic and military power grows in the face of relative American decline. And complicating that assessment, China rising in the company of other rising regional powers.

A region of this kind might turn out to be as peaceful and as prosperous for Australia as the one we have had since the end of the Vietnam War; a place where all powers have a role and where Australia is open to have whatever relationship it wants with any of them. But then again it might not turn out like this. The region may become more problematic.

This is why a defence policy is a must-have contingency against adverse developments. But importantly, a defence policy is not enough on its own: it has to be woven into a view of the region and that view can only be encapsulated within a foreign policy.

Too often, Australia has created problems for itself when its defence policy has gotten ahead of its foreign policy; Vietnam and Iraq are prime examples.

Let me conclude on this point.

Cooperative regionalism was the idea that propelled me down the path of having Asia Pacific states meet at head of government level in

1992. That initiative was of its essence, positive, outgoing and alert to opportunity, carrying with it a message of participation with invitations to inclusiveness.

These characteristics must, I believe, be the hallmarks of an Australian foreign policy in these new times.

We should never return to a posture of fear or reaction of the kind that prevailed during the Menzies years nor should we look to position ourselves as a comfortable accessory tucked under someone else's armpit.

If John Curtin had lived in these times, I would be pretty sure he would be saying much the same thing.

3

LEADERSHIP AND CHANGE

Second Asian Leadership Conference 2008,
Seoul,
21 February 2008

The Second Asian Leadership Conference in South Korea hosted by the principal broadsheet newspaper, the Chosun Ilbo, *and attended by a number of former leaders, presented Paul Keating with an opportunity to lay out some of his own views on the contemporary international scene. Here, delivered extemporaneously, is the response Paul Keating made to earlier contributions by Henry Kissinger, Goh Chok Tong and Ichiro Ozawa. The relatively short intervention concentrates down the Keating world view: the unprecedented 60-year-long period of peace and prosperity; the lost post-Cold War opportunity of putting together a new representative structure of world power; the legitimacy of a rising China and the folly of endeavouring to contain it; the political obduracy of Japan's political establishment, especially towards China; and the need for China to pursue a more propitious economic policy, allowing its real exchange rate to reconfigure its economy while leavening economic issues between itself and the United States.*

I WOULD LIKE TO CONCENTRATE on the essence of Senior Minister Goh's keynote address and broadly endorse his appeal for a new world structure. This is something he and I spoke of when we were both Prime Ministers in 1992. In fact it was that thought, a new structure, which drove the APEC construct and the APEC Leaders' Meeting. We saw the opportunity at the end of the Cold War of open regionalism and while we were able to have an influence on this part of the world, given the limitations on the influence of our countries and their size, we were not able to have commensurate influence elsewhere.

We need to see the world in the following terms. There were three long waves of growth in the twentieth century: 1909 to 1929, then nothing until 1947; then a second wave from 1947 till 1974 and then the third wave, in which we are still currently, which began in 1982. So we are now in the twenty-sixth year of this third long period of prosperity, and if we remove the eight years between 1974 and 1982, we have, pretty much, enjoyed a 60-year continuous period of growth. This is unprecedented.

Along with that, of course, we have had a contiguous period of peace; in fact in modern history you had to have grown up at the end of the Napoleonic Wars to have witnessed a similar period of peace, before the Franco–Prussian Wars, and somewhat later, the First World War. So it is the peace, the absence of world wars and the prosperity which has got us to this point. We have now seen, as a result of US magnanimity, the development of Japan, South Korea and Western Europe. But now we are seeing an altogether different influence, on which the US has had only a moderate bearing, and that is the growth of East Asia.

When the Cold War finished we had an opportunity to put together a new world order, where the big states like India and China were more adequately represented in the structure of world power. Instead, the G8 contains countries like Italy and Canada, not countries like India or China. The ball on that structure was dropped at the beginning of the Clinton presidency. Through two Clinton presidencies we had no movement from the template of 1947. When we had an opportunity, with the George W Bush presidency, to move away from the template of 1947, I believe that administration opted for the wrong policy—a policy of exceptionalism, giving up liberal internationalism at a time when it could have worked most powerfully for the United States. As a result, four American presidential terms have gone by without us coming to a new settlement about power in the world, with these great states of a billion or more people each, rising both socially and economically. So the reordering and reweighting is now long overdue: it is to be hoped that the next American President will start thinking about a more representative system of world governance and how that system will better guarantee American security and stability 30 years from now. We have to move on from the framework we developed at the end of the Second World War.

If we look at the world economy, the majority of us depended on the United States for its locomotive energy. The United States economy is $12 trillion of GDP: $12 thousand billion and it grows at roughly 3 per cent a year. That's $360 billion of new wealth. If you look at China, albeit about $4 trillion of GDP, in US-dollar terms, and growing at 11 per cent, thereby generating about $440 billion of new wealth. Let us not split hairs, call it about $400 billion each of new wealth. So the increment to wealth, progress and a generally better world has come with the advent of China.

One of the lessons I want to see come from a conference like this is that we pick up the lessons of Europe at the end of the nineteenth century. Efforts then to contain Bismarck's creation, the German Empire, by Russia, Britain and France, among other things, ended in tears with the First World War. There were other influences, of course, in Germany itself which led to that outcome, but nevertheless, in the West, those states cavilled at Bismarck's creation. For most of the last 30 years, the West has cavilled, perhaps quietly cavilled, at Deng Xiaoping's creation.

I think it would be a grave mistake by the world or indeed, for any state to try and contain China. China, I believe, is a force for stability. It is a legitimate partner of the United States in the quest for stability. And here the operative word is *stability*, which has given us the peace, the growth, freed us from human misery and lifted our incomes.

So what should we do to maintain that stability and the peace? First and foremost, I believe that China must be welcomed as a new major player in the world, and given appropriate recognition and standing in world forums.

Which brings me to the point Senior Minister Goh Chok Tong made earlier about Japan and China. It is a great pity that 70 years on since Manchuria that the enmities between Japan and China still exist. And it's a great wonder that the Liberal Democratic Party and Japanese people more generally, clever as they are, in some way, 70 years later are still trying to prove a point about militarism in the 1930s.

Japan with 160 million people, with a rapidly deteriorating demographic, should be seizing this point in history to find a lasting accommodation with China. And that accommodation with China can be had. The Chinese want it, and I should think the great body of Japanese people would want it. But the political system, especially the LDP, has dragged the chain and dragged itself along for half a century in denial of truth and what is right.

If China and Japan reach a point of equilibrium, what matters in North Korea now will matter far less. Henry Kissinger's point this morning is entirely correct. That is, if North Korea gets away with nuclear proliferation, other nuclear horses will also bolt. We cannot wait for a situation where the acquisition of weapons in North Korea becomes an excuse for either China or Japan to consider lifting their military profiles, supposedly in protection of themselves, but in reality frightening each other while destabilising the region. This is another reason I think we have now long passed the point where the old unrepresentative UN structure of governance can obtain much longer. With one vote, a little Pacific island has the same vote as China, which is, of course, nonsense. A nonsense structure produces a nonsense organisation and this is why the UN has withered as an independent force.

We have reached the point where we cannot go on pretending that what is happening in the East Asian hemisphere is not a seminal change to the world and that it is other than pro-stability.

Let me conclude with some points about the economic situation. Thirty years ago China was an agrarian country. Today it is the largest manufacturing state. Of course its real exchange rate had to rise. But attempts by the government of China to deny this by pushing down the nominal exchange rate will end in tears with many economic distortions. Inflation is one of them. I notice inflation in China is already running at 7 per cent. This had to happen. We have a big problem in respect of world financial imbalances. The United States needs a competitive depreciation against the rest of the world to repair its current account. It cannot get it. It cannot get it because China has been tying, opportunistically, its currency to the US dollar, while the Bank of Japan shadows the US dollar daily. What we have is a shadow dollar area which now makes up a very large part of world GDP. This means that America's adjustment falls much more heavily on those currencies which wear their heart on their sleeve; pricing themselves on volume and not by official intervention. The euro and the Australian dollar come to mind. China has to grow up and go its own way, as should Japan, instead of running permanently in the shadow and coattails of the United States. The American Federal Reserve can no longer pursue a policy, as we saw under Alan Greenspan, of offering a 1 per cent or 2 per cent cash rate and expect to fund its current account and budget deficits, especially with a falling currency. If it were not for Chinese and East Asian savings, the Americans would have difficulty funding their obligations. And without that cheap money policy their banks and financial institutions would not have stuffed their households full of cheap mortgages of the kind we are seeing default now.

It seems to me that it is within our hands and our scope to maintain a continuing economic expansion. It is also within our scope to maintain and develop proper structures for peace. That includes East Asia but also includes Europe. The mistaken policy of expanding NATO with Hungary, Poland and the Czech Republic, taking NATO's border right up to the west of the Ukraine, began the alienation of Russia. We brought Russia to within reach of our own camp in 1990 and now we've lost it. So a policy of magnanimity and representativeness—let's call it that—should apply also within Europe. That is, part of a more stable, wider world structure, where the US is the first amongst equals. Let's say a more sustainable, longer run structure.

4

APEC
Australia's Biggest Seat at its Biggest Table
Evatt Foundation,
Sydney,
23 August 2007

*As Prime Minister, Paul Keating proposed and with Bill Clinton had
built the APEC Leaders' Meeting. Fifteen years on from its inaugural
gathering, Australia was to host the 2007 meeting in Sydney under
the stewardship of John Howard. To mark the occasion, the Evatt
Foundation invited Paul Keating to sketch out the history of the APEC
meeting and to address the contingency issues which the 2007 meeting
might address. Paul Keating urges John Howard to lift his gaze and the
focus of the meeting by putting strategic issues on the agenda, such as
the armaments race taking place in North Asia. He also re-emphasises
that Australia's vital interests reside in the East Asian hemisphere and
not in the Middle East, and urges Australia to be itself rather than a
derivative power masquerading as someone else's deputy.*

SITTING DOWN TO A PRIVATE dinner one night in Tokyo as a guest of
my Treasury counterpart, the Japanese Minister of Finance, Kiichi
Miyazawa, in a moment of candour, asked me whether I thought the
Chinese would attack Japan.

Taken aback by the question, and one put so seriously, I immediately
replied, 'No, I do not'.

To which Mr Miyazawa then said quizzically, 'But why not?'

Both questions sent a political shiver through me, coming as they did from such an accomplished and worldly figure as Miyazawa.

What that conversation did for me was to underline something I had well known but had not concentrated upon: the unresolved issues between Japan and China flowing from their history during the Second World War and the period leading up to it.

Mr Miyazawa in the same conversation then asked me for a pen sketch of the personality of Mr Li Peng, the then Chinese Premier and other senior members of the Chinese politbureau.

Those remarks made it apparent to me that not only had the leadership of Japan's government, the Liberal Democratic Party, no understanding of Chinese thinking, but worse than that, had never met Chinese leaders.

Japan's imperial history and the history of the Cold War which followed it had kept the leadership of these two great nations apart to simmer in ignorance, resentment and mistrust.

It was the antipathies within this relationship that led me to conclude that something radical had to be done about the political architecture of north Asia and that that architecture had to also include the United States, Japan's strategic guarantor.

This was the major dynamic which encouraged me, as Prime Minister, to propose a head of government meeting among the major powers of the Asia Pacific. An idea of an Australian Prime Minister who knew that Australia's security would be put at risk if the countries of north Asia again resorted to military violence. And, not just Australia's security—the region's.

This was in 1992, fewer than three years after the Soviet Union had imploded, the Berlin Wall had come down and the Cold War had ended.

Twelve days after I had become Prime Minister, on 21 December 1991, I had the privilege of meeting and hosting a visit to Australia by the President of the United States George Herbert Bush—the second only visit by an American president to this country. On New Year's Day 1992 at Kirribilli House, I put to President Bush the idea of developing a heads of government body in the Asia Pacific to take the opportunity of regionalism of a kind which had formerly been put out of bounds by the bipolarity of the Cold War.

Until that time, United States policy in the Pacific had mostly been conducted by the United States Navy. The great majority of us really only remembered one head of government meeting between a Chinese Communist Party leader and an American president and that was the famous one held between Mao Zedong and President Richard Nixon.

There existed no political framework within which an American President, a Chinese President and a Japanese Prime Minister could meet one another, save for meetings of the high summitry kind which, however infrequent, could only ever include any two of them.

As a middle power, I saw Australia as having the opportunity of helping to reshape the political architecture of East Asia and the Asia Pacific in general, thereby adjusting power in the world to better suit Australia's interests. But it goes without saying that that which suited Australia's interests, conducting our national life in a context of peace and prosperity, would similarly suit the Asia Pacific, a region riven by bad history, massively damaged by conflicts and weighed down by poverty.

At the Kirribilli House meeting, President Bush's national security adviser, General Brent Scowcroft, told me that I had outlined to the President a strategy which the Americans had not themselves conceived and which, he said, the Americans were not in a position to put together. He said the moment the United States sought to approach China with a head of government apparatus which also included Japan, the Chinese would back off if the Japanese themselves had not done so.

President Bush also agreed with my proposition that such a body should necessarily include the countries of ASEAN, especially Indonesia, but Indonesia until that time had been one of the leaders of the non-aligned movement and there was no guarantee that even if we were able to bring in the Chinese and the Japanese, that we could do the same with the Indonesians.

The meeting finished with me promising the President that I would feel out heads of government around the region and that I would write to him more formally with an express proposal.

This I did on 3 April 1992, outlining the proposition and the progress in consultation I had made in the interim.

The President wrote back to me on 29 April 1992, saying, 'I believe the most effective means of moving your suggestion forward at the proper time would be for Australia to take the lead. Too prominent a US role could be counterproductive'.

I took the President at his word and wrote to Mr Kiichi Miyazawa in Japan, who had since become Prime Minister. He replied on 8 May 1992, saying that 'the support of other members of our region, above all the ASEAN countries, will be an essential requirement for success'. He then suggested I further discuss with the ASEAN countries the possibility of them joining Australia in taking up the initiative. And by referring to ASEAN, he meant, in the main, Indonesia. The Japanese viewed ASEAN as Indonesia with the other Southeast Asian states more or less tacked on.

So, there it was—I had to get the shy and cautious President Soeharto to agree, despite Indonesia's non-aligned status, to be part of a new open regionalism and if I got Soeharto, I would get Miyazawa, and if I got Miyazawa I would get Li Peng, and if I got Li Peng, I would get George Bush.

As it turned out, I got them all, but by the time I had, George H Bush had been replaced by Bill Clinton as President of the United States, so I had to begin afresh with a new US administration. So, this I did.

However, many people will recall that Bill Clinton had won the 1992 presidential election on the slogan 'It's the economy, stupid', attacking as he had, President Bush for what Clinton had described as Bush's adventurism in Iraq in 1991.

President Clinton made it plain to me that he would support an Asia Pacific Leaders' Meeting, provided the body had the complexion of an economic cooperation and trade body. Even though my proposal was for a highly strategic head of government grouping focused on the big political issues, Clinton was only prepared to entertain it if it had the look and feel of an economic and trade body.

This was why, in the end, I chose the APEC template for the Leaders' Meeting. In my mind there was nothing particularly common between APEC, the recently formed economic grouping which Bob Hawke had first proposed and the highly strategic body I had in mind. Mine could have been a grouping of just a dozen major states, but I chose to carry the acronym APEC onto the Leaders' Meeting to best secure Clinton's support.

In an initiative that proved again that good ideas generally find traction, President Clinton extended an invitation to an inaugural Asia Pacific Leaders' Meeting in 1993 in Seattle, the home of those two great American corporations, Boeing and Microsoft. He had chosen that city to paint a commercial and economic picture of the event, when in fact, of course, the event itself completely resembled the strategic body it truly was.

There is much debate now in academic circles about APEC, its structure and its agenda and what may be referred to as a kind of crowding out by other Asia Pacific regional fora.

In the regionalism which the end of the Cold War facilitated, in this part of the world, we have ASEAN, we have ASEAN Plus 3, we have the ASEAN Regional Forum, the East Asia Summit, as well as APEC itself, its Leaders' Meeting and its ministerial groups.

There are proposals around to sort these structures into economic and trade and military and security groupings, with the paramount political body being separate.

While much of this appeals to the neat and tidy mind, and I hope I have one of those myself, we risk mucking about with the Leaders' Meeting where we have a structure now where the United States President attends in person. Not the Secretary of State, but the President. And ditto for the President of China and the Prime Minister of Japan and the President of Indonesia.

This structure is of inestimable strategic value. Now we know that each year the American bureaucracy will be involved in preparing for the Leaders' Meeting to put the President in a position to be well briefed and to raise issues as needs be. Part of that brief will relate to the round of bilateral meetings which will precede and follow the full plenary session of the leaders. Not only does this give each leader the chance to meet counterparts, but it efficiently allows the doing of strategic business within the context of what is seen as an economic cooperation meeting. In other words, no preceding preening being required or huffing and puffing necessary—things which were always associated with summit meetings.

If there is any problem with the APEC structure, it is not that it is attended by some of the most powerful people in the world, it is that it is attended by too many of the not so powerful. When countries like Papua New Guinea, Chile and Peru were invited to join APEC, it was expanded such as to make it less efficient, with the interests of the principal players in East Asia being diluted to the interests of a greater whole.

This expanded compliment was a gift from the foreign ministers' club. A club which works on the more the merrier principle, not understanding that leaders will only turn up to organisations if those organisations are capable of doing things. Foreign ministers have a compulsion of never sending a customer away unsatisfied. It was that compulsion, to find a place for everybody, which expanded APEC to its current membership of twenty-one.

Nevertheless, oversized or not, the most important thing about the APEC Leaders' Meeting is that it actually exists. That there is actually a forum where leaders can get to know one another, develop better levels of understanding and with that, some modicum of trust.

In the lead-up to this, the Sydney meeting of the APEC leaders, all manner of economic and trade issues are being suggested for the agenda, such as climate change and multilateral trade facilitation.

Normally, the success or otherwise of an APEC meeting depends on the imagination and ability of the host head of government to fashion the agenda and to see new initiatives into place. An international climate change declaration has been suggested for John Howard, as has further progress towards multilateral trade facilitation in the Doha context.

These matters are no doubt virtuous enough and John Howard, uncharacteristically, might have a burst of inspiration about them. I hope he does. But, for the meeting to concentrate on these things only, does, I believe, under-rate and under-sell its capacity for more difficult topics; topics of the strategic variety like the arms race currently being run in north Asia and the risk posed by the continued proliferation of nuclear weapons.

These topics are not capable of being resolved in the local strategic talk-shop, the ASEAN Regional Forum. That organisation, by the way, was established with the help of Australia, most particularly through the work of Gareth Evans, the then foreign minister.

Discussion in the ASEAN Regional Forum is useful and valuable but it is only the heads of government who can really make a difference. Certainly, heads of government are not going to move on issues unworked or unprepared, but they can work on the grand topics if they are somewhat pre-cooked and prepared. This is where the APEC leaders or even some subgroup of the full meeting can do truly useful work.

As things stand, the most dangerous part of the world is not the Middle East, though of course that is dangerous, nor even those always simmering tensions between India and Pakistan. In my opinion the most seriously dangerous part of the world is North Asia, within that triangle of unresolved tensions between China and Japan and the Korean peninsula.

In the 60 years since the end of hostilities in the Second World War, the antipathy between China and Japan has only intensified. The ruling Liberal Democratic Party in Japan maintains the pretence that Japan was only defending its interests in the Pacific theatre of the Second World War, while the Chinese resent this denial and lack of atonement for atrocities against them by declaring that they will never suffer Japanese hegemony ever again.

Whether you put it down to that underlying tension or not, we are now witnessing an arms race on either side of the Sea of Japan. For a country which has long prided itself on the 'self-defence' nature of its armed forces, eschewing an offensive armoury, Japan's latest weapon acquisitions blur the line between defence and offence.

Japan has, for a long time now, been developing a competent blue-water navy including VTOL and helicopter-type aircraft carriers, as well as squadrons of its own fighter jets with mid-air refuelling capabilities, giving it reach and projection. Japan has also expressed interest in acquiring the American-designed and built F-22 Raptor, a stealth fighter designed to carry off offensive tasks such as penetrating air space dominated by others.

China, for its part, has grown its airforce to around 2500 combat-capable aircraft plus roughly 800 combat-capable naval aircraft. Many of these aircraft do date from earlier periods, yet China has acquired fourth-generation fighter aircraft such as 140 Russian SU-30s and 60 Jian-10s. China also has nuclear-attack submarine capability as well as its nuclear-tipped ICBM missiles.

There is a view that China's aircraft and missile delivery system build-up is designed more from a defensive standpoint, to complicate any future US or Japanese calculations in the event either one or both of those states seek to come to Taiwan's aid. Defensive or otherwise, this build-up is part of the continuing growth in armaments in North Asia.

South Korea, alert to the bristling equipment procurement of its neighbours and the ever present threat from the North, is now seriously upgrading its defence material to give it at least a fighting chance in any skirmish.

Meanwhile, back at the ranch, the Pakistanis have been supplying nuclear technology and materials to North Korea, which has proudly declared itself to be a nuclear weapons state with both the capacity to build nuclear weapons and to competently deliver them around the region. Something which horrifies the Japanese.

These issues, I believe, should be at the top of the APEC leaders' agenda. Yes, Doha is important. Climate change is important. But who is going to pop their head up on this one?

This is an issue which I believe Australia should place squarely on the leaders' agenda because we would be one of the countries to suffer from any outbreak of hostilities in this part of the world. Not to mention the other countries of the region.

Now is the time to get the focus on these things. To get a real conversation going about political and strategic accommodations in North Asia. To encourage China to include a future for Japan in its regional view of things and to oblige Japan to include a point of accommodation with China which goes to Japan's economic future, its declining population and some real recognition of the none-too-laudable parts of its twentieth-century history.

Real leadership of the APEC meeting is about getting these matters on to the agenda. In the first instance, all will resist it. The Chinese won't like it; the Japanese won't like it; and the Americans would probably regard it as an intrusion into the international game they usually conduct. But an Australian Prime Minister, particularly as host, should be able to do it. Certainly, no-one else will.

Australian foreign policy can make a difference but you have to dare to try.

The problem is, these issues are accentuating themselves. They are not going away, and American diplomacy, by itself, is unlikely to be effective in dealing with it unless it is pro-active and resolute. Frankly, I think this is hoping for too much.

These issues have to be worked on. They will not vanish because they are not being talked about. Look at the failure of US and NATO policy towards Russia.

Last week, Russian President Vladimir Putin decided to resume long-range nuclear bomber patrols over the Atlantic, Pacific and the Arctic for the first time since 1992. And Putin's office is backgrounding people that Russia may soon resume production of the TU-160 and TU-95 nuclear bombers.

Can you believe that?

This is happening because of Russian grievances about being left out of US and European arrangements since the end of the Cold War and by decisions of the US and NATO to build missile defence facilities around Russia's borders.

The US is now losing all influence over Russia. We do not want the same thing happening in our neck of the woods with China and Japan.

Let me recap here: I first proposed the APEC leaders' structure and built the consensus for it. And I knew what motivated me in doing it. It was to deal with the unresolved tensions between China and Japan and the latent capacity for conflict by building a broad regional body which included the United States with the direct involvement of its president.

Those aims and that motivation are as relevant today, fifteen years on, as they were then.

If APEC has become a talk-shop of debatable output, it is because the leaders who have shaped its agenda since its early and optimistic days have lacked an understanding of what it really is and what it is capable of.

International leaders like George Bush and Hu Jintao or Indonesia's Yudhoyono or Russia's Putin are hardly going to have their hearts racing over a discussion about trade facilitation or the removal of non-tariff barriers. This is the stuff of trade and foreign ministers' meetings, save for the big sweeps like the Bogor Trade Declaration which occupied centre stage at the second APEC meeting in Indonesia in 1994.

Officials are excellent at the incremental game of moving things like trade and facilitation agendas forward, but they are not good when it comes to divining strategic goals. Few of them think strategically, none has strategic power.

And the issues which existed at the beginning of the 1990s are not the issues which dominate now.

Then, China was on the ropes after Tiananmen Square and India was only just beginning the gradual opening of its economy.

The world is now a very different place and one of the things that makes it different are those security issues which attend great powers when they come among the world at large. Issues of the kind which attended Germany when Bismarck launched his creation on Europe in the third quarter of the nineteenth century. And we all know what that led to.

The nuclear genie which was set free in 1945 can now be possessed by any number of half-competent states and many of them are possessing it. But absent are the political command and weapons control systems that locked the genie down so successfully during the Cold War years.

Australia these days is a relatively small player in the world. There was a time when we punched well above our weight. For the moment, those days are over. I helped put the APEC Leaders' Meeting in place, and for our trouble we got a permanent seat at the table. It remains the most important table we sit at, certainly at head of government level. But before we become fascinated with the plethora of regional fora around us, we should at least appreciate what we have and what we can lay our name to.

One of the greatest pieces of software which Australia developed in the 1980s and mid-1990s was foreign policy and within our gift was APEC, the APEC Leaders' Meeting, the ASEAN Regional Forum, the Chemical Weapons Convention and the Cambodian Peace Accords, among other things, including the Canberra Commission on the Elimination of Nuclear Weapons.

None of that is happening today. These days we dance to someone else's tune, as our commitment in the Middle East makes clear.

Australia's vital interests are in East Asia. They are not in North America or Southern Africa or Europe. They are here, here where we live, in the fastest growing part of the world. It is in this region that Australia's destiny lies; it is only in this region that our security can be found and that will only happen when our foreign policies and our economic and trade policies are in appropriate and sensible alignment.

The Howard government's ambivalence towards Asia and its willingness to throw our strategic eggs solely in the North American basket will cost us dearly down the years. We must go to Asia as Australians and not as some derivative outfit pretending to be someone else's deputy. The quicker we get back to being ourselves, the earlier will be our true integration with the region around us and our influence over it.

5

THE DEATH OF PRESIDENT SOEHARTO
Sydney,
31 January 2008

Paul Keating's article on the death of President Soeharto of Indonesia,
published in the Sydney Morning Herald *and* The Age, *lays out*
the case as to why Soeharto had been Australia's principal strategic
benefactor between 1965 and 2005. How Soeharto had provided the
strategic ballast to Southeast Asia at a time when he was rescuing
100 million Indonesians from abject poverty.

Paul Keating takes to task the Australian media, especially the
Fairfax press and the ABC, for what he calls their get-square policy
on Soeharto over the death of five Australian journalists in Balibo in
Timor. He reminded readers that the Sydney Morning Herald *in its*
rabidness had actually editorialised in favour of Australia mounting
a military invasion of Indonesian East Timor. The article paints a
portrait of Soeharto at odds with the stereotypical one common to the
Australian media.

THE DEATH OF SOEHARTO, THE former President of Indonesia, gives all
Australians a chance to assess the value of his life and the relationship
between Indonesia and Australia.

More than any figure in the post-Second World War period, including
any American president, President Soeharto, by his judgement, goodwill
and good sense, had the greatest positive impact on Australia's strategic
environment and, hence, on its history.

In the 40 years since he came to power in 1965, Indonesia has been the ballast in Southeast Asian stability and the foundation stone upon which ASEAN was built.

Soeharto took a nation of 120 million people, racked by political turmoil and poverty, from near disintegration to the orderly, ordered and prosperous state that it is today.

In 1965, countries like Nigeria and Zimbabwe were in the same position as Indonesia then. Today, those countries are economic and social wrecks. By contrast, Indonesia is a model of harmony, cohesion and progress. And the principal reason for that is Soeharto.

We can only imagine what Australia's strategic position would be like if Indonesia's 230 million people degenerated into a fractured lawless state reminiscent of Nigeria or Zimbabwe.

For the last 40 years, we have been spending roughly 2 per cent of GDP on defence—about $20 billion a year in today's dollars. That figure would be more like seven to eight times that, about $150 billion today, if Indonesia had become a fractured, politically stricken state.

Had General Soeharto's New Order Government not displaced the Sukarno government and the massive PKI Communist Party, the postwar history of Australia would have been completely different. A Communist-dominated Indonesia would have destabilised Australia and all of Southeast Asia.

So why have Australians regarded Indonesia so suspiciously, especially over the last quarter century, when it is evident that Indonesia has been at the fulcrum of our strategic stability?

Unfortunately, I think the answer is Timor and the wilful reporting of Indonesian affairs in Australia by the Australian press.

That press has, in the main, been the Fairfax press and the ABC. Most particularly and especially the *Sydney Morning Herald* and, to a lesser extent, *The Age*.

This rancour and the misrepresentation of the true state of Indonesian social and economic life can be attributed to the get-square policy of the media in Australia for the deaths of the Balibo Five. The five Australian journalists who were encouraged to report from a war zone by their irresponsible proprietors and who were shot and killed by the Indonesian military in Timor.

This event was sheeted back to Soeharto by journalists of the broadsheet press. From that moment, in their eyes, Soeharto became a cruel and intolerant repressor whose life's work in saving Indonesia from destruction was to be viewed, and only viewed, through the prism of Timor.

Rarely did journalists ever mention that Soeharto was President for ten years before he did anything about Timor. He was happy to leave the poverty-stricken and neglected enclave in his archipelago to Portugal, with its 300-year history of hopeless colonisation. Soeharto had enough trouble dragging Indonesia from poverty without needing to tack on another backward province.

But in mid-1975, Communist-allied military officers took control in Portugal and its colonies abroad were taken over by avowedly Marxist regimes. In Timor, a leftist group calling itself the Revolutionary Front for an Independent East Timor, or Fretilin, staged a coup, igniting a civil war.

When Fretilin overran the colony by force, Soeharto's government became alarmed. This happened at the height of the Cold War. Saigon had fallen in April of that year. Fretilin then appealed to China and Vietnam for help. Fearing a Cuba on his doorstep, Soeharto reluctantly decided on military intervention.

In his 33 years as President, he embarked upon no other foreign exploit. And he would not have bothered with Timor, had Fretilin not made the going too rough. Indeed, Ramos Horta told the *Sydney Morning Herald* in 1996 that 'the immaturity, irresponsibility and bad judgment of the East Timorese provoked Indonesia into doing what it did'. Xanana Gusmao also told anyone who would listen that it had been a 'bad mistake' for Fretilin to present itself as a Marxist outfit in 1975.

But none of this stopped a phalanx of Australian journalists, mostly from the Fairfax stable and the ABC's *Four Corners*, from reporting Indonesian affairs from that time, such that Australians could only view the great economic transformation of Indonesia and the alleviation of its poverty and its tolerance primarily through the warped and shattered prism of Timor.

The *Sydney Morning Herald* even editorialised in favour of an Australian invasion of Timor, then Indonesian territory. That is, right upfront about it, the *Sydney Morning Herald* urged the Australian government to invade Indonesia. So rabid has Fairfax been about Indonesia and so recreant of Australia's national interest has it been.

Even as late as this week, the *Herald* claimed the achievements of Soeharto's New Order Government were built on sand, nominating Indonesia reeling from crisis to crisis after 1998 when the *Herald* knows that Soeharto did precisely the right thing in calling the IMF in to help and that the IMF, operating under US Treasury prescriptions, kicked the country and Soeharto to pieces.

The decline in Indonesia after 30 years of 7 per cent compound growth under Soeharto had little to do with Soeharto and everything to do with the Asian financial crisis and the short-sighted and ill-informed IMF.

But, more than that, Australian journalists knew but failed to effectively communicate that not only did Soeharto hold his country together, he insisted that Indonesia be a secular state; that is, a Muslim country but not an Islamic or fundamentalist one. In other words, not an Iran.

Wouldn't you imagine that such an issue would be a matter of high and primary importance to communicate to the Australian community? That on our doorstep, there is a secular Indonesian state and not a religious one, run by Sharia law? And wouldn't you, in all reasonableness, give Soeharto full marks for keeping that vast archipelago as a civil society unrepressed by fundamentalism?

Look what happened to us in Bali at the hands of a handful, literally a handful, of Islamic fundamentalists. Imagine the turmoil for Australia if the whole 230 million of Indonesia had a fundamentalist objection to us. But this jaded bunch of Australian journalists could only report how Soeharto was corrupt because his son Tommy might have elbowed his way into some carried equity with an American telephone company or his daughter something with a road builder. True as those generalisations might have been, in terms of the weight of Australia's interests, the deeds of Soeharto's public life massively outweigh anything in his private affairs.

I got to know Soeharto quite well. He was clever and utterly decisive and had a kind view of Australia. The peace and order of his country, its religious and ethnic tolerance, and the peace and the order of Southeast Asia came from his goodwill towards neighbouring states and from his wisdom. He was self-effacing and shy to a fault. One had to tease him out of himself to get him going, but once he got going, his intellectualism took over.

Soeharto lived in what we would call in Australia a rather old and shabby McMansion in Jakarta. I have been there on a number of occasions. He lived as simply as anyone of his high standing could live.

But *Time* magazine claimed that Soeharto has stashed away $30-billion-odd, as if those ning-nongs would know, presumably so he could race off to live it up in Miami or in the Bahamas. Errant nonsense. Soeharto was an Indonesian who was always going to remain an Indonesian. He lived a simple life and could never have changed that.

I do not doubt that his rapacious family had the better of him and got away with lumps of capital that they had not earned. Soeharto was a disciplined leader, but not a disciplined father. But to compare him with the likes of Marcos is nothing short of dastardly.

The descriptions of Soeharto as a brutal dictator living a corrupt high life at the expense of his people and running an expansionist military regime are untrue. Even Soeharto's annexation of Timor was not expansionist. It had everything to do with national security and nothing to do with territory.

Like all leaders, Soeharto had his failings. His greatest failing was to underestimate the nature of the society he had nurtured. As his economic stewardship had led to food sufficiency, education, health and declines in infant mortality, so too those changes had given rise to a middle class as incomes rose. Soeharto should have let political representation grow as incomes grew. But he distrusted the political classes. He believed that they would not put the national interest first, had no administrative ability and were utterly indecisive, if not corrupt. He told me this on a number of occasions. He would not let the reins go. Partly because he did not want to lose them, partly because he really had no one to give them to.

Soeharto's problem was he had too little faith in his own people, the very people he cared for most.

Whatever political transition he may have wished to have had, it all blew up on him with the Asian financial crisis of 1997–98. He had no democratic transition in place and in the economic chaos, political forces wanted him to go.

In January 1998, nearly two years after I had left the prime minister-ship of Australia, at my own initiative and my own expense, I flew to Jakarta to see him the day he signed the IMF agreement with the IMF Managing Director, Michel Camdessus.

The IMF had tragically overplayed its hand the previous November and Soeharto was giving it a chance to dig itself out of a hole. He had a small window of opportunity. I thought that as a former head of government who was on friendly terms with him, I at least owed him advice of a kind I knew he would never get inside Indonesia: to take the opportunity of the IMF interregnum to say that he, Soeharto, would contest the next election but that he would not complete the term. That he would stay long enough to see the IMF reforms into place and then hand the presidency over to his Vice President.

Had he taken this advice, the process of political transformation would have been completely orderly. And a new administration could set up the organs of democracy.

I discussed this issue with Lee Kuan Yew in Singapore and Prime Minister Goh Chok Tong, both of whom had Soeharto's and Indonesia's best interests at heart. Both gentlemen believed that I was in a better position to broach this subject with President Soeharto than either of them. For two hours I had President Soeharto in his house with his State Secretary Moerdiano and his interpreter Widodo. Fifteen minutes into the conversation when I was making the case why he should step down, he stopped Widodo's translation and took my advice in English directly. Moerdiano said to me in an aside at the door, 'I think you have got him'.

Soeharto followed me to the door, put his arms around my shoulders and said 'God bless you' as I left. As it turned out, I didn't quite have him, and he hung on thinking he could slip through one more time.

But the crisis and the behaviour of the IMF with the American Treasury had marooned him. Completely determined to act constitutionally, he turned over his singular power, at his own initiative, to his Vice President to avoid any upheaval of the kind Indonesia had experienced during earlier transitions.

The new president, Habibie, then, by all due process, picked up the reins of government to deal with the ongoing financial reconstruction and the long process of democratisation.

When the Attorney General Robert McClelland and I arrived in Indonesia for his funeral last Monday, we drove the 30-odd kilometres from the airport at Solo to the mausoleum where he would be buried alongside his wife. For not one metre of those 30-odd kilometres was there no person present. In some places they would be six and eight deep, all holding their baskets of petals to throw at his cortège. They all knew they were burying the builder of their society and all felt the moment.

How many Australian leaders would have a million or so people to grieve for them beside the roadway? Soeharto's funeral was a tribute to what his life truly meant. I felt honoured to have been there but more than that, to have known him.

6

JOHN CURTIN'S WORLD AND OURS

The John Curtin Prime Ministerial Library Anniversary Lecture,
Curtin University of Technology,
Perth,
5 July 2002

*Paul Keating uses the 2002 John Curtin Memorial Lecture to
sketch out his views on political leadership: how Prime Minister
Curtin had urged Australians to think about a new world: one of
engagement with our neighbours, guided by an Australian foreign
policy operating from an Australian national economy. In the address
he further develops his theme on the need for a representative and
cooperative world structure where the vast states of India and China
are given a place in the institutional power sharing, and how US
exceptionalism of the George W Bush variety could not suffice as an
organising principle of world governance. In the address Paul Keating
also speaks of the long waves of world economic growth, suggesting
that the then current growth phase, which had begun in 1982, would
end 25 years later, in 2007. The address was given six years before the
Global Financial Crisis of 2008.*

EVEN IF WE ARE ABLE to interrogate the people involved, even if we take
part ourselves in the events we describe, the causes and consequences
of human actions will always be wrapped in doubt and seen quite
differently by different observers. Perhaps this is especially true of

political actions, which play across so much broader an arena of human activity than most.

So those of us looking back from 2002 need to approach John Curtin with due caution.

Leaders are significant in history. There is more to history than the determinism of events; personalities do matter, the scope of their minds matters, their courage matters, their capacity to make people believe, matters. And leaders carry that singular burden, responsibility. Being trustee of the nation's safety and its future directions, and the pressure that that involves, makes a leader's thought processes different from other ministers or officials.

Those of us who have been in public life know that an important decision can emerge from an unlikely juncture of policy, fact, reflection and emotion. A Cabinet discussion can veer from one point to another guided by contributions which can propel an argument way beyond or way beside that which might have been expected when the discussion opened.

The same with leaders. While most who matter develop their minds with the gymnastics of the issues they encounter, and the vagaries of public life in general, they are, in the end, all prisoners of their own DNA: their own prejudices, their own experiences, their upbringing.

Talking about leaders today is difficult enough; talking about them 60 years ago is little more than speculation. We know things they said and believed, the events they were associated with, even the ambience that surrounded them. We can get at certain things, their motives, etcetera. But we cannot know them. We may revere them, and that may be important to us, but we cannot know them.

I became Prime Minister in December 1991, a few weeks after the fiftieth anniversary of Curtin's appointment as Prime Minister. My four years as Prime Minister tracked his four years, from the fiftieth anniversary of the fall of Singapore in February 1992 right through to the fiftieth anniversary of VP Day in 1995, though he, of course, had gone by VP Day. Through each twist and turn of the Pacific War I felt I was in the lee of Curtin's trajectory or at least, in some way, connected to his consciousness of the events. As much as I thought I knew of the Pacific War, the punctuation of those four years by anniversaries of events of strategic significance drove the meaning of it home to me more poignantly.

A number of people have remarked that, next to Curtin, among Australian Prime Ministers, I had made more speeches on the war than anyone else and I am sure this is true. I do not claim anything by it other than that it gave me a much closer idea of the travails Curtin endured and the sequence in which he endured them.

And they make a second point—that history is made but often not as the makers should like it. John Curtin would have much preferred to have been a great peacetime Prime Minister, whereas I was never more at home than when my back was to the wall. Not that in my ministerial life I had not spent much of my time in that position—I had—but I might have enjoyed some more competent enemies than the remnants of our failed upper class, the Liberals with whom I seemed to be slated to always deal.

So it is difficult to pin Curtin down. We can talk about the ebb and flow of events; we can discern some coordinates. There is a certain clarity to them and some of the general experiences that Labor governments have had.

For one reason or another, Labor governments somehow seem to end up with the rough end of the historical pineapple.

The Labor government of Hughes found itself in the mayhem of the First World War. Scullin inherited the whirlwind of the Depression. The Whitlam government came to office virtually at the end of the postwar wave of growth, as inflation was beginning to accelerate. The Hawke government came to it after years of structural and fiscal neglect by Fraser and Howard, with investment falling and inflation flying, though fortunately at the beginning of another long technological wave of activity.

There have been three such long waves of growth and development in the twentieth century: 1904 to 1929, 1947 to 1974 and 1982 until now. Each has a duration of about 25 years. The first was driven by the internal combustion engine and petrochemicals, the second by aviation, plastics and consumption and the third by the information revolution, the personal computer and the growth of digital technology generally and by more open international product and financial markets.

Curtin was around in the trough between 1929 and 1947. And not just the trough, the dumper of the Second World War. Conscripted to serve in the political vacuum created by Menzies, his first ministerial job was that of Prime Minister.

Curtin was, I believe, correct in calling the return of Australia's Sixth Division Australia's Dunkirk and in saying that the 'fall of Singapore opens the battle for Australia'.

In many respects his predicament was very much akin to Churchill's. Churchill became Prime Minister in 1940 when the strategy of the Conservative government of Chamberlain collapsed. The Conservatives hated Liberals more than they did Labor people and even though Churchill had rejoined their ranks they regarded him as illegitimate; an unrepentant adventurer, a bounder. They hated giving him the job. The British establishment was torn between what it might have to do—defend Britain—and what it preferred to do—come to terms with Hitler. But in their own conniving way they knew there could be no terms without the ability to fight on and that Halifax, their favourite man, was not up to it.

So they took Churchill. Within weeks, Hitler had subjugated Holland and Belgium and was already controlling northern France. The standoff at Calais and Dunkirk followed.

In a similar way, Curtin got the job after Menzies' leadership had collapsed, just before the Japanese overran the Malaya Peninsula and Singapore. He expected the battle for Australia at the same time that Churchill had expected the Battle of Britain.

Island nations, both of them, Australia and Britain were shrouded by a screen of enemies. Britain's battle did come; Australia's was thwarted by our defence at Kokoda, by the Americans in the Coral Sea and at Midway where Japan's naval projection capacity was dealt a terminal blow. But Curtin was not to know these things when Singapore fell and the Dutch East Indies was overrun. He had to steel himself for the fight and the country with him.

A tough call for a fellow who for a large part of the 1930s was left loitering on the political periphery.

John Edwards, in a lecture last year, made the important point that Curtin not only provided the leadership through the worst of the war, he also provided it for the coming peace. Curtin, thinking of Australia as a continent and all of those within it as one nation, believed we should have a national economy, with a national income tax and a central bank. Instruments that allowed the Commonwealth government to run fiscal and monetary policy on a national basis.

The Curtin political meteorite burnt its way across the heavens broadly straddling two other significant political events: Menzies' collapse in 1941 and his renaissance in 1949. The four years of Chifley were largely filled with the postwar reconstruction which began with Curtin's White Paper and the putting in place of the mechanics of a return to a peacetime economy.

The greatest direct political beneficiary of Curtin's leadership was Menzies. He left Curtin in the maelstrom of history in 1941 and, being the complete opportunist, climbed back to power on Curtin's insightful economic work and Chifley's painstaking efforts in reordering the economic pieces.

A political dandy of the Edwardian kind, Menzies ingratiated himself to an electorate tired of sacrifice and hankering for easier and better times.

But history's prizes go to the leaders who make the turns and it was Curtin, and Chifley with him, who made the turn. The strategic turn away from Britain to the United States and the economic turn from six state economies to a national one. And with the migration policy, a recognition that Australia had to engage the world, that it could not exist in splendid isolation, that it had to eschew exclusiveness in favour of magnanimity and not go on conjuring distinctions between the civic and the human community. These were very big changes.

By dint of conscientiousness, passion and commitment Curtin served Australia with high distinction and built up a huge head of goodwill for the Labor Party and for his administration.

Words are the currency of politics and John Curtin understood the power of words. He had a good turn of phrase, a sharpness of mind, a 'studied elegance', according to the *Sydney Morning Herald* at the time. He was a storyteller.

One of the important jobs of political leaders is to interpret the future to the present. At its essence this task means knowing deep within oneself what the story is and then conveying it in words sharp and potent enough to seize the attention of an electorate that is half-listening at best and persuading them to it.

But words can be used either to obscure or to clarify. To fudge debate or to sharpen it. As we can see in Australia at this moment, words are being used to blur meaning and to distort reality. Phrases like 'Pacific solution' or 'practical reconciliation' or 'queue jumpers' come to mind.

In public life there is nothing more noble than the well argued, articulate political speech. A political personality is developed to think, to reason, to explain and to propose matters of state. The political speech, old as it is as a medium, is hard to beat. It deserves to survive political spin, the ten-second grab, the simple, uncritical, anonymous questions at the doorstop. All the devices that absolve the politician from explaining, indeed, thinking.

Curtin used language to turn a nation's head; to divine a new world and to lead Australia into it.

If we think of the indelible stamp Curtin left on Australia it is, most obviously, in the area of foreign policy. The war, I suppose, as much as what he made of it, did that. And in particular, the turn to the United States, notwithstanding his deep reluctance to rely only on that commitment. A turn made necessary by Japan's attack on Australia; a turn made possible by Japan's attack on the United States. But it changed everything that came after.

Foreign policy is, of course, always a continuum. It has to deal with the world as we really find it rather than one we might prefer. Before

Curtin, Australia never really had a foreign policy. Today it is the way we define ourselves to the world; a mosaic which comprehends, or should comprehend, the manifest complexities that the modern nation must deal with.

Australian foreign policy has been conceived taking into account the many issues and influences. Perhaps the primary one has been the limited scale of our population. Currently there are nineteen million of us and perhaps we have always seemed larger by virtue of the fact that, unique to us, we inhabit a continent.

Population has invariably been the driver of GDP and with a limited population Australia has had, in world terms, modest levels of gross domestic product. In other words, we have never possessed the economic power to either defend ourselves or to project military power. So the unilateralist option has not been one for us.

It is fair to say that both sides of the political debate recognise that reality. But notwithstanding the reality, two distinct or contending ideas have emerged as to how Australia secures itself in the world.

The conservative side of politics has largely kept to the view that Australia, in Menzies' phrase, needed 'great and powerful friends' to protect us.

The long thread of this policy began with the conservative view that Australia did not need a foreign policy at all because the policy of the imperial government was the relevant policy; the one upon which we were entitled to rely.

Indeed, in 1938 RG Casey, the conservative External Affairs Minister, said:

> As to a foreign policy for Australia, personally I am against those who say we should have an Australian foreign policy simply for the sake of having it. British foreign policy may be regarded in a very real sense as Australian foreign policy.

Following the fall of Singapore and the collapse of British power in East Asia, the imperial policy view was no longer credible. Almost seamlessly, Menzies' Liberal Party switched to the United States, investing that country with the role of our new protector-in-chief. And you do not need to be a political scientist to know that that view has been maintained with the Harold Holt mantras about LBJ and more latterly, John Howard's ambition to be the regional deputy.

The alternate contending view is that we should use our limited economic and strategic strength to build coalitions with likeminded countries, especially those in the region, rather than to bet everything on a strategic guarantor. This view largely characterises the Labor side of the discussion from Bert Evatt's work at the founding of the United Nations, through that of John Dawkins in establishing the Cairns Group on global trade, or of Gareth Evans in developing the ASEAN Regional Forum. Indeed, my own work in establishing the APEC Leaders' Meeting goes to the very core of what coalition-building and regionalism is all about.

But there is not a definite template here; after all, a Labor prime minister, John Curtin, established the alliance with the United States. However, it is clear that the first approach—the great and powerful friends one—has broadly been championed by conservative governments, while the coalition and institutional pathway has been broadly followed by Labor governments.

But you can also cut the debate about Australia's place in the world in a different and more complex way. In some ways the Australian community seems to divide into four main groups, crossing traditional political categories.

The first group—the Hansonites at the extreme end—want to isolate both the economy and the society from the outside world. Their economic agenda is to rebuild the tariff walls, their social one to keep out the foreigners and to return to a mythical golden age of Aussie values.

The second group—the anti-globalisation demonstrators and elements of the Democrats and the Greens—want to internationalise social issues but nationalise the economy. They oppose *globalisation* in its economic manifestation—free international trade, easy foreign direct investment—but are perfectly comfortable supporting extra-territorial claims for human rights or environmental action.

A third group believes the reverse. Parts of the Business Council of Australia and many in John Howard's Liberal Party would find a home here. They are all in favour of internationalising the economy, giving free rein to the free market, but they are damned if they think foreigners and international bodies like the UN should have anything to say about social policies here in Australia.

A fourth group—and it's obviously the one to which I belong—believes that for a country like Australia, with a small population tucked away in a corner of the Asia Pacific, economic openness, social inclusiveness and engagement with the outside world is the only way in which we can hope to prosper. The only approach that will give us the economic growth, the social confidence and the physical security to survive over the next century.

And we are going to need all of that, because the world we are entering looks increasingly dangerous.

With the end of the Cold War the Americans cried victory and walked off the field.

The ideological and geopolitical ambitions which began at the turn of the twentieth century played themselves to a standstill in 1989.

From 1990 onwards, the Americans and the rest of us had the chance to think about a new world in which ideology had essentially evaporated and we had the opportunity for the first time to think about running the world cooperatively.

In 1945, the American administration of Franklin Roosevelt had made a magnanimous effort to try to reshape Europe and the world. This time, however, it isn't the spirit of FDR in charge but the ghost of Manifest Destiny.

As the decade ended and the new millennium began it was clear that we were living in the Age of the Americans.

We found ourselves in a unipolar world where the US could make decisions about its strategic power outside any multilateral context. Once the Cold War ended, and the check of Soviet power was removed, the US was able to intervene with impunity—and so it did, with a frequency unmatched during the Cold War, in Panama, the Gulf War, Somalia,

Haiti, Bosnia and Kosovo. New technologies such as smart missiles made such interventions more feasible and less costly in terms of men and treasure.

The size of the US economy is around $10 trillion in GDP. Japan is $5 trillion, half its size. And Europe is about the same as the US.

But this does not give us a multipolar world.

The two largest single economies are the United States and Japan. Never in world history have we seen a position where the second-largest economic power has been a strategic client of the largest economic power. But we have witnessed this with Japan now for 50 years. This situation has let Japan rebuild itself, but it has denied it the confidence to stand on its own feet as a pole in its own right in what might otherwise have been a multipolar world.

The single market in 1992 and the advent of the euro have produced a Europe-wide economy for the first time. But while Europe is integrated economically it is not integrated politically. Certainly not militarily.

As a consequence, Europe has lacked the political and military unity to mark itself out as a strategic power. And the largest state in the EU, Germany, has for 50 years remained outside the permanent membership of the UN Security Council. Its capacity to act internationally in other ways was also impeded by the Allied settlement of 1945.

Only one large nation has the confidence and inner sense of itself to stand up and be counted. And this is China, the largest country in the world. China will inevitably be the epicentre of East Asia and a pole in its own right, but for the time being it is poor and preoccupied with its own development.

The 1990s saw the spread of globalisation and the huge accumulated attendant benefits to the US. Washington promoted the economics of globalisation—free and open product and financial markets. And it needed to have its savings augmented. It wanted a high-growth economy and therefore required its current account to be funded. Globalisation provided the wherewithal for this. But the US does not understand that a globalised economy requires a polity of similar scale to support it. That you cannot expect to draw benefits from integrated, interdependent markets while operating in a world that is unrepresentative and which is not run cooperatively.

Then came September 11. The terrorist attacks did not change the world. But they did change the United States. They also revealed the world more clearly and the trends in the international system which had been developing since the Cold War ended.

On the one hand, and in some parts of the globe, it was clear that the nation state had never been stronger. Not since the Roman Empire have we seen one country so dominate the world as the United States does now. It is the largest economy in the world and the only country with global military reach.

It spends as much on defence as the next eight highest-spending countries in the world combined. The entire GDP of Russia, its Cold War competitor, is just slightly more than American defence spending alone.

And despite the weaknesses revealed by the collapses of Enron and WorldCom, the US has a flexible and dynamic economy, and dominance in important technologies including IT and biotech.

Above all, it has willpower, a quality essential to any great power. FDR called it its 'righteous might'.

But elsewhere, a different world exists. A world in which the writ of the nation state does not run, where the rule of law cannot be enforced, where poverty, anarchy and disease destroy hope. Space where terrorist groups like Al Qaeda can grow and thrive.

Looking at the AIDS-devastated swathes of Africa or the ruins of Afghanistan or, in Australia's own front yard, the growing anarchy in Solomon Islands or Papua New Guinea, we see a world in which notions of national sovereignty are entirely artificial. Where the nation state does not provide the bare minimum of protection for its citizens.

To this point, I think most observers of the international situation would agree with the analysis.

Where the disagreement comes is over what we can or should do about this new form of unipolarity.

The emerging Bush doctrine, endorsed by John Howard, devalues deterrence in favour of pre-emption.

The sophisticated argument goes this way. You can only use military deterrence when there is a state able to be deterred. You can only use international law and multilateral rules where you have nations able to abide by them. And because the parts of the world where terrorists spawn often have no governments to deter, the US is entitled to take pre-emptive action in order to protect its own people.

The blunter—but perhaps more honest—argument goes like this. The United States has never been more powerful; its central strategic objective, therefore, should be to minimise any constraints on its power, whether in the form of direct competition from other states or pressure from multilateral organisations.

Either way, the emerging reality is that the old rules of national sovereignty, built up fitfully over centuries, no longer apply in large parts of the world; or, rather, they do not apply where the US determines they no longer apply.

So we have seen the US trying to weaken multilateral treaties that might otherwise constrain the undisciplined ambitions of many states. These make a long list now: the Anti-Ballistic Missile Treaty, the Comprehensive Test Ban Treaty, the Chemical Weapons Convention, the International Criminal Court, with potentially devastating implications for peacekeeping in Bosnia and elsewhere, the Kyoto Protocols and so on.

But the problem for the rest of us is that this unilateralist response from the US administration is not just to the anarchic world in which Al Qaeda can operate. It is also a response to the world where the nation state continues to operate—where the growing interconnections of a globalising economy and the information age make multilateral cooperation more important than ever before.

We need to ask ourselves whether US exceptionalism is an adequate central organising principle on which to build a new world.

Is it an enduring model that will help—in twenty, in ten, even in five years' time—Australia to understand the world better and to fund a place in it?

Does a war on terrorism provide a sufficient framework for understanding the role of the developing countries in the international community?

Does it help Australia to deal with the part of the world of greatest importance to it—Asia and the South Pacific?

Above all, does this model offer a way forward?

I do not think it does.

Australians are among the closest allies the US has. We share aspects of its culture and understand it better than most of the world does. There is great sentiment between us. But the US is the last remaining ideological great power. Does President Bush's rhetoric speak to us? I don't think so. And if it does not speak to us, how can it speak to the other great cultures—China, India, Africa? What can it say to them?

I'm in favour of pursuing terrorists globally. I'm in favour of Australian participation in a coalition to do it. I'm even in favour of pre-emptive action, including sometimes, in some limited circumstances, military pre-emption.

But why is the debate we are having couched *only* in terms of military pre-emption? Other forms of pre-emption exist. They are harder, though, and require knowledge, commitment, statecraft of a high order and sophisticated diplomacy. They do not always deliver quick results. But, as I suspect we are about to find in Israel and Palestine, and perhaps in Iraq too, they last longer.

Noting that 'America's founding fathers warned against the perils of power in the absence of checks and balances', the American scholar Kenneth Waltz asks, 'Is unbalanced power less of a danger in international than in national politics?'

And the answer is, of course, it isn't.

In 1944 Curtin said this:

Our remaining task is to think and plan so that [the] world [of our sons and daughters] may in truth be a new world. There can be no going back to the good old days. They were not good and they have truly become old. We have to point the way to better days.

Nearly 60 years on, his new world is our old one. The world of the Bretton Woods institutions laid the foundation for economic stability and postwar prosperity; the GATT promoted free trade and helped us avoid the disastrous protectionism of the 1920s and 1930s; the United Nations, for all its faults, helped us to think of the world as a global community and, at times, to act like that.

But the world is still set up on the victory of the Second World War. Germany and Japan—the world's second-largest economy and the largest European economy—are not in the UN Security Council. Vast states like China and India have no institutional place in any power-sharing structures. The Group of Eight is a rich countries' club that includes Italy but not Brazil.

The great achievements of the IMF and the World Bank have run into the sand. The IMF became an arm of US foreign policy, as we saw in the disastrous demands for conditionality that it imposed on Indonesia, and from which our nearest neighbour is still recovering.

The IMF's prescriptions in times of economic crisis have caused far more human suffering than they have resolved economic problems.

Those are not my words, or the words of a radical student demonstrating on the streets but those of the Nobel Laureate for economics and former Chief Economist at the World Bank, Joseph Stiglitz. Yet the proposals for change in the IMF we heard after the Asian financial crisis have drifted out of sight.

The GATT, now the WTO, helped provide the basis for the most rapid and extensive period of economic growth the world has ever known. But China's entry to it is about the only bright light on the international trade horizon.

Faced with the understandable demands of the developing economies for reform of the agriculture and textiles market, the developed countries got cold feet and the new Doha Round looks sick before it properly begins. We are seeing a rush back to bilateral and even unilateral arrangements.

Australia's salvation does not lie there. A Free Trade Agreement with the United States that requires us to abandon the social safety net of the Pharmaceutical Benefits Scheme, as the American pharmaceutical industry is demanding, is not worth having.

George Bush has increased punitive tariffs of up to 30 per cent on steel. US farm-subsidy programs have risen by 80 per cent. New tariffs have been imposed on Canadian timber, despite the existence of a Free Trade Agreement. Entirely new subsidies have been imposed on commodities such as peanuts. Recalling these developments, the *Financial Review*'s Peter Hartcher recently described the past four months as the 'bitterest betrayal of free trade hopes'.

We should know by now that events constantly happen to disrupt our complacent view of the natural order. We would be fools to think that the unipolar moment we now see will endure.

Australia's security and our prosperity, as always, will be best found, and most easily negotiated, in the region around us, in Asia and the Pacific. That is where Australia's interests coalesce and no amount of squirming or denying or pitiful claims by the Howard government that Labor had an Asia-only policy can change that.

We can maintain, and must maintain, our traditional linkages with the United States. But we must tell them, and show them, that unilateralism can never be a satisfactory world model. We must argue the case for cooperative management of the world and for inclusive institutions.

The United States will be a major power in the world for as far ahead as any of us can see. But it will not be the only power. It may think that it can exist like a gated community behind the golden padlock of national missile defence, with a military able to strike out at offenders in a Mad Max world left outside. But that will not secure its people, and it will certainly not secure us.

If Australia is not a foreign-policy maker, we will end up a foreign-policy taker. As John Curtin said: 'we have to point the way to better days'.

The government and Labor will both put forward White Papers on Australia's foreign policy before the next election. Whether they think about it often or not, Australians have a deep interest in the outcome of the debate.

John Curtin began us thinking in our own terms, and this is probably his long-term legacy. We should take the lessons to heart knowing that, essentially, we are on our own. That our safety and prosperity can only be guaranteed by our engagement with the rest of the world, by our energy, our ingenuity, our self-respect, our confidence in ourselves and our charity. I should think Curtin might regard this as memorial enough.

7

CHINA AND ITS CHALLENGES

Peninsula Palace Hotel,
Beijing,
3 September 2004

*Paul Keating's China and its Challenges provided, in 2004, a somewhat
futuristic forecast as to how and in which ways China might develop.
He says the 'China Project' knows no precedence in world economic
history and that Deng Xiaoping and his policy of openness and
engagement was never slated to materialise. Paul Keating explains that
he does not see China as a strategic competitor of the United States
or of other nations; rather, he sees China adding economic and social
value to the region and to the world.*

WHAT IS HAPPENING IN CHINA knows no precedence in world history.

Never before have 1¼ billion people dragged themselves from
poverty and at such an astounding pace.

Having missed the Industrial Revolution and all its benefits, China
today, after its mid-twentieth-century upheavals, is catapulting itself
into the post-industrial age. Given the recentness of its shift from a
predominantly agrarian economy, one could say without too much
hyperbole or stretch of the imagination that in the last 25 years, China
has done the equivalent of leaping from the eighteenth century to the
twenty-first century in a single bound. In economic or human terms
there has been nothing like it.

And the imagination of it came essentially from the creativity in one man's head: Deng Xiaoping. Of all the great people of the twentieth century—those who shaped and influenced it, like Winston Churchill and Franklin Roosevelt—no twentieth-century leader will have a greater influence on the twenty-first century than Deng. What he did in the 1970s changed the world or certainly, the way the world will work in the future.

Leaders in wartime can often enjoy huge mandates for the exercise of power. But in peacetime, these mandates are much harder to come by. Deng Xiaoping's reformation of China occurred at a time of external peace, albeit after the astringent experiences of Mao's Cultural Revolution.

But the fact is that Deng was not slated to materialise. He did not have to be there. China could very well have gone down a different pathway. We should never fail to consider or lose sight of the consequences of what that other pathway might have been. The construct of modern China cannot be taken for granted.

Underpinning Deng's great vision were two powerful yet simple notions: openness and engagement. Yet underlying these was a more powerful imperative: giving the creativity of his people a chance to express itself. Letting it run much more freely. While at the same time lining up the sinews of power to make the openness happen and to keep it happening. Coupled with this, Deng had the ability to choose real leaders among China's promising political community. And so, too, have his successors, in the party and in the government.

One would never have thought that a Communist party rooted in a huge agrarian base would bet its political future on economic growth. And growth brought about by openness. But that, in fact, is what has happened.

And much has been achieved. At the big turning in 1978, Deng said he wanted to quadruple output by the end of the century. This target has been more than accomplished.

The 1990s, the decade which saw China's growth and wealth accelerate so markedly and compound, was also its most peaceful decade in centuries. Now, the premium for China has to be on steadiness. Its challenge is to keep the growth going, to keep the country resourced, holding itself together by means of an acceptable distribution of wealth. And in the compelling context of keeping an external peace.

China's progress will, I believe, move in lockstep with its magnanimity. Great states who know what they are and what they stand for don't need to be capricious or skittish. Or even defensive.

I think China sees itself and will place itself at the epicentre of a prosperous and cooperative community of east Asian states. China will probably do more for its neighbours than its neighbours are likely to do for it. But in the doing of it, by its wisdom, underwriting the longevity of its own reformation.

We can see these influences already in the current trade outcomes. China has substantial trade deficits with Japan, South Korea, Taiwan, Australia and the Association of South East Asian Nations (ASEAN). It is generating output in these countries for the Chinese market. It is tugging them along.

Concerned about the preponderance of world foreign direct investment (FDI) going to China at the expense of its neighbours, it is itself investing in its own supply chain in these countries. Chinese foreign direct investment will be a significant factor in east Asian hemispheric growth.

The proposed regional free-trade zone between China and the ASEAN countries is another indication of China's grander view of the region and itself.

We can also see this in its foreign policy. The development of ASEAN Plus Three which, in reality, is China plus two plus ASEAN. It is China reaching out in communal terms in major economic matters and, while doing it, taking the security discussion with it into forums in which it is influential.

Strategically, China's size and steadiness add important ballast to the region. A region dominated by three powers: China, Japan and the United States. China will become a competitor of the United States through its economic integration and the growth of its output. But not, I believe, a strategic competitor—if by strategic we mean having the ability to project military power. China will try to protect its sources of raw materials and supplies but the growth in its military establishment is unlikely to be about force projection of the kind that makes the United States the sole superpower.

But having said that, nor does it seem that there will be any rush to a rapprochement between itself and Japan. For China and Japan, it is very much a case of business as usual though with concealed but growing enmities. Japan is increasingly apprehensive about the rise of Chinese power. Not that there is any inherent capacity on the part of Japan to interact or to deal more effectively with the world around it. Except to say that there is evidence that Japan sees itself taking a more serious security role.

China's participation in the six power talks on North Korea and its role in nuclear diplomacy is helping to cement its position as a regional power and reliable interlocutor.

It is very clear that these days, China stands for 'order' and not 'disorder', certainly of the variety it might have been seen to stand for some decades ago. This is comforting for Japan, for the countries of the region and for the United States. All of these things give China a better place in the strategic firmament.

One issue above all could change this. The situation across the Taiwan Strait. This requires the most careful handling. The consequences of miscalculation by any party would be terrible for all of us, and would spread far beyond East Asia. The worrying thing is that history abounds with examples of just such miscalculations. Europe in 1914 is a case in point. This situation requires all parties to exercise wisdom and statesmanship of a very high order.

The central principle, however, is clear. Any problems across the Strait have to be resolved within the framework of One China. That policy has been accepted by all the key countries including the United States. That principle should be expressed clearly and forthrightly to the authorities in Taipei. But China's leaders will also have to carry a heavy weight of responsibility. The situation will require China to continue exercising restraint, even in the face of provocation. It will require the kind of magnanimity I referred to earlier.

Two very bad things happened at the end of the 1990s but as it turned out these were quite good things for China. The first was the 1997 financial crisis, the other was the events of 11 September 2001.

China clearly benefited from the financial crisis in 1997. The first benefit was that the crisis brought home at a very important point in Chinese economic history that command or top-down intermediated economies were not as robust as previously thought. China's toying with the idea of a set of its own *chaebol*; a bit of state capitalism, as the shaper and driver of its economy, was thrown out the window when South Korea revealed the fragility of its economic and commercial structures. As was also seen in places like Thailand. The decisions taken that year by the leadership and the government to build the economy around individuals and small to medium-sized enterprises in an open, competitive model, reinforced by WTO processes, is probably the greatest single benefit from the crisis. And the next most important economic step in China's modern history save for Deng's seminal 1970s changes.

The crisis also saw flows of foreign direct investment moving increasingly towards China, such that by 1999 China took 85 per cent of the region's total foreign direct investment, where it was 25 per cent in the early 1980s. China also involved itself in IMF packages for its neighbours and by not depreciating its currency, played a better than neighbourly role at a time of economic stress for others. China learned a lot but it also gained a lot.

The attack on the World Trade Center on 11 September 2001 altered the international strategic settings. Before this event, China was suffering from a pariah complex with the current United States administration. And worryingly so. Within months of this cataclysm, the focus of the United States had shifted from China and issues such as national missile defence to the hills of Afghanistan. China, espousing the cause of 'order', played a constructive role in the resistance to terrorism, setting China up as a strut in the global system. The smooth step change from Jiang Zemin and Zhu Rongji to Hu Jintao and Wen Jiabao consolidated this position.

These two, large but negative events taught China a lot and encouraged China to pick up its game and make the most of the opportunity.

September 11, 2001 and the war in Iraq are events which have altered the world's strategic compass. And internecine bouts of terrorism keep things off balance. Yet, when we assess the current position of China in world terms, our assessments have to be discerned through this veil of events.

But by any objective assessment, the longitude and latitude of major strategic circumstances has rarely been better.

- Save for the Balkans, we have not seen a major European conflict for 60 years.
- The European Disease—best exemplified by the wars between Germany and France—has given way to unprecedented cooperation.
- François Mitterand and Helmut Kohl put together a vision for a United Europe with a single market and a single currency; a monetary base larger than the US dollar; and a united Germany in NATO.
- The collapse of the Soviet Union and the end of the Cold War.
- Now the EU—expanding to 25 nations including states like Poland, Latvia, Lithuania etc.
- Pan Asian regionalism including states such as Vietnam and Cambodia joining ASEAN.
- Indonesia holding itself together to become a democratic state.
- India gradually opening its economy—dealing with large income disparities.

The world never looked as good or as solid as this at any time in the twentieth century.

Perhaps the event that adds a new and optimistic quality to this constructive world outlook is China's emergence as a major economic and political power. Its rise should be assessed in this new and more promising context.

We live, so it is said, in a unipolar world where the United States, with the major economy and superpower force projection, stamps itself out as unique. Yet, economically, the world is much more multipolar; intensely interconnected by trade and investment and integrated through communications.

In this interconnected multipolar economic world, nation states matter less and governments are less important. And there is also the overlay of the cultural divisions between the Middle East and the West. Yet for all this, all four bits or factors live in the one space:

- the unipolar United States with its geopolitical power and force projection;
- the multipolar economic world with its intense trade and investment interconnections;
- the declining influence of the nation state in this globalised homogenisation; and
- the cultural divide with the Middle East.

China can more than make its way in these new and somewhat conflicting contexts. It can be a very large piece in this economic and strategic jigsaw picture.

Let me now turn to China's economic growth and its impact on the world more broadly. And on East Asia in particular.

China's growth and its integration with the rest of the world very much mirrors the experience of those other economies which grew rapidly in the twentieth century. Ones which successfully integrated themselves as world trade opened up; Japan, South Korea and the ASEAN countries being cases in point.

China, by contrast, is likely to have a much bigger impact on the global economy as, when market freedoms are permitted reasonable expression, population is the principal driver of GDP. China will be a supplier of lower priced labour-intensive products. Products which will benefit the developed countries in providing price competition while restraining global inflation. It will also be a market for the high value exports of the same economies.

Developing countries will find a new and growing market for their exports as the Chinese economy soaks up primary commodities and primary-stage manufactures, manufactures that are capable of being reprocessed. This, especially, will be the case in the region around China where, as a regional engine of growth, it is likely, in the not too distant future, to overtake Japan. Its role as a regional reprocessor and manufacturer of exports to the world will have an induction effect upon the exports of countries in the immediate neighbourhood. Inducing them to grow more rapidly.

China has been a major receiver of foreign direct investment. This has raised factor productivity, inducing faster labour productivity and lowering unit labour costs. And, of course, this has been backed by a large pool of unskilled people whose transition to skilling, incrementally, has maintained China's competitiveness. This should remain the case even in the event that China's currency appreciates into the future. Human capital has been growing strongly as labour has been reallocated from the low-productivity agricultural sector to the higher-productivity manufacturing sector. And so far so good.

But, even in China, the supply of marginally priced labour is not endless. Already a quarter of the agricultural workforce has migrated to urban industrial centres. And in places such as Guangzhou and Shenzhen, shortages of appropriately skilled workers is leading to a rise in the real price of labour. This is best accommodated and paid for by increasing levels of productivity, otherwise wage costs will drift into inflation, pulling back competitiveness and raising the cost of capital. Skilling and vocational education are the instruments that can best turn the flow of farm workers into higher order increments to the manufacturing and service workforce.

China is also facing the challenge of continued structural reform; reform which has been a significant factor in its productivity increases. This has been the case since the mid-1980s. We can chart the growth in productivity from the liberalisation of agriculture in the early 1980s and the introduction of more open and market-oriented changes from the early 1990s. The productivity growth induced by these changes, especially labour migration to higher productivity sectors, is the central factor in the higher output growth of China over the past twenty years.

China has clocked up a very impressive annual rate of output growth exceeding 9 per cent. But of course 9 per cent off a small base, while impressive, is more easily achieved than maintaining 9 per cent from a larger base. To keep up these rates of growth, China must sustain high rates of capital accumulation.

One of China's great assets is its high rate of national savings. The Chinese are a thrifty people, with household savings at around 45 per cent of GDP. But China's financial sector will have to become more open, flexible, commercial and adaptable in providing credit. Without it, capital accumulation at a desirable rate is going to be much harder to achieve.

An important element in financial growth is competent risk management. Something Chinese institutions are yet to come to terms with. Thriving financial systems have at their core not only the ability to create credit but lending circumstances where the loans do not impact upon the capital of the institutions involved.

It is very important for China to move away from a system where banks do most of the financial intermediation. An economy built around individual and small-to-medium enterprises must have a competent capital market, and the presence of a competent capital market will put the banks where they ought to be: providing personal and consumer credit, housing finance and finance to small business.

A situation where banks have hegemony within the financial system and are subject of a central bank with implicit guarantees off the national budget and whose practices are influenced by the bureaucracy can never make the contribution to Chinese national growth that China so desperately needs. A capital market and a set of well-managed banks is an imperative.

In basic terms, the labour surplus coming off agriculture will not be sufficient to keep the economy gingered up. Structural changes will have to be made. And one of the laggards is the financial sector and its institutions. Financial innovation is the key to higher rates of capital formation.

As I said earlier, for the world at large, China's integration, with acceleration flowing from the WTO mandates, is likely to represent a larger change to the global economy than the integration exercises of other countries in the twentieth century. China is likely to have a bigger impact on the world economy than did the reindustrialisation of Germany or of Japan or of the newly industrialising economies. But with that shock comes an opportunity. And that opportunity represents a challenge for the rest of the world to structurally adapt to the reality of China. This will be doubly true if India continues to integrate itself with the world economy at its current trajectory.

Developed economies, particularly those with deteriorating demographics, should recognise these important changes in the international division of labour, and rather than resist them, take the benefit of them by accelerating their own trade liberalisation and integration. A tsunami of deflationary lower-priced products from China inevitably means higher real disposable incomes in developed countries, leaving developed countries to do what they do best: sophisticate further their service sectors and concentrate on the higher orders of technical innovation.

There is no doubt that China is becoming the new engine of global growth, underlining again the urgent need for a new round of multilateral trade liberalisation to keep the sinews of reciprocal trade open and growing.

The China 'project' knows no precedence in world economic history. China can continue this progress as its economic base expands. But it can only do this in an environment of stability and peace.

8

A PROSPECT OF EUROPE

Robert Schuman Lecture,
University of New South Wales,
Sydney,
4 September 1997

Invited by the University of New South Wales to give the Robert Schuman Lecture, Paul Keating uses the opportunity to talk about developments in contemporary Europe: the enlargement and deepening of the European Union, the development of the single currency, the euro, and the involvement of Russia in European affairs. In the lecture Paul Keating argues the single currency should be established around the core economies of Germany, France and the Netherlands, suggesting that the early entry of peripheral states might put the undertaking at risk in a manner that became evident in the European financial crisis of 2010–11. Paul Keating lays out the story of Australia's cultural relationship with Europe though claiming Australia's connection to the broader Europe is compromised by Australia retaining the monarch of Great Britain as its head of state. He says Australia should take its republic with courage and grace, rather than have it wrung out of the political system because the monarchy's time is coming to a close. He further argues that Australia has unfinished business with Europe notwithstanding the fact that all Australia's political interests come together in Asia.

IT WAS AN HONOUR FOR me to be invited to give this Robert Schuman lecture on Australia and Europe.

I have called this speech 'A Prospect of Europe', but in fact I want to talk about prospects for Europe in the plural. Prospects in almost all the different meanings the *Macquarie Dictionary* gives us: a 'contemplation of something future or expected'; a view over a region or in a particular direction; even 'something in view as a source of profit'.

Let me begin by paying tribute to Robert Schuman, in whose honour the lecture is being given. Not, as some people might have assumed given my personal interests, the great German Romantic composer—though I am happy to pay tribute to him as well—but the French Foreign Minister who proposed the establishment of the European Iron and Steel Community, the progenitor of the European Union.

After the Second World War, as if to make up for the tragic miscalculations of earlier generations of European leaders, Europe seemed to burst with pent-up intellectual energy and commitment to public service. Thinkers like Monnet, and politicians like Spaak, De Gasperi and Adenauer, came forward.

On the other side of the Atlantic they were mirrored by an outstanding group of American public servants like Dean Acheson, George Marshall and John McCloy, the group responsible for the Marshall Plan, which Churchill called 'the most unsordid act in history'.

It's a much-noted fact that a disproportionate number of the European leaders who remoulded the continent came from the frontiers of their societies and cultures.

Robert Schuman was the best example. His family had originally come from Alsace. He studied law in Germany and spoke German fluently. Although imprisoned by the Nazis during the war, he had been unshakeably convinced since the end of the First World War that Franco–German reconciliation was vital for peace. He was a religious Catholic, personally quiet and introverted, politically shrewd.

But as Jean Monnet said of Schuman, what he had above all was a 'lucid vision of Europe's future'.

In May 1950, Schuman was due to visit London as French Foreign Minister, to discuss with Dean Acheson and Ernest Bevin the future of Germany. Germany wanted to increase its steel production, which was still limited by Allied decree. It was already clear that the Americans would support them in this. Schuman was worried about the long-term implications for France of such an agreement.

It was at this point that Jean Monnet suggested to Schuman's office—and Schuman seized on—the ideas which became the Schuman Plan—the starting point for the uniting of Europe.

Monnet proposed to use Germany's desire to increase steel production as a lever to place all Franco–German coal and steel production under an international authority, with the participation of the other countries of Europe. This new community would be supervised by a High Authority, able to make binding decisions. Monnet saw this binding Authority as laying the foundations for the European Federation which he believed was indispensable to the maintenance of peace.

Schuman put the proposal first to Adenauer, who was immediately enthusiastic, then to the French Cabinet. Within three weeks Germany, Italy, Belgium, the Netherlands and Luxembourg all accepted the invitation to negotiate. Britain declined, however. It still did not see its future in Europe. Dean Acheson called this decision Britain's 'great mistake of the postwar period'.

The Schuman Plan conference met in Paris in July 1950, and despite the difficult and complex negotiations, the Treaty of Paris, establishing the European Coal and Steel Community, was signed in April 1951.

It was the basis for one of the greatest and perhaps unlikeliest developments of this century—the transformation of the greater part of Europe into a single market.

In a sense the work of Schuman and his colleagues in the 1950s was about constraint. Constraint—in which Germany willingly acquiesced— of Germany's capacity to threaten the security of its neighbours again; constraint, more broadly of nationalism in favour of a pan-European consciousness; constraint of Soviet power through collective defence.

That search for constraint, and the development of the institutions which would preserve it—the European Union and NATO—guided Europe's development through the second half of this century. The search for binding ties culminated in the development of a single market among all the member countries of the EU.

It has been a remarkable achievement.

But nearly half a century after Schuman's work, the world is going through a period of change even more radical than the one he confronted. The Cold War has ended. The information revolution and economic globalisation are transforming the way the international system operates. Asia is emerging again as a global centre of power.

The European institutions which developed during the first historic phase of European unity face fundamental changes.

Constraint is no longer the answer to the strategic dilemma facing Europe. Growth is the issue—how to broaden the EU's membership, how to enlarge the definitions of European security, how to expand the European economies.

In a political sense the last of these is the most immediate problem. And the need has emerged from another aspect of European constraint. Constraint of growth and structural change in favour of the protection of existing jobs, low inflation and the economic status quo.

The result, compared with the United States, has been—in continental Europe anyway—insufficient economic growth and persistent unemployment. As Lester Thurow records in his book *The Future of Capitalism*, not one net new job was created in Western Europe between 1973 and 1994. Europe's unemployment rates, which had been about half those of the United States through the 1950s and 1960s, had risen by the mid-1990s to be more than double American rates. German unemployment, for example, is at its highest levels since the 1930s.

It was partly in response to this problem that Chancellor Kohl and President Mitterrand, representing the two countries at the core of the EU, gave the mandate to Jacques Delors to move Europe towards tighter economic integration. First, through the *Single European Act* of 1987, which provided for the removal of all barriers to trade and established the framework for foreign policy cooperation, and then through the 1993 Maastricht Treaty, which set out the arrangements for economic and monetary union.

These leaders recognised that the central question for Europe was how flexible its economies were going to be in the new global environment. In this context, the single market had an important political dimension. Not just in deepening European integration, and especially the nexus between France and Germany, but in making the task of domestic reform easier for national governments by allowing them to appeal to, or blame, externally imposed pressure for needed economic reform.

Despite much talk about whether the Maastricht convergence criteria will be met in time for monetary union to go ahead in 1999, I am sure it will happen. This will be for political reasons as much as economic. In particular, Germany's credibility is so heavily tied up in it.

But when it happens, the economic impact will be every bit as significant as its proponents argue. When there is one price for the currency and a freer flow of investment, there will be an equilibration of labour markets and productivity across Europe. That can only mean structural change of a kind America is continuing to go through, and that Australia is going through. By removing from the economic system one lever of flexibility—the exchange rate—flexibility will be forced upon other important areas.

And with structural changes will come an improved capacity to employ people. As Germany and France move, as I believe they must, to become much more service-oriented economies with a higher component of information in their economies, unemployment will be relieved, income will be lifted and Europe's economic paradigm will be changed.

The alternative to economic and monetary union would, I am sure, be a disaster. The integration process would stall and the always potent sentiments for protectionism and economic nationalism would reappear.

We are seeing them reemerging now in the results of the French elections and in the public mood in Germany. A drift back towards caution and protecting jobs with state intervention and a resistance to structural change.

If these sentiments prevail, Europe has no hope of dealing decisively with its unemployment problem. The single currency is in many respects the major hope.

But success depends on the new European central bank keeping two objectives clearly in mind: not simply price stability, the staple responsibility of central banks, but also growth and activity. For it will only be by growth that sufficient aggregate employment can be created.

It is important that effective monetary management is not compromised. Price stability should remain important. But the leaders and governments should understand that the growth imperative can only be dealt with positively by taking the policy changes that will make their economies more supple and more dynamic.

It won't be easy. Members will soon run into the problems of dealing with a centralised monetary policy in the variable context of broadly unrestrained national fiscal policies. It will quickly become clear that it is not just the technicalities of monetary policy which will be affected, but virtually every aspect of Europe's economic, fiscal and social policy.

But it is the only way the Union can move to greater integration.

It is not just Europe which will be changed by monetary union, however. The euro will alter global capital markets as well. It will become an increasingly competitive reserve currency with the US dollar. Present candidates for the single currency have bond markets worth over \$500 billion, compared with \$680 billion for the US dollar and \$260 billion for the yen.

Another effect of the Economic and Monetary Union (EMU) will be to underline the reality of a two-speed Europe. Indeed the EMU itself will, I believe, become a two-speed issue. So much has been said and written about the Maastricht criteria, as if meeting a budget deficit of 3 per cent of GDP matters completely, but a deficit of 3.2 per cent represents a dismal failure. Or, worse, that reference principally to budget deficit criteria is the best way of assessing the worthiness of potential entrants.

The criteria should be much broader and with a touch of realpolitik about them.

I believe the single currency should be based around the principal economies of Western Europe, those with a durable economic performance. They pick themselves out: Germany, France, the Netherlands. And I believe the United Kingdom should be there, and from the start.

A group like this with a substantial monetary and economic base can provide the foundation the currency will need if it is to become the powerful instrument of integration it should be.

After some period of operation and a time for proper observation of the currency's impact on Europe's economic performance, other countries could then be considered.

I do believe the whole issue might be delayed and compromised if other countries beyond this group are brought into the fold in the first instance.

More broadly, the two-speed approach will be essential if Europe is to handle effectively the related issue of how to take into the Union the new democracies now knocking on its door.

In fact, it is possible that a two-speed Europe will bring about full union much faster than a process of waiting until a confluence of criteria is met by all.

The emergence of a group of former communist countries in central and eastern Europe determined to establish their place as Europeans raises the prospect of a union of 25 members by early next century. Already Hungary, Poland, the Czech Republic, Estonia, Slovenia and Cyprus have been offered entry.

This widening of the union will bring changes to almost every aspect of the EU.

For one thing, it will be a much more diverse union. The average GDP per head of the new applicants is just 13 per cent of the EU average.

Many questions will arise.

How can the constitutional arrangements drawn up for a group of twelve serve the interests of a much larger and more diverse group? Voting by qualified majority seems certain to be extended, but what will the implications be? How will Europe accommodate a very different political and security agenda? Which of the rush of new applicants will be accepted? How will Europe deal with Turkey, the gateway to the Islamic world?

It has been politically difficult for the present EU members to accede to the demands of those who are knocking at the door, and the response has been cautious.

The public reaction in Western Europe to the subsidies which will flow to the poorer EU members, both present and potential, has been increasingly loud. It has already forced the Commission to propose that there should be no shift in its expenditure of 1.27 per cent of Union gross national product (GNP).

But although these are difficult matters, they are by no means insurmountable. And it is essential for Europe and the world that the prospect of pulling together the European Union continues with all speed.

Partly as a result of the reluctance of current members to move faster in expanding EU membership, I believe a great security mistake is being made in Europe with the decision to expand NATO. There is no doubt this was seen by some in Europe as a softer option than EU expansion.

NATO and the Atlantic alliance served the cause of western security well. They helped ensure that the Cold War finally ended in ways which serve open, democratic interests. But NATO is the wrong institution to perform the job it is now being asked to perform.

The decision to expand NATO by inviting Poland, Hungary and the Czech Republic to participate and to hold out the prospect to others—in other words, to move Europe's military demarcation point to the very borders of the former Soviet Union—is, I believe, an error which may rank in the end with the strategic miscalculations which prevented Germany from taking its full place in the international system at the beginning of this century.

The great question for Europe is no longer how to embed Germany in Europe—that has been achieved—but how to involve Russia in a way which secures the continent during the next century.

And there was a very obvious absence of statecraft here. The Russians, under Mikhail Gorbachev, conceded that East Germany could remain in NATO as part of a united Germany. But now just half a dozen years later NATO has climbed up to the western border of the Ukraine. This message can be read in only one way: that although Russia has become a democracy, in the consciousness of western Europe it remains the state to be watched, the potential enemy.

NATO's declaration at the Copenhagen summit of 1991 was admirable. It said 'We do not wish to isolate any country, nor to see a new division of the Continent. Our objective is to create a Europe whole and free.' But that sentiment sits impossibly with the expansion of the institution. The fundamental point of principle that NATO enlargement should 'contribute to stability and security in the entire Euro-Atlantic region and not pose a threat to any nation' is simply incompatible with enlargement.

The words used to explain NATO's expansion have been nuanced, and the dangers have been acknowledged. But however careful the words are, whatever the window dressing of the Permanent NATO–Russia Joint Council, everybody knows that Russia is the reason for NATO's expansion.

The decision is dangerous for several reasons. It will fuel insecurity in Russia and strengthen those strains of Russian thought, including the nationalists and former Communists in the Parliament, which are opposed to full engagement with the West. It will make more likely the restoration of military links between Russia and some of its former dependencies. It will make arms control, and especially nuclear arms control, more difficult to achieve. President Yeltsin's offer to 'take the tips off the warheads' might have been described as a misstatement, or even the unconscious utterance of official briefing, but what are the chances of that happening now, with NATO creeping towards Russia's western borders?

And NATO expansion will do much less to strengthen the new democracies of eastern Europe than would enlargement of the EU. New strains will be opened up between the ins and the outs among those countries.

It will also weaken NATO itself. The financial costs will be high and NATO's effectiveness and credibility will be diminished. An American commitment to defend the border of Poland and the Ukraine in all circumstances simply lacks political credibility.

The reasons Poland and the other countries of Eastern Europe believe their security is served in this way are obvious, and historically understandable. But I do not believe either European or global security will be helped by this decision.

The better option, even now, would be to build on existing institutions like the Organization for Security and Co-operation in Europe (OSCE), or new mechanisms like President Clinton's January 1994 Partnership for Peace proposals, to intensify military and political cooperation and improve transparency throughout Europe.

The world needs Europe now because the world we are moving into is not one we have any experience in dealing with. It will require the highest levels of statesmanship and leadership, including from Europe, if we are to take advantage of the opportunities while avoiding the traps.

And perhaps we might reflect upon what sort of world it will be.

One idea which has received a good deal of attention has been the suggestion that it will be one in which the ideological divisions of the Cold War are replaced by divisions along the faultlines of civilisations.

The best known proponent of this view is an American political scientist, Professor Samuel Huntington from Harvard University.

Over the course of a long political career, you get accused of many unflattering things. But I have to say that the most spectacular of all the charges against me came from the same Professor Huntington, who accused me of precipitating the fall of a civilisation.

The central idea in his book, *The Clash of Civilizations and the Remaking of World Order*, is that the ideological divisions of the Cold War will be succeeded by a world divided along the faultlines of civilisations. It is a much more elaborate and footnoted version of the words of that grand old imperialist Rudyard Kipling, 'East is East and West is West and never the twain shall meet'.

In a section about Australia and the changes my colleagues and I were trying to bring to Australia's relationship with the region, Professor

Huntington writes that 'At the beginning of the twenty-second century historians might look back on the Keating–Evans choice [of engagement with Asia] as a major marker in the decline of the West'.

In a way, it's a flattering accusation, I suppose. It's certainly a reminder that there is nothing much about hyperbole that a politician can teach an academic in full flight. But I can confidently reassure the professor that future historians will be doing no such thing.

The choice I was said to have made in the early 1990s was that Australia should 'defect from the West, redefine itself as an Asian society, and cultivate close ties with its geographical neighbours'. The last claim is right; the first two are rubbish. Though perhaps it can be said in the book's defence that the then Opposition was making the same claims in those days.

The evidence Professor Huntington gathers to support his charges reveals ignorance about Australian politics and economics, not much comprehension of the complexity of political and economic relationships in Asia over the past decade, and no knowledge at all of what I have actually said about Australia's foreign policy.

Paul Keating 'liked to say', Professor Huntington asserts confidently, that I was going to change Australia from being '"the odd man out to the odd man in" in Asia'. Despite Professor Huntington's authoritative quotation marks, I liked to say no such thing, and I never did.

What I did say, and many times, was that Australia was not Asian or European or American or anything except Australian. This is what history and geography have delivered us. It is the only option we have and one which we have every reason to celebrate.

The problem the professor has with Australia is that we are untidy. We shouldn't be where we are. We ruin the neatness of it all. Like an obsessive housekeeper, he wants to sweep us back where he assumes we belong.

But we're too large to be swept and our interests do not impel us to go voluntarily. We belong somewhere very different from where the professor wants to put us.

So when I was invited to give this lecture I also thought it might be a good forum to defend myself against the charge of bringing civilisation as we know it to an end.

For this reason, the second of the prospects of Europe I want to talk about is the view of the continent from Australia.

I certainly believe that, in a way which has never been true in the past, all Australia's principal interests now come together in Asia. As Prime Minister I wanted to sharpen the focus on the region around us. This is the part of the world we live in. This is where we can have the most influence and where we can make a difference. It is where our future predominantly lies. It remains in my view the foreign-policy area where investment of time by Australian political leaders is most needed and can have the greatest impact.

And because the stakes for Australia were and are so high, and because there were powerful cultural and historical forces resisting this transition, I wanted to make our intention abundantly clear.

The issues facing Europe—enlarging and deepening the EU, managing the transition from communism in Eastern Europe, constructing new security mechanisms—are very important globally, but they are areas in which Australia can do little more than express opinions.

The obvious truth—obvious to me and my colleagues anyway—is that the more Australia is integrated into this part of the world and the closer our relations are with our Asian neighbours, the greater will be our relevance to Europe and our influence there on the things that matter to us.

Nothing in my view of Australia's role in the world can be taken as suggesting that Europe is not important to Australia's future. The economic relationship is vital and growing, our cultural and scientific links are vigorous. Global issues important to Australia, ranging from trade liberalisation to greenhouse gases, won't be solved without Europe's participation.

And much more fundamentally than these issues, Australia's relationship with Europe is an ineradicable part of what makes us Australian. No matter how we shape our future in this part of the world, the legacy of our links with Europe is entrenched in the structure of our society, the forms of our institutions, and in the way we think about the world.

No matter how Australia changes in the future, that will remain.

More than 2.3 million Australians were born in Europe and a further 2.6 million had one or both parents born there. My children are among them.

For many Australians, as for me, Europe is important beyond the facts of our history and the vigour of our economic relationships. I love visiting Paris and—dare I mention?—Berlin. I love the civilised architecture and the human scale of the best European cities—their compactness. I respond to the place from which has come the music I love most. Few things have moved me more on my overseas trips as Prime Minister than the civic reception in the village of Tynagh in Ireland from which my great grandparents had set off all those years ago.

We have heard often since the last election the mantra that Australia doesn't have to choose between our history and our geography. It appears again in the Howard government's recently released White Paper on foreign policy.

But just think about that assertion for a minute. What could it possibly mean? No choice we can make as a nation lies between our history and our geography. We can hardly change either of them. They are immutable. The only choice we can make as a nation is the choice about our future.

And as Robert Schuman and the other great European reformers in the middle of the century understood so profoundly, you sometimes have to break away from the past to get the future right.

It seems to me that we have never got the prospect of Europe from Australia right. Too often, the perspective has been distorted. We have managed simultaneously to hold two different views of the place. On the one hand Europe has been a distant, too easily romanticised place; on the other an overwhelming presence.

Australia's modern origins involved us in no great act of differentiation from Europe. Unlike the United States, we had no puritan sense of moral separateness, no New Jerusalem to build, no shining city on a hill. We did not need to redefine ourselves in revolutionary ways against the place most of us had come from.

We were exiles from a *home*—and that word was being used about Britain without irony by some Australians well into my adult life—long after this country should have been home. We looked to Europe for our psychological as well as physical security in a world where we did not feel we belonged.

We did not seize our independence, but were set adrift, some of us still complaining about it. Australia took until 1943 even to ratify the 1931 Statute of Westminster, which conferred dominion status on the whiter parts of the British Empire. A full five years earlier, Sir Robert Menzies had explained the delay to Parliament by saying that 'quite a number of responsible people are troubled about the proposal to adopt the Statute of Westminster for the reason that they feel it may give some support to the idea of separatism from Great Britain'.

Australia's struggle has not been to avoid the foreign entanglements the early American revolutionaries feared. On the contrary, we set about searching them out, roping them in, dragging them down and clutching them tight.

This isn't an argument for revolution. The absence of blood in the streets is not something we should regret. One of Australia's achievements has been to have built a society like this without great strains or great violence. That is something to be proud of.

And it isn't an argument for isolationism either. We have to be part of the world and to help shape it.

But we still have unfinished business in our relationship with Europe—and I don't mean just Britain, but Europe as a whole—which we must address before the relationship can flower fully. It revolves around the constitutional reform agenda and the creation of a republic.

It is of the utmost importance that the decision by Australians to become a republic is not something which emerges simply as a reaction to external events or external perceptions. It must be something we do for ourselves, and for our own reasons, something with a bit of verve and expectancy about it—not something which is wrung out of the political system, which we slump into because there seems no good alternative, or because time has run out, or as a reaction to developments in Britain, whether a change in the person of the monarch or even constitutional change there.

It is sometimes suggested that the best thing for us to do would be to wait for the end of this Queen's reign before introducing changes. But that would be the worst reason to act. It would suggest that the move to a republic was not a decision which Australians wanted to make for our own reasons and in our own interests, but was somehow connected with judgements about the person of the monarch.

And it would be the worst time to act—a time of sorrow, and a moment decided by chance rather than as an independent act of will by Australians. And in any case, her successor will immediately assume the throne.

The choice by Australians to become a republic must be taken with courage and grace. And I say *taken,* because it is the act of taking which will give our sovereignty its strength.

I believe this constitutional change will strengthen, not weaken, our relationship with Britain. As I said in Australia House in London:

> *it is not because our affections for Great Britain are reduced, or the friendship between us frailer, or our respect and admiration for the culture and institutions Britain has bequeathed us in any way diminished, that now, in this last decade of our first century as a nation, we are considering the option of becoming a republic. It is not because the machinery is broken that we wish to change it. It is because a great many Australians (in all likelihood, a majority of Australians) believe the machinery is no longer the most appropriate.*

Britain will remain one of Europe's major powers and a very important partner for Australia in the new Europe.

But the image of Australia as a branch office of Britain is tenacious, as recent British public-opinion polling has demonstrated. Both governments want to change that perception. The New Images program which is running at present in Australia was something John Major and I endorsed as part of the effort to place the relationship on a more modern footing.

But the only action which will seriously achieve that will be the first state visit to London by the President of Australia.

The act of becoming a republic will also make it easier for us to look at Europe from a perspective other than London's. And easier for the other countries of Europe to look at us with fresh eyes.

We have to get beyond the perception that 'Europe' is best understood when filtered through British sensibilities. The prospect of Europe from Westminster Bridge can be very distorting. We can't afford not to understand the rest of the continent on its own terms. Our businesses and our media suffer particularly from this affliction. Far too little of the news we receive about Europe comes from correspondents who are based outside London.

We do not give ourselves the chance we should have in Europe while we still have the monarch of Great Britain as our head of state.

The republic must come because we are convinced it is right for us, not because of what it says to others. But the idea that the identity of our head of state has no effect on the way others perceive Australia—and through this on some very hard-headed economic and political interests—is nonsense, just as the proposition that the offensive nostrums of Pauline Hanson would have no effect was nonsense.

In this very fundamental sense, the measure of how far Australia has come to terms with itself and its position in the world will be measured more by the nature of our relationship with Europe than with Asia.

But assuming we make these changes in perception, the outlook for Australia's relationship with Europe is very bright.

So, let me turn finally to another prospect of Europe, the prospect defined by the *Macquarie Dictionary* as 'something in view as a source of profit'. Because there are remarkably good opportunities opened up in both directions, especially by the changes now underway in the global economy.

In a globalised world we cannot ignore one of the one three great economic groupings. The fifteen current members of the European

Union, with their population of 370 million, now form the world's largest trader.

Australia's two-way trade with the EU is now 18 per cent of our total.

But in a globalised world the investment figures are particularly important. The EU is Australia's largest source of foreign investment, including foreign direct investment, and our major host for overseas investment.

Thirty per cent of foreign investment in Australia comes from Europe. Hundreds of large European companies are based here and many of them have found that Australia is an excellent base for their Asian operations. Over 80 have regional operating centres here.

Australian investment in the other direction is also strong—nearly $40 billion. Almost half this investment is in Britain. There is absolutely nothing wrong with this, and much to commend it—provided that investment is going there because it offers the best opportunities not just because of fear by Australian companies of crossing the Channel. I'm not sure that is always the case.

The value of sales generated by Australian direct investment in the EU significantly exceeds Australia's annual exports of both goods and services to Europe.

Our exports to Europe are still dominated by traditional commodities like wool, coal and iron ore. But even though we are seeing strong growth in elaborately transformed manufactures, our overall export figures have slipped in relative importance. Transport costs, lower economic growth in Europe compared with Asia, and the complexity, cost and unpredictability of the EU regulatory regime all play a part. But there is no doubt that Australia also has to perform much better in getting our goods into European markets. Happily, things are looking better than for some time on the agriculture front. Reality is catching up with the Common Agricultural Policy (CAP), one of the enduring items of dispute between us. It was less the fact that Europe wanted to support its farmers that we objected to than the way they did it—especially the export subsidies which distorted the international markets for our efficient primary producers. For a variety of reasons—only partly

Australian persuasiveness, I think—the EU has not engaged in predatory subsidies of exports recently.

And at a more fundamental level the sort of reforms to the CAP which were first introduced in 1992 will have to continue. Aid to farmers already absorbs half the EU's budget. And the Union's enlargement to the east will increase arable land by 55 per cent. One quarter of Poland's workforce is in agriculture.

Australia and other agricultural exporters will have to watch carefully that the EU's expansion does not result in a series of new deals which harm our interests.

Under the Uruguay Round outcome further multilateral negotiations on agriculture need to begin by 1999. If we move to a new Millennium Multilateral Trade Round, Europe will be integral to it and we will have to ensure that agriculture is a key part of the negotiations.

Our opportunities for cooperation with Europe go much further than trade and investment of course. Our science and technology agreement signed in February 1994 was the first for the EU with a non-EU member. We are negotiating a mutual recognition agreement. Our cultural exchanges, official and unofficial, are important in both directions.

The importance of new structures to underpin these avenues for cooperation is the reason why as Prime Minister I proposed to Jacques Delors that Australia and the EU negotiate a treaty-level agreement to provide a framework for our future relations.

Unfortunately that high-level agreement fell before the present Australian government's problems over the human-rights clauses. So although I am pleased we have a Joint Declaration, I am sorry it is of less status and value than it might have been.

Australia and Asia have important lessons to learn from the experience of Europe this century. Above all, the importance of institution building and ways of facilitating easy contact between political leaders. Europe is the best example we have of how closer economic integration can restrain conflict.

As Jean Monnet once said, 'Nothing is lasting without institutions'. Our institutions in this part of the world will be very different from

Europe's, reflecting not just different cultural and political experiences but different times. But they need architects—and stonemasons and carpenters—with the same sort of vision these Europeans had.

We're staggering to the end of the twentieth century, and there won't be nearly as much to lament about its passing as there should have been.

This may have been the American century, but it was Europe which set the tone. The strategic blunders which marked European statesmanship around the end of the last century did more than anything else to generate the carnage of totalitarianism and two world wars.

But Europe at the end of this century is a source of great hope. It has shown, thanks to Schuman and Monnet and all their successors, a capacity to remake itself and to overcome deep-seated rivalries. And even where the rivalries still erupt, as in the Balkans, Europe has developed mechanisms and institutions for dealing with human rights and encouraging democracy. This has had a global impact.

For the rest of us, the new Europe will be more promising than the old, I think. Less inward-looking, perhaps less self-satisfied at times, more likely to play a larger role in the world because its agenda will be broader.

European diplomats will respond that they already take such interest, and it is true. But interest is different from leadership—and that is what we need more of from Europe. An ability to put itself into the minds of others.

We often hear talk of the next century being the century of Asia or the century of the Pacific.

But I don't think the world will be like that anymore.

Regionalism will be important, and it has much further to go, especially in the Asia Pacific, than we have yet seen. The pressures generated by the new economy and multilateral problems like the environment will make sure of that.

But those same pressures will also ensure that, while Asia will be more influential in the world, no one area will be able to dominate the global agenda in the way Europe and North America did in this century.

Robert Schuman was born in Luxembourg, a state whose national motto is 'We want to stay as we are'. It's a cry from the heart that most people can understand.

We all want that in some way, or at some level. But, as Robert Schuman knew, Europe could not stay as it had been. And in Australia we must know that we cannot either.

9

ELIMINATING NUCLEAR WEAPONS
A *Survival Guide for the Twenty-first Century*
University of New South Wales,
Sydney,
25 November 1998

*Paul Keating saw the end of the Cold War, that epiphany at the end of
the twentieth century, as an unprecedented and probably unrepeatable
opportunity to create a new international strategic environment—one
free of nuclear weapons. With the Cold War over, a concrete program
of weapons elimination was possible; lacking was the imagination and
the will. But no government had ever contemplated yet put its name
to a report urging the complete elimination of nuclear weapons. The
Labor government in Australia was the first to do so. In 1995 Paul
Keating established the Canberra Commission on the Elimination of
Nuclear Weapons. The Commission produced the first ever handbook
of practical measures to move the world down the path to better
nuclear safety and to a point of full nuclear elimination. The Report
stressed that there could be no nuclear non-proliferation without
de-proliferation—the notion that some states could have nuclear
weapons but others not. The Report was a milestone in the international
debate. Upon completion it was presented to the Howard government,
which refused to promote its recommendations.*

IN EARLIER LECTURES AT THIS university I have spoken mostly about
Australia and its place in the world. Tonight I want to discuss a darker

and more dangerous subject, one that threatens to cast a long shadow over the twenty-first century.

I am talking about the continuing inability of the international community, and more particularly the great powers, to take the steps necessary to eliminate nuclear weapons from the world.

In some ways, I suppose, I am an unexpected campaigner for nuclear disarmament. I am a realist about international affairs and I don't have great faith in the inherent goodwill of the nation state. I have never seen much point in the politics of symbolism. During the Cold War I thought ideas of unilateral disarmament were naïve and dangerous.

And yet the issue of nuclear weapons worries me more than any other when I think about the sort of world young Australians will inherit.

Over the past decade the world has undergone deep changes. The Cold War, which defined our international system for 50 years, has ended and the information revolution is transforming our lives and societies. But in many ways our institutions, and our ways of thinking, have not adjusted. As a result, we find ourselves on the verge of the twenty-first century dangerously close to repeating the mistakes of this one.

One reason for this is the human tendency to avert our eyes from problems, to hope that if we do not look directly at them, they will disappear.

In the aftermath of the Cold War, this was what we did. No image in the twentieth century has seared our collective consciousness like that of the mushroom cloud. And in our minds that image of the bomb defined the Cold War. So although nuclear weapons had originally been conceived for a different conflict, we assumed that because the Cold War was over, the weapons that defined it had miraculously disappeared as well.

For most Australians, the realisation that this was not so came with the announcement by President Chirac, on 13 June 1995, that France would conduct a series of eight underground nuclear-weapons tests at Mururoa Atoll in French Polynesia.

In making this decision the newly elected President was following China in breaking an international moratorium on testing that had been in place since January 1993.

The resumption had been foreshadowed during the French election campaign, so it was not unexpected. But the outcry in Australia was immediate and strong.

In response to the tests, the government I led took a series of measures including recalling the Ambassador to France, curtailing defence contacts, and coordinating protest action in the United Nations and other international bodies, including the South Pacific Forum, which Australia was chairing that year.

This did not much diminish the public clamour. The government was being urged to break diplomatic relations with France, cut off all trade, and dispatch Australian warships to stop the tests. Sections of the media, especially commercial radio, were running a campaign that became more anti-French than anti-nuclear. It seemed at times as if the smoke of the Battle of Agincourt had only just cleared. At several points I had to underline publicly that our opposition was to the nuclear tests, not to the people of France.

The selfishness and cynicism of the Chirac decision appalled me and I was deeply concerned by the provocation it provided to some of the threshold nuclear states. But I was not interested in the sort of theatrical and ultimately pointless gestures that were being urged upon us. Trade sanctions would have harmed Australia more than France. I was certainly not prepared to permit Australia's military forces to be used for symbolic reasons. Short of going to war with France, which was absurd, the only option for the warships would have been to steam around in circles while the French exploded their bombs. This would have underlined not Australia's strength but our impotence.

The more I thought about the French tests, the more I came to feel that the understandable public outrage was in a sense directed at a symptom rather than a cause of the problem.

The French had reminded everyone of what we all wanted to forget—the unique, sickening sense of insecurity which comes from knowing that weapons exist in the arsenals of governments which have the capacity to destroy humankind. The problem, in other words, was the continued existence of nuclear weapons in the world.

As I reflected on this, I thought we had an unprecedented and possibly unrepeatable opportunity to begin to move to a new strategic environment which offered not just a reduction in the number of nuclear weapons, but their elimination. The Gulf War had shown that new, accurate, conventional weapons could accomplish the military purposes for which nuclear weapons had once been intended, but without such appalling, indiscriminate consequences. The Cold War had ended, all the declared nuclear powers were at least on speaking terms, and the proliferation of nuclear weapons had, for the time being, been reasonably contained. There was no prospect, however, that this situation would continue into the indefinite future.

The goal of a nuclear-weapons-free world was not new. It had been a long-term aim of the Labor Party and a goal that had been articulated forcefully by others.

But as long as the Cold War raged, the ambition was unachievable. Now, however, we had an opportunity to develop a concrete program to achieve a nuclear weapons-free world.

The successful negotiation of the chemical weapons convention in which Australia had played an important diplomatic role had shown that it *was* possible to put the genie back in the bottle; that a whole class of weapons of mass destruction could be abolished. And Article VI of the Nuclear Non-Proliferation Treaty, which had only recently been indefinitely extended, committed the nuclear-weapons states to 'pursue negotiations in good faith on effective measures relating to cessation of the nuclear arms race at an early date and to nuclear disarmament'.

But of course the task of ridding the world of nuclear weapons was not something Australia could accomplish unilaterally. We had none of our own to eliminate and we were committed not to get them. We were well respected internationally for our arms control expertise. But we were now entering a domain where the deepest national security interests of the United States, Russia, China, Britain and France were involved.

Every country was directly affected by the nuclear threat, but nothing could happen without the five nuclear powers.

We decided, therefore, that the most useful thing we could do was to try to shape the international debate. Anti-nuclear groups had written many reports about the problems of nuclear weapons but, until that time, no government had ever put its name behind a report committed to their elimination. I wanted to put the authority of a sovereign government behind the push to rid the world of nuclear weapons.

So in October 1995 we announced the formation of a commission comprising a group of eminent scientists, disarmament experts, military strategists and statesmen and asked them to develop 'concrete and realistic steps for achieving a nuclear-weapons-free world'.

The emphasis was to be on 'concrete and realistic'. I saw no point in another rhetorical statement that nuclear weapons were evil and should be abolished. Any report which was to have a chance of convincing the hard-headed defence establishments of North America and Europe to change their positions had to be grounded in a deep understanding of what elimination meant, both technically and strategically.

These are matters of the greatest complexity and profundity. They are not easily resolved. The problems include verification—that is, how you can be sure everyone abides by an agreement; dealing with break-outs—situations in which one country tries to snatch strategic advantage by breaking the agreement; and the broader implications of such a major change in the global-security environment for issues such as the deterrence of chemical and biological weapons and of conventional war.

We were very lucky to get together an outstanding group of commissioners. The members included Joseph Rotblat, who had won the Nobel Peace Prize for his work with the Pugwash Foundation; General Lee Butler, who had been responsible until 1994 for all United States strategic nuclear forces; Field Marshal Lord Carver, the former chief of the British Defence Staff; Robert McNamara, the former US Secretary of Defense and President of the World Bank; and a number of internationally regarded disarmament experts. The distinguished

Australian strategic thinker, Professor Robert O'Neill, was a member, as was Richard Butler, then the Australian Ambassador to the United Nations, now the UN's Chief Weapons Inspector. I believed the group should also include someone with direct political experience, so I invited Michel Rocard, the former French Prime Minister, to participate.

These were not people who had come down in the last shower. They had very different backgrounds and brought different assumptions about nuclear weapons to their work. Some were long-time peace activists; some had had nuclear weapons directly in their control. If this diverse and distinguished group could agree on the road ahead, we hoped they would be able to persuade others.

We provided resources to permit the group to commission more detailed papers from expert advisers on specific dimensions of the move to a nuclear-weapons-free world. This brought a range of international scholars into the project. Their work has provided a rich resource lode for further debate about this issue.

By the time the commission reported in August 1996, it was made to the conservative Howard government which replaced mine in March 1996.

The recommendations were based on the fundamental assumption that 'the proposition that large numbers of nuclear weapons can be retained in perpetuity and never used—accidentally or by decision—defies credibility. The only complete defence is the elimination of nuclear weapons and the assurance that they will never be produced again'.

The report recommended a number of immediate steps to reduce the dangers of nuclear war as well as longer-term moves towards the larger goal of the elimination of nuclear weapons.

The immediate steps proposed included taking nuclear forces off alert; removing warheads from delivery vehicles; ending the deployment of non-strategic nuclear weapons; ending nuclear testing; initiating another round of negotiations between the US and Russia to reduce their arsenals; and a joint agreement by nuclear-weapons states not to be the first to use nuclear weapons.

The commissioners also recommended a series of reinforcing steps to build on these foundations. These included measures to prevent further horizontal proliferation, not only by countries but by terrorist groups, the development of verification arrangements for a nuclear-weapons-free world, and the cessation of the production of fissile materials for nuclear explosive purposes.

As we hoped, the recommendations were realistic and practical. The commissioners did not ask for unilateral disarmament or suggest any measure that might threaten security during the process. However, they did make the fundamentally important point that, in the end, the decisions that need to be taken are not technical decisions but political ones.

It was a good start. But many excellent reports lie languishing on shelves in ministries around the world. The next step was the diplomatic one of trying to persuade others to embrace the ideas and adopt the policies.

One of my regrets about losing the 1996 election—and I have several—is the opportunity I lost to pursue the report's recommendations as Prime Minister. I would have taken the report to the United Nations General Assembly to launch it myself. It would have been high on my agenda for discussions with President Clinton and the leaders of the other nuclear states.

But beyond receiving the report in August and lodging it at the United Nations, the Howard government did not endorse its recommendations or try to sell them more widely. The Canberra Commission was associated with the government I led, and it had been labelled a 'stunt' by the foreign minister, Alexander Downer, in the political atmosphere of the time. So the political momentum—at least on Australia's part—lapsed.

This is a great pity, and not just for Australia. But other governments, I am glad to say, have taken up the cause.

In June this year the foreign ministers of Brazil, Egypt, Ireland, Mexico, New Zealand, Slovenia, South Africa and Sweden formed a new international coalition—called the New Agenda Coalition—to push for the elimination of nuclear weapons. They explicitly drew inspiration from the Canberra Commission.

In August, in another parallel with the Canberra Commission, Japan convened the Tokyo Forum, a meeting of eighteen prominent diplomatic and strategic experts from sixteen countries to discuss the impact of nuclear testing and issues of nuclear disarmament and non-proliferation. I think I can reasonably say that the Canberra Commission Report brought a new atmosphere to the debate, an optimism that something better was possible.

Three years after we convened the Canberra Commission report, what is the international environment for such initiatives? I want to turn now to the current situation and the prospects for the future.

On the positive side, the Comprehensive Test Ban Treaty was finally adopted in 1996 and some progress has been made in opening the way for negotiations on a treaty to limit the production of fissile material for weapons.

But almost all other news on the nuclear front has been bad. Twenty thousand nuclear warheads still have the capacity to destroy the world many times. Two of the states on the nuclear threshold, India and Pakistan, have now stepped over it. Another regime with a known nuclear program, North Korea, tested a medium-range ballistic missile in August. Meanwhile, Russia's capacity to control and store its existing nuclear arsenal is atrophying. And the strategic arms negotiations between the major nuclear powers are not going anywhere. Russia has still not ratified START II. Russia, China and the United States have still not ratified the Comprehensive Test Ban Treaty. Across the board, in other words, the impetus for change has stalled.

After years of developing its nuclear capability yet never declaring itself a nuclear power, the new Indian government openly tested weapons on 11 and 13 May this year. India can undoubtedly deploy reliable fission weapons on a wide range of delivery systems including ballistic missiles. It probably has 60 to 80 weapons.

Pakistan, India's long-standing rival, responded with its own tests on 28 and 30 May. Pakistan's nuclear arms are not as sophisticated or numerous as India's, but it has technical capacities which at some time it may be tempted to share with its Middle Eastern neighbours.

Then in August we saw the successful test by North Korea of a three-stage missile capable of carrying conventional or nuclear warheads over 5500 kilometres. The test suggested North Korea has also made progress on a longer-range missile that would enable it to strike targets throughout Asia.

The 1994 Framework Agreement, under which North Korea agreed to freeze its nuclear program in exchange for heavy fuel oil, help in building two light-water nuclear reactors and an eventual end to the economic embargo, is now under pressure again. North Korea has reportedly continued to work on missile launch facilities, and just this week we have seen Pyongyang deny the United States access to an underground facility that Americans believe to be a nuclear installation.

After the Indian nuclear tests, President Clinton said forcefully and accurately that 'to think that you have to manifest your greatness by behaviour that recalls the worst events of the twentieth century on the edge of the twenty-first, when everybody else is trying to leave the nuclear age behind, is just wrong'.

But the problem, of course, is that no one else does seem to be trying to leave the nuclear age behind, or not at least with any noticeable degree of urgency. And this, the non-nuclear powers note, is despite the fact that in order to secure the indefinite extension of the Nuclear Non-Proliferation Treaty in 1995, the five declared nuclear weapons states recommitted themselves to pursue measures of complete and general nuclear disarmament.

The essential issue here is that you can't have *non*-proliferation without *de*-proliferation.

It is not just states that we need to worry about as a source of new nuclear threats, but terrorists and other groups as well.

Nuclear weapons are not hard to make. You can get instructions for a workable device off the Internet. Graham Allison, Director of the Centre for Science and International Affairs at Harvard University's Kennedy School of Government, put it this way:

*if a state or a terrorist group obtained as little as 30 pounds of highly
enriched uranium, or less than half that weight in plutonium, they
could produce a nuclear device in a matter of a month or two with
design information that is publicly available, equipment that is readily
available in the commercial market, and modest levels of technical
competence represented in graduates of any respectable engineering
program.*

The only difficulty is access to fissile material. That is why we need
to address much more comprehensively the problems of 'nuclear over-
hang'—essentially the security of stored nuclear weapons and excess
fissile material in Russia. This is a second area that has become more
dangerous since the Canberra Commission report.

At more than 90 sites across Russia, 715 tons of nuclear material are
stored. This is enough to fuel 40,000 weapons.

Guarding this deadly treasure are military officers and soldiers whose
morale is low and who have sometimes not been paid for months. In 1996
the then Director of Central Intelligence, John Deutch, told the U.S.
Congress that of the tons of weapons-useable nuclear material distributed
to various centres around Russia over the past 40 years, *none* had what
would be regarded in the United States as sufficient accountability.

Last July, thousands of scientists at the nuclear city of Arzamas-16
went on strike after months without pay. The Russian Ministry of Atomic
Energy MINATOM has told its personnel that they can no longer rely
on government funds to support them and that they need to market
their goods and services.

The dangers are real. In November 1993, a Russian naval officer
walked out of a shipyard in Murmansk with about 10 pounds of highly
enriched uranium and went looking for a buyer while it was stored in his
garage. In August 1994, almost a pound of weapons-useable plutonium
was seized by German police in Munich.

It is not just in Russia: the reported theft of approximately 130 barrels
of enriched uranium waste from storage in South Africa was reported
in the press in August 1994.

Through the Cooperative Threat Reduction Program of 1991—named the Nunn–Lugar program after the senators who co-sponsored the bill—the United States provides about $400 million a year to help secure poorly guarded Russian nuclear facilities and to help destroy weapons earmarked for destruction under current arms-control negotiations. But this accounts for only one-sixth of 1 per cent of the US defence budget. The Nunn–Lugar program is a solid investment, producing lasting security dividends. It could easily be doubled or tripled. And if the build-down is to continue, it will have to be.

Some people willingly concede the dangers that nuclear material could be diverted to rogue states or terrorists. But that just proves we need nuclear weapons, they say, in order to protect ourselves against these very prospects.

But the argument is circular. It is the argument that we *need* nuclear weapons because we *have* nuclear weapons. It is not an argument we think persuasive when applied to biological or chemical weapons.

In an outstanding article in a new collection of essays called *The Force of Reason* to be published shortly in honour of Joseph Rotblat, a leading member of the Canberra Commission, Professor John Holdren of Harvard University, says that such criminal threats 'could well be the dominant nuclear threat in the next century'. He argues that the threat is not only 'greatly aggravated by the continued existence of national nuclear arsenals, but nuclear deterrence is likely to be useless against it (because terrorists and other criminals may not be locatable, or if locatable, could not responsibly be attacked with nuclear weapons)'.

The state of the Russian nuclear arsenal has other dangerous consequences. Thousands of Russian nuclear systems are on hair-trigger alert, ready to launch at the United States in fifteen minutes. The deteriorating condition of Russian early-warning systems and the erosion of military command and control heightens the danger of an accidental or unauthorised launch. It increases the incentive for the Russians to adopt a 'use them or lose them' strategy for their strategic arsenal. We reportedly came very close to such a situation in 1995 when a Norwegian research rocket was mistaken for a United States missile attack and the whole Russian system went on alert.

The economic collapse and the decline in conventional military capabilities tempts Russia to place extra weight on its nuclear forces to compensate. This is the reason Moscow has abandoned its long-standing declaratory policy of 'No First Use' of nuclear weapons.

Meanwhile, the strategic nuclear negotiations are stalled. The burst of activity from the conclusion of the Intermediate Nuclear Forces treaty of 1987, through START I in 1991, which halved long-range missiles, to START II in January 1993, which imposed a further 50 per cent cut in strategic nuclear forces, has run into the sand. And Russian hardliners are pointing to the expansion of NATO to the borders of the old Soviet Union as a reason for Russia to maintain its nuclear capabilities. The Russian Parliament has refused to ratify the START II treaty, which it believes advantages the United States. Russia cannot afford to modernise and replace ageing and decaying nuclear forces and it is slipping inexorably further behind the United States' numbers and capabilities. It simply cannot afford its vast nuclear arsenal and is seeking much larger cuts.

In the United States political pressure is growing for a National Missile Defense System to respond to a perceived evolving ballistic missile threat. This would certainly mean abrogating the 1972 Anti-Ballistic Missile treaty and would cause the Russians to walk away from START I and II, fearing that the United States could quickly upgrade a missile defence system into a shield behind which it could launch a first strike.

In this depressing landscape—a period in arms control negotiations that some have called 'the great frustration'—the agenda for action set out in the Canberra Commission report remains highly relevant.

First we need to urge the steps recommended by the Canberra Commission to de-alert the nuclear arsenals—to lengthen the fuse by extending real launch preparation time. This means removing vital parts of the systems. An agreement between the Russians and the Americans in 1994 to de-target missiles was essentially meaningless.

Original targets can be fed back into the computer in seconds. But de-alerting—in other words, standing the missiles down—will require an effective and intrusive inspection system.

Second, we need to press speedily ahead with negotiation of the fission material cut-off treaty which will halt the production of fissile material (that is, weapons-grade plutonium and uranium) for nuclear weapons. This treaty will begin negotiations next January in the United Nations Conference on Disarmament, but the scale and scope of the negotiations are still not agreed.

The fissile cut-off treaty will be a companion to the Comprehensive Test Ban Treaty. Banning tests constrains technological improvements. The fission treaty will constrain the production of the material that goes in them.

Third, we need to urge Russia and the United States to move as quickly as possible to leap-frog START II with a new and radical START III which rectifies the emerging numerical inequality in favour of the United States and gets nuclear numbers down so low that the other nuclear weapons states are brought into the negotiations.

For my part, however, I do not think such measures will be enough.

I don't believe that any objective short of zero will be able to generate the political consensus necessary to stop an eventual break-out. Even if only a handful of weapons are held by Washington and Moscow and Beijing, even if they are held in 'strategic escrow' under some form of international supervision as General Stansfield Turner and others have suggested, I find it impossible to imagine why a future South American government, or some future African leader, convinced that Africa has been abused and marginalised, will not understand the disproportionate strategic advantages that accrue to states with even crude nuclear weapons and will not ask: why not us?

And there is no defensible answer to that question. That is why I believe only a full commitment to, and an active program to secure, the elimination of nuclear weapons will ever be sufficient to secure our safety.

Even so, the goal of elimination can't be accomplished by the arms control route alone.

It is also—even essentially—a debate about global power and influence and I believe it will only be resolved in that context. We have come to see nuclear weapons as the ultimate global status symbol. Membership of the United Nations Security Council remains coterminous with the possession of nuclear weapons. And United Nations reform, so high on everyone's agenda when the Cold War ended, has faltered.

The senior adviser to the Indian Prime Minister on security issues defended India's decision to declare itself a nuclear state by writing that his country was 'assigned a particular place in the world order and not treated as a subject responding to our own interests'. That frustration lies at the heart of India's decision to test. I'm not arguing that countries should be rewarded for flouting international norms. But I do not think we can create an adequate architecture for the world without finding a place in it for the democratic government that speaks for the one billion people of India.

More broadly, a larger and more sustainable role has to be found for China, India and Japan. And with the EU's expansion, and the creation of the euro, Europe urgently needs to address the fundamentals of its own structure to see how it can act more effectively beyond its own continent.

The link between nuclear weapons and the broad strategic environment is particularly important to Australia and its region.

In North Asia, more than any other part of the world—more, even, than the Middle East—a combination of historical animosities, unresolved relationships, territorial disputes and technologically sophisticated economies makes it distressingly plausible to envisage conditions emerging which might induce Japan or South Korea or Taiwan to seek nuclear weapons. The further introduction of nuclear weapons into the North Asian strategic equation would be catastrophic.

A very senior Chinese leader once told me—decisively and with great passion—that China would never permit Japan to possess nuclear weapons. It would act to pre-empt such a situation arising.

This raises again the urgent need for a more structured defence and security framework in the Asia Pacific, one which can provide transparency and reassurance at a time of growing uncertainty. The ASEAN Regional Forum has been a good first step, but it can't carry us through pressures ahead. I had hoped the APEC Leaders' Meeting might be able to develop as an umbrella on top of a regional security forum, but that hope is dimming as APEC membership expands and its energy diminishes. This is an issue of the highest priority for the region, and a program to eliminate nuclear weapons globally must also comprehend the more general problem of regional security.

People might well say this is an argument about which Australians can do little. Our capacity to influence the world is limited.

But Australia has shown it can play an active part in the global debate. We have an internationally regarded body of officials working on arms control issues. They form a national—in fact, an international—asset whose expertise should be preserved.

We can raise our voice. Both major Australian political parties are committed to the alliance relationship with the United States. This allows us at least the privilege of having our arguments heard. We should be using our voice as powerfully and persuasively as we can, and not just with the administration but with Congress as well.

I believe the government should seriously consider suggestions that have been made to reconvene the Canberra Commission, probably with a different membership, to re-examine in current circumstances its practical and realistic program for moving to a world without nuclear weapons. As a firm ally of the United States, with a high reputation in international arms control negotiations, Australia has a better chance than any other country to refocus international debate on the final goal of abolishing nuclear weapons. The government would have my enthusiastic support for such an initiative.

But this is not just a matter for governments. Increasingly, the international agenda can be shaped from outside. We have seen this with the success of the international campaign against landmines.

We face a long struggle to get rid of nuclear weapons and we might not succeed. But you can be absolutely sure that if the pressure is not kept on governments, if the issues and alternatives are not debated, if the voice of public opinion is not raised, then the line of least resistance will be taken.

And that line will always be to let things slide—to hope that in the next hundred years some new, more ruthless or more able Saddam Hussein or Kim Jong-Il won't emerge, that somehow the skills of Russian nuclear scientists now on the market will not be made available to some terrorist group, and that we will get through it all unscathed.

I want to end this lecture by quoting not a politician or an anti-nuclear activist but a man from the heart of the nuclear establishment. General Lee Butler was the former head of United States Strategic Nuclear Command, and a key member of the Canberra Commission panel.

Accepting the prestigious Henry L Stimson award for distinguished public service last year, General Butler said he was dismayed that:

> *even among more serious commentators, the lessons of fifty years at the nuclear brink can be so grievously misread, that the assertions and assumptions underpinning an era of desperate threats and risks prevail unchallenged, that a handful of nations cling to the impossible notion that the power of nuclear weapons is so immense their use can be threatened with impunity, yet their proliferation contained. Albert Einstein recognised this hazardous but very human tendency many years ago, when he warned that 'the power of the atom has changed everything save our modes of thinking, and thus we drift toward unparalleled catastrophe.'*

I hope that is wrong. But drifting is the right word to describe what all of us—nuclear and non-nuclear powers alike—have been doing over the past few years.

And those who think there are no risks, who believe we are sure to glide safely past the rocks and shoals because we have done so before, should at least reflect on the history of the last issue I spoke of in this auditorium—the Asian economic crisis. The economic, social and political uncertainty we are seeing around us seemed unimaginable in 1997, to even the most informed and sober observers. Just so, ten years earlier, would the disappearance of the Soviet Union have seemed unimaginable.

And however unlikely nuclear catastrophe may seem to us now, here in Sydney on this peaceful November evening, if our judgements are wrong, the consequences will be terrible and ineradicable.

Our challenge—as always, in everything—is one of imagination.

10

OBSESSION REVISITED

Transformation Public Lecture Series,
Seymour Centre,
Sydney,
29 March 2000

Paul Keating's 'Obsession Revisited' was a major speech on foreign policy delivered against the backdrop of the Howard government's steady movement towards a more unilateralist security option for Australia—a more exclusive relationship with the United States at the expense of multilateral coalition building, especially in Asia. Paul Keating predicts the US unipolar moment will pass, making it necessary for a small country like Australia to build coalitions and institutions, in what he sees as a world of shifting networks and strategic alliances. He reminds his audience that the old Asia is gone forever and that Australia is in a weaker position than at any time in the last 30 years because it is now less involved—while projecting faded, sepia-toned images of what and who we are.

The transformation I want to discuss tonight is Australia's relationship with and engagement of Asia—the essence and subject of my book, *Engagement*.

The way we come to terms with our place in the world and the relationships we develop with our neighbours seems to me to be one of the very large issues in Australia's national life.

Like Federation a century ago, like the great decision to adopt a mass migration policy after the Second World War, like reconciliation with indigenous Australians, it is one of the ideas around which we must define ourselves one way or another. For reasons I will come back to later, I think a lot hangs off this question for our country's future.

Alexander Downer has accused me of having an obsession with Asia. It's a line he also used about me when I was Prime Minister.

I have to say I was flattered. It has always struck me as an odd insult for an Australian foreign minister, even one like Alexander Downer, to want to fling at a political enemy.

The proposition that an Australian political leader might be obsessed with the region immediately around us, with the countries that take two-thirds of our exports, where our security is shaped, where increasing numbers of our people come from, seems rather reassuring to me.

Matter of fact, I wish we had such a leader now.

But, in fact, what obsessed me was not Asia itself but the future of Australia. It's just that I thought then, and believe now, that a closer relationship with our neighbours is critical to that future.

That is why I have written the book, *Engagement*, which is not so much the story of what my colleagues and I did about Australian foreign policy in government during the first half of the 1990s as why we did it.

I begin *Engagement* by saying that the book is part of a long and unfinished story, the story of how Australia has slowly come to terms with the facts of our geography and our place in the world.

From the first speech I gave about foreign policy as Prime Minister I made it clear that this was not a new endeavour for Australia. Committed and far-sighted men and women had been working for decades outside and inside our political system to strengthen our ties with Asia. Some of them are in this audience tonight.

But in 1991 when I took over from Bob Hawke I thought that the world was changing in ways that made Asia more relevant to us than it had ever been before. The Cold War had ended unexpectedly, transforming the international landscape. It provided new potential for regional cooperation that had been impossible while the world was divided into two competing camps.

It was now possible to heal the rifts between Indochina and the rest of Southeast Asia, for example, and to think about the creation of a cross-regional organisation like APEC.

Secondly, economic globalisation was changing the way the economic system operated, and it was bringing unprecedented growth to Asia. The Asian miracle in the 1980s and early 1990s represented the greatest single increment to growth in human history.

More people had been lifted out of poverty more quickly than ever before. For the first time, Australia was situated next to the fastest-growing area of the world, rather than half the globe away from it.

Finally, the information revolution was beginning to transform the whole idea of sovereignty and what it meant. Its implications were still unclear. The 1991 edition of the *Macquarie Dictionary*, published in the year I became Prime Minister, doesn't have an entry for the word 'Internet'. But the effect of digital technology and cheaper and more flexible communications was to change the meaning of foreign policy. The clear divisions of old between foreign and domestic policy were being eroded. Virtually every aspect of our daily lives, from the gas we use to cool our refrigerator to the interest rate we pay on our mortgages to the sport we watch on television now has some sort of international dimension.

In my view, these changes meant that Australian interests coalesced in Asia in a way that had never been true before. That didn't mean that we were claiming to be Asian. On the contrary, as I always said, we are not Asians, or Europeans or North Americans or anything except Australians. When you have a continent to yourselves, when your people have come here from almost every country in the world and when indigenous Australians have been here for perhaps 60,000 years, that is the only way you can relate to your neighbours.

But if we are not Asian, we are certainly an essential and rightful member of the Asia Pacific community. Australia is one of the region's great integrators. Our resources helped fuel Asian economic growth, our educational institutions helped train regional leaders, our defence forces from the Second World War onwards showed our commitment to the region's security.

That is not to deny that we have important interests elsewhere, including Europe. But the measure of Australia's success in foreign policy, the place where our interests are most direct and where we can shape developments most effectively is in the Asia Pacific.

Australian foreign policy is determined by many things, but fundamental to it is the fact that we are only 19 million people. We inhabit a continent but we don't have the clout—either the economic power or the population size or the political leverage—to do what we need to do by ourselves. There's no unilateralist option for Australia.

All sides in the Australian foreign-policy debate have acknowledged that underlying reality. But throughout our modern history two distinct responses to it have emerged: two contending ideas about Australia and the world.

The first response, seen largely on the conservative side of politics, has been that given our circumstances Australia needs to seek out, in Robert Menzies' famous phrase, 'Great and powerful friends' to protect us.

That strand in Australian foreign policy began, of course, with the view that Australia did not need a foreign policy at all, because imperial policy, set in London, would keep us safe.

As late as 1938, Menzies' External Affairs Minister, RG Casey, could say—and this is quite typical of views expressed at the time:

> I believe that the future and the fortunes of Australia are bound up indissolubly with those of Great Britain, and that is why I say I am an Imperialist as well as an Australian.
>
> As to a foreign policy for Australia, personally I am against those who say we should have an Australian foreign policy simply for the sake of having it. British foreign policy may be regarded in a very real sense as Australian foreign policy.

After the Second World War had comprehensively swept that view away, the job of protector-in-chief was allocated to the United States. We had the 'All the way with LBJ' mantras of Harold Holt. The same theme lives on, of course, in John Howard's aspirations to be a regional deputy.

The alternative approach to leveraging our limited global influence, rather than relying on powerful patrons, has been to build coalitions of interests with smaller countries and to try, where institutions did not exist that served Australia's interests, to use such coalitions to build our own forums. Bert Evatt's role in the founding of the United Nations was the principal early example of that line of thinking but there have been plenty since.

In my time in government this sort of approach led to the founding of the Cairns Group by John Dawkins to pursue Australian interests in global trade, to Gareth Evans' role in developing the ASEAN Regional Forum, to the Canberra Commission on the Elimination of Nuclear Weapons, and most notably to APEC and the APEC Leaders' Meetings.

I don't want to caricature the two ideas. It was Labor, after all, which established the US Alliance under John Curtin, and elements of both approaches blend in the policy mix of all Australian governments. But it remains true that the first approach has been most characteristic of conservative governments and the latter of Labor governments.

The initial argument I want to make tonight is that the world is changing in ways that will make the first approach—bilateralism and the support of great and powerful friends—much less relevant to Australia's future than the second approach—coalition- and institution-building—and that our foreign policy needs to prepare for this shift.

The reason for the change is partly that this immediate post-Cold War period in which the United States so comprehensively dominates the global system—the 'unipolar moment' as some have dubbed it—will pass. It will be replaced by a multipolar world in which stronger centres of power will emerge in Europe, China, India and so on. Such a world will be more fluid than any we have known since the Second World War.

A second reason for the change is globalisation. This will continue to inject an international dimension into almost every aspect of our lives and to constrain even further the power of governments. More power—and I'm talking here about power to shape international public policy—will shift to global or regional multilateral bodies, such as the World Trade Organization or international criminal courts or environmental forums. Europe is a model for what is to come.

In the other direction, power will also seep away to non-state structures—multinational corporations, non-government organisations and advocacy groups.

If Microsoft were a country it would now be an economy bigger than Canada, and would be eligible for membership of the Group of Seven industrialised countries.

But the information revolution has also empowered the economically weak. It has given advocacy groups unprecedented capabilities to organise, enabling them to form networks rapidly and inexpensively, and to influence governments in new, more effective ways. We have seen such power used to seal the fate of the Multilateral Agreement on Investment and to bring into force the Ottawa Convention on Landmines.

John Lewis Gaddis, the distinguished American historian, recently put the problem states are facing like this:

A laissez-faire economic model is emerging at the global level a century after the invention of the welfare state limited laissez-faire economies at the national level. The social and political compromises that saved capitalism through an expansion of state authority early in the twentieth century no longer constrain it. And states now are as ill-positioned as towns and villages were then to resist the buffeting of markets or to relieve the dislocations they can produce.

The power of the state is being eroded at the very point when people want government to be able to do more. Think of the calls for more services in regional areas, for greater investment in education, for the preservation of distinctive culture.

I think globalisation is a good and exciting development. It has helped transform Australia for the better, and it has helped transform Asia for the better as well. It is the key, in my view, to getting development to the poorest 20 per cent of the world's people who still account for only 1 per cent of global GDP.

But despite the advances it offers, there is no doubt that globalisation has left some people worse off. The benefits of globalisation are clear but they are relatively diffuse. Its costs, however, are often sharply specific. And those who have paid a price for globalisation are fighting back. We have seen the backlash highlighted recently by the demonstrators who took to the streets at the World Trade Organization meeting in Seattle to protest about free trade.

We will undoubtedly hear more from such groups unless we deal effectively with globalisation's impact on different groups in society and address the widening wealth gaps within individual societies that globalisation tends to make worse.

In a globalised world, governments have to do more than simply appoint a regulator and sit back to watch the creative destruction at work. They have an important role in ensuring that globalisation's centralising tendencies don't drive out the small.

Markets are powerful and useful mechanisms, but they can't do this. It requires effective government and good public policy.

I'm not arguing for stronger states in the mid-twentieth-century sense. But I certainly believe we need healthy, confident states if we are to respond effectively to globalisation's challenges. And critical to the health of our states are institutions of governance that are understood by, and have the support of, the citizens whose interests they serve.

Robert Hughes wrote recently about 'the fraying of America' as a result of the success of what he called 'popular demagoguery', which was 'sceptical of authority and prey to superstition; its language corroded by fake pity and euphemism'. This had led to what he termed a 'distrust of formal politics'.

I'm the last person, of course, to argue that institutions do not need to change in response to changes in society, but the fraying and distrust Hughes speaks about in America is also evident in Australia, and for some of the same reasons.

It is fanned by elements of the media, especially the talkback shock-jocks.

The problem is that the delegitimising of politics to which the media contribute will have serious implications for all Australians.

Whatever its shortcomings, the federal parliament remains the most representational forum in the country—elected by every adult Australian. And, in an age of fragmentation, it is the only place where we can make the trade-offs between increasingly vociferous single-interest groups which are necessary if we are to address the problems of globalisation.

But however we handle these challenges, the inexorable force of globalisation will continue to change the world in ways that make coalition- and institution-building more important to Australian foreign policy than the support of Great and Powerful Friends.

As a result of these developments, Australians will find ourselves increasingly on our own, far less able to rely on others to defend our interests for us. The Cold War days when the Alliance provided us with a template for making most international decisions are long gone. In the twenty-first century, nations, like businesses, will be operating in a world of shifting networks and strategic alliances.

My second argument tonight is that these changes to the international system have important implications for Australia and its relationship with Asia. If we are moving into a world in which *ad hoc* coalition-building is more important, Asia is where we will principally have to do this.

Our interests—economic, environmental, security and so on—will continue to be focused there. They are not going to shift suddenly to Africa or Eastern Europe. So it will be even more important to make sure we are part of any new networks that emerge within the region.

That, of course was the thinking behind the Labor government's work on the ASEAN Regional Forum and on APEC and the APEC Leaders' Meetings. It also lay behind my disagreement with Dr Mahathir Mohamed about whether the institutions in this part of the world should be Asia-only institutions, or Asia Pacific ones.

Over the past year or so we have seen greater support for Asia-only forums of which Australia is not part. ASEAN-plus summit meetings have effectively created the East Asia Economic Group proposed by Dr Mahathir.

If we are to work with Asia more closely, however—and this is my third argument—we need to understand that it is a new Asia we are dealing with, and which is dealing with us.

After the first flurry of Hansonism, and the dangerous ambiguity of John Howard's response—it was all about freedom of expression, you will remember, after the nightmare years of conformity and political correctness into which Australians were allegedly frog-marched during Labor's term—the conventional wisdom in Australian politics became that Australians did not like being told about Asia, or encouraged into engagement with it, and it was better if the subject was discreetly avoided. I think there is still a lot of this in the current political debate.

Whatever the focus-group polling may say at a particular time—and I've never been much of a fan of them—I believe most Australians *are* interested in engagement with Asia and see its importance. I also believe, however, that some of us have a problem in thinking about it.

In the same way that Victorian England regarded the Worthy Poor, or antebellum American southerners felt sentimental about warm-hearted Mammies, Australians have a dangerous inclination to want our neighbours to be Little Brown Brothers—Fuzzy Wuzzy Angels whom we can help and who assist us in their gratitude.

We like to think of ourselves as dispensers of aid and purveyors of moral rectitude, doing Good Works by means of aid programs like the Colombo Plan or peace-keeping operations like Timor. We are in favour of that sort of Asia, but we don't want the neighbours to get all uppity on us.

Psychologically, the Asian economic crisis caused a sense of relief for some Australians: Labor had been wrong. We didn't need to worry about Asian economic growth after all. We could continue to think about Asia as we always had: in an economic and moral hierarchy with us on top. Australian politicians embraced a rather distasteful and altogether premature triumphalism.

The violence after the East Timor referendum had the same sort of impact and it was exacerbated by some of the media coverage.

Richard Walsh wrote a brave article in the Melbourne *Age* recently. To my knowledge he was the first independent observer and journalist to comment on the sort of reporting we saw over Timor last year, when a lot of the Australian reaction, including the government's reaction, was shaped by the media. He recalled the *Sydney Morning Herald*'s front-page lead story by Lindsay Murdoch that Dili police station was piled high with thousands of corpses.

According to Walsh:

Desperate for circulation, even the best papers succumb to a kind of creeping tabloidism. For example, newspaper editors almost certainly hoped for a lift in sales during last year's crisis in Timor. If reporting is dramatic, if there is widespread belief that hundreds of thousands of people are being massacred, this compounds the effect. History will show that the Australian media grossly exaggerated the mayhem in Timor which is not to deny there was widespread property damage and appalling loss of life.

He is right on both counts.

The old Asia has gone forever. We face a different China, a new India, a transformed Indonesia. The World Bank again predicts East Asia will be the fastest growing region in the world in the first decade of the next century. Thanks to the information revolution, which shines its intense spotlight on government and business alike, it will be a more democratic and less centralised Asia. It will also be more assertive. Asian countries will increasingly want to go their own way, under their own terms. They will not easily forget the economic and social impact of the IMF's initial flawed prescriptions for the Asian crisis, imposing capital-account solutions on a current-account crisis.

The first signs of this new assertiveness have been seen in the ASEAN-plus summit meetings in Manila, in the suggestions from the ASEAN secretary-general that APEC should abandon its Leaders' Meetings, and in debates about an Asian monetary facility. And more is to come.

In this new and more assertive Asia, I think Australia is in a weaker position than at any time I can remember over the past 30 years. Weaker because we are less involved. Unsure of how much we want to be there. Too content to look on from the sidelines, as an observer rather than a shaper.

In the foreign policy White Paper it issued after it came to office, the Howard government differentiated itself from Labor by emphasising bilateralism as a 'central feature' of its foreign policy. They were also determined, as they put it, to 'invigorate' the relationship with the United States, which they did in part by developing high-profile new military arrangements under ANZUS.

Pro-forma statements about the importance of Asia were injected into the government's intermittent speeches on the subject but the message was that the incoming government would be reweighting Australia's international priorities away from Asia.

It was coded in the words that Australia did not have to choose between its history and its geography, as though we could ever change either, or in messages from Alexander Downer that Labor had been too 'frantic' about Asia.

We are also in a weaker position in Asia, however, because of the faded, sepia-toned images of Australia we have been projecting into the region.

I argued the case for a republic because of what it says to ourselves rather than what it says to others. And I argued the case for reconciliation with indigenous Australians because of its moral force rather than because of what the international community thinks. But there is no doubt that these issues, like mandatory sentencing, are relevant to our efforts to assert our proper place in the world and in our region.

They are not, as the coalition argued when I was in government, 'distractions' from the main game. They are intrinsic to it.

Much of our relationship with Asia will come to be viewed through the prism of defence.

The government is to issue a new White Paper on defence. This is welcome. I believe that security is the primary responsibility of any government and I am in favour of a strong defence force for Australia. Under Labor, the percentage of our GDP going to defence was consistently higher than it has been under the Howard government.

However, as this debate proceeds, I think it is essential that Australians understand that the principal determinant of our security will not be the size and effectiveness of our defence forces, or the vigour of the defence alliance with the United States, important as these are.

Much more important will be an active, imaginative effort to construct our own security with our neighbours in the form of strong bilateral relationships and effective multilateral institutions. We need to find our security *in* Asia, not from Asia.

Indonesia will be central to this process.

Before I became Prime Minister I said publicly that Indonesia was our great under-developed relationship. With 200 million people, it is the fourth most populous country in the world and the largest Islamic country. It is central to our security—as we are to its security. The rest of Southeast Asia cannot develop fully in peace and prosperity unless Indonesia is also doing so. I don't believe that we can say Australia has come to terms with our region until our relationship with Indonesia is based on more solid and enduring foundations.

I've been accused by some commentators in the media, especially the *Sydney Morning Herald*, of being part of a sinister 'Indonesia lobby'.

It is interesting to see the way that phrase is bandied about in the way the 'China lobby' tag was used by the right-wingers in the United States 50 years ago to pillory those who were accused of 'losing China' after the Communist revolution—as though China was ever anyone else's to lose.

The phrase is currently used to try to suggest that those who are interested in better relations between Indonesia and Australia are working not in the interests of Australia but of Indonesia, and that the two are mutually incompatible.

Members of the lobby seemed to include anyone who took Indonesia seriously. Distinguished academics like Harold Crouch from the Australian National University, whose books were banned by Jakarta, found themselves on the list, presumably solely because they knew what they were talking about.

All I can say is that if there was an Indonesia lobby, you wouldn't want to hire it for a serious job. At the time I became Prime Minister, the heads of government of Australia and Indonesia, Bob Hawke and President Soeharto—two neighbouring countries—had not met for nearly a decade. Imagine what we would think if the heads of government of France and Germany had not met for such a period. In Bob Hawke's memoir of his years as Prime Minister the word 'Indonesia' is only mentioned once. Most Australian journalists were barred from Indonesia. Most defence cooperation projects were suspended. Almost all official contact was conducted by our two foreign ministries.

One of my objectives in office was to shift our defence relationship with Indonesia from one based primarily on ties between our military forces to one whose central focus was shared strategic dialogue. This was the purpose of the security treaty, the Agreement on Maintaining Security.

I deeply regret that that treaty was abrogated by President Habibie upon provocation from John Howard. Without it, Indonesia remains the great black hole in the middle of Australia's regional security network, sandwiched between the Five Power Defence Arrangement with Malaysia and Singapore, the joint Declaration of Principles with Papua New Guinea and our defence relationship with New Zealand. We are all periphery and no centre.

I began this lecture by saying that I believe this issue of engagement with Asia is one of the great themes of Australian life in these first decades of the twenty-first century. I want to make it clear that I am not interested in point-scoring about Australia and Asia. I don't care who contributes to greater engagement. I just want it to be done, and if the Howard government is part of it, I should be happy to applaud.

But the job of engagement with Asia is not a task governments can or should undertake alone.

Like all national transformations, this one has to be as much social and cultural as it is political and economic, and it has to involve all of us: businesspeople, students, journalists, artists, film makers, universities, sports fans, bookshop owners. You name it. It has to happen in the relationships between people.

In October 1994 I said in a speech to the Asia-Australia Institute that I hoped Australia would become a country in which:

- more and more Australians speak the language of our neighbours
- our business people are a familiar and valued part of the commercial landscape of the Asia Pacific
- we are making full use of the great resource of the growing number of Australians of Asian background
- our defence and strategic links with the countries around us are deeper than ever
- our national identity is clearer to us and our neighbours through the appointment of an Australian as our head of state
- our national culture is shaped by, and helps to shape, the cultures around us.

It still seems to me to be a useful, modest and easily attainable checklist.

Some of the transformations governments and societies have to go through are tough and demanding. Remaking our economy in the 1980s and 1990s was one of those.

But this issue of engagement with Asia is not like that. I ask myself: how is it possible to look at the rich cultures and the old societies around us, at the opportunities and challenges they present, and not see this as one of the most exhilarating and enjoyable challenges Australia has faced?

Perhaps we won't feel relaxed and comfortable about it—but excited and energised is an excellent substitute.

11

REGIONAL ECONOMIC COOPERATION AND INTEGRATION

The 2002 International Seminar Series,
Jakarta,
25 April 2002

*Invited to address a conference in Indonesia on regional economic
cooperation, Paul Keating took the opportunity to hammer away
at two of his foreign policy themes: the importance of a broadening
relationship between Australia and Indonesia, and the value of open
regionalism to the East Asian hemisphere. The address ranges across
such issues as the 1997 Asian economic crisis, including the damaging
role of the IMF, the nature and character of regional bodies such as
APEC and ASEAN Plus Three, noting again China's economic growth
and the inappropriateness of George W Bush's unilateralism as a
sustainable leadership model for world governance.*

IN SO MANY WAYS INDONESIA is a different country from the one I
first visited as Prime Minister in the early 1990s. Democratisation,
decentralisation, reform and constitutional change have transformed
the political landscape. Economically, the country is still dealing with
the consequences of the Asian financial crisis which made life so much
harder for millions of ordinary Indonesians.

I know from my own experience how difficult the task of reforming
institutions and confronting vested interests can be. So I greatly admire

the efforts of those Indonesians who are building a culture of account-ability and transparency here.

But underneath the obvious changes in Indonesia, much remains the same. A rich culture, a warm people and a tolerant society. These are what make Indonesia unique and why I am always so happy to come back here.

Well before I became Prime Minister, I told the Australian people that I regarded my country's most underdeveloped major relationship as the one we had with Indonesia, our nearest, largest neighbour.

The Australia–Indonesia relationship had a political and defence dimension to it, but it lacked the depth of trade, economic and financial contacts and the educational, cultural and people-to-people ties that ought to underpin relations between two close neighbours. It lacked what Gareth Evans used to call *ballast*, the weighting of interests that would keep the ship on a steady keel during a political storm.

So my initial focus was on trying to broaden the relationship. On my first visit here as Prime Minister in 1992, President Soeharto and I agreed to establish a ministerial forum that would engage a range of other departments and agencies—trade, finance, transport, science and so on—in the relationship. I also worked to try to encourage new non-governmental links in trade and investment, education and culture, including by expanding the teaching of Bahasa Indonesia in Australian schools. I am glad that a lot of this work is still going on.

But the second way in which I wanted to broaden the Australia-Indonesia relationship was by working with Indonesia to tackle some of the wider issues of regional economic cooperation and integration, including APEC. So I am glad to be talking about these matters again today.

Ten years ago, the frozen international landscape of the Cold War was beginning to thaw. After 50 years, this was an unexpected and welcome development. The most important immediate impact on the international environment was to open up opportunities for regional cooperation and integration. Relationships that had been impossible under the Cold War's bipolar structure suddenly showed new potential.

For example, the European Union was able to begin dialogue with the former Communist countries of Eastern Europe. And in this part of the world, ASEAN expanded by bringing in the countries of Indochina. It was also possible for us to build APEC, the first ever regional organisation to include all the countries of East Asia, including China.

At the same time, the globalisation of manufacturing processes and easier capital flows were leading to an economic boom in Asia. The so-called Asian Miracle brought with it a new sense of regional identity and self-confidence.

It was a time when it seemed possible to do new things, to try to remake the world along better lines.

But just as Indonesia has changed over the past five years, so has the environment for regional cooperation. We now live in a very different region.

The most immediate change to the regional environment came with the Asian financial crisis in 1997. Perhaps no-one could have prevented that disaster. It had its roots in an expectation that unsustainable exchange rates would continue indefinitely and in dangerously sloppy lending practices by Western and local banks. But certainly we could have lessened its impact.

In my view—and it is a view I put forcefully to senior US administration and IMF figures at the time and since—this mishandling bore down terribly unfairly on Indonesia.

Of course there were weaknesses in the Indonesian economy that needed to be addressed, just as there were in the other affected countries. But the tragedy is that some of the medicine that the IMF and its allies touted so confidently as a sure-fire remedy, and then force-fed to the patients, turned out to be snake oil. It made their condition even worse.

That whole approach was one of the most significant failures of international public policy over the past 25 years. Its economic and social impact is still being felt.

The crisis changed the dynamics of regional cooperation. It deflated a lot of that regional optimism and generated a new caution about the pace of economic reform. It also increased scepticism about *outside* advice and gave new voice to economic nationalist sentiments.

The second important way the region has changed over the past five years has been through the impact of China's continuing economic growth. China's GDP grew by 9.7 per cent a year on average between 1989 and 2000 and real urban incomes doubled. It is now the second largest economy in the world by purchasing power parity measurements, and the destination for 85 per cent of all foreign direct investment coming to Asia.

As a result, it has become a much more powerful competitor for export markets. But the growth of domestic demand, and its WTO-mandated commitment to openness, have also made it a more important market and economic partner for its neighbours.

In my mind, there is little doubt that over the course of this century China will become much stronger economically, more powerful strategically and more confident politically.

Ten years ago it might have been possible to talk about economic integration in Asia without China. That is no longer possible.

A third obvious change—this time external to the region—has been the impact of the terrorist attacks in the United States last year.

I don't believe as some commentators claimed that the world was changed utterly by the events of September 11. On the contrary, I think we got to understand the world better. It is not excusing terrorism to see in those events a reminder to us of the divisions that continue to exist globally between a 'contented centre' and the problems on the margins, and the dangers we face if we ignore them.

The attacks did profoundly change one very important thing, however. They gave Americans a new sense of their own vulnerability. As a result, the United States, the world's largest economy and the only military power with global reach, has become more openly unilateralist in its approach to the world.

So how have these developments changed the prospects for regional cooperation and integration in Asia? What should we be looking for in the first decade of the twenty-first century compared with the last decade of the twentieth?

Before talking about regionalism, however, it is necessary to say something about globalisation.

Globalisation has continued to transform Asia. We saw it in the volatile capital movements around the time of the financial crisis and in the continuing direct and immediate links between what happens in the regional economy and the global one. The recent fate of Asian electronics exports is a good example.

Globalisation is not going away. The technological changes that drive it cannot be uninvented, so it continues to transform the way countries interact.

In my view, the challenge for governments is not to try to circumvent globalisation but to harness and direct it in ways that bring its many benefits to ordinary men and women.

But one obvious question is whether, in an age of globalisation, regional cooperation and integration still makes sense.

After all, by making information more easily available and facilitating transactions, globalisation brings closer the ideal of an efficient global market. Indonesian manufacturers can find markets anywhere on earth. Market forces are themselves driving a harmonisation of product standards and regulations, as manufacturers themselves adjust to the needs of their markets.

In a world in which distance is shrinking, perhaps physical closeness no longer matters so much. So do we still need regional arrangements in a world in which sellers and buyers can be linked up instantaneously on the Internet and transactions can be made at the click of a computer mouse?

My answer is yes.

One reason is that while changes in the private sector may be happening automatically, as a result of market forces, the issue for governments is how to deal with the reverse side of the process.

For governments, globalisation raises a range of new and difficult issues: harmonising legislation, protecting taxation revenues, improving corporate governance and accountancy standards. They also have to address increasingly urgent transnational problems like environmental degradation and terrorism.

Markets alone won't resolve these challenges. Nor can they be dealt with by national legislation alone or within the borders of individual states. They require international cooperation; multilateral cooperation.

But existing global organisations are often too large or slow-moving to respond effectively. The sheer scale of the United Nations and other large multilateral bodies can restrict the capacity of smaller countries, especially, to participate effectively in their work, to get any kind of worthwhile result.

Faced with these problems at the global level, tighter, more flexible, regional organisations have been able to fill some of the gaps.

They can address the growing number of issues that are too large for the nation-state to handle and too limited or too urgent for global action. That is the essence of it.

Regional cooperation also has the useful byproduct of strengthening bilateral relations, by increasing the opportunities for contact by political leaders and making that contact easier and less formal.

The European Union, ASEAN and APEC all have political and strategic as well as economic purposes. Economic cooperation is one of the ways they build deeper and more lasting political relationships.

The broadest of the existing regional organisations, of course, is APEC.

I have to admit that I feel less confident about APEC than I did ten years ago. The Asian financial crisis weakened the forum, partly because it did so little during the initial stages. And members have shied away from some of the most politically difficult trade-liberalisation aims.

Just as importantly, the organisation suffered from reckless expansion in numbers to include economies such as Peru and Russia that simply do not have the same interests in the great trans-Pacific flows of trade and capital that bound the original members. The larger the membership of a regional organisation becomes, the harder it is to keep the focus clear.

These failures might not matter so much if it was possible to see among current members any real champions for APEC, leaders prepared to expend energy and political capital to keep the organisation moving forward. But it is hard to identify any. And if regional organisations don't face such internal prodding, they tend to slump back into a state of bureaucratic sleepiness in which the process becomes as important as the outcome.

APEC has some important things in its favour, however. Its Leaders' Meetings have shown themselves time and again to be a useful and practical way of enabling regional heads of government to maintain links and contacts, even at times of stress in bilateral relations. We saw that when President Bush was able to visit Shanghai so soon after the spy plane incident.

And the vital role US markets, investment flows and security policy will continue to play in this region means that a trans-Pacific forum engaging the United States at the highest level about these issues—and which includes Japan and China—will have a continuing vital usefulness for all of us.

But, partly because of its size, APEC can no longer fulfil so easily some of the other community-building functions of regional organisations.

One of the consequences of the financial crisis was to turn the debate about regional integration inwards again, to East Asia.

Financial issues emerged as a more urgent and obvious focus for cooperation. Japan's first proposal in 1997 for an Asian Monetary Fund met opposition from the United States, the IMF and China, but it began a debate which has led to some concrete outcomes.

In May 2000, the new ASEAN Plus Three grouping—which has been another manifestation of the narrower regional focus after the crisis—created a network of regional currency-swap arrangements. The same grouping is trying to regularise meetings of finance and trade officials.

At the subregional level, the oldest and most important of the organisations is, of course, ASEAN. Like APEC, it has had some difficulties in maintaining focus after its expansion to include the countries of Indochina. Its new members are at very different levels of development. Nevertheless it remains important to Southeast Asia's capacity to develop confidently and cohesively.

We have seen a flurry of new proposals for economic cooperation, but not much movement. Various dialogues about free-trade areas are continuing but without sign of early movement.

AFTA—the ASEAN Free Trade Area—has moved haltingly. Proposals for a China–ASEAN free trade agreement within ten years were announced in November 2000 and Japan has also proposed a comprehensive economic initiative with ASEAN which would include free trade. Discussions about a link between AFTA and the Australia New Zealand Closer Economic Relations Trade Agreement have been underway since my government first proposed them in 1995.

I think it is fair to say that it will be some time before we see concrete results from this dialogue. Elements of competition and cooperation continue to balance themselves evenly in the debate about Asian regional economic cooperation. Competition between China and Japan, between Japan and South Korea, between some of the ASEAN countries, between China and the other developing economies remains absolute.

This links into the second of the changes I talked about: China's economic growth.

I believe the world is far better off with a growing and self-confident China than with a weak and uncertain one. But it can be uncomfortable to live next door to a giant. The experience can generate resentment and a feeling of powerlessness on the part of smaller neighbours.

In these circumstances, other Asian countries need to have confidence that their voices will be heard. That they can shape the region as well as belong to it. For these reasons, I think it is vital that China enters the regional and global stage in the context of successful, working regional organisations. I think the signs so far are positive.

The final change I mentioned in the region was the impact of September 11.

The main point I want to make here is the simple one that American unilateralism is simply not a sustainable leadership model for the world.

One lesson we must all learn—not as a result of terrorist attacks, but because it is morally essential—is that the developed world cannot just take the economic benefits of globalisation and ignore the demands from other parts of the globe for a voice and for representation. Such action will simply store up fiery resentment which will eventually manifest itself in ever more dangerous ways.

A globalised international economy has to mean a more representative international polity. This the United States continually fails to understand. And regional organisations themselves have an important part to play in a more representative international order.

So although there have been disappointments in regional cooperation and integration, we should not give up on the process.

Just as Asia's interests and problems differ from those of other parts of the world, so will the forms and structures of its regional bodies. Compared with Europe, Asian countries are at very different stages of economic development. And the patterns of interaction between, say, North Asia and Southeast Asia, have been less intense than Europe's. As a result, Asia is likely to develop a more variegated regional architecture. Nothing monolithic or highly structured.

Let me end by saying something about Australia and Indonesia, a subject I feel strongly about.

This might not be a fashionable sentiment in either Canberra or Jakarta at present, but I continue to believe firmly that Australia and Indonesia together have a major contribution to make to regional cooperation and integration; indeed, to their own safety, security and development.

We have shown it in the past in two areas in particular. The success of the Cambodia peace settlement and the establishment of APEC Leaders' Meetings both depended critically on close cooperation between our two countries.

This idea lay behind the Agreement on Maintaining Security which we signed in 1996 but which fell victim to domestic politicking during the East Timor troubles.

The agreement provided for Australia and Indonesia to consult regularly about their common security, including adverse challenges to it, and to develop such cooperation as would benefit them *and* the region.

415

In other words, we saw the Australia–Indonesia relationship as an integral part of wider regional cooperation. It is a vision well worth remembering today.

If I had one piece of advice for Indonesians, it would be the same advice that I have been offering my friends here for a long time now. Indonesia needs to be energetic and creative about communicating its own realities to the outside world and identifying strategic partnerships that will help them with this. That is one of the reasons this conference is important.

Like China or India or the United States, Indonesia is so large that it can become self-absorbed. Given the challenges the Indonesian people face, that is hardly surprising. But I urge Indonesians to look outwards as well.

Indonesia is at the epicentre of Southeast Asia. The success of regional cooperation and integration in this part of the world will continue to depend vitally on Indonesia's active participation.

President Megawati recently made an important speech in India in which she said that 'the main foundation upon which [Indonesia's] national stability is built' is tolerance.

That is one of the enduring strengths of Indonesian society. And at this particular time, it has never been more important for the international community to understand and appreciate the structure and outlook of the world's most populous Islamic society.

12

AUSTRALIA AND ASIA

Lazard Frères Symposium,
Sydney,
15 May 2001

*Delivered to a financial market audience, Paul Keating's 'Australia
and Asia' addresses his continued advocacy that Australia's destiny
lay inexorably with Asia. He reminds his audience that Australia is
more alone in the world than ever before. He says the core of what
is happening in Asia goes to how the rest of the world handles the
emergence of China. He makes clear his view that China is not the
old Soviet Union nurturing some tradition of Russian expansionism.
The address criticises the George W Bush administration for its
early stigmatisation of China as the looming Evil Empire Mark II
and goes on to discuss regional developments, including in Japan
and in Indonesia. Paul Keating concludes the address by urging
that Australia resume its role as an architect of Asian regionalism
and upbraids the Howard government for its lack of diligence
and imagination.*

WHEN I THINK ABOUT OUR future, I begin with one main proposition:
that this is a period in which Australia is going to be more alone in
the world than ever.

In a way, this is a paradox, because one impact of globalisation
and the information revolution is to make the world smaller and more

crowded. But it also makes the global environment more competitive, more fluid and much less sentimental.

And unlike the pioneers of Federation one hundred years ago, we have no patron to look after us.

No imperial preferences to guarantee us markets. No Royal Navy to steam to our rescue in time of trouble. No massive population to give us unearned weight in the international system. No voice to speak up for us in the world unless we do it ourselves.

If you face a prospect like this, you have two broad ways of dealing with it.

You can take the Hansonite approach and hunker down against an unfriendly external environment, cutting yourself off economically and politically. This approach is attractive to some, but it just won't work, at least on terms that would be acceptable to most Australians. The inevitable result will be falling living standards.

Or you can draw self-confidently on your national strengths and declare the place open: open to immigration, to economic competition, to ideas, to new technology.

I think that is the only approach that will deliver this country—or any country—success in the information age.

One of the most important consequences of this is that the most important national development responsibilities of the twenty-first century do not lie with vast infrastructure projects but with the development of our human capital, our people.

At present Australia's investment in education and research is falling. School retention rates have actually declined under this government and our universities are precariously close to the edge in maintaining their international reputation. That reputation is all that sustains our increasingly valuable education exports.

Our human capital requirements also mean we must be open to skilled migration. Reports of Indian students being beaten in Melbourne, or televised pictures of asylum seekers being treated harshly in remote detention centres, do us more harm in the message we send to skilled young people around the world than other images we may seek to project. The notion that as a society, we are suspicious of foreigners must surely be poison to those otherwise willing to place their trust in us.

Unless we address these questions, we'll have a long, barren time to regret it.

We live in a world in which image and brand matter for countries as much as companies. The job of being Australian Prime Minister these days is in important ways about management of the national brand. As trade becomes a larger part of our economy, and services and technology manufactures become a larger part of our trade, our national brand matters more.

This is because when people in other countries make decisions about where to go for a holiday or educate their children or buy parts for the next generation of aircraft or make their technology investment, they factor into those decisions a complex range of interests and emotions. Much more complex than the issues of price and security of supply that govern decisions about where to source steaming coal or wheat.

Openness also puts a new premium on our capacity to deal effectively with the outside world, because the external environment has the capacity to shape domestic outcomes much more directly.

For Australia, this means getting our relations with Asia right.

Since the Asian financial crisis there has been a whisper around that the last Labor government got carried away with Asia. Alexander Downer accuses me of being 'obsessed' with it. But it's not Asia I'm obsessed with, but Australia's future. And this region is where our future lies.

Of course Australians will make their fortunes where they can, and Europe and America will continue to have a lot to offer us. But nothing we can do will greatly affect the outcome of developments in those parts of the world. We are observers there, not players.

Asia is where all our interests come together. It will still be the fastest growing area of the world over the next decade; it is where our main security and defence interests lie; where an increasing number of Australians come from.

Our trade is already back to where it was before the 1997 financial crisis, and it will only grow, because there is a natural complementarity between what we produce and what Asia needs; not just minerals, energy and agriculture but services and sophisticated manufactures as well.

We're hearing a lot about whether Australia is destined to be a branch-office economy. We're far less likely to end up with a hollowed-out capability if Asia is where our business is focused. There are tremendous opportunities in the region and Australians are well placed to take them up.

But over the short term, and—unless we all play our cards right—perhaps longer, Asia faces some serious problems, and I now want to turn to these.

I'm a long-term optimist about Asia, but it is hard not to be a short-term pessimist.

Almost all the indicators look worse than they did six months ago. The economic outlook is weaker, the politics are getting harder and the security issues are more uncertain.

At the core of what is happening in Asia is the issue of how the rest of the world handles China's emergence as a great power. It was the international system's failure in the late nineteenth century to manage Germany and Japan's growth that set the twentieth century on its disastrous course.

We looked for a while as though we were going to avoid repeating this error with China, but I'm now less sure.

The United States, China and Japan form an unstable triangle within which these problems will have to be resolved. But domestic politics rather than statecraft seems increasingly to be driving policy.

The American side of the US–China relationship has always had a strong element of domestic politics in it, dating at least from the post-Second World War debate about who 'lost' China—as though it was ever America's to lose. Under the Bush administration, however, public debate about China is increasingly being marked by hysteria and overstatement. We face a real danger that China is being assigned a role as the Evil Empire Mark II.

For any one except the American Right, China wouldn't survive an audition for this part. Economically, it is doing everything asked of it, in moving steadily towards a more open and rules-based economic system, avoiding competitive devaluation during the Asian financial crisis, and moving to join the WTO. Non-state-owned businesses now account for 60 per cent of China's GDP.

Politically, reform is slower, but it is happening. Personal space for ordinary Chinese is growing, not least with 80 million mobile-phone users and 22 million on the Internet. Legal structures are getting stronger and experiments with local-level elections have been held.

And in foreign policy China has been helpful and cooperative—as with its hosting of APEC later this year. In terms of cross-Straits relations, Beijing's approach to Taiwan since last year's review of policy at the leadership retreat has been a model of restraint. And its behaviour is beginning to have an effect in opinion polls. For the first time, more than 15 per cent of Taiwanese voters now support the 'one country, two systems' option for reunification.

In other words, China is not the Soviet Union. After the Second World War, a combination of Stalin's paranoia, Moscow's ideological commitment to world revolution, direct military confrontation across the vulnerable plains of northern Europe and the legacy of historical traditions of Russian imperialism made containment a viable and sensible policy. There was a genuine struggle and the West needed to win it.

But China does not have the Russian tradition of expansionism—its policy weakness was the reverse of Russia's: it turned away from the outside world from the middle of the millennium, with disastrous results. Its brand of communism is no longer of the proselytising sort. It is not seeking to confront the West.

The important question is not *whether* China becomes a great power: it almost certainly will. Deng Xiaoping settled that when he introduced the economic reform program.

The important thing is *how* it becomes a great power—that is, whether it is brought smoothly into the world within a framework of robust multilateralism, or whether it has to elbow its way into the international arena. That will help shape its approach to global stability.

Although China's entry into the world as a large, confident and richer power will be uncomfortable for its neighbours from time to time, it will not be nearly as uncomfortable as a poor and fragmented China would be.

According to the World Bank, China is now the second largest economy in the world, measured by purchasing power parity. Around the middle of the century, on current trends, it will become the largest.

The strategic situation of the second half of the twentieth century with the world's second largest economy—Japan—being a strategic client of the largest—the United States—was always historically unique and not going to continue into the twenty-first.

Some element of strategic competition between China and the United States is inevitable, especially as China develops a larger and more effective power projection capability and becomes, for the first time in its history, a sea and air power as well as a continental one. But that is not incompatible with a broadly cooperative approach to the management of international issues.

However, the George W Bush administration seems in danger of placing China in the enemy camp, ostentatiously 'reviewing' its relations, abandoning—whether deliberately or not—the former position of 'strategic ambiguity' over the US's willingness to defend Taiwan against any Chinese military threat, and pursuing an expensive and probably technically unfeasible National Missile Defense (NMD) program, which has the capacity to disrupt and remake the whole Asian security agenda, including by reinforcing the Sino–Russian relationship.

In China itself, domestic politics are also playing a growing part in shaping foreign and economic policy. As we saw in the response to the bombing of the Chinese embassy in Belgrade and the recent spy plane incident, a genuine, nationalist public opinion is emerging in China with the capacity to influence government policy. That is going to make the relationship with the United States harder to manage.

In addition, most of the current leaders, including Jiang Zemin and Zhu Rongji, will retire over the next two years. Their likely replacements, Hu Jintao and Wen Jiabao, will follow the same policy direction, but political nervousness within the leadership means that we are seeing a reluctance to make major policy changes as well as a general tightening up on the domestic security front.

On the Japanese side of the triangle, domestic politics are playing a new role too. Prime Minister Koizumi is an unknown quantity. We have now seen a decade of structural decline in Japan. Deep changes in its economic structures and political culture are certainly needed if it is to move back to growth and therefore help the rest of the region.

Koizumi is calling for more rapid write-off for banks' bad debts (now estimated at perhaps $500 billion); the introduction of unemployment benefits to make it easier for companies to lay off workers; unspecified reform of the pension system (which is probably under-funded by $3 trillion—or 100 per cent of GDP); capping of government spending at $245 billion; and the privatisation of the postal savings bank.

Perhaps Koizumi will deliver. We must all hope so, although even if he does, the short-term effects, at least, of the reforms will be an interim period of even sharper economic decline.

Two important questions remain open.

The first is whether Koizumi genuinely represents change in the LDP—and therefore in the structure of Japanese society—or whether the old powerbrokers are just using him to put on a new public face before the 29 July Upper House elections, and will then stymie his attempts at reform.

The second question about him is whether he will use old-fashioned nationalism to gather the necessary public support for his changes and what the impact of this will be on Japan's neighbours.

Koizumi seems to be foreshadowing a more 'normal' Japanese stance in the world. That need not be a bad thing—the current client relationship between Japan and the United States won't continue indefinitely, and the world could do with more open and imaginative leadership from Japan. And, thankfully, Koizumi seems to have backed away from earlier proposals to change the peace clause in the constitution and to pay a public, as opposed to private, visit to the Yasukuni shrine. But the dynamics of Japan's relations with its neighbours are going to become more complex as a result.

All this strategic juggling is happening against a backdrop of renewed economic uncertainty in Asia.

The IMF projects world economic growth at 3.2 per cent this year, with the US at 1.5 per cent and Japan at 0.5 per cent. With the American and Japanese economies slowing, developing Asia will face enormous difficulties.

Only China, growing at 7 per cent, and India, are reasonably strong. Southeast Asian growth is expected almost to halve to 3.5 per cent.

Since the Asian economic crisis, financial and corporate restructuring in most of the affected countries has been much slower than needed. In almost every case, the political clout of the major investors has proved more resilient than the power of the reform institutions, and governments have been concerned about the systemic or social implications of allowing important firms to fail.

South Korea, for example, has made some good economic progress and it is now less vulnerable to balance-of-payments crises. But the corporate sector remains one of the most heavily indebted in the world and its profitability is too low. South Korea seems unable to break out of its *chaebol* mould. (One of the few good results of the Asian economic crisis was that it came just in time to prevent China following down the South Korean *chaebol* route in the reform of its state-owned enterprises.)

This general economic gloom will be reinforced if tensions in the Sino–US relationship cause a further delay in China's entry to the WTO beyond the Qatar meeting in November. With a new focus by the US on regional free trade in the Americas, and anti-globalisation sentiment growing, the membership of the most populous country in the world is about the only thing on the horizon that might give the WTO and the international trading system generally a kick-along.

All these developments are putting much greater pressure on Southeast Asia, the part of the region closest to Australia.

The ASEAN countries are feeling the competitive impact of China, not just in competition for export markets but, most importantly, for foreign direct investment (FDI). Southeast Asia used to attract 60 per cent of all foreign investment going to East Asia. Now the figure is around 20 per cent, with China the overwhelming beneficiary. A decline in FDI will have ramifications not just for economic growth and employment, but for technology transfer as well.

Almost all the individual ASEAN countries face problems. Malaysia is entering a much more uncertain phase, with the transition from Prime Minister Mahathir getting closer and the results more uncertain. In Thailand it seems unlikely that Thaksin will be able to deliver both the populist policies that got him elected and economic growth. His rhetoric is developing a more nationalist edge to it. The Philippines is still hostage to the political uncertainty that followed Gloria Arroyo's replacement of Estrada.

But the country that really matters here is Indonesia and its 210 million people. Southeast Asia cannot recover without a growing and stable Indonesia.

Economically, the rupiah is still around 11,500 to the US dollar. This is putting huge pressure on the central government's debt service obligations: two-thirds of central government expenditure is going into servicing international and domestic debt.

Bank restructuring under the Indonesian Bank Restructuring Agency hasn't come close to addressing the underlying problems with the financial system. FDI is still flowing out. Unrest in Aceh is threatening supplies of natural gas, which provides 20 per cent of the nation's export revenue and 5 per cent of its annual budget.

The security situation in Aceh, Irian Jaya and Maluku is deteriorating.

The chances that Indonesia's parliament will vote to dismiss President Wahid some time in the next couple of months are growing. The key will be Vice President Megawati. She is reluctant to move directly against President Wahid, but is eventually likely to do so.

The prospect, in other words, is for several more years of uncertainty. And if Australia learned one lesson from the past 30 years in Southeast Asia, it is that the ASEAN region needs Indonesia as a leader.

This uncertainty in the region has a direct relevance for Australia.

We don't have the option of averting our eyes and waiting for events to take their course.

We need urgently to resume our role as an architect of regional institutions—the sort of role we played in developing APEC and the ASEAN Regional Forum.

By multilateralising the interests of the great powers like China and the United States, APEC helped create an environment that was much more conducive for small and medium-sized countries like Australia.

But now a lot of the action is passing to the ASEAN Plus Three group (that is, Southeast Asia plus China, Japan and South Korea). The most recent agreement on currency-swap arrangements—a precursor perhaps to eventual closer monetary cooperation—was taken without Australian involvement.

The key lesson of the past five years of the Howard government has been that Australia cannot afford to have ten years on and ten years off with Asia. Consistency and continuity are vital—as are diligence and imagination.

Australia does not have to choose between Asia and the rest of the world. It has always been true that the greater the influence we have on developments in Asia, the more use we will be to the United States and Europe, and the more influence we will have globally.

13

NOTES ON THE STATE OF THE WORLD
Melbourne,
25 July 2001

There is perennially a question in the mind of the Australian people as to what our leaders really think about important issues. Paul Keating's 'Notes on the State of the World' address, delivered extemporaneously to a private business audience in Melbourne, provides a hard-hitting, no-nonsense assessment of how he saw the world in July 2001, two months before the attacks on New York in September of that year. He underlines the lost opportunity by the United States in wasting a decade at the end of the Cold War, on triumphalism and dot-com booms, while failing to develop a new order to run the world. Just before September 11 and the Iraq war which followed, he saw the US adopting an introspective, insular unipolarity—eschewing the liberal internationalism that had allowed it to so successfully manage the Western alliance against the Soviet Union. In the speech, Paul Keating spells out what this means for Australia—including snapshots of contemporary developments in China, Japan and Indonesia. He uses elements of his recently delivered Lazard Frères address in this private talk.

WE NEED TO GET THINKING about the security and sovereignty of Australia. This is not guaranteed.

The Cold War world was tense, but within its bipolar structure the capacity to do massive violence was managed. This has led people to assume that this is the way it will always be.

But that is a dangerous assumption. When the US won the Cold War, it cried victory and walked off the field, leaving no structure behind.

We thought at the time of the Gulf War that we were moving towards some sort of UN-based system of international management, but that turned out to be simply a myth.

What we have seen since 1991 is a decade of US growth, wealth and triumphalism, but no attempt to create a new international order which reflects the great body of states, including ones like China and India.

There was a view when the George W Bush administration came to power that it would lift the foreign policy bar above the low level of the Clinton years. That hasn't happened. Europeans and others just cannot understand why Americans express such feelings of vulnerability at a time when it is, without question, the most powerful economy in the world and which spends more on defence than the next *eight* highest-spending countries in the world combined.

The US is becoming more introspective and now we have a President who has not only turned his back on nuclear disarmament but is promoting a new nuclear arms race by failing to ratify the Comprehensive Test Ban Treaty and seeking to overturn the Anti-Ballistic Missile (ABM) treaty—all in the cause of seeking to insulate and isolate the United States from the rest of the world. The world is not being cooperatively run, which forces the likes of Vladimir Putin and Jiang Zemin to come together, as they did recently to urge the US not to go down the path of another nuclear arms race. They are vowing to resist US hegemony.

If we assume that the US wants to dump arms control treaties that don't suit it and cocoon itself behind some sort of missile shield, it does not take a great leap of political science to consider that the US won't be party again to the kind of peace-keeping and peace-making missions we've seen of it in the past. We risk ending up with a world that resembles more a *Mad Max* film than the sort of order established after the Second World War in which we had participation by all the powers.

The new Bush administration is surely running a policy which is at odds with that kind of order. It is militantly asserting a unilateral approach—on the environment, on Kyoto, on weapons systems. We've seen the strength of isolationist exceptionalism in American politics before: the view that the US is a society apart from others, a strain of thinking that goes right back to the first Puritan settlers. Splendid isolation is not a real-world position in an interconnected world.

There are questions here for Australian policy. Should we rejoice in the new American exceptionalism? Should we be fawning supplicants of our US ally, or should we be doing all we can to try to persuade Washington to help create a liberal international order which is nuclear-free, inclusive and where violence can be managed? In other words, a new society of nations that includes China, India and especially Russia.

We're at a fork in the road and have to decide whether we go uncritically down the pathway towards defence-force integration in the American orbit or whether we decide that our real future is with the people of this part of the world. Does Australia go down the path of finding its security *in* Asia and the world? Or do we adopt the Howard credo of seeking our security from the world by nipping and tucking under Uncle Sam's arms?

Or do we follow the path of New Zealand, which seems to have decided that its national aim is limited to being the largest Polynesian state?

At the moment we are witnessing demonstrations against the G8 and the World Trade Organization (WTO). The reason we are seeing this mindless resistance to globalisation at the G8 meeting and elsewhere is that global political leadership hasn't kept pace with the economics.

People who suffer the harsher effects of globalisation aren't satisfied that leaving the world to be sorted out by multinational corporations is necessarily a right or good thing. And they are right. Remember Galbraith saying the tribulations at the margin can upset the content-ment at the centre.

Let me now turn to Asia. At the core of what is happening in Asia is the issue of how the rest of the world handles China's emergence as a great power. It was the international system's failure in the late-nineteenth century to manage Germany and Japan's growth that set the twentieth century on its disastrous course.

The triangle between the United States, Japan and China has its antecedence in the postwar history—in the set of strategic guarantees given to Japan by the United States. These are not natural arrangements. As a consequence, they are inherently unstable. Especially as domestic politics, as much as statecrafe, is often the driver.

The American side of the US–China relationship has always had a strong element of domestic politics in it, dating at least from the post-Second World War debate about who *lost* China—as though it was ever America's to lose. Under the Bush administration, however, public debate about China is increasingly being marked by hysteria and overstatement (from Donald Rumsfeld and the Defense Department more than Colin Powell and the State Department.) We face a real danger that China is being assigned a role as the Evil Empire Mark II.

For anyone except the American Right, China wouldn't survive an audition for this part. Economically, it is doing everything asked of it, in moving steadily towards a more open and rules-based economic system, avoiding competitive devaluation during the Asian financial crisis, and moving to join the WTO. Non-state-owned businesses now account for 60 per cent of China's GDP.

Politically, reform is slower, but it is happening. Personal space for ordinary Chinese is growing, not least with 80 million mobile-phone users and 22 million on the Internet. Legal structures are getting stronger and experiments with local-level elections have been held.

And in foreign policy China has been helpful and cooperative—as with its hosting of APEC later this year. In terms of cross-Straits relations, Beijing's approach to Taiwan since last year's review of policy at the leadership retreat has been a model of restraint. And its behaviour is beginning to have an effect in opinion polls. For the first time, more than 15 per cent of Taiwanese voters now support the 'one country, two systems' option for reunification.

In other words, China is not the Soviet Union. After the Second World War, a combination of Stalin's paranoia, Moscow's ideological commitment to world revolution, direct military confrontation across the vulnerable plains of northern Europe and the legacy of historical traditions of Russian imperialism made containment a viable and sensible policy. There was a genuine struggle and the West needed to win it.

But China does not have the Russian tradition of expansionism—its policy weakness was the reverse of Russia's: it turned away from the outside world from the middle of the millennium, with disastrous results. Its brand of communism is no longer of the proselytising sort. It is not seeking to confront the West.

The important question is not *whether* China becomes a great power: it almost certainly will. Deng Xiaoping settled that when he introduced the economic reform program.

The important thing is *how* it becomes a great power—that is, whether it is brought smoothly into the world within a framework of robust multilateralism, or whether it has to elbow its way into the international arena. That will help shape its approach to global stability.

Although China's entry into the world as a large, confident and richer power will be uncomfortable for its neighbours from time to time, it will not be nearly as uncomfortable as a poor and fragmented China would be.

According to the World Bank, China is now the second largest economy in the world, measured by purchasing power parity. Around the middle of the century, on current trends, it will become the largest.

The strategic situation of the second half of the twentieth century with the world's second largest economy—Japan—being a strategic client of the largest—the United States—was always historically unique and not going to continue into the twenty-first.

Some element of strategic competition between China and the United States is inevitable, especially as China develops a larger and more effective power projection capability and becomes, for the first time in its history, a sea and air power as well as a continental one. But that is not incompatible with a broadly cooperative approach to the management of international issues.

However, the Bush administration seems in danger of placing China in the enemy camp, ostentatiously *reviewing* its relations, abandoning—whether deliberately or not—the former position of strategic ambiguity over the US's willingness to defend Taiwan against any Chinese military threat, and pursuing National Missile Defense which, as we have seen, has the capacity to disrupt and remake the whole Asian security agenda, including by reinforcing the Sino–Russian relationship.

In China itself, domestic politics are also playing a growing part in shaping foreign and economic policy. It was evident in the response to the bombing of the Chinese embassy in Belgrade and the spy plane incident, that a genuine, nationalist public opinion is emerging in China with the capacity to influence government policy. That is going to make the relationship with the United States harder to manage.

In addition, most of the current leaders, including Jiang Zemin and Zhu Rongji, will retire over the next two years. Their likely replacements, Hu Jintao and Wen Jiabao, will follow the same policy direction, but political nervousness within the leadership means that we are seeing a reluctance to make major policy changes as well as a general tightening up on the domestic security front.

On the Japanese side of the triangle, domestic politics are playing a new role too. Prime Minister Koizumi is an unknown quantity. We have now seen a decade of structural decline in Japan. Deep changes in its economic structures and political culture are certainly needed if it is to move back to growth and therefore help the rest of the region.

Koizumi is calling for more rapid write-off for banks' bad debts (now estimated at perhaps $500 billion); the introduction of unemployment benefits to make it easier for companies to lay off workers; unspecified reform of the pension system (which is probably under-funded by $3 trillion—or 100 per cent of GDP); capping of government spending at $245 billion; and the privatisation of the postal savings bank, which basically operates as an extra-parliamentary slush fund for the Liberal Democratic Party (LDP).

Perhaps Koizumi will deliver. We must all hope so, although even if he does, the short-term effects, at least, of the reforms will be an interim period of even sharper economic decline.

Two important questions remain open.

The first is whether Koizumi genuinely represents change in the LDP—and therefore in the structure of Japanese society—or whether the old powerbrokers are just using him to put on a new public face before the 29 July Upper House elections, and will then stymie his attempts at reform.

The second question about him is whether he will use old-fashioned nationalism to gather the necessary public support for his changes and what the impact of this will be on Japan's neighbours.

Koizumi seems to be foreshadowing a more 'normal' Japanese stance in the world. That need not be a bad thing—the current client relationship between Japan and the United States won't continue indefinitely, and the world could do with more open and imaginative leadership from Japan. But the dynamics of Japan's relations with its neighbours are going to become more complex as a result. We've seen another sharp dispute between Japan, South Korea and China over the Japanese treatment of the war in school textbooks.

But the country that really matters to Australia is Indonesia and its 210 million people. Southeast Asia cannot recover without a growing and stable Indonesia.

Megawati's elevation may help stabilise the situation. She will be more predictable than Wahid, and should be able to keep the Indonesian military, the TNI, onside, but the period between now and the next election in 2004 will be full of uncertainties.

With Megawati's election the rupiah has strengthened but at 10,000 to the US dollar the pressures on the central government's debt service obligations are still intense: almost two-thirds of central government expenditure is going into servicing international and domestic debt. Standard & Poors gives Indonesia a credit rating of CCC-plus, the lowest in the world.

Growth next year is expected to be just 3.5 per cent. Bank restructuring under the Indonesian Bank Restructuring Agency hasn't come close to addressing the underlying problems with the financial system. Foreign direct investment is still flowing out. Unrest in Aceh is threatening supplies of natural gas, which provides 20 per cent of the nation's export revenue and 5 per cent of its annual budget. Inflation is running at 12 per cent.

The security situation in Aceh, Irian Jaya and Maluku is deteriorating.

The prospect, in other words, is for several more years of uncertainty. And if Australia learned one lesson from the past 30 years in Southeast Asia, it is that the ASEAN region needs Indonesia as a leader.

Finally, let me say some things about Australia. Australia is going backwards in the region politically and economically. Our regional horizon is sinking into the Arafura Sea.

The low dollar is keeping our exports up, and the percentage going to Asia is back where it was before the financial crisis, but strategically we are going nowhere in shaping the regional architecture; ASEAN Plus Three, the ASEAN Free Trade Area—Closer Economic Relations (AFTA–CER) arrangements fell apart and little is happening with regional financial institutions.

The key lesson of the past five years under John Howard has been that Australia cannot afford to have ten years on and ten years off with Asia. Consistency and continuity are vital. Australia does not have to choose between Asia and the rest of the world. It has always been true that the greater the influence we have on developments in Asia, the more use we will be to the United States and Europe and the more influence we will have globally.

14

THE PERILOUS MOMENT
Indonesia, Australia and the Asian Crisis
University of New South Wales,
Sydney,
25 March 1998

As a piece of writing and as a history, Paul Keating's 'Perilous Moment' speech describing the Asian economic crisis of 1997–98 is compelling reading for anyone interested in this crucial time in Asia and for the world economy. The speech weaves the threads of the varied and complex issues into a tapestry, which provides the reader with accessible images. It traces the history of the crisis from the first attack on the Thai baht in May 1997 to the contagion which followed, especially in Indonesia. It tells how the International Monetary Fund overplayed its hand with a complete reordering of the Indonesian economy through its intrusive program of so-called 'structural conditionality'. Paul Keating explains how this crisis affects Australia and how Australia should stand by Indonesia. Prophetically, he said with financial contagion facilitated by rapid communications, 'we are likely to have less warning of future crises—and when they come, the swings they generate are likely to be larger'.

IT IS TEN MONTHS SINCE we saw the first signs of the Asian economic crisis with an attack by speculators on the Thai baht in May 1997. Since then, the crisis has unravelled in unpredictable ways across Asia. It is not over yet, and it presents Australia and the other countries of the region with a complex and dangerous challenge.

That challenge is not just economic, although the implications for individual economies, including Australia's, are serious. It is political and strategic as well. The whole direction in which the Asia Pacific has been moving—towards economic and political openness, towards a sense of Pacific community—is at risk. It is a perilous moment and there are real questions in my mind about whether we and our institutions can meet it successfully.

I want to talk tonight about why the Asian economies suddenly look so shaky, why the problems seem worse in Indonesia—the country of greatest immediate concern to Australia—what the implications are for our global and regional institutions, and what Australia should be doing about it.

This is the first region-wide crisis we have seen in Asia since it became one of the central pillars of the global economic system.

No-one predicted its timing or its precise cadence. And no-one understands with certainty whether it will spread further or how long its resolution will take.

But one of the important causes certainly lies in currency exchange rates, and the impact of rapid movements of currency which the information revolution has facilitated.

Its beginnings can be traced back to 1985. That was the year when, in response to growing US concern about the size of its trade deficit with Japan, the G5 industrial countries agreed in the Plaza Accord to take coordinated policy actions to push the US dollar lower. The result of their efforts, as they intended, was that the yen appreciated strongly against the US dollar.

That rising yen increased costs for Japanese exporters and encouraged them to move off-shore. Asia was the preferred destination, in part because the pegs Asian governments had established between their currencies and the US dollar made production costs cheap.

Over the next decade, this link with the dollar served Asian countries well. It facilitated the long boom in foreign direct investment into the region, with all the associated benefits, including technology transfer, which came with it. From the mid-1980s, Japanese companies built as much manufacturing capacity in continental Asia as exists in France. Businesses borrowed dollars cheaply at low rates of interest, thinking that the fixed tie with the American dollar gave them a natural hedge.

But then the game changed. In the two years after 1995, the US dollar rose 60 per cent against the yen, dragging the pegged Asian currencies up with it. As these economies became less competitive, their current accounts were exposed to much greater scrutiny, especially as regional exports fell after 1996.

The artificiality of the dollar pegs became more obvious, and devaluation became inevitable.

Stephen Grenville, the Deputy Governor of the Reserve Bank of Australia, recently described the crucial combination of elements in the crisis as 'the large volatile foreign capital flows, plus fragile financial sectors' which made these economies very vulnerable to changes of confidence.

In effect, the pressures of growth had become too great for the inadequate structures of the Asian countries to cope with. Their economic systems lacked transparency, banks were often seriously under-regulated, lending was politically directed and legal structures were inadequate.

The contagion spread with astonishing speed. In the markets, as the academic Jeffrey Sachs put it: 'Euphoria turned to panic without missing a beat.'

The economies of Thailand and South Korea, Malaysia, the Philippines and Indonesia came under scrutiny, then pressure.

But nowhere has the pressure been more intense than in Indonesia, and nowhere in Southeast Asia will the consequences be more serious. The reasons this should be so are matters of the greatest importance to Australia.

I said as Prime Minister that no country was more important to Australia than Indonesia. That reality will be brought sharply home to us over the next twelve months.

Clearly, what happens in Indonesia affects Australia's prosperity and security directly. We can't isolate ourselves from the consequences of large-scale economic, social or political uncertainty among the 200 million people living on an archipelago which stretches over 5000 kilometres across our north.

But developments in Indonesia affect Australia indirectly as well, because what happens there will determine—not simply shape or mould but *determine*—how quickly and peacefully the rest of Southeast Asia can develop.

This was a lesson which was clear to us more than 30 years ago, as Australians and our neighbours in the region watched with relief the transfer of power from President Sukarno to General Soeharto and the establishment of the New Order Government.

It is important to recall that time. Indonesia's economy was in chaos, inflation reached 1000 per cent, and as part of its policy of confrontation against Malaysia, the Indonesian government had launched attacks on its nearest neighbours. Australia was directly, if unofficially, involved in that military conflict.

The consequences of those developments in Indonesia in 1965 and 1966 have shaped Australia's environment for the past 30 years. As I have said before, the coming to power of the New Order Government was the single most beneficial strategic development for Australia in the postwar years.

In abandoning the dangerous international adventurism of his predecessor, President Soeharto provided the solid underpinning for successful regional cooperation through ASEAN and later APEC.

He refocused the efforts of the Indonesian government on economic and social development. The New Order Government delivered consistent economic growth of around 7 per cent a year.

And, just as importantly, the growth was spread widely. According to the World Bank, poverty was reduced more rapidly in Indonesia than in any other country it has studied.

The social indicators were equally strong. Over the past 25 years, the number of Indonesians living in absolute poverty fell from 60 per cent to 11 per cent, infant mortality was halved and life expectancy rose by seventeen years. Literacy rates were up from 39 per cent in 1960 to more than 80 per cent now. Economic modernisation and family-planning successes mean that there are some 50 million fewer Indonesians than would otherwise have been the case.

As a result of these developments, Australia was saved literally billions of dollars in defence expenditure and a market was created for trade worth $A5 billion last year.

Until this current crisis, Indonesia had been one of Asia's great success stories. In addition to a high growth rate, its current account deficit was less than 4 per cent, its budget was in balance and inflation under 10 per cent.

As in Thailand, Indonesia's economic problems began when its government was unable to sustain its informal currency peg between the rupiah and the US dollar. Indonesia had benefited greatly from that peg and the inflow of foreign direct investment it brought. But one of the consequences of opening up the economy was to give the financial and currency markets of New York and London and Frankfurt a significant influence on the Indonesian economy. I don't think this change was fully understood in Jakarta.

As the Indonesian economy came under greater scrutiny, problems everyone had known about—and lived with—like a weak banking sector, a lack of transparency in the economy, and political direction of investment decisions were put under the microscope.

Capital started leaving Indonesia, capital inflow slumped and confidence evaporated in the local market. The problems were magnified because an estimated 75 per cent of the offshore private-sector debt of around $74 billion was unhedged.

As the rupiah came under pressure, the Indonesian government realised it did not have the resources to defend the peg. In August 1997—quite early in the crisis—it decided to float the currency.

But neither that action, nor its extensive economic deregulation package in September, nor an IMF package in November, which the

Indonesian government was praised for seeking in a timely way, were sufficient to restore market confidence.

The annual budget delivered in January had some strong points, but was undermined by out-of-date economic assumptions, especially about the value of the currency. The government was forced back to the IMF to negotiate another, even larger, $43 billion, package of support.

This package, which was signed on 15 January, surprised almost all observers with its comprehensiveness. It involved extensive economic restructuring, including fundamental reform of the financial sector, and the dismantling of most government monopolies. 'Sweeping away all the restrictions,' was the way the IMF put it.

But despite these measures, the rupiah has not recovered. From a rate of 2430 to the US dollar in mid-1997, it has dropped to a current level of around 10,000. In these circumstances, Indonesia's high foreign debt of $120 billion becomes an insupportable burden. In essence, the Indonesian government has lost control of the pace of its adjustment to the global economy.

To give some idea of what Indonesia has to cope with, the decline in the rupiah's value is the equivalent of the Australian dollar falling from 75 cents to 10. No government can cope with that. The current rate of exchange is quite unreal: a fiction which bears no relationship to the strengths of the Indonesia economy.

As the Governor of the Reserve Bank of Australia, Ian Macfarlane, has pointed out, 'Falls of this size defy economic logic and serve no useful economic purpose . . . There is no value to Indonesia, to the region or the world in now having an exchange rate at a quarter of its former level.'

But Indonesia's economic problems are not confined to the financial sector. In parallel with the currency crisis, the widespread El Niño drought has brought smaller rice harvests and food shortages as well as catastrophic forest fires in East Kalimantan.

This depressed economic outlook, and the impact of many of the IMF reforms, will have serious social consequences. These cannot be avoided.

Fuel subsidies will be cut and food will rise in price. At the same time, the unemployment results of the currency collapse will be felt more strongly. Official estimates, almost certainly too low, are for a 50 per cent increase in the number of unemployed to 6.5 million during the course of the year.

The Indonesian economy is expected to contract by at least 5 per cent this year. And inflation is already rising and is expected to hit 40 per cent. Hyperinflation is possible.

These economic problems raise the likelihood of social unrest. Resentment against Chinese shopkeepers could lead to further looting and rioting with unforeseeable consequences. The leadership of the Indonesian armed forces is strong and competent but, in such circumstances, discipline will be tested.

This is not just a matter of foreign-policy concern. It is a human tragedy. The economic decline has dashed the prospects for tens of millions of ordinary Indonesians, who for the first time had been seeing some real improvements in their lives and better hopes for their children.

Why did it happen? Why have markets punished Indonesia so much more severely than other Asian countries in demonstrably worse macroeconomic shape?

The main reason is that the future of the Indonesian economy became caught up in judgements about its political system.

This was partly unfortunate timing. The onset of the crisis coincided with what was always going to be an uncertain political period in Indonesia leading up to the presidential elections. Markets like certainty and the Indonesian political timetable meant they couldn't have it.

Aspects of Indonesia's own response to the crisis contributed to the difficulty. It sent out mixed and sometimes confusing messages—as in the uncertainty about the currency board proposal. And it has backtracked on some important issues in the agreement with the IMF (as well as on some trivial issues which had a symbolic importance internationally).

The regrettable truth is that times like these require directness and clarity rather than Javanese obliqueness.

But most importantly, in my opinion, Indonesia was disproportionately punished because a grossly inaccurate view had taken hold in some quarters in Europe and North America that it was some sort of rogue state, to be talked about in the same breath as Mobutu's Zaire or Marcos's Philippines. Partly as a result of East Timor and a domestic dispute over political fundraising in the United States, Indonesia had become a symbol and a caricature rather than a real, complex and deeply important country.

Indonesia has not been good at telling its own story. It is noticeable how few voices exist in the United States or Europe willing to speak out for Indonesia—I'm not talking about the government here but the country and people.

The result was that the international goals for dealing with the crisis, and the performance measurements against which Indonesia would be judged, were expanded and restructured to include, explicitly, wholesale economic and social reform, and, implicitly, a change in the political leadership.

So the IMF's demands included not just measures to allow orderly economic adjustment but a complete reordering of the Indonesian economy.

It seized the opportunity to try to impose in one sweep an extensive and intrusive program of change. Some of the reforms it demanded were badly needed and will greatly strengthen the Indonesian economy when it recovers. But they have made that recovery more difficult by changing Indonesia's political dynamics and imposing goals which were politically unachievable, and therefore delaying any restoration of confidence.

It is important to remember that despite Indonesia's rapid growth it remains a developing economy with serious problems of administrative efficiency—just in getting the government's writ to run. It ought not be surprising if it has run into difficulty implementing a complex package of reforms which I doubt that Australia, with a smaller population and better communications, could have put in place in two months.

It was noticeable that almost before the ink was dry on the January agreement, prominent voices in the United States and Europe were casting doubts on Indonesia's willingness to comply. This had elements of a self-fulfilling prophecy about it. It undercut, almost immediately, the very confidence the measures were designed to restore.

Some of the commentary we are seeing about Indonesia has a chilling tone to it. Those who argue that the screws should be tightened on President Soeharto and the government because this will somehow force political change show tragically little understanding of what the consequences of widespread unrest in Indonesia would be for real people in the real world.

The IMF has done its job with good intentions, but I agree with those who argue it has been the wrong job. Or perhaps the right job, but in the wrong time and manner.

I am certainly not arguing against further reform. I fully agree with the need for greater transparency and economic and political openness. This is a line I have pressed in APEC and around the region.

The immediate need, however, is to stabilise the rupiah and get it back to a figure around 5000 to the US dollar.

This can't be done without wholesale reform of the banking and finance sectors, and the satisfactory rescheduling of Indonesia's corporate debt. But it doesn't require the immediate dismantling of the clove monopoly, however worthy a goal that might be.

The essential requirement is to get confidence back into the investment community, both domestic and international.

To do this Indonesia has to directly address the question of the private debt owed to overseas creditors. So long as this issue is unresolved, solvency will not be restored to the bulk of the corporate sector and the rupiah will continue to hover at unrealistically low levels.

In part this might be done by the large Indonesian companies converting debt into equity, or at least acknowledging that even at any reasonable exchange rate the corporate debt will still be too high and will require dealing with. A move along these lines would help confidence in the rupiah.

The new government has already announced plans to restructure its 164 state-owned companies and has foreshadowed the development of strategic partnerships with foreign firms. It will find benefits in moving speedily on this front.

The signs over the past few days have been hopeful that sensible dialogue is underway again between the IMF and the new Indonesian government.

Having originally left the central issue of private-sector debt largely to lenders and borrowers, the IMF is now involved in discussions with the Indonesian government on the matter.

And it appears ready to accept that some of its original macro-economic goals relating to rates of economic growth, inflation and the current-account deficit are unreachable, and that the social impact of some of its demands, like the immediate dismantling of the state-controlled food monopoly and cuts in subsidies to food and medicine, would be too severe.

The two sides also appear to be at least discussing a new way of stabilising the currency by adopting some sort of currency band system.

But even if Indonesia and the IMF reach agreement, under the best circumstances imaginable it will be a long tough road to recovery in Indonesia.

I believe Australian policy through this critical period has to be based on this one fundamental: *we stand with Indonesia*.

It is the same message the Labor government sent to the young republic during the revolution. We are with Indonesia whatever happens.

Australia cannot insulate itself from the future of the 200 million people who are our nearest Asian neighbours. And we should not try to do so.

I know that the statement 'We stand with Indonesia' begs some important questions. Is standing with Indonesia the same thing as standing with the Indonesian government? *How* exactly do we stand with Indonesia? What are the practical things we can do? What is the crossover point between helpful neighbourliness and counterproductive intrusiveness?

But these are exactly the questions we should be debating.

My point is that if you approach policy formulation from that starting principle you reach different conclusions from those which follow if you begin from other points like 'How can Australia firewall itself from the impact of what is happening?' or 'How can Australia best bring about political and social change in the region?'

Well before I became Prime Minister I was concerned that despite the long efforts of committed people in both countries to build friendship, the relationship between Australia and Indonesia seemed little more than a thin foreign policy veneer. I believed Australia faced serious dangers if it entered the twenty-first century without trying to build a relationship of trust and substance with our nearest Asian neighbour.

Significant misunderstandings persisted in the public mind on both sides. Research we commissioned in 1994 showed that fewer than one in five of the Indonesians surveyed saw Australia as a modern or advanced society, only 2 per cent were aware of Australian manufactures and mining products, and a depressingly large two-thirds believed the White Australia Policy was still in operation.

On Australia's side, suspicion of Indonesia as a long-term threat to the country persisted. It was fuelled by an equal level of ignorance about modern Indonesian society. Some in Australia believed that geography made Indonesia a permanent threat to this country.

What both President Soeharto and I tried to do was to construct a framework for a relationship which would endure after we had passed from the scene. I certainly valued my friendship with him, but I was also conscious that our friendship would not be enough to change the nature of the relationship. What we had to do was to increase substantially the number of stakeholders in it.

So on my first visit to Jakarta as Prime Minister in 1992 we established a new ministerial forum to meet every two years and to bring together ministers from a whole range of economic and social portfolios. We wanted the different areas of government to discover new opportunities for cooperation.

On the defence side we developed the Agreement on Maintaining Security as an historic declaration of trust between us, a recognition that Australia and Indonesia had common, not conflicting, security interests in the region, and in appropriate circumstances could respond through common measures.

We improved the foundations for trade and economic ties. A major trade promotion in Jakarta in 1994 was attended by the largest number of Australian business people ever to attend a trade fair abroad.

But we also knew this had to be more than a government-to-government relationship.

We worked to build up the number of people outside government with a stake in the relationship, supporting Indonesian-language teaching and setting up the Australia–Indonesia Merdeka Fellowship scheme to bring outstanding Indonesians to Australia and send outstanding Australians in mid-career to Indonesia.

To underpin all this, I made six visits to Indonesia between 1992 and 1995. This was more than the total of all previous visits by Australian Prime Ministers in the preceding twenty years.

None of this was done with short-term politics in mind.

For that reason I was genuinely pleased to hear Indonesia ministers talk with obvious satisfaction about the commitment of their counter-parts in the Howard government to the Australia Indonesia Ministerial Forum in October 1996.

But the depth of our accomplishments, and the work of so many other Australians in and out of government over the past 50 years, will be tested in coming months.

In the policy now being developed, our aim has to be what will cause least pain to the Indonesian people and what will get growth going again. Australia's role is not to stand in judgement over Indonesia, marking boxes with ticks and crosses and awarding points for adherence to IMF packages before deciding whether or not we should respond to Indonesia's needs.

In this crisis Australia needs to be a miner and distributor of ideas.

This isn't just a job for government but for business and universities as well—for anyone who can understand and interpret what is going on. Over a period of nearly 50 years, Australian universities, beginning with people like Sir John Crawford and Heinz Arndt, have maintained a level of scholarship on Indonesia which is among the highest in the world. Now is the time for contemporary Indonesia scholars to contribute to the debate.

Australia can't compete with the large economies in offering multi-billion-dollar loans to Indonesia. But we should be a principal coordinator of support and a major deliverer of services and advice in areas like information, education, applied systems and public administration.

We should be substantially increasing our support to enable Indonesian students to continue studying in Australia during this period.

Food will be critical in the months. I think the government has its priorities right in looking to the humanitarian task ahead. But the Labor Party's proposal to broaden this into a mini-Marshall Plan involving not only the World Bank but the FAO and the World Food Program, together with an international coalition of aid donors, deserves the government's support.

This is a regional, not just a national, crisis. Indonesia is the epicentre of Southeast Asia and we need to work as closely as possible with our other neighbours in trying to address the causes and consequences of Indonesia's problems.

I can't tell what will happen in Indonesia over the coming months. But I am much more confident than many. We have been treated to a good deal of coverage—some of it shrill—about what lies ahead, including prophecies of the break-up of the archipelago, or a renewal of the massacres of 1965, or flotillas of refugees fleeing Java.

I can confidently offer advice about what we will *not* see. Historical analogy is generally a lousy way of predicting the future, and it is especially so in this case.

This is a very different Indonesia from the country of 1965 and 1966.

In the weeks and months ahead, my earnest advice to you is to discard immediately any newspaper articles or television reports you come across which include phrases about Years of Living Dangerously.

In some ways, the political stability over the years of the New Order Government has disguised to the outside world the speed of change in

Indonesia since 1966. The country has been transformed from a rural to an industrial economy, from a village to an urban society, from a largely illiterate society to one where education is spread widely. Agriculture made up half the economy in 1966. Now it is around 20 per cent. A large middle class of around 15 million has emerged.

And because of these achievements, Indonesia is no longer the country it was. With its integration into the world economy have come changing expectations about the kind of society it should be.

Formally or informally, issues like the place of *pribumi* business in the economy, the long-term role of the army and whether it retains its dual functions in the security and political areas, ways of addressing differences in the rates of development between the central and outer islands, and means of getting greater public participation in politics are all being debated in Indonesia.

So change isn't going to stop now. It will continue just as it has continued in other Asian societies, and in our own. But it is change which must come from within.

One great danger is that as the political and social consequences of the economic downturn become clearer, Indonesia and other countries of the region will turn inwards and conclude that engagement with the world was the cause of their problems, rather than the source of their growth. (And it is worth recalling that despite the experience of the past twelve months, Asia in recent years has seen the largest and fastest surge of growth in human history.)

Prime Minister Goh of Singapore has spoken of the danger of a broadening of this sentiment to include a reassessment of the region's relations with the West.

Voices in Asia are now being raised in favour of greater autonomy. This is fine. Asian countries can be as autonomous as they like. But they have to accept that a trade-off exists between autonomy and growth. In a world revolutionised by information technology, autonomy won't deliver enough jobs to absorb the growing number of young job-seekers.

And the domestic savings on which these economies have depended will no longer be sufficient. They will continue to need access to international financial markets and to the technology and expertise which foreign direct investment can provide.

Asia does not have to play according to the Authorised Economic Version or the Wall Street Model. There are obvious cultural dimensions to the way Asian economies work, just as there are to the American or German or Australian economies.

But Asia *does* have to play by the rules which facilitate growth.

You can't attract investment without an economic rate of return and you can't get the best sort of investment without providing the opportunity to litigate your interests. The challenge for these countries is to find ways of preserving their cultural autonomy and the different social, and inevitably financial, obligations which accompany it while improving transparency.

If this danger of an inward-looking Asia is to be avoided, the best antidote to it will come through the policy prescriptions and examples of the regional great powers—Japan, China and the United States.

In particular, the speed with which Asia emerges from recession and the longer-term strategic impact of the crisis will depend on whether Japan can stimulate its economy and use it to drive growth elsewhere; China can cope with its huge domestic challenges and withstand the strong pressures it will face to devalue its own currency; and the US economy continues to grow and to remain open to Asian exports.

Japan's response to this crisis so far has been deeply disappointing. The original victim of the Asian economic crisis, it is still mired in a long structural recession.

It is likely to see negative growth this year. At the same time, its trade surplus rose 88 per cent in February over the same month a year ago. And its imports were down from every Asian country.

One of the most effective ways through Asia's current problems would be for Japan to resume its role as the regional engine of growth and expand its capacity to absorb some of its neighbours' exports.

Japan has generously contributed to the IMF packages and Prime Minister Hashimoto has been personally involved in the problems of Indonesia. But what has been absent is much of a sense of Japan taking a leadership role in the region, generating ideas, marshalling support and making decisions about its own economy in full cognisance of their impact on its neighbours.

When we look back at this crisis in coming years, I believe the thing for which it will be remembered is not that Asian economic growth suddenly stumbled. That was always going to happen in one form or another. The historically significant thing about it will be the way China handled the first region-wide crisis since it reasserted its role as a great power.

China's neighbours have been looking carefully at the way it responds to these current difficulties as a measure of the way it will behave in future, as a test of the sort of power it will be.

By any measure, the results so far have been encouraging.

Although the massive devaluations of other Asian currencies will impose new pressures on China's exports, cutting its growth rate back to under 8 per cent, the government has promised to avoid any competitive devaluation of the yuan. It has justified this decision precisely in terms of the harmful impact such action would have on its neighbours.

China has instead adopted a policy of expanding domestic consumption. It has begun a public-works program equal to 1 per cent of economic output.

But just as important has been the example China has provided. It has demonstrated that the best way out of the crisis is by continuing bold reform rather than retreating into introspection and caution.

It has taken on the huge challenges of reforming the state-owned enterprises and the banking system. It has begun the largest restructuring of the machinery of government since 1949. It has signalled new measures to encourage foreign investment in China's infrastructure. On the political front it has announced that it will sign the International Covenant on Civil and Political Rights.

No-one, least of all President Jiang or Premier Zhu, would underestimate the huge difficulties of keeping reform and growth going in an economy of 1.2 billion people, but China's handling of its response to this crisis suggests that it is conscious of the responsibilities of leadership and capable of acting beyond narrowly defined national interests.

The United States has now had a period of prolonged economic growth, from the first cycle of investment associated with the digital economy—beginning in 1992. This has been fed by a stockmarket which can shift capital effectively and efficiently out of unproductive sectors into productive sectors. With luck, the Asian crisis will help the United States continue to grow by feeding in deflationary effects.

However, virtually all the Asian economies will be basing their strategies for economic recovery on even more competitive exports. And the United States market is the one they will be looking to.

But the United States foreign-trade deficit for the last three months of 1997 was already the highest ever recorded and seems set to grow. A further surge of Asian imports will fuel protectionist sentiments in Congress. This will be happening at a difficult point in the electoral cycle.

Although the administration has been heavily involved in seeking solutions to the current economic crisis, it is hard in the post-Cold War United States to find congressional or public acknowledgement of the link between American prosperity and the rest of the world, or indeed much interest in the outside world at all. The forces standing in favour of a confident United States multilateralism seem to be losing ground.

A growing problem for the rest of us is that the cost to the United States administration of securing US public and congressional support for international issues like United Nations funding or the current IMF replenishment is increased demands that these organisations demonstrate that they serve specific American goals and ideals. This situation is untenable over the long term for both the United States and the international community.

It was openness and links across the Pacific which delivered Asia's enormous growth. This crisis has demonstrated yet again how central those trans-Pacific links are. But they require careful tending on both sides of the ocean.

Asian economies are looking at a lengthy and painful period of adjustment. It took Australia about five years to fully exploit its new competitiveness in the 1980s. We turned a huge nominal depreciation of the exchange rate in 1985–86 into a real depreciation. That is, we captured the competitiveness.

But we didn't start really seeing the longer-term results in our export performance and our import replacement performance until about four or five years later—in 1990. But I believe that the adjustment time in Asia will be shorter because the voices of so many people looking for better lives for themselves and their families won't be denied.

The underlying factors underpinning Asian growth have not changed: young demographics, high savings rates, sensible macroeconomic policies, entrepreneurial cultures, the high value placed on education.

And if regional governments can get through this immediate period and take advantage of the reforms now being imposed on them, and the competitiveness benefits which the devaluations provide, they will have tremendous horsepower for the next stage of economic growth. The IMF may not have all the answers, but it has provided governments with the authority to make reforms which they could not have drawn down from their own political system.

But the long-term problems for Asia haven't gone away. In a sense, the *real* Asian economic crisis is still out there, waiting.

This is the crisis of funding and building the infrastructure required to support more than two billion people, to feed and educate them and deal with the profound environmental consequences of that growth.

Asia's energy demand is doubling every twelve years with all the consequences that has for air quality and global warming.

In the early 1990s, around 500 million East Asians lived in towns. By 2020 this figure will have trebled to 1.5 billion. This demographic shift from the countryside to the cities will put a huge strain on basic services like water, sanitation and shelter. Only half the urban populations in developing Asian countries currently have access to safe water supplies and 42 per cent to sanitation.

Food is a looming issue, too. We are already seeing across the region the consequences of unconstrained heavy use of fertilisers, irrigation and pesticides. Agricultural productivity is better, but at the expense of soil erosion, salinity and the pollution of water resources. How will the region supply itself with food without destroying the land for future generations?

These looming problems have largely been forgotten in the current turmoil. But they will require even greater attention once the current crisis has passed.

Unfortunately, as we have seen over the months since last July, global and regional organisations are nowhere near ready to respond effectively to the new challenges of globalisation, and the changes it is bringing to the international system.

Throughout this past year, the principal institutions we might have looked to for help have been out of breath, or behind the play, or playing the wrong game.

Many writers have commented, and all of us know intuitively anyway, that the pace of global change is quickening. It is still fewer than ten years since the Soviet Union collapsed, and with it the whole postwar international order. Now, only a few years later, we are seeing an economic crisis in Asia that threatens to hobble the region which had promised to be the world's economic growth engine as we enter the twenty-first century.

History is made up of discontinuities. But surely one of the main lessons of the past decade is that those discontinuities are becoming more frequent and deeper.

In other words, it is not the speed of change which should concern us most, but the fact that change seems to be becoming inherently more sudden and less predictable.

The reason lies in the profound impact on the international system of the information revolution in all its various forms, including the way it has made economic globalisation possible and has accelerated the mobility of capital, information and ideas.

The Asian economic crisis has been an obvious example of this.

We are likely to have less warning of future crises and therefore fewer opportunities to avert them. And when they come, the swings they generate are likely to be larger. We do not as yet fully understand the new system's dynamic and that we need to update and modify our institutions and practices to reduce the risks inherent in it.

The IMF has had a lead role in this crisis, but it is a very different, much broader, role than the sort of balance-of-payments crises it has had to contend with in the past. The officers of national finance ministries which make up and run the IMF haven't been able to assimilate properly the political dimensions of the new job they are now being asked to perform.

The momentum for changes to the processes and policies of the IMF is now probably unstoppable.

The G7 has had a go at thinking about the crisis, but its problem in these circumstance is that the interests of its European members demonstrably don't extend to the political stability of Southeast Asia.

APEC ought to have been ideally placed to respond to the region's difficulties because it is an economic organisation which includes all the countries most affected.

One problem which has clearly emerged has been the absence of a strong APEC secretariat with institutional backing able to bring issues and current data to the attention of member economies.

But more basically, APEC has been hobbled by the agreement last year to add Russia to its membership.

I think this decision was an act of international vandalism. I would have opposed it to the end. It was a fundamental mistake which was made worse because it was designed in part to atone for another fundamental mistake: the 1997 decision to expand NATO to the European borders of the old Soviet Union.

I'm certainly not anti-Russian and I well understand its long-term importance as a great power. But its participation in APEC has already changed the dynamics of the organisation.

Under no conceivable stretch of the imagination is Russia currently part of the Asia Pacific economy. And its strategic and political priorities are totally different from those of APEC's other members.

Precisely because it is such an important power in its own right, its participation will make it harder to use APEC and the Leaders'

Meetings as a focused and effective forum to oversee and coordinate the various responses to the economic crisis. Russian membership makes it impossible, for example, to contemplate using APEC as the basis for a financial fund to address future balance-of-payments problems in the region, because the potential additional demands it would generate are just too great.

The Declaration which emerged from the Leaders' Meeting in Vancouver last November described APEC as the 'region's most comprehensive economic forum' and 'particularly well placed to play a pivotal role in fostering dialogue and cooperation'. It asked APEC finance ministers and central bankers to accelerate their work. It talked about an increasing role for APEC.

Well, we haven't been swept aside in the rush.

This year's APEC meeting in Kuala Lumpur has to send firm messages that Asia remains on the path to openness. This isn't just a matter of making declarations but of taking specific actions which will restore confidence within the region and in key markets that Asia can resume its growth path.

This means showing a determination to move forward on the Bogor free trade and investment agenda.

It means giving some clear support to the development of more structured cooperation between regional central banks.

But if APEC is to get anywhere, the bulk of the work to achieve it has to be going on now. It will be useless for leaders simply to turn up in Kuala Lumpur in September and expect to put something together in those couple of days.

I'm not prepared to write APEC off yet. But if it doesn't show its relevance to the Asian economies this year it will write itself off.

What happens to any individual international organisation isn't in the least important.

But APEC matters because it embodies a big idea—that of an open Asia Pacific region. And that idea lies at the core of how we can best overcome this mess.

On the trade front, the message has to be sent out strongly that the world is not in the business of building barriers. We need China in the WTO, and as quickly as possible. I hope this will be one of the outcomes of President Clinton's proposed visits to China in June.

More broadly, this would be an excellent moment to press ahead with the proposed Millennium Round of trade negotiations.

Let me end by returning to the subject of Australia and Asia.

I believe the changes Australia made internally in the 1980s and 1990s have prepared us well to cope with the challenges we now face. We went voluntarily through much of the painful integration into the global economy that our neighbours are experiencing.

I also believe the progress we have made in forging closer bilateral and regional ties will help both Australia and the countries around us.

But I have to note that a few worrying signs about Australia's relationship with Asia are emerging.

For example, I was taken to task by the *Sydney Morning Herald* last week.

This is not a new phenomenon, of course, or one which strikes fear in the heart. But it is worth mentioning because the criticism has broader implications.

I was criticised for a speech I made in Singapore in 1996, from which the editorial quoted. I had said that Australia's 'engagement with the region around us is not just commercial. And it is not just the result of some crude economic determinism. It goes—and must go—much deeper than that. It goes to a genuine desire for partnership and real involvement . . . Australia needs to seek its security in Asia rather than from Asia'.

This view was described by the newspaper as 'light-headed'.

But to assert, as those words of mine do, that Australia's engagement with Asia has a political, security and cultural dimension as well as an economic one, and requires a genuine national commitment on our part, seems to me so deeply true, so basic to Australian interests, so blindingly self-evident, that it is perhaps only a *Sydney Morning Herald* editorialist who could take exception to it.

But unfortunately there are other hints of revisionism around. A sort of *sotto voce* whisper that the Labor government rather overdid the whole Asia thing and that we are now paying the price. Some of the old brigade obviously think Asia's recent economic problems mean that Australia can heave a sigh of relief and head for the safety of old friends and familiar geography.

Others argue that some historically determined conflagration is coming in Indonesia and that Australia should distance itself from it by tiptoeing quietly to the side of the field in the hope that no-one will notice we are there.

This is dangerous nonsense.

Australia must have a deep and continuous commitment to Asia— and for reasons that lie at the heart of our national interests. None of that has changed as a result of recent developments.

The intrinsic economic complementarities between Australia and Asia have not changed. Australia has not suddenly developed security interests in Africa rather than Asia.

Australian engagement with Asia is not a temporary enthusiasm. Asia is not a flavour of the month. We have not been on a ten-day package tour from which we can return with a couple of T-shirts and a handful of colour prints for the album. Australia can't bolt on the Evinrude and motor off to the coast of California.

If we know anything about dealing with Asia it is the importance of building relationships for the long term.

That's the business Australia needs to be in now.

15

LEADERSHIP, ASIA AND THE DIGITAL ECONOMY

BusinessWeek Digital Economy Forum,
Singapore,
18 June 1999

In addressing the topic of leadership, Asia and the digital economy,
Paul Keating says the end of the Cold War and the advent of the
digital economy are global transforming events. He strands together
related thoughts, lamenting the lost opportunities of the 1990s—no
forging of a new international structure to include states like China
and India and no attempt to deal with nuclear weapons the greatest lost
opportunity. He says the digital revolution, while changing the world,
plays particularly to Asia's strengths: young demographics and high
savings. Paul Keating argues the new world is best understood by the
young, who will prosper from the openness that digital communication
facilitates. He says if Asia gets openness right—politically—managing
the dimensions of information, the digital revolution will further
underwrite Asia's prosperity into the twenty-first century.

SINGAPORE IS A GOOD CITY in which to think about the future. From
its origins as an entrepot port, it has always had a strong sense of where
its strategic advantages lie, and what it needs to do to preserve them.

That will be an increasingly useful attribute for all societies in the
information age, when the fundamentals of our economies seem under
constant assault.

Singaporeans know they cannot hide from change and therefore that they must try to shape it. They teach us a vital lesson: when you face things and begin to do what must be done, you liberate ideas about what can be done.

I have been asked to talk tonight about leadership, Asia and the digital economy. Not an easy topic, but a broad one.

Leadership comes in many forms, and it expresses its influence in different ways. The leadership skills required to build a great company are not necessarily the same as those needed by a successful political leader. Military leadership requires different skills from those of musicians or writers who point the way down cultural paths.

But the best definition I know is one of the simplest, and it applies to leadership in all its forms: leadership is the job of interpreting the future to the present.

A couple of weeks ago I was addressing a group of young people in Sydney and making the point that the familiar dichotomy between age and experience is no longer very relevant. The people who have most experience of the world we are moving into are, in fact, the young. They certainly understand the practical facts of the digital world but; more than that, they are culturally at home in it. They have internalised the social changes it is bringing with it.

I'm not making an argument against age and wisdom. With each passing year I find myself more attracted to Confucian principles of respect for the elderly. And history's lessons have to be understood and remembered if we are not to repeat our errors. But if Asia is looking for leadership in the digital age, the place to look first is among the young.

I gained my own leadership experience in public life. I have often described this as the ultimate high wire act. The stakes are high, the opportunities great. It requires balance, grace, training and bucket loads of adrenalin. Done well, it is beautiful to behold and incomparably satisfying for the person on the wire. But all the while you know that a proportion of the spectators, however much they cheer you on, is secretly hoping that you will plummet spectacularly and entertainingly to the ground. You have to try to disappoint them.

I became Prime Minister of Australia at the end of 1991. Two transforming global events were underway.

The first was the end of the Cold War. This was a fundamental change in the international system. One of the two poles in a bipolar world suddenly ceased to exist. Almost no-one, least of all the two main protagonists, expected this. New opportunities and new uncertainties emerged, but no-one was quite sure what to make of them.

In this region, for example, the end of the Cold War made it possible for Vietnam to take its place in ASEAN and for us to develop broadly based regional organisations like APEC. But at the same time, America's strategic interest in Southeast Asia was diminished. We saw what that meant in practical terms during the Asian economic crisis, when there was little incentive for Washington to soften the most rigorous and unreasonable demands of the IMF and the World Bank.

But now we are near the end of the nineties, I'm afraid we will look back on a decade of too many wasted opportunities. Collectively we have failed to rise to the leadership challenges the end of the Cold War provided.

Instead of forging new paths to reform the international system, we slipped back into the well-worn ruts of the old tracks.

For example, if it is to reflect new international realities, a globalised world requires more comprehensive institutions than the G7 and a United Nations Security Council which comprises the victors of a war now more than half a century behind us.

It requires active engagement with the two most populous countries in the world, China and India, rather than attempts to sideline or marginalise them. We should have had China in the WTO by now, but instead we found Washington unable to take yes for an answer when it turned down the offers Zhu Rongji brought with him to America. The US–China relationship will shape this region in the early years of the next century but we can see how easy it is for both sides to slip back into familiar patterns of suspicion.

A globalised world requires us to develop international trade and financial organisations that reflect more fully the role of the developing world in the international economy and take its interests into account. There has been talk about opening up the IMF and the World Bank, but it hasn't gone far enough.

We have also failed to address the issue of nuclear weapons in the world. This has been the greatest lost opportunity of the post-Cold War era. Future generations will blame us, and so they should.

Twenty thousand nuclear warheads are still in the arsenals of the nuclear powers and have the capacity to destroy the world many times. Two of the states on the nuclear threshold, India and Pakistan have stepped over it. Another regime with a known nuclear program, North Korea, has tested a medium range ballistic missile.

Meanwhile, Russia's capacity to control and store its existing nuclear weapons is atrophying. And the strategic arms negotiations between the major nuclear powers are not going anywhere. Across the board, the impetus for change has stalled.

The reason for this is that you cannot have nuclear non-proliferation without nuclear de-proliferation. Unless the United States and the other nuclear powers are prepared to contemplate a world without their nuclear weapons, they will certainly be joined in the nuclear club by others who can't see why prohibitions should apply only to them.

We have heard suggestions in recent weeks that the NATO intervention in Kosovo represents a new approach to the way the international system operates. It is true that this is the first time we have seen force used on such a scale to change the internal policies of a government. And it is the first time NATO, a defensive alliance, has been used for offensive purposes.

But however understandable the humanitarian impulse behind the operation may have been, I am not sure how successful the operation will be over the longer term. And, most importantly, I don't believe it is easily replicable. For that reason it is not a template that can be used regularly or often for changing the behaviour of future governments like Serbia's. But on the other side of the ledger, the fact that it was done outside United Nations auspices has further marginalised Russia and China and made them more resentful and suspicious of western aims.

The impetus at the end of the Second World War, with Roosevelt's promotion of the San Francisco conference, was for an inclusive approach to the world. After the end of the Cold War, however, the expansion of NATO to the borders of the old Soviet Union defined Russia out of the European security system.

The second event changing the world through the 1990s has been, of course, the digital revolution. This transformed the ease, speed and cost of processing and communicating information. It facilitated the globalisation of the production and distribution of manufactured goods (and increasingly of services), and in doing this it fundamentally altered familiar international economic relationships.

I had spent most of the 1980s as the Australian Treasurer involved in opening up the Australian economy to the world: deregulating the financial system and introducing it to international competition, floating the dollar and dismantling the tariff barriers which had always sheltered Australian industry, making it sleepy and uncompetitive.

I could see that in a period of rapid change this was the only choice Australia had which did not condemn us to irrelevance and decline. And I believed that market-oriented policies were the best way of getting economic growth and therefore improving the lives of ordinary Australians.

In this approach the Australian Labor government pioneered the policies that have become known as the Third Way in Britain. And fifteen years of reform laid the basis for the Australian economy to emerge strongly from the Asian economic crisis.

But when I became Prime Minister, I knew the country also had to address a broader agenda. I wanted to continue the economic changes, including by addressing our national savings problem through compulsory superannuation. But there were other issues.

If Australia was to take its proper place in the new post-Cold War world, I thought we had to move much more quickly to build strong bilateral and regional relationships with the countries around us. We had to make clear that Asia was the place where all Australia's interests coalesced.

We also needed to confront the issue of our treatment of indigenous Australians. We could not argue to the region that Australia had changed if we marginalised our original inhabitants.

And we needed to begin the process of making Australia a republic. It seemed ridiculous to me that we should enter the second century of our existence as a Commonwealth while borrowing the head of state of another country. However you do the polling, more than half of all Australians don't think this situation adequately represents our country.

These issues were not just important socially. They had an economic relevance too. The information revolution has created a world in which it is almost impossible to disentangle domestic from international policies.

In Australia's case, once our economy began to depend more heavily on the export of services rather than bulk commodities, the way we presented ourselves to the world became more important. Decisions about where to educate your children, or seek health care, or look for legal assistance, or buy your entertainment are quite different from decisions based essentially on cost and reliability of supply which affect decisions on where to source steaming coal or other commodities. They involve much more subjective decisions about the 'brand' of the place you are buying from.

Australia, like every other country, also had to think about the great unanswered question of the information age. Will the digital revolution result in a fundamental diffusion of power within societies and between economies? Or will it deliver instead the sort of concentration of power that accompanied the industrial revolution a century ago in the form of robber baron capitalism?

The jury is still out on that.

By making direct relationships between producers and consumers possible in a way we haven't experienced since the first appearance of the mass market, the digital economy is squeezing out the middleman. E-commerce over the internet will generate an estimated $300 billion annually in the next five years. But will the large simply get larger?

The United States is home to three quarters of the global software industry. It is set to dominate the initial stages, at any rate, of the electronic commerce industry. What place can the rest of us find for ourselves?

This is also a problem that Asia has to face.

This region has been through a harsh, and in some ways unnecessary, economic crisis. I have been consistently optimistic about the speed with which it will recover and the new strength its economies will have when it does so. The IMF and World Bank reforms were administered too bluntly, especially in Indonesia, but they will make these economies enormously competitive as growth resumes.

But a fundamental question that Asian societies now have to ask themselves is: competitive at what?

Asia's economic crisis had many causes. But a central factor was the global capital spending boom of the mid-nineties and the excess productive capacity it produced. As capital spending surged, capacity utilisation rates began to fall. And because Asia produced the low-tech products like steel, ships, cars and commodities that were the part of world output most sensitive to economic cycles, it happened most sharply here.

Obviously these manufactured goods were an important part of the initial growth spurt of the Asian miracle. They will continue to be important for the region's economies. But present world production capacity exceeds expected consumption by at least a third, and the downward pressures on prices are likely to continue. And compared with the first stage of Asia's growth spurt, competition will be more intense. Many more parts of the world—Latin America, Eastern Europe, India—are involved in global commerce.

In other words, I don't believe Asia can rely for the growth it needs on the resumption of a bottomless stream of manufactured exports to the United States. It needs to embed itself in the new tech, as well as the old.

The opportunities are there. India has shown that the potential to out-source back office functions is not only changing the geographical distribution of jobs in the developed world, but the global distribution of jobs as well. And Singapore and Malaysia have both developed comprehensive policy approaches to new technology.

Asia already has many of the attributes for success in a digital world. Successful economies in future will be constructed around good education systems, effective research and development, and sound investment in infrastructure. Most Asian countries know this and the best are acting upon it. And the region's high savings and young demographics will continue to help it.

Asia also has enormous advantages through its capacity to leapfrog generations of technology. This is most important in telecommunications. Countries like China are moving straight into fibre optics and wireless communications.

The new communications technologies can overcome some of the environmental problems that might otherwise impede Asia's growth. Congestion in the region's cities will be relieved by more efficient distribution systems and supply chains. Better communications systems, especially broadband technology, will also help address the huge and growing educational and health needs of the region.

There is an old saying that information is power. That is no longer true. Information swirls around us in thick clouds. As the demands for transparency from governments and corporations continue to grow, the amount of information in the public domain will increase exponentially. Power now lies with those who can access, collate and assess information. That is just as true for businesses looking for markets, for soldiers looking for battlefield advantage and for governments wanting to maximise their national interests.

Power relativities among nations are changing in the direction of those societies that can handle all the dimensions of information. If Asian economies are to succeed beyond the stage of mass manufacturing, they will need agile and flexible economies that can understand foreign markets and learn rapidly from them.

It will be impossible to reach the highest levels of economic success without open societies; that is, communities in which information flows freely both between its members and from outside it and which have rapid and effective transmission lines conveying views and reactions to the leadership. This will be just as true for companies dealing with consumers as for governments dealing with their citizens. I don't believe there is one model of an open society, and it doesn't have to be a western model, but it does have to involve a questioning and involving education system, the easy movement of people and the rapid transmission of ideas.

The economist David Hale recently pointed out that emerging markets currently represent 45 per cent of global output, 70 per cent of the world's land area and 99 per cent of the projected growth of the labour force in the early decades of the next century. But they account for only about 6 per cent of global stock market capitalisation. Provided economic reform continues, it will be impossible to sustain over time this imbalance between stock market capitalisation and economic endowments.

If Asia adjusts to the requirements of openness and the digital age—politically and philosophically, as well as technically—this will continue to be the fastest growing region of the world into the next century.

Whether you are in Australia or Asia, in business or government, interpreting the future to the present has rarely been harder or more important than it is now.

16

IMPLICATIONS FOR THE STRATEGIC ARCHITECTURE OF THE ASIAN HEMISPHERE

APEC's Sixth Leaders' Summit Meeting,
1998 Pacific Rim Forum,
Shanghai,
22 September 1998

As the progenitor of the APEC Leaders' Meeting, Paul Keating's
thoughts about the organisation were pertinent, particularly as the
views in this major speech were given just two years after he had left
the prime ministership and the effective 'secretaryship' of APEC. The
conference held in Shangai just before the Kuala Lumpur meeting of
APEC gave him the opportunity to reflect upon and provide guidance
to the organisation. Paul Keating says the 1997 Asian crisis was one of
the world's biggest economic challenges since the Second World War
and that the crisis marked China's re-entry as a major participant in the
international system. He argues the Washington-based institutions—the
IMF, the World Bank and the G7—had demonstrated an incapacity to
supervise the system and to put effective remedial policies into place.

IT IS VERY GOOD TO be here in Shanghai which is one of the great cities of the world. But it is also an ideal place to hold a conference like this at this time.

When we look back on this, the Asia economic crisis, one of the most important things we will remember about it is the way it marked

China's re-entry as a major participant in the international system. During the crisis, China has been a creative shaper of responses. It has looked beyond its own borders and its own immediate interests. This is not an easy task for a developing country facing as many challenges as China. But the message it has sent the region by holding back from a competitive devaluation of the RMB, by active participation in the IMF packages of support for its neighbours, and, above all, by its own continuing commitment to policies of reform and openness, is a welcome one.

This session of the conference is about APEC, and especially the prospects for the November Leaders' Meeting in Kuala Lumpur under the chairmanship of Dr Mahathir Mohamed, the Prime Minister of Malaysia.

Many issues will be on the agenda for that meeting, but one fundamental question will be answered there: whether, as an institution, APEC has reached the end of the road.

It is important to set out clearly what is at stake here.

First, this region is experiencing its most serious economic challenge since the end of the Second World War. The region as a whole has moved into recession. According to the World Bank, no nation in the past 50 years has experienced such precipitate economic collapse as Indonesia. The economy of the world's fourth most populous country may shrink by 20 per cent this year. Thailand's GDP is likely to fall by 7 per cent, South Korea's by 6 per cent and Hong Kong's by 4 per cent. The Daewoo Economic Research Institute estimates that domestic consumption in South Korea plunged 28 per cent during the first half of this year compared with 13.4 per cent in the United States during the height of the Great Depression. Regional stockmarkets have fallen more than half since their peak.

Second, this economic crisis is already producing devastating social consequences. Tens of millions of Asians have been pushed back into poverty. Human suffering is growing daily. Every child who drops out of school, or misses out on a vaccination against a debilitating disease, will have a human lifetime's impact on the economies and societies of the region. The crisis has also reignited ugly ethnic divisions in societies like Indonesia's.

Third, these economic and social problems can spread beyond national borders and generate security tensions. Bilateral relationships in Southeast Asia have already been strained by the economic crisis. We can expect more of this.

Fourth, the Asian crisis has now spread and threatens to have a global impact. Deflation is a looming problem. Japan has just posted its worst economic growth figures since the Second World War. Russia and Latin America face dangerous strains. Wim Duisenberg of the European Central Bank acknowledges that the international turmoil will have a 'dampening effect' on European growth. Too much weight is placed on the continuation of unwavering strength in the United States economy at a time it faces what is likely to be a debilitating political crisis. As Alan Greenspan said recently, the United States cannot forever be an oasis of prosperity.

APEC's November meeting should be an ideal vehicle for coordinating action to address these problems. APEC represents all the key Asia Pacific economies. The two largest economies in the world—the United States and Japan—and the most populous nation—China—are members. So are the developing economies which have been most directly affected by the crisis. Unlike the IMF or the G7, APEC allows the voices of all those affected to be heard.

But unless the APEC forum can show in November that it has the will and capacity to do something about Asia Pacific economic cooperation during the worst crisis of the past half-century, it might as well pack its bags, declare that a decade is enough, and let its officials move on to more productive enterprises.

APEC might loll around in the corners of Asia Pacific consciousness for a while yet, but unless it can deliver results this year, in these dangerous circumstances, it will have demonstrated only its own impotence. Its pronouncements will no longer be taken seriously. Sometimes organisations lose sight of what they are there for. They become institutionalised and formalised, and the process becomes more important than the goal.

If that happens to APEC it will be a great tragedy. It will rob the region of an institution which is probably irreplaceable in its current format, and one which is capable of facilitating political and strategic dialogue at a time when this is badly needed.

When I wrote to other APEC leaders in 1992 suggesting that we strengthen APEC's institutional structures by adding an informal Leaders' Meeting, I had strategic as well as economic purposes in mind. I believed the absence of any mechanism in this part of the world to enable heads of government to meet collectively was a real inhibition to the development of the Asia Pacific. We were missing out on the benefits of frequent informal contact, and the insight and opportunities that come from it, which the Europeans got through the EU, or Latin America through the OAS.

I also believed that only meetings at the level of leaders could give APEC the political horsepower it needed to develop a really ambitious economic and social agenda. The leaders' engagement in these annual meetings raises the political stakes and increases the pressure for significant outcomes.

So, thanks to President Clinton's invitation to his colleagues to meet in Seattle in 1993, the Asia Pacific has a structure in place which can provide leadership during this crisis, if the will is there to exercise it.

It has to be said that APEC's record so far has not been good. As a source of ideas and responses to the Asian crisis during the past year, APEC has been the invisible man.

Leaders will meet in Kuala Lumpur in a very different atmosphere from Vancouver twelve months ago. Month by month, the economic indicators have been adjusted downwards and the contagion effects of the crisis have become clearer.

A debate has been opened up within the region on the subject of where blame lies for the economic slump. Does it lie with speculators and outside interests who have abused the growing economic openness in the region? Does it lie with inadequate financial structures, and corruption and cronyism in some regional economies? Does it lie in unrealistic and overly restrictive demands by multilateral organisations like the IMF?

This is a very good debate to have. It is impossible to look back at the scarifying developments in Asia over the past twelve months without concluding that the policy responses of governments and international institutions have been seriously flawed.

If the consequence of addressing the sort of capital-account problems a number of regional countries experienced is to plunge the region, and possibly the world, into recession, then either our understanding of what is happening or our prescriptions for dealing with it are seriously flawed. There must be a better way of responding to such events than by pushing millions of people back into poverty.

APEC in Kuala Lumpur will inevitably and properly be caught up in discussing these questions about economic openness and its consequences, if only because Malaysia, the host nation, has reimposed capital controls.

For my part, I am all in favour of policy responses which accept different paths and different speeds, which acknowledge that political and social environments vary from country to country and have to be handled in different ways. In fact, that is what the APEC approach has been about from the beginning. It is what distinguishes it from other multilateral economic organisations. APEC's diversity of membership requires it to exercise such flexibility.

But it is vital that all those paths lead to the same destination, and that progress along them is steady. And that destination, in my view, must be a world in which trade and investment and ideas move freely and openly around. That is the core of the Bogor Declaration.

Why should we choose that destination? Because it offers the greatest growth prospects to lift the millions of people in the Asia Pacific who still live in poverty into a better life. And because, in the end, it is the only way technology will let us move.

We are living in an Age of Convergence. This is more than simply the economic and financial process of globalisation. Globalisation is one form of convergence—a convergence in the way goods are made and distributed and in the way capital is allocated. Between 1980 and 1992 world trade grew at twice the rate of world output, and more than one third of all international trade is now conducted by firms trading within their own structures. Foreign direct investment doubled between 1988 and 1993.

But the Age of Convergence is broader. It encompasses the radical social and political realignment brought on by technological changes and the information revolution.

Convergence blurs the margins of many aspects of our lives. Barriers erode and elide. Technologies merge. And as they do, the nature of the work we do changes, and the way we live our lives and conduct our social relationships change. That is as true for a farmer in rural Thailand as for an industrial worker in the American Midwest.

At the international level, convergence is breaking down formerly impervious barriers between nation states.

We can't un-invent the information revolution. Neither can we stop its consequences, or channel them in one preferred direction. Technology takes us inevitably, irrevocably, in the direction of a converging world.

But support for economic openness does not require every economy from Chile to China to adopt the same policy responses at the same time. Globalisation is a process, not an outcome.

The first question to be asked about APEC's response to Asia's current crisis is whether it, or any other institution, can do much about it. Does what is happening simply reflect powerful underlying economic forces which are beyond any effective policy response? Is there, in the end, nothing useful we can do beyond sitting back and waiting for the Invisible Hand to finish slapping us about the head?

Obviously I believe there are things we can do. Bad policies got us into this crisis—the absence of effective prudential regulation, policy decisions to tie various Asian currencies to the US dollar, misguided and damaging responses once the crisis was upon us. In the same way, better policies can help us find our way out.

It is true that APEC cannot solve the problem alone. But it can identify and coordinate more effective responses. It can focus debate. It can change the mood of the marketplace and the dynamics of regional recovery.

I believe the Kuala Lumpur meeting needs to deliver results in five areas.

First, a primary aim of the meeting should be a reassertion of the idea of APEC as the embodiment of an Asia Pacific community. In the traumatic events of the past twelve months, this has often been overlooked. But if ever there was a need to reinforce such a sense of community this is the time. Economic strains in individual economies are causing countries to focus inwards again, to blame external forces for their problems.

This renewed commitment to the idea of community should be at the centre of the Kuala Lumpur outcome. I don't mean by this simply a rhetorical sentence or two in a joint declaration talking about the value of cooperation. Instead, the meeting itself should be used as a genuine exchange between the leaders to refocus themselves, and through them the people of the region, on its underlying interdependence. That can be one of the great benefits of the APEC format in which leaders meet together without officials or formal agendas.

Whatever the flaws in the responses to the economic downturn have been, at every stage we have been reminded of how interdependent the regional links are. The United States and Japan are critical to any recovery. The United States remains the key export market for the region. Japan's recession deepens the crisis for its neighbours, and, despite its problems, it remains a vital source of capital. China's policy responses, as I said earlier, will have a significant impact on its neighbours. Most of the direct financial support to the economies which are suffering most, even when channelled through the IMF, has come from regional partners including Japan, Australia and China.

The Kuala Lumpur meeting will do a great service if it reminds regional leaders of that truth and its consequences.

A second outcome from Kuala Lumpur should be to provide practical evidence that the region is not putting up the shutters and turning inwards, that it remains committed to a process of continuing openness. But this requires action if it is to be believed, not just assertions.

Last year in Vancouver the APEC leaders proclaimed that APEC's goals, including the achievement of free and open trade in the region by the dates set out in the Bogor Declaration, were 'ambitious and unequivocal'. They designated fifteen major sectors for 'early voluntary sectoral liberalisation', with nine to be advanced through 1998 with a view to implementation beginning in 1999.

There could hardly be a clearer test of APEC's continued commitment to openness than whether it delivers on this promise.

If it does so, APEC will have sent a powerful message of optimism about recovery in the region. But if it not only fails to take its trade commitments further, but actually backs away from a commitment made by leaders only twelve months ago, the organisation's credibility will suffer a further damaging blow. Some of the larger APEC members, including Japan, are showing a reluctance to acknowledge this fact.

Third, APEC has to show that it offers something to the weakest economies as well as the strongest ones. APEC has always had a development as well as a trade dimension, and this is the time to step that up. Other organisations like the World Bank and the United Nations, as well as bilateral aid programs, may have a more central development role, but if APEC members are to continue to be committed to the process of liberalisation, the nexus between economic openness and development needs to be reinforced in the consciousness of all regional countries.

In this area, education should be a priority for APEC because human capital is at the core of everything the economies of the region might want to achieve. Even if it is outside its usual area of operations, APEC should coordinate action to keep children and young people in education through this crisis, whether through scholarships or large-scale technical assistance.

Fourth, APEC should try to coordinate a broad response to getting trade flowing again. This is a natural extension of its trade facilitation agenda. Necessary banking reforms are shrinking the sizes of banks and, as managers are forced to review their loan portfolios, trade finance assets are often among the first and most easily discarded. As we saw in South Korea, this can have a devastating and almost instantaneous effect on trade, and through it on the broader economy. APEC is a good forum in which to exchange experiences and coordinate policies on this issue.

Fifth, APEC should help shape the broader international debate on some of the questions thrown up by the Asian crisis, including the management of capital flows.

Such a debate is also taking place in other international forums like the G7, the G22 and various UN bodies. Does it matter whether APEC is also engaged in it? I believe it matters greatly.

APEC's broad membership of developed and developing economies gives it a distinct viewpoint on these matters and its members include those most seriously hurt by the crisis. But, most importantly, the only way we will achieve effective changes to global institutions for the twenty-first century is if all those affected are included in the dialogue.

Over the past year scepticism about the prescriptions of wise, Washington-based international economists has understandably risen. International economic diplomacy needs to be opened up. The face it presents to the world is a great deal more secretive, exclusive and arrogant than that of its more traditional political or trade counterparts. Broader debate in APEC—not just among finance ministers—is one way of addressing this problem.

One of the distinctive things about APEC is the importance of the chairmanship. As it is such a loosely structured organisation, without a powerful secretariat or formal processes, its outcomes are shaped heavily by the approach adopted by the country chairing it. Like all his predecessors, Dr Mahathir will have an important personal role in shaping the outcome. He has a chance to deliver some fresh region-wide initiatives which will also shape global developments at a critical moment. The results of the meeting will be an important reflection on Malaysia's role in the world.

But APEC will find success harder to achieve this year because of its expanded membership. As Prime Minister, I was opposed to Russia, Chile and Peru joining APEC, not because of any animus to those countries but because I believed they would shift its focus away from the vital economic, strategic and political links which govern the relationship between East Asia and North America and which are so critical to APEC's original members.

I was also opposed to Asia-only bodies—a judgement that has been reinforced by this crisis. The United States and its relationship with Japan and the other economies of Asia, including China, will be central to recovery. These are problems which bridge the North Pacific and they require bridging solutions.

The question of APEC's membership is directly relevant to the architecture of the post-Cold War world.

Last year I described the decision to invite Russia to join as an act of international vandalism. My argument was not that Russia should be kept out of this part of the world. I don't believe in a new containment strategy for Russia any more than I believe in containing China. North Asian security can't be resolved without Russia, and eventually it will have a great influence on the Asia Pacific economy.

But the decision to admit it to membership this year was taken without serious thought about what was good for APEC. Its membership changes the agenda, adds a major country whose current economic links with the region are miniscule, and makes harder, by sheer weight of numbers, the chances for genuine dialogue in the Leaders' Meetings.

Russia's membership was supported by the United States in part, I believe, to atone for another bad decision—to expand NATO to the borders of the old Soviet Union. This sent a signal to Russia that it wasn't wanted as part of the European system. Instead it was offered APEC membership as a consolation prize in the Asia Pacific.

I hope I am wrong and that Russia and Peru will demonstrate that APEC has become a central part of their foreign policy and a major shaper of their international economic policy, but I doubt it. Better, however, an APEC with the wrong membership than no APEC at all.

The global institutions we created after the Second World War fail to reflect the demands of the age we have entered. This has been apparent for a number of years. Reform of the United Nations was on the international agenda earlier in the decade, although nothing much has happened. It is absurd, for example, that membership of the United Nations Security Council has no place for the second- and third-largest economic powers in the world, Japan and Germany, and that membership is still coterminus with the possession of nuclear weapons.

The events of the past twelve months—economic and strategic—have reinforced the structural problems of our key institutions. The IMF, the World Bank, the G7, have all revealed weaknesses in doing jobs for which they were not designed, in a world which has fundamentally changed since the end of the Cold War.

The United States is revelling in its unipolar moment. Its leadership has been, and remains, essential. President Clinton's announcements last week, including the special meeting of the G22 to examine the financial architecture of the twenty-first century, were enlightened and welcome.

But the United States cannot bear the weight of leading the world alone, and in a healthy international system it should not be expected to do so. Equally, it has to accept leadership from others, and not just when it has already pointed out the direction it wants the rest of us to go in.

The recent entry of India and Pakistan into the nuclear club was another reminder of how high the stakes are. The senior adviser to the Indian Prime Minister on defence and security issues wrote in defence of the nuclear tests that India was 'assigned a particular place in the world order and not treated as a subject responding to our own interests'. It is not necessary to support India's decision to test—which I strongly oppose—to acknowledge the more general frustration.

A larger and more sustainable role has to be found for China, India and Japan. And with the EU's expansion and the creation of the euro, Europe needs to address the fundamentals of its own structure, including the rotating presidency, to see how it can act more effectively beyond its own continent.

It seems to me that one absolute precondition for recovery in Asia and for a healthier global environment is systemic change in Japan.

Japan lies at the core of Asia's problems. It now accounts for 70 per cent of East Asian GDP, up from 60 per cent before the crisis. Yet instead of pulling the rest of the region along, Japan is in the eighth year of a structural recession and heading for at least ten. When the world's second-largest economy is unable to help global growth, we have an unsustainable situation.

Japan's economy has recorded its worst growth figures since the Second World War. But for the first twenty days of July it had a merchandise trade surplus of $US6 billion, a rise of 84 per cent on the previous year.

Even as its economy contracts, Japan's national policy game has remained on track: more and more exports to the world product markets, and the sustenance of large current-account surpluses underpinned by high domestic savings.

The Liberal Democratic Party conscripted two generations of Japanese to save in order to fund the big industrial companies which then marched out to conquer the product markets of the world. Instead of calling on domestic demand, the LDP has maintained its focus on these core economic objectives for 50 years. It did not change economic direction even when its success guaranteed it a fair share of world trade. There is no evidence it can change track now.

In 1995, after the currency reached 89 yen to the United States dollar, the US Treasury let Japan off the restructuring hook by intervening to support a lower yen. Yet when the financial systems of the other Asian economies started to seize up under the strain of the subsequent appreciation of the dollar against the yen, the US Treasury, with the IMF, demanded strong structural medicine for the Asian Tigers of a kind earlier American actions had absolved Japan from applying.

The only thing which will get Japan out of its present problems is a complete reform of the political system to dismantle the cosy, amorphous alliance between officials, politicians, bankers and industrialists and to make politicians more accountable to the real interests of Japanese electors. Fiscal stimulus won't do it. Since 1992 the Japanese government has spent nearly $US700 billion on stimulus packages which have failed to stimulate.

This system has to change. And, as it changes, a more balanced relationship needs to emerge between China, Japan and the United States, one in which Japan and China can develop a relationship which is not mediated almost exclusively through the prism of the United States—Japan relationship.

APEC has already had a role making this triangular relationship healthier. The informal meetings between President Clinton and President Jiang at APEC leaders' forums since 1993 no doubt made arrangement of President Clinton's successful visit to China easier, and its outcomes more productive, if only because each side was working with much better knowledge of the other's positions.

In APEC, the Asia Pacific region has an institution which, with the right leadership, provides an enduring framework for regional relations into the twenty-first century. Despite its recent expansion of membership, it has the right scope and the right aims.

It has an ambitious trade and economic agenda which requires constant tending.

Beyond that, this crisis has again demonstrated how intertwined are economic, political and security issues. It is inevitable that the political and strategic dialogue which now takes place in the ASEAN Regional Forum will, over time, flow upwards to the APEC structure and that the Leaders' Meetings will provide an umbrella over the ARF as well.

But if that is to happen, it needs to survive this crisis.

I remain a long-term optimist about Asia and about the world. I believe the problems we are seeing are transitional and that the world is on a long convergence-generated upswing.

But the intervening period is going to be dangerous and complex. It will require committed and imaginative leadership. Without it, we could easily replicate the mistakes which made this century so dire.

Nothing was predetermined about the twentieth century's savage pattern of world wars and global depression. Bad decisions shaped developments and bad decisions will do so again.

For its part, APEC needs to recall its own objectives set out in the Seoul Declaration. These are 'to sustain the growth and development of the region for the common good of its peoples and in this way to contribute to the growth and development of the world economy'.

That is the test—APEC's own test—which the leaders face in November.

17

CHINA AND THE CHALLENGE OF ASIAN REGIONALISM

China in the Twenty-first Century

Chinese People's Institute of Foreign Affairs,
Beijing,
10 September 2001

The Chinese People's Institute of Foreign Affairs long served as China's de-facto foreign office during the years of diplomatic closure under Mao Zedong. A conference, to celebrate the Institute's diplomatic utility, attended by many heads of government, was held in Beijing over a number of days including 11 September 2001, the day of the terrorist attacks on New York City and the Pentagon. Paul Keating's speech is cast against the backdrop of the international order with particular reference to China. He says there is a hollowness at the core of the international system for which Asia should compensate by developing new forums for regional cooperation. He applauds China's decision to join the World Trade Organization and suggests that China will play a constructive leadership role in building regional organisations.

MAY I THANK THE CHINESE People's Institute of Foreign Affairs not just for arranging this conference, but for the valuable work it has done over many years in facilitating interaction and understanding between the Chinese people and the world.

My subject today is China and the challenge of Asian regionalism.

I believe that the post-Cold War world has been one of greatly missed opportunities. Our international architecture bears no real resemblance to the realities of the new world. There is a hollowness at the core of the international system. It is essentially unled. Our international structures simply haven't kept pace with the economic forces powering around the world, lubricated by globalisation.

The UN Security Council still comprises the victors of the Second World War and leaves important states like Japan, Germany and India out in the cold. The IMF and the World Bank have undergone some reform, but not nearly enough, as we saw during the Asian financial crisis of 1997–98, when loans to Indonesia were weighed down with damaging and counter-productive conditionality. The self-appointed G8 is even more unrepresentative of important forces in the world. It is an old world club.

Faced with this void at the global level, I strongly believe that if Asia is to avoid in the twenty-first century the problems so many of its people suffered in the twentieth century, it needs to develop and support new forms of cooperation—but regional cooperation.

The need for effective regionalism has been driven in part by the profound impact on the international community of two revolutions—one, a revolution in the integration and speed of global patterns of production and flows of capital, and the other in the cost and speed of distribution of information. These are the interlinked processes we call globalisation.

These forces were part of the complex mix of pressures which helped to bring about the unexpected epiphany of the end of the Cold War.

Throughout the Cold War years, regionalism in Asia was constrained by political divisions. But the collapse of the bipolar global structure we had known for half a century meant that it was possible to think about a whole new range of connections, things that were beyond our reach not long before, such as the formation of APEC, with membership by the three Chinese economies, and the expansion of ASEAN to include the countries of Indochina.

If the end of the Cold War opened up possibilities for closer regional cooperation, the forces of globalisation drove home the necessity.

I am an unapologetic believer in the benefits of globalisation. We have seen the way it has helped lift millions of people in Asia out of poverty. But I accept that any force this powerful will generate a range of problems of its own.

For example, in a world in which more businesses and processes of production operate across national borders, differing regulations and standards can sharply increase costs, so governments have come under growing pressure from companies to harmonise such arrangements. With faster, more open financial flows, national agencies find it harder to monitor and control taxation and corporate governance. Environmental problems and security issues like terrorism pay no regard to national boundaries.

None of these problems can be resolved by national legislation alone or within the borders of individual states. They can only be dealt with by international cooperation: multilaterally.

But what sort of international cooperation? Existing global organisations are often too large or slow-moving. The sheer scale of the United Nations and other large multilateral bodies can restrict the capacity of smaller countries, especially, to participate effectively in their work, to get any kind of worthwhile result.

Faced with these flaws at the global level, smaller, more flexible, regional organisations have been able to fill some of the gaps. They can address the growing number of issues that are too large for the nation-state to handle and too limited or too urgent for global action. That is the essence of it.

Regional cooperation also has the useful byproduct of strengthening bilateral relations, by increasing the opportunities for contact by political leaders and making that contact easier and less formal. Without the APEC Leaders' Meeting, for example, it would be very difficult to have arranged President Bush's visit to Shanghai this year. Or to get China's WTO membership back on track at the APEC meeting in New Zealand. Such facilitation benefits apply to countries of all sizes. I know myself how useful it can be for an Australian Prime Minister to be able to meet informally and regularly the leaders of our neighbouring countries.

Asian regionalism has been slower to develop than Europe's and it is still less highly structured. There are historical reasons for this, of course. European integration was driven by the devastating experience of the First and Second World Wars. No-one was more important to its recent history than Chancellor Kohl, who is with us at this conference.

Just as Asia's interests and problems differ from those in other parts of the world, so will the forms and structures of its regional bodies. Compared with Europe, Asian countries are at very different stages of economic development. And the patterns of interaction between, say, North Asia and Southeast Asia, have been less intense than Europe's. As a result, Asia is likely to develop a more variegated regional architecture. Nothing monolithic.

I believe it is vital to us that we retain an overarching Asia Pacific regionalism with APEC as its umbrella organisation. APEC brings the three key economies of the United States, Japan and China together in one forum. Each of them will be critical in its own way to Asia's capacity to sustain growth and development over the coming decades.

For China, regionalism will extend west as well as east. It faces tough economic and social challenges in ensuring that development in its western provinces maintains pace with the coastal areas. Regional cooperation can help this effort. The inauguration in June of the Shanghai Cooperation Organization, comprising China, Russia and the Central Asian republics of Kazakhstan, Tajikistan, Kyrgyzstan and Uzbekistan was a significant step forward in regional cooperation.

At the subregional level, organisations like ASEAN and the South Pacific Forum will continue to have an important role. ASEAN has been weakened recently by the effects of the Asian financial crisis, the uncertain political situation in Indonesia and its expansion to include new members at very different levels of development, but its health will remain critical to Southeast Asia's capacity to develop confidently and cohesively.

Asian regionalism will also weave different areas together in fresh ways. One example of this is in the work of the ASEAN Plus Three grouping, to which China has made a central contribution.

China will, in fact, be critical to almost all the dimensions of Asian regionalism. Over the course of this century China will become much stronger economically, more powerful strategically and more confident politically.

But size can overwhelm. It can be uncomfortable to live next door to a giant. The experience can generate resentment and a feeling of powerlessness on the part of smaller neighbours. Already China is attracting the greater part of foreign direct investment coming to Asia (85 per cent) and it is an increasingly competitive exporter.

In these circumstances, other Asian countries need to have confidence that their voices will be heard. By linking them with others and providing additional networks of communication, regional organisations can do that more effectively and less overbearingly than can bilateral relations. Successful Asian regionalism needs to ensure that small and medium countries have a sense of ownership of regional organisations. Shaping as well as belonging.

You can't find many positive things to say about the Asian financial crisis, but one of its beneficial outcomes was that it provided China with an opportunity to exercise a constructive leadership role. China offered support for the IMF packages, refused to take advantage of the temporary problems of its neighbours by a competitive devaluation of the RMB, focused on domestic demand for its own economic growth and contributed to efforts to secure a more effective regional financial response during any future crisis.

Its contribution during this period was noted and welcomed by its neighbours. It was a demonstration of the importance of leadership in carrying regionalism forward.

Perhaps the most important outcome of the crisis was to confirm to China's leaders that the models of development around it in East Asia were inappropriate for it.

Reform models that followed the state capitalism of the South Korean *chaebol* variety or the top-down intermediation of the Japanese sort could have robbed China of its greatest asset: the creativity and initiative of its one-and-a-quarter-billion people.

If China's economy is set up around small and medium business enterprises and around the capacity of individuals to excel, its progress will have no parallel in history. The government of China, I believe, understands this. So did Deng Xiaoping.

Asian regionalism has a long way to go before it is fully mature. Opportunities for progress exist in several different areas.

Economically, I believe China's continuing growth is likely to lead to new pressures for more open and integrated regional economic structures. For example, ASEAN leaders are already speaking of the need to reinvigorate the ASEAN Free Trade Agreement in order to meet the new challenges of competition from China. And China has spoken of the possibility of more open economic ties between Southeast Asia and China.

At the Shanghai Leaders' Meeting of APEC in October, China again has the opportunity to provide leadership at a worrying time for the world community.

The international economic outlook does not look promising. Leading economic indicators in the United States, Europe and Japan all point in negative directions. And on this side of the Pacific, many of the developing countries are in recession or just avoiding it. One of the few bright spots on the international horizon has been the continuing strength of the Chinese economy and the successful negotiation of China's entry to the WTO. Perhaps the only bright spot.

China's decision to negotiate WTO membership was not only brave, but correct, for the reasons I mentioned earlier. In my view it will also do more to shape a prosperous future for Asia than any other single decision of recent decades. In a great many respects, over time, it will change the way the world works. WTO membership will strengthen the Chinese economy and improve the living standards of the ordinary Chinese people by introducing an economic model which lifts productivity, lowers prices and gives Chinese working people higher real incomes.

That is one promising signal to the world at this difficult time. The APEC meeting provides a further opportunity for China and the other APEC members to demonstrate to international markets and to their own people that the political will and skill exists to keep Asian economies growing, and to support further movement towards freer global trade.

The second major area in which opportunities exist for progress in regional cooperation is with security. Asia has nothing to compare with the CSCE process in Europe although in both the Taiwan Strait and on the Korean peninsula it faces potentially dangerous points of conflict. Asia's security relationships still tend to be bilateral and directed across the Pacific in hubs and spokes. The ASEAN Regional Forum has been a useful interim body but its structure and membership is not ideal for the task.

The need for more effective mechanisms for regional security dialogues is pressing. I don't underestimate the complexity of the task. The direct bilateral interests of several great powers interact. But I am certain of one thing: unilateralism of the sort we have seen from the United States administration with its proposals to abrogate arms control agreements is not the way forward. Confidence-building, transparency and dialogue have to play a greater part in Asia's future.

Left to their own devices, regional groupings, like any other organisations, tend to slump back into a state of bureaucratic lassitude. We have seen plenty of examples of this phenomenon in Asia. Regional organisations need to be prodded and challenged; their agendas need to be constantly refreshed; they require imaginative thinking. This will only come—both the impetus and the authority—from political leaders.

One of the reasons I am optimistic about Asia in the twenty-first century is that I am optimistic that China will play a constructive leadership role in developing and tending regional organisations.

AUSTRALIAN AND INTERNATIONAL ECONOMIC POLICY

1

AUSTRALIA
The New Economic Template
Planning Institute of Australia,
National Conference,
Hobart,
23 February 2004

*Paul Keating's 2004 speech to the Planning Institute of Australia
provides a history of the Australian economy as it was in the postwar
years and how it came to be reformed by the seminal economic changes
he presided over as both Treasurer and Prime Minister. The speech
paints the colours and atmosphere of the old economy, as it does the
reasons for the changes and the nature of the changes themselves. The
speech carries the authenticity that could only have come from the
author of the reforms. Paul Keating goes on to share his faith in the
influence of long, technology waves as the key driver of world economic
growth. He tells his audience that the current prosperity phase, which
began in 1982 would, according to trend, be likely to end in 2007 or
2008. The last line of the speech warns the audience not to be exposed
'in or after 2007'.*

AUSTRALIA IS NOW IN ITS third economy.

Its first, the colonial one, was based almost exclusively around
agriculture. The second also had a strong agricultural component but
was augmented by mining and manufacturing. That economy, which

started gathering momentum in the 1880s, more or less, lasted for one hundred years to the 1980s.

Its earliest stages saw the growth of the gold industry and later other minerals, as it did the nascent manufacturing industry which then prospered under protection.

Because that economy was protected, paying for its imports by resort to the primary-export sector, it was given a name: it was called the Australian Defence Model.

It earned that name from the principal characteristics of the economy. The Australian Defence Model ran on a triangle of policy: first, strong export income arising from high commodity prices under strong terms of trade; second, the high level of national income paid for a high tariff, which was set to protect manufacturing industry against imports; and third, the higher cost of goods inflated by the tariff was afforded by arbitrarily set wages—wages set by a national tribunal.

The Australian economy ran on those three legs for a century. The model was reinforced by an administratively determined exchange rate and interest rates. Quantitative restrictions were also set for the levels of lending by banks and lending institutions.

The model worked for so long because most people gained something from it. Farmers and miners occupied a place of primacy in the economic system; manufacturers lived and prospered under the tariff; workers garnered a living wage under Australia's unique system of industrial arbitration.

Because everybody had something from the model, in latter years it was given a new name: 'the Australian Settlement'.

All was well until the model broke down. It broke down when the 'terms of trade' moved sharply against Australia between the mid-1960s and the mid-1980s. The prices of the things we sold the world experienced a secular decline in value while the prices of the things we bought from abroad rose in value. As our national income suffered this sustained decline, the first leg of the triangle broke down. The dramatic reduction in our national income meant that the tariff became unaffordable. Real wages were out of line with our national income while the central wage tribunals sought to maintain wages without adequate reference to our more straitened economic circumstances.

Our competitiveness was becoming more out of line with comparative countries while the onset of double-digit inflation for over a decade since the 1970s rendered the economy broadly uncompetitive.

That uncompetitiveness was compounded by an overly valued exchange rate set administratively to encourage import competition so as to apply downward pressure on local prices from import-competing industries. The exchange rate at these levels automatically militated against the competitiveness of our agricultural and mining producers, thereby reducing our national income even further.

This was the economy I inherited as Treasurer in March 1983: an economy that had simply run out of puff.

The model had made Australia an industrial backwater, relying on the lifeline of ever decreasing relative export income. The country had become an industrial museum, with manufacturers eschewing innovation, while unions used the centralised wage-fixing machinery to increase real wages. And not only that—to have the nominal growth of wages indexed to the inflation rate.

Of course, no such economic outcome, however glacial, could fail to be noticed. In fact, the terms of trade started their long secular decline around 1965—the year Robert Menzies retired as Prime Minister. Indeed, a succession of governments and, might I say, Treasurers, watched these outcomes over a twenty-year period.

In the early stages of this long 'terms of trade' decline, coupled as it was with a rise in protection, some could be forgiven for not comprehending that a secular change was underway and that the Australian Defence Model had outlived its usefulness.

But by 1975 nobody could fail to notice that the trends were deadly. At the end of the Whitlam government nominal wages growth had reached unprecedented levels, igniting a bout of double-digit inflation. This came courtesy of the ACTU under an accommodating policy set up by the Whitlam government minister Clyde Cameron.

But with the advent of the Fraser government and under the treasur-erships of Philip Lynch and John Howard, no remedial policies were put into place. In fact, during Howard's period as Treasurer, tariff protection rose sharply while double-digit inflation was maintained by a wages breakout, facilitated by his own fantasies about how the labour market should work. He was promoting open wage outcomes in a structure which was still centralised and award-based. A structure that operated on the principle of comparative wage justice. So when metalworkers procured an increase under the Metals Construction Award, that same increase would leapfrog its way into other awards; for instance, into the Metals Manufacturing Awards. This was called a 'wage round'. Howard sat glibly by while all this happened around him. He finished as Treasurer with the place in economic ruin. Indeed, centralised wage fixation stayed in place until the Keating government abolished it for a system of enterprise bargaining in 1993.

The policy of the Whitlam and Fraser governments was to see no evil, hear no evil and certainly not mention any evil. For to mention it meant the structure had to change. And not change at the margins but change completely. No-one was prepared to take that on—no-one would own up. One broken piece was incapable of being repaired; because of the inter-relationships, the whole model had to be broken up.

Let me digress here and say this. Many senior people in public life speak of their regard and affection for the Australian public. You hear these things said all the time, by rote. But I am afraid there were hardly any whose regard and affection for the Australian people went so far as to provide those same people with the truth. The affection should compel one to give the public a real break: to tell them how it really is. For, in not letting the public in on the problem, the political system treated them like fools; worse, it allowed their prosperity to be hijacked by political convenience and calculated neglect.

The fact was, to take on the task of economic repair in earnest, required the dismantling of the old model.

As Treasurer and later Prime Minister, it fell to me and my colleagues in the Hawke–Keating government to do it. But the doing of it required the discerning of a new model, one which took account of our changing economic circumstances and which would serve the country better and sustainably.

That new model has been put into place. It took thirteen years, between 1983 and 1996, but it is now there.

Fundamentally, it is an open, competitive model, the obverse of the old defence model.

Instead of the country being ring-fenced with tariffs, with a managed exchange rate and exchange controls and with wages set in the aggregate by national tribunals, the Australian economy now has a completely international complexion. Its leitmotif is flexibility.

Gone are the old rigidities; the country now has open financial, product and labour markets, as free as any comparable country. And it now also enjoys endemically low inflation. The end result is that the economy enjoys a flexibility today which was unthinkable twenty years ago.

Indeed, the changes undertaken by the Labor government between 1983 and 1996 were so profound that they have, more or less, become the model for OECD member countries.

In short, in Australia, an economic revolution took place. One which has, on average, doubled Australia's economic rate of growth and doubled Australia's rate of trend productivity.

In the ten years to 1983, GDP averaged 1.8 per cent. In the ten years to 2003, GDP averaged 3.6 per cent—it doubled. And when an economy's growth rate does that, it produces a massive increment to wealth.

In the ten years to 1985, trend productivity averaged 1.25 per cent; it now averages 2.7 per cent—more than double. This productivity, along with the recession in 1990, broke the back of inflation.

We went into the 1990 recession with the broadest measure of inflation, the non-farm GDP deflator at 4.5 per cent; we came out of the recession with it at 1 per cent. In the twelve years since, inflation has ticked over at an average level of 2.5 per cent, largely held in place by the growth in productivity arising from the Labor government's structural changes. Most important among those was the move to enterprise bargaining in the labour market in 1993. But other express changes like competition policy have helped in keeping productivity up and prices down.

This has led to what I call the 'daily double'—rising real wages with falling unit labour costs.

As a result of these structural changes, real wages have grown by about 2 per cent a year since 1992. For the decade 1992 to 2002, this has meant an increase in *real* incomes, incomes after inflation of 20 per cent; the biggest increase in any decade of the twentieth century. Is it any wonder the place feels wealthier?

It is productivity which determines real income growth. The irony is that it took a Labor government to move the country to a productivity-based culture.

But higher real incomes are only part of the story. Higher disposable income is an altogether different story. Higher disposable income in Australia has been achieved by the interaction of three influences: the first, higher real wages; the second, falling prices through the tariff cuts and competition policy; and the third, falling interest rates following the resultant fall in inflation. Taken together, higher real wages, falling prices and lower interest rates have kicked along consumption and added mightily to the service sector of the economy. It has also kicked along property values.

This is why Australia feels better, because it is better.

Indeed, since September 1991, Australia's economy began its now continuous thirteen-year stretch of growth.

The size of the economy has doubled. Inflation, which had averaged 8.5 per cent a year throughout the 1980s, fell to an average of 2.5 per cent between 1991 and 2004. And the unemployment rate fell by half from 10.5 per cent to 5 per cent over the same period.

These rates of continuous growth are not only remarkable by Australian historic standards—they are remarkable against all other developed economies. Growing at an average of 3.6 per cent a year over the period, Australia has easily outstripped the United States at

2.6 per cent, the United Kingdom at 2.3 per cent, Germany at 1.8 per cent and Japan at 1.4 per cent.

And I am sure you will give me the latitude to say that none of this had anything to do with John Howard or Peter Costello. Apart from the Howard government's GST, no other important structural change has been put into place. And I do not regard a GST, a tax change, as having important structural influences. A GST does not change economic behaviour, it simply collects revenue. Howard and Costello have simply traded off the structural benefits bequeathed to them by my government. They have made hay while the sun has shone, providing buckets of revenue to the annual budgets in measures that they could hardly believe.

And endemically low inflation—2.5 per cent recurring—they simply put that in their pocket. Wouldn't have had the wit to put it into place themselves but smiled like Cheshire cats as each quarterly set of national accounts confirmed its maintenance.

Let me say a few other things about productivity.

Productivity, of its essence, is about getting more output from fewer people. But those people, in a growth economy, are then released to higher paid, more interesting jobs.

For example, in manufacturing, output has exploded while employment has shrunk. Products have therefore become much cheaper and because they are cheaper, our living standards rise. They rise because less of our income is spent buying them.

In fact, the decline in manufacturing employment is not unique to Australia—manufacturing is disappearing generally in developed countries. For instance, in the United States, manufacturing absolute employment today is at the same level it was in 1958, yet manufacturing production in the US is up by 358 per cent. Productivity has soared.

Coupled with that is a new division in the international division of labour. Old tech—manufacturing—now largely hails from the East, from North Asia, especially China. But this concentration of manufacturing output in North Asia is giving us lower prices and a huge increase in the value of our commodities.

Our national income is going up while prices are coming down. China is giving the world a wave of deflation; quality goods at lower prices.

All these changes are central to your conference topic because these changes are impacting on our cities.

The Fordist model of regional production has now largely gone. Towns and regions built on one factory or industry are becoming a thing of the past. 'Just in time' manufacturing and inventory management mean that production is decentralised—the digital economy facilitates not only a dispersion of product but higher productivity. The Internet, as it develops, will further revolutionise production and marketing. It is likely that people in centres of output will be able to remain remote from centres of production. This, in turn, will lead to changes in the distribution of population; remembering, that all the while, real income growth is pumping growth into services, our country's major employer.

As the centre of gravity of production shifts to the East, the division of labour becomes central. Ours must be shaped by education. The premium will be on knowledge, not on widgets. Creativity is where the premium will grow. Whether that will be in financial services, or software, or in film, leisure or care—this is where our bread will be buttered. It will be what is in our heads rather than in our hands that will matter.

I have long believed that product innovation and creativity drives long or extended waves of economic growth. For instance, Thomas Edison's electric lightbulb led to the building of power stations with electricity reticulated through sub-stations and cables. Twenty-odd years on, this led to the development of domestic heaters and radios. A decade or two after that, it became washing machines and air-conditioners. These world-changing innovations and discoveries say and do more for the pattern of economic growth than only macroeconomic management by national governments.

In our time, the development of microprocessing and, with it, the personal computer, has now led to a revolution in direct communication via the Internet. This has and will produce much more investment, as it will productivity.

Technology drives not simply economic growth but waves of economic growth. As technologies mature, they promote another cycle of investment.

The twentieth century saw three long waves of economic growth, each technology-driven. These were in the years 1904 to 1929, 1947 to 1974 and 1982 until now.

The 1904 to 1929 wave was driven by electricity and petrochemicals, the 1947 to 1974 wave was driven by motor vehicles, aviation and plastics, while the international economy from 1982 until now has been broadly shaped by telecommunications and digital technology.

One has to construct a picture of the extended nature of technological influences and to see them in a continuum. And overlaying these long, driving technology waves are business or investment cycles. These are known as Juglar cycles. That is, the technology is providing the locomotive reason to the general propensity to invest. But all periods of investment tend to run in cycles and run over. When conditions are propitious to invest, companies tend to invest all at the same time. We then find that we have had a glut of investment, so this is generally followed by an investment recession to bring the stock of capital back to a point of equilibrium.

In this current long wave, we have already had two investment cycles: 1982 to 1990 and 1992 to 2000. The third investment or Juglar cycle began in May 2003, when business investment in America restarted after a three-year business investment recession.

In the twentieth century these cycles—the underlying buoyancy or upswing from technology—have lasted approximately 25 years. By this reckoning, this current long wave and this, the third business cycle, would end around 2007 or 2008. By this time, the digital technology may have drawn down much of the productivity which the technology facilitates. At the moment, it is keeping incomes up and unit labour costs down. For instance, in America in the September quarter of 2003, productivity rose by 9.6 per cent, while unit labour costs fell by 5.6 per cent. No wonder profits are big—these are truly staggering numbers and they should fuel the US economy for the next few years. But buoyant as these figures are, they will die when the endgame comes, so we should be keeping our eyes peeled for the natural decline, which, as I say, on past trends, should be in three to four years from now—2007 or 2008.

It is also prudent to understand that there are other influences on growth at the moment which go beyond the technology imperative. In the United States, fiscal policy is now hugely expansionary, with the Bush tax cuts and the defence spending working its way back through the military industrial complex into the economy. As well, US monetary policy, courtesy of Mr Greenspan, is similarly accommodating.

Through a series of events from the Asian crisis in 1997–98, through the Russian debt crisis, through September 11, 2001, through the accounting scandals like Enron, through SARS, the US Federal Reserve has kept monetary conditions soft so as not to slow US or world growth. This has led and is leading to a great compression in the risk premium attached to certain categories of investment. There is very little difference in the yields between investment-grade bonds and junk bonds. And not simply with investment-grade bonds; the differential with Treasury bonds is similarly compressed. At some point, the official interest-rate structure will have to change, to return to something more normal. But with the party having begun again just a year ago, Mr Greenspan is probably reluctant to take the punchbowl away just yet.

Finally, I want to say something about China.

A new factor in the world growth equation is China. What is happening in China today knows no precedence in world economic history—one and a quarter billion people pulling themselves from poverty. China is already a growth engine of the world economy. As I said earlier, its goods are lowering prices around the world. We have had the happy position of rising real wages and falling prices: wages up, widgets down.

There is no doubt that China, by way of its exports, is providing a strong subsidy to the inflation rate of the developed world.

I will conclude on this note.

There is every chance that Mr Greenspan will keep the party going for a fair bit longer. But whether he does or he does not, the natural end of the long wave will eke its influence anyway. China is a new influence and not one that was around during the two previous long waves. Will the advent of China and its burgeoning economy alter the otherwise pre-destined technological end of the current wave? For my part, I don't think so.

So, in the next few years, I think investment levels will start to fall off. The moral of that story has to be, don't be exposed in or after 2007. It could be dangerous.

2

THE STORY OF MODERN SUPERANNUATION

Australian Pensions and Investment Summit,
Sanctuary Cove, Queensland,
31 October 2007

*Paul Keating's 'The Story of Modern Superannuation' tracks the
twists and turns in the development of national superannuation, in
a narrative that could only have been written by the person at the
helm. The address provides an insight into the Keating policy mind:
how long-term objectives are reached by laying out blocks in a policy
construct informed by industrial and economic opportunity. The
narrative records the various stages in the building of Australia's $1.4
trillion pool of superannuation savings and its impact on the living
standards of Australia's retired. Paul Keating also makes note of the
impact compulsory superannuation has had on the broadening and
deepening of Australia's capital markets with the overall superannuation
pool standing at 110 per cent of GDP.*

BEFORE 1985, AUSTRALIA HAD RELIED on the taxpayer-provided age
pension as its principal post-employment income system. Up until then,
private retirement income under the superannuation provisions applied
to the upper end of the commercial sector and to employees in the
public sector. The great majority of working Australians had no viable
access to the generosity of the superannuation tax provisions.

The reason for this, in part, was that superannuation was so concessionally taxed in budgetary terms, its universal extension was prohibitive. Superannuation was taxed at the marginal personal tax rate of only 5 per cent of the accumulated sum; for most people, an effective tax rate of 3 per cent. And the accumulations were not subject to preservation: they could be cashed out at any time during a working life. After paying the 3 per cent tax, a person could then, subject to the income and assets tests, apply for the age pension.

So, in 1983 as Treasurer, to lay the groundwork for the extension of the superannuation provisions to the whole workforce, I announced a radical change to the taxation treatment of superannuation generally. That change preserved the concessionality of the system to 1983 while changing the tax treatment of superannuation post-1983. This meant that those people who, for a large part of their working lives had enjoyed the concessionality of the superannuation provisions, would have those accumulations protected under a 'grandfathering' concession—that is, with no retrospectivity—while income after 1983 would be taxed on a less concessional but sustainable long-term basis. This led to what famously became the 'pre- and post-1983' tax calculations.

At the same time, I took the opportunity of introducing rollover provisions to the superannuation system. These allowed employees, for the first time, to roll over rather than cash out a superannuation accumulation as they left an employer, into what was described as an 'Approved Deposit Fund'. This protected the accumulation from immediate taxation, allowing the rolled accumulation to continue enjoying compound earnings.

Rollover vehicles or ADFs usually had the same rates of return as the industry generally. This meant that someone between jobs could maintain their superannuation coverage without having it truncated by a termination. This was especially important for women, many of whom left the workforce to have children, only to find upon their return they had disbursed their accumulation, obliging them to begin again, but from the first dollar. Having lost the compounding effects at termination, they were unlikely to build a meaningful sum into the future.

Notwithstanding that the new taxation treatment of superannuation was less concessionary than the give-away 3 per cent arrangement, it was still highly concessionary, such that it should not be available simply as a vehicle for protecting income. Accordingly, I announced in 1987 that *preservation* would be a condition of the concessionality of the superannuation tax provisions, meaning that for the first time, people could not, in a discretionary way, cash out a superannuation accumulation before age 55.

These changes—the new tax treatment, rollovers and preservation—laid the groundwork for the development of a universal system of superannuation coverage. A system designed to augment the age pension for income in retirement.

The first move towards universal access under the newly shaped superannuation provisions came as part of the then government's Accord with the Australian Council of Trade Unions. Led by Bill Kelty, the ACTU and its constituent unions had participated in a series of wage settlements designed to restrain wages growth following the unsustainable increases presided over by the earlier Fraser government.

Both the Labor government and the ACTU believed that the profit share in the economy had to be restored to reignite private investment. At the time, unemployment and inflation were both hovering around 10 per cent. The ACTU and its constituent unions had demonstrated complete fidelity to this undertaking, so when the ACTU approached the Conciliation and Arbitration Commission in the National Wage Case of September 1985, the government supported the ACTU's claim that three percentage points of wages should be contributed by employers to a superannuation account in the name of each individual worker. In supporting the unions before the Commission, I wanted unions to enjoy a structural or ongoing benefit in recognition of their years of wage responsibility. Bill Kelty and I were both of a mind to add the layer of private retirement incomes to the industrial agenda as part of an expanded social wage.

In February 1986, the Commission found in the ACTU's and the government's favour, agreeing that up to three percentage points of wages could be vested in each employee's name through a process of award negotiation between individual trade unions, employer groups and enterprises. The negotiation involved the splitting of productivity with employers. It also went to deciding what part of the wages growth would be paid as cash—as take-home pay—and what part would be withheld by the employer as employee savings—to go to superannuation.

Objecting, employer groups took the matter of superannuation contributions in industrial awards to the High Court. The High Court subsequently cleared the way, agreeing that superannuation contributions could form part of the industrial negotiation process.

To legislatively underpin the new system, as Treasurer I introduced the *Occupational Superannuation Standards Act 1987*, setting for the first time separate prudential standards for the management of superannuation accumulations and their benefits. The *Act* also included:

(i) the vesting of benefits in the employee, not the employer, prior to retirement;
(ii) preservation of all benefits to age 55;
(iii) greater member involvement in the control of superannuation funds; and
(iv) a requirement that funds submit returns to the regulatory authority to certify compliance with the required standards.

In 1988, I outlined further sweeping change to the tax treatment of superannuation. In the 'Taxation of Superannuation' statement I announced that in future, the tax treatment of superannuation would be brought into line with the tax treatment of other forms of savings such as bank deposits. This was that income would be taxed on the way into the superannuation account, as with the after-tax income of deposits in a bank account; that earnings in the super account would be taxed as they accumulate, as interest in a bank account accumulates and is taxed; and that funds would be free to be taken out, as savings can be freely taken from a bank account.

In the statement, the new tax rates were nominated. Tax at a rate of 15 per cent was to be applied to all employer contributions and to tax-deductible contributions made by those who were self-employed. A further tax, at a nominal 15 per cent, was to be applied to the earnings within a fund. But in the same statement, I also announced the extension of the revolutionary dividend imputation system to superannuation. This was a milestone reform. It meant that the imputation credits attaching to dividends paid on equities owned by a fund could be streamed to the benefit of that fund, thereby reducing the nominal 15 per cent tax on fund earnings to something approaching an effective 5 per cent. This rate of tax on income was concessional compared with the level of tax on other forms of income.

In the same 'Taxation of Superannuation' statement, a Reasonable Benefits Limit or RBL regime was introduced to limit the total amount of concessionally taxed superannuation any one person could receive over a lifetime. This was designed to stop chief executive officers and people at the top of industry on the cusp of retirement protecting income by being awarded large sums by way of employer superannuation contributions.

The RBL was introduced as an equity measure to make certain that the concessionality of the superannuation taxation provisions were shared fairly across the community and not concentrated to the benefit of a few.

In 1990, under a new variation of the Accord, Accord Mark VI, the ACTU approached the Conciliation and Arbitration Commission to approve the industrial negotiation of a further three percentage points of superannuation contributions under the Award system—to bring the quantum under award superannuation to 6 per cent of wages. The claim was also supported by the government before the Commission. Despite this, the Commission found in favour of the employer groups, rejecting out of hand the ACTU's claim for the further Award contribution. Overcoming the affront to the Accord process, this decision caused me as Treasurer to make a commitment to the ACTU—to its Secretary Bill Kelty and its negotiator Iain Ross. That commitment was that, under the Corporations power of the Constitution, the government would legislate for at least a further three percentage points of wage-equivalent superannuation contributions to be paid on behalf of all employees. This included bringing the first three percentage points to those employees who lacked the bargaining power industrially to secure it in the first instance—in the main, part-time workers and the low-paid, a high proportion of whom were women.

I resigned as Treasurer on 3 June 1991 after challenging Bob Hawke for the Prime Ministership.

The 1991 Budget process was to begin in the second week of July. The then Hawke Cabinet under the new Treasurer was of a strong mind not to proceed with a compulsory charge for superannuation. Treasury had never supported the growth of award superannuation and saw a guarantee charge as simply another cost to revenue. The intimation that the government may walk away from the earlier undertaking I had given the ACTU brought a strong rebuke from the unions.

Bill Kelty and Iain Ross made clear to Bob Hawke and to Treasurer John Kerin that if the government walked away from compulsory superannuation, to at least 6 per cent of wages, the ACTU would no longer operate general wages policy within the Accord framework.

The government was nonetheless, quite stubborn. It was listening to the Treasury.

It also suited Hawke to adopt the Treasury line; to put him at distance with me and the policy commitment I had made. It was to demonstrate that Hawke possessed an independent policy mind. So to put more pressure on the issue, on 25 July 1991 I made a comprehensive speech on superannuation to the Australian Graduate School of Management at the University of New South Wales.

The speech sketched out a future for the superannuation system under a compulsory model. In the speech, I argued the government should legislate a mandatory twelve percentage point charge to be paid by employers as part of productivity sharing under the Accord wage restraint model.

The 25 July speech, while given out of office, remains the key speech in the forward design of the Australian superannuation system. Before that time, owing to the piecemeal negotiated nature of award superannuation, it was not possible to pull all the threads together in a comprehensive policy speech. The proposed jump to a fully mandated universal scheme made such a speech conceivable.

As it turned out, the speech was widely reported, sharply lifting the bar on Bob Hawke and the government during the budget process. Hawke could feel his grip on the Prime Ministership getting a good shake and he did not want the ACTU battalions siding with me.

The Graduate School of Management speech and continued ACTU pressure from Bill Kelty and Iain Ross pushed the government over the line in confirming the undertaking I had given as Treasurer. The Budget Speech of 20 August 1991 set out a 9 per cent target for the guarantee charge but said a further 3 per cent, that is, the full 12 per cent, would be considered, including reaching it by way of tax cuts. Before the Graduate School of Management speech neither the figures 9 nor 12 were ever mentioned by the government in relation to superannuation, including by Hawke.

The Budget speech also included a line that confirmed the government had registered the fierceness of the ACTU's warnings. It said: *Improvements in superannuation will be taken into account in future Accord processes.* There was no doubt about that.

Owing to the continued wage restraint by the trade unions and the structural reforms engendered by the government, trend productivity was increasing and later had more than doubled to three percentage points per annum. This meant that significant real wages growth could then be afforded, including a diversion of a substantial cash equivalent to savings via superannuation, while still underwriting a fall in unit labour costs.

I replaced Bob Hawke as Prime Minister on 21 December 1991. On 2 April 1992, an even newer Treasurer, John Dawkins, introduced the Superannuation Guarantee Charge Bill. Under this path-breaking legislation, employer contributions to superannuation would rise from four percentage points of ordinary-time earnings from 1 July 1992 to nine percentage points of ordinary-time earnings by July 2002. It is now a matter of record that that growth in contributions did occur, and that the whole system matured at nine percentage points of earnings on 1 July 2002.

It is worth reminding people that in every year the Superannuation Guarantee Charge (SGC) grew by a further one percentage point of employer contributions towards the 9 per cent target, unit labour costs fell markedly. This meant that the cost of superannuation was never borne by employers. It was absorbed into the overall wage cost. Indeed, in each year of the SGC growth between 1992 and 2002, the profit share in the economy rose. The growth in trend productivity over the period was so large it paid for generous wage settlements, including superannuation, while accommodating a higher and higher share of national income going to profits. And those wages and profits were paid consistent with an inflation rate of 2.5 per cent, on average, across the period.

In other words, had employers not paid nine percentage points of wages as superannuation contributions to employee superannuation accounts, they would have paid it in cash as wages. Otherwise, the profit share in GDP would have risen to unprecedented levels and would have shot beyond any reasonable bounds.

When you hear conservatives these days speak of superannuation as a tax on employers they are either ill-informed or they are lying. The fall in unit labour costs and the upward shift in the profit share during the period of the SGC is simply a matter of statistical record. It is not a matter of argument.

That said, not all that needed to be done had been done.

Superannuation at nine percentage points of wages, while extraordinary in western world terms, is not sufficient to reach an income replacement rate of 70 per cent in retirement. That is, for employees to enjoy in retirement an income equal to 70 per cent of their earnings before retirement.

For people on 100 to 200 per cent of average weekly earnings, nine percentage points of superannuation contributions across a working life will equate to a replacement rate of about 40 per cent in retirement, well short of the 70 per cent it should be. And given the fact that a great body of the workforce was born in the 1940s and early 1950s, there were not enough years before retirement for those people to accrue accumulations sufficient to fund a replacement income anything like 70 per cent.

So, in the Budget of 1995, the Treasurer Ralph Willis announced the government's intention of lifting superannuation contributions for all employees from nine percentage points of wages to fifteen percentage points by the same 2002 income year. In other words, seeking to frontload or boost the level of superannuation contributions to better meet the needs of the 'baby boomer' generation in retirement.

In that Budget, the Treasurer foreshadowed that the next three rounds of personal income tax cuts would be paid as savings rather than as cash—a completely new idea, one designed to bring the superannuation contributions of each employee to the equivalent of twelve percentage points of wages.

But there was a condition. It had been agreed with the ACTU under Accord Mark VIII that a new principle would be established within the wages system, whereby a *co-payment* would be made by each employee to their own superannuation account, matching that provided by the government by way of the tax cuts. This would amount to one percentage point of wages to be paid by the employer on behalf of each employee to their superannuation fund in lieu of one percentage point of cash which would have otherwise gone to their wage packet. This one percentage point was to have been withheld and paid over each of the three years, 1997–98, 1998–99 and 1999–2000. Three percentage points in all.

Those three percentage points of personal saving, matching the government's three percentage point tax cuts, summed up to six percentage points, bringing the overall level of superannuation contributions to fifteen percentage points, as the Superannuation Guarantee Charge concomitantly reached its ninth percentage point in the final year of its growth, 2002.

The two streams were designed to come together to be in place for that year. It is now history that the arrangement was thwarted. Had it happened, Australia would have had the foremost retirement income system in the world, one which would have met the larger requirements of the baby boomer generation, while giving young people joining the workforce at 22 a replacement rate of just on 100 per cent of average weekly earnings as they reached age 60.

It took a conservative government to sink the plan. You do not expect much from conservative governments, but you do expect them to believe in thrift. A Labor government procures the agreement of the whole workforce to save 15 per cent of its wages for retirement and a Liberal government comes along to destroy the last and vital six percentage points of it.

In the 1996 election campaign John Howard promised to maintain the value of the Keating government's 1995 Budget superannuation measures. But Howard walked away from that commitment as a 'non-core' promise in his Treasurer Peter Costello's first Budget by legislating to remove the 1995 Labor tax cuts payable to superannuation. They actually had to negotiate and legislate their destruction. Upon the withdrawal of the government's three-percentage point wage-equivalent tax cuts, the ACTU withdrew its Accord commitment to the employee three-percentage point *co-payment*. So, a full six percentage points of wages to superannuation was lost. Lost to the individuals, lost to the nation. Over a working life, a superannuant lost the equivalent of $300,000 in accumulation in today's dollars. And what did it save the Budget? In national savings terms, the tax cuts amounted to a bare transfer of Commonwealth savings to private savings, but preserved way into the future under superannuation's preservation provisions. Far less likely to be spent than those savings lying on the Cabinet table, waiting to be plundered by the Howard spending ministers. Which, within a year or two, they were.

As the number of retirees on the age pension is expected to more than double from the present three million to seven million by 2025, the national budget will be put under stress as the intergenerational burden falls more substantially on Generations X and Y. And they will have John Howard and Peter Costello to thank for it.

The point is the Labor government in which I was Treasurer had the foresight, as far back as 1983, to see that the demographic bulge in the Australian population beginning in 2010 and rising through 2030 was a major problem, and that something substantial had to be done in dealing with it. And done early. Fortunately, the action taken since 1985–86 in increasing award then mandatory contributions to superannuation, now to a level of nine percentage points of wages, will save future generations from the budgetary stress that would otherwise have been occasioned by the sole call on the age pension system. We have at least got that far.

But as I said earlier, nine percentage points is not enough. The universal system, now too little too late for the baby boomers, has to rise to at least twelve percentage points to reach a 70 per cent replacement rate for their children, Generations X and Y. This can be done. But we have to begin with the extra three percentage points virtually immediately.

Right now Peter Costello is out encouraging people in the top decile of incomes to invest up to $1 million in superannuation before 30 June of this year. The great body of working people got next to nothing from the Howard government's recent superannuation changes—with their superannuation contributions jammed at 9 per cent. Now Costello is abandoning the Reasonable Benefits Limits by allowing retirees over 60 years to invest up to $1 million in superannuation and take the benefits tax free. There is no doubt about the Tories: devoid of imagination or policy ambition, they always look for the main chance—to look after the wealthy.

The fact is, the Howard government despises superannuation. The idea that organisations of working people should manage large sums of money in the economy is anathema to it. If it could have gotten rid of the Superannuation Guarantee Charge, it would have. Fortunately, it did not get control of the Senate until well after the SGC had topped out at 9 per cent.

Superannuation, with the SGC contributions, is now an accumulation of just on $1 trillion in national terms. Let me repeat that: $1 trillion for just the twenty million of us. That pool of savings has transformed the Australian capital markets and has dramatically reduced the cost of capital in Australia. Even at 9 percentage points, the pool when fully mature should top out at 200 per cent of GDP. A remarkable number. But the donkeys of the Liberal Party, understanding none of this, would destroy mandatory superannuation if they had had half a chance.

In 1989 my then colleague Brian Howe and I outlined the Labor government's retirement income policy. In a document, *Better Incomes: Retirement Income Policy into the Next Century*, we explained we were moving Australia towards a retirement income system based on three pillars:

(i) a taxpayer-provided age pension, the basic anti-destitution payment;
(ii) a mandated fully funded, privately managed occupational contribution scheme, superannuation; and
(iii) a voluntary retirement savings system of discretionary superannuation contributions encouraged and supported by the concessionality of the tax system.

That system will work for Australia. It establishes a working interface between the age pension and superannuation savings, with an asset taper withdrawal of certain sums of pension for every $1000 of assets. Based on the current age pension, a single retiree would lose all entitlement to the public pension should their assets (excluding their home) exceed $494,000 or, in the case of a couple, $785,000. Who could object to that? This interface between the age pension and privately provided superannuation works efficiently and is fair.

The challenge with superannuation can be summed up in one word: adequacy. The mandatory system must rise to a minimum 12 per cent of wages if we are to have a mature scheme. And, with that, any hope of shuffling the baby boomers through without inordinate stresses on the Budget onto those younger Australians who will have to fund it. And young Australians need the 12 per cent of wages working for them, and they need it from age 22 all the way to age 60.

As with all things, something on this scale requires imagination. It also requires conscientiousness and for leaders and ministers to take responsibility. We have already left most comparable countries well behind. But to add to mandatory superannuation from here will require an extra dimension. It will require the defeat of the Howard government. Only a Labor government will return to the as yet unfinished retirement and savings agenda. But the years are ticking by, and with each one we lose the compounding effect on the savings and the wider opportunity to set the nation up for the future.

3

AFTER THE CRISIS
The Emerging Order
World Steel Association,
Sydney,
12 April 2011

Paul Keating's speech to the World Steel Association sketches out how
he sees the world developing after the Global Financial Crisis. In the
speech, he points out that the emerging economies now account for 60
per cent of global expansion, compared to 25 per cent a decade ago. He
paints a picture of globalisation moving in two separate and distinct
'tectonic' plates: one hosting the trade and investment of the transatlantic
world, the other the trade and investment of the developing world. He
believes that for the first time since the Industrial Revolution, the link or
relationship between population and GDP is being re-established—where,
due to productivity, the countries with the biggest populations will again
have the biggest GDPs. In this scenario, China overtakes the United
States as the largest economy in the world. Paul Keating also uses the
speech to underline the importance of geopolitical and strategic structures
being adapted to accommodate this vast and fundamental change.

IN A SPEECH A NUMBER of years ago, I reminded the audience that the
Industrial Revolution broke the link or relationship between population
and GDP. And that it had the effect of doing this for two centuries.

Before 1820, the work most people were engaged in was agricultural
and that work, country to country, was mostly of equal value. Therefore,

the countries with the largest populations had the largest GDP. This is why China was the largest country by GDP before 1820.

That equation was upset by the onset of industrial innovation and mechanisation, which came with the Industrial revolution. Very quickly, a relatively small country like Britain had a larger GDP than a vast country like China.

So what is happening in China and India today is no different to that which happened in Britain in the nineteenth century, to Germany and to Europe later in that century and, following that, to the United States. All that is different is the scale.

We now have a productivity revolution across the globe. And that revolution is re-establishing the nexus between population and GDP of a kind which existed down through time to the nineteenth century. In essence, the world is being remade.

But we have a guide to that new world. And that guide is the *mother* of all emerging economies—Japan.

Having industrialised earlier in the twentieth century, by 1955 Japan had a per capita output at 20 per cent of US output. This is exactly where China is today.

In Japan that output per capita rose to a peak of 90 per cent of US output in 1990. Were China to reach a per capita output of just 50 per cent of US output—which could happen within 20 to 30 years—China's economy would likely be twice that of the United States by way of overall GDP. With China enjoying overall GDP possibly as large as the United States and Europe combined, this implies large change in the way the world works.

Much of this simply reflects the balance of populations: the *West* today—the US, Europe, Canada, Australia, New Zealand, etcetera—represents 11 per cent of world population. By contrast, China and India today represent a combined 37 per cent of world population.

By applying the West's productivity co-efficient, that is, by equilibrating productivity across the globe, the distinction between developed and developing economies will disappear.

This year, the emerging economies will account for about 60 per cent of global expansion. A decade ago, that figure was 25 per cent. This leads me to believe that globalisation will become much more a developing country phenomenon. For instance, China is now Brazil's biggest trading partner and largest investor.

There is a view in the West that globalisation has some kind of pyramid structure, with the United States and Europe at the apex, with the bigger developing states like China, India and Brazil battling their way from the base towards the apex. I think that image is entirely erroneous.

I think globalisation is a horizontal phenomenon, played out between the developed world and the developing world. It is conceivable that globalisation will broadly arrange itself into two recognisable tectonic plates: one plate will host the trade and investment of the transatlantic world, the other will host the trade and investment of the developing world. That world will be made up of countries like China, India, Russia, Brazil and the countries of continental Africa.

The top-down conceit of the old G7 structure will atomise as globalisation becomes more developing countries-centric. Also apparent and reinforcing is the huge loss of prestige by the West in its management, or let's say mismanagement, of the international financial system— particularly the damage done to the US and European economies. The fact that the developing world, or most of it, trotted through the global financial crisis, is not lost on those countries. The Bretton Woods institutions now do not enjoy the clout or prestige they had.

This change, the movement towards developing countries and their economies, is also altering the strategic equilibrium of the world.

The United States, in particular, will need to adjust to a far more multipolar world. The unipolar moment, which the United States occupied, has come and gone. This will not mean that the United States will not remain powerful and relevant—it will. It will remain the top dog at the top table. But it will be a table of a number of dogs, and large ones into the bargain.

Let me return my focus to Japan.

As I said, Japan is the mother of all emerging economies. During the postwar period, Japan was to the world what China is today—the leading emerging market.

In fact, Japan experienced even higher rates of growth than has China. Japan's equity markets, despite all the early risks of investing in them, turned out to be the best in the world for four straight decades—the 1950s, 1960s, 1970s and 1980s. Indeed, one could have invested in Japan and kept all one's investments there for 40 years and still outperformed all other markets.

For instance, real equity returns per annum between 1950 and 1990 were 14 per cent for Japan against 7.7 per cent for the United States. Virtually double the return on equity for 40 consecutive years.

This gives us some idea of the likely scale of the equity markets of emerging Asia. And the debt markets too.

Much of this will go to how and with what speed China opens its financial markets. And this, in some substantial part, goes to the exchange rate system by which China manages its currency. It will also go to the pace of the internationalisation of the renminbi. Currently the Chinese government is taking active steps to promote the use of the renminbi in funding its trade.

The management system of the renminbi is now seriously distorting China's industrial development. It is internalising the wrong price signals. As a result, scarce economic and material resources are being directed towards investment, with a heavy preponderance on export industries and budget-mandated infrastructure.

The exchange rate is the most important price in the economy. It is one of the mechanisms, perhaps the principal one, for directing economic resources to the most productive places. Developing countries, which have relied on exports to kickstart their development, tend to find it very hard to break the habit: they feel obliged to underwrite the business of exporters by keeping the exchange rate down and by subsidising factor input costs.

While export industries have provided the high demand for steel and steel products, the future domestic development of China should do the same. China is the biggest producer of steel in the world and much of that goes to the investment side of the economy—to capital structures, to manufacturing plants, to public infrastructure, to railways. A greater shift to domestic consumption would simply change the pattern of steel consumption in China rather than, necessarily, its volume.

The story of modern China is fundamentally a story of urbanisation—and urban areas are full of people who rely on services. The service industries are easily the most labour intensive. They create the kinds of jobs which the Chinese economy needs. As capital intensification in the manufacturing process in China rises, relatively fewer people will be employed producing a greater level of product. There comes a point where further capital intensification becomes counterproductive for employment, especially when many industrial plants are remote from where people live. It is to enhance consumption in the cities as distinct from investment generally, that China's financial and material resources should best be directed.

This is being proposed under China's new Five Year Plan, but the pace of the shift and the breaking of old habits in China's capital-intensive-cum-export model will require more than simply administrative direction, no matter how conscientious or effective China's government may be. Such a mammoth change requires the hidden hand of financial imperative. And the best place this can materialise is via the exchange rate.

The full convertibility of the renminbi will accelerate this trend: it will also help in the long-awaited rebalancing of the world economy.

This would obviate the need for the central bank of China to recycle developing-country capital inflow into foreign-exchange reserves; rather, using that income to develop China more broadly and more quickly.

Locking away, now, the equivalent of over US$3 trillion, US$3000 billion in foreign-exchange reserves, earning minimal rates of interest and losing capital value as the US dollar declines, does not seem to be an optimal way of managing financial assets. These assets should be used more sensibly to promote a more rapid and even pathway to growth within China, than currently.

Full convertibility—a full and open float of the renminbi, free of exchange controls—will allow the exchange rate to find its appropriate level free of daily central-bank interventions. The current management system camouflages the real exchange rate while seeking to keep a lower nominal exchange rate, for reasons of competitiveness.

The system currently works in this way: each day the People's Bank of China sets a price at which it will buy and sell all other currencies. All capital inflow is then purchased by the PBoC by it issuing local currency. The wave of that local currency then floods through the financial system, providing massive amounts of liquidity, which drives along investment and finances price increases. A system made so liquid each day simply funds higher levels of investment than would otherwise be the case—it also promotes and finances inflation.

It means that, notwithstanding an ambitious government bond-selling program to mop up liquidity, China's financial system is always saturated. The current exchange-rate management system makes it virtually impossible for China to run an effective monetary policy. This means simply that attempts to trick up the real exchange rate invariably end in tears: inflation races away while scarce capital resources continue to be placed in the wrong industries. Imports are more expensive than they ought to be; consumers pay higher prices than necessary, while exporters put the proceeds in their pockets, without real regard for the cost to the nation.

The current exchange-rate system is also inhibiting China's development in other important ways. China is a country financially intermediated by banks. Banks do the capital raising and the lending. But China, at this stage of its economic development, should now be building public capital markets. This is not happening and the reason, again, is the exchange rate. The system of exchange controls which attends a managed system means it is impossible to provide fungibility of the kind which is part and parcel of a mature capital markets structure. Not only is this bad for the major industries in China, it is also bad for savings institutions and the public, who are not able to invest in such instruments. The public are left to invest their hard won savings in the banks, which pay them an abysmal deposit rate, while the banks, all government controlled, take commercial risks with their funds.

Let me conclude where I began.

The nexus between population and GDP is re-establishing itself. The equilibration of productivity across the globe will mean that the largest states by population will again be the largest states by way of GDP. As I said, this will change the way the world works. These great states will not just present themselves or re-present themselves economically, they will also present geopolitically and strategically.

Throughout history, great states have claimed strategic space for themselves. Save perhaps for Japan in the second half of the twentieth century, they have insisted upon it.

Europe and its offshoots like the United States have run the world for 300 years. That period is now over. The development of an effective and representative world structure of governance will now be paramount as we make our way through the twenty-first century. Inclusion will need to be the byword.

Resolution around these issues and those structures will be as important to the peace and prosperity of us all as are changes in the international economy.

Steel is a product synonymous with development; demand for it will continue to grow in volume as the world continues to adapt and prosper. But the continuity of its growth will depend upon the peaceful resolution of the geostrategic issues, as much as it will on matters of macroeconomic performance and trade.

The transition we are living through is the largest in world economic history. We have to take notice of the lessons of the past and make certain this great transformation happens with understanding and magnanimity.

4

SUPERANNUATION
Turbocharging Retirement Incomes
Global Pension and Investment Forum,
Monte Carlo,
7 February 2007

Addressing an Organisation for Economic Co-operation and
Development (OECD)-sponsored conference on pension adequacy,
Paul Keating laid out the rationale for the fundamental changes
to Australia's superannuation and retirement income system which
he presided over both as Prime Minister and Treasurer. He explains
Australia's three pillars retirement system: the government-provided
age pension; the 9 per cent Superannuation Guarantee Charge or
private savings; and the voluntary top-up 'super' contributions. In the
address, he says from 1983 he could see that the age pension alone
could not sustain an adequate level of income for retirees, particularly
when the bulk of the baby-boom generation was leaving the workforce.
Paul Keating says most OECD countries have lost at least 25 years in
savings by not acting to deal with the intergenerational consequences
of ageing. But, because Australia did act, and early, from 1985,
he notes that Australia now has a superannuation savings pool of
$1 trillion, amounting to over 100 per cent of GDP, an enormous
sum for a workforce of ten million people. He reminds his audience
that the political class—the politicians—can make all the difference
in transformative national schemes of this kind, if they face up to the
urgency and are decisive.

WHEN I FIRST BEGAN ATTENDING IMF, World Bank and OECD meetings in 1983, the big issues then on the agenda related to macroeconomic policy and macroeconomic management.

There was no consensus in those days as to how economic policy might best be managed between Keynesian nostrums of deficit budgeting to fill out overall demand, including the pressure those kinds of policies put on bond markets and interest rates, and the more classical approaches to economic management, which would have preferred every budget to be in surplus with monetary growth tightly constrained.

1970s inflation was still with us, economies were growing at a snail's pace and more often than not, the wage share in GDP had dislocated profits and, with it, investment. Of course, higher unemployment blighted most economies.

These days, two decades later, there *is* a consensus as to how economies should be managed, where fiscal and monetary policies enjoy a much clearer role in the scheme of overall economic management.

Now, in developed countries, there is as much attention being paid to microeconomic issues such as taxation, education, skills formation, etcetera, as there is to macroeconomic policy. Of course, in the last decade or two, product innovation has played a starring role in the transmission and use of information with its ability to change the way we live while lifting productivity and incomes.

Since this current long economic wave of growth began in 1982, over those 25 years so much has been achieved in world output and wealth.

At the same time, something else has happened. Those of us who were at work in 1982 are 25 years older. If we were born in the 1940s, as so many of the 1980s workforce were, we are at or near retiring age.

The decline in population replacement rates during that period of prosperity has given most western countries an ageing demographic where larger retired and near-retired communities depend or will depend on a relatively smaller force of younger workers to sustain them.

Demographers have been pointing to these statistical absolutes for aeons, yet the great majority of governments in the developed world focused on the macro and microeconomic issues I have just mentioned.

It is only now that governments of some of the major countries are beginning to focus on the enormous out year costs of their pension systems and the sustainability of those systems.

Governments around the world took the attitude that solutions to this problem could be postponed or at least handed on to the next generation of politicians. All sorts of remedies have been wished up: more immigration of younger people, higher participation rates by women in the workforce, older workers staying in employment beyond usual retiring ages, more factor productivity, etcetera.

However helpful some of these remedies or supplementations may be, the costs involved in providing retirement incomes for ever expanding ageing populations is so large as to dwarf the otherwise helpful influences flowing from most of the suggested remedies.

As we know, demographics take a long time to change. Higher workforce participation can provide useful supplementation while older people can work longer until they either tire out or become infirm.

The fact is, most countries have lost 25 important years in savings, a time when, with the combined power of good earnings through three business cycles and compound interest, we might have seen ballooning accumulations which could have been used to improve the adequacy of retirement savings and incomes while augmenting the budgetary provision of public aged pensions.

Implicit in what I am saying is that the greater array of pension arrangements, whether they be public, or public and private, or only private, are unlikely to produce adequate pensions in retirement.

In the modern age, most societies believe they have an obligation to those who have already worked and contributed. More than that, there is the broader commitment to social equity and the avoidance of destitution. Built on those notions is the idea of consumption-smoothing, removing or diminishing that precipitous downward step which, all too often, characterises income in retirement.

I come to this subject with my own experience as Treasurer of the Commonwealth of Australia between 1983 and 1991 and Prime Minister between 1991 and 1996.

During this period, the Labor governments in which I participated and later led, effected a fundamental transformation of the Australian economy, one which has now seen Australia through a fifteen-year continuous expansion. And a low inflationary one at that.

From the beginning, in 1983, I could see that the public pension in Australia, known as the age pension, could not be sustained without income and asset testing and that in the event it was sustained, as the demographics began to deteriorate after 2010, the burden would detrimentally affect the budget and, with it, its regressive intergenerational impact on the young.

I also knew that it was extremely unfair and inequitable that the tax provisions which went to fund the private pension provision, which in Australia is called 'superannuation', for those in the top end of industry and the public sector, was not available to the workforce at large. For I knew that those who were able to access these provisions were in a far better position to smooth their income between work and retirement.

Underpinning that belief was the acceptance that a two-tier or two-pillar retirement income system delivered and was likely to deliver a more adequate and more sustainable income in retirement than the basic government, single-pillar age pension was able to provide.

So, beginning in 1983, I introduced changes to the taxation treatment of taking lump sums which had become an exceptionally tax-effective means of voiding retirement savings early, forgoing the capacity to ever produce annuity income. Two years later, in 1985, having changed those tax arrangements, I was able, in budgetary terms, to afford the movement towards the first occupational-funded private pension provisioning for the whole workforce.

This first occurred 22 years ago. And in January of this year, 2007, that system crossed one trillion dollars in accumulations. Or, 110 per cent of GDP. A big sum for a workforce of ten million and a population of twenty million.

During this time, the government also adopted the policy of discouraging the growth of employer-provided defined benefit schemes. We could see the time coming when those schemes had insufficient assets to cover their liabilities and where all too often retirees had their benefits, or some part of them, decided by liquidators.

We were not motivated in this to shift risk from employers to employees. Rather, with the disappearance of many companies, either by corporate misadventure or bad management or structural change, the maintenance of defined benefits schemes was making the lot of the corporation far less flexible, though not necessarily improving the likelihood of providing, in the ultimate, the actual benefits so defined.

It is true that working people in accumulation schemes are more or less left to the vagaries of national economic growth and the performance of product and financial markets. But the same influences which bear upon those vagaries also bear upon a corporation's ability to meet the promise of the benefits. It is not easy to insulate anyone over time from the fluctuations of the economic cycle.

In 1985, and in the context of an Accord or broad incomes policy with the trade unions of Australia, I negotiated a national wage settlement, where three percentage points of wages contributed over three years would be allocated to savings, which would be 'preserved' in private pension accounts to age 55, managed by the 'for-profit' financial management industry. When the 3 per cent scheme had reached 60 per cent of workforce coverage by industrial negotiation between unions and employers, in 1992, as Prime Minister, I legislated what is known as the 'Superannuation Guarantee Charge'. The SGC, as it is called, made it mandatory for employers to hold back and put away a total of nine percentage points of the wages and salaries of each employee into their individual superannuation account. These contributions were made in one-percentage-point increments, over a period of nine years. Or, in the 60 per cent of cases where the 3 per cent had already been contributed, an additional six percentage points of wages was contributed over the ensuing nine years. By 2001, the whole workforce had the mandatory nine percentage points of their income being saved annually for their retirement.

In the context of massive reforms to the product and labour markets during that decade, national trend productivity more than doubled to 3 per cent annually.

This meant that there was a 2 per cent real increase in incomes in each year of the 1990s; 20 per cent real in all. The 9 per cent Superannuation Guarantee Charge essentially split off some of that income into savings; that is, workers took home less in cash as the 2 per cent real increase in wages also paid for the superannuation.

That said, this two-pillar approach had and has at its foundation the basic building block of the taxpayer-funded, means-tested, age pension. Because many people were already in their forties or fifties when occupational superannuation was introduced in the mid-1980s, there was not enough time or accumulation to make a dramatic difference to their reliance upon the age pension in retirement.

Nevertheless, to effect a working interface between the age pension and superannuation savings, a pension assets taper withdrawal of a certain amount of pension was set for every $1000 of assets. Based on the current Australian age pension, this would see a single retiree lose all entitlement to the public pension once their assets (excluding their home) reached $494,000 or, in the case of a couple, $785,000.

As mandated and voluntary retirement savings grow, naturally, the asset base of each superannuant will grow, easing their reliance on the taxpayer-provided age pension, while at the same time providing an income in retirement equal to or much nearer the one they enjoyed just prior to retirement.

In fact, if an Australian employee joins the workforce at 22 and retires at 60 and his or her fund earns an average of 6 per cent over the period, that person will retire on or near 70 per cent of average weekly earnings. Today this is around $40,000. At a contribution rate of 15 per cent those retirement savings will fund an income of around 100 per cent of average weekly earnings. At either level, it would mean that such a superannuant would be making no call, whatsoever, on the budgetary provided pension.

The Australian system also has a third pillar. This is voluntary private superannuation and other savings which are encouraged by the concessionality of the Australian tax system. The mandated savings system currently tops out at 9 per cent of all wages and salaries. But employees are encouraged to salary sacrifice so as to add to the 9 per cent wages being put away as savings by their employer. As people get older, naturally, they tend to think more about retirement and are thus more prone to salary sacrifice. The concessionality of the Australian tax system encourages them to do just that.

In short, Australia's retirement income system has a three-pillar structure. A taxpayer-provided age pension or basic safety net; a mandated, fully funded, privately managed occupational contribution scheme; and a voluntary retirement savings system, encouraged and supported by the concessionality of the tax system.

A de facto fourth pillar, as I indicated earlier, is that the Australian retirement income system is not characterised by Defined Benefit schemes, owing to the ambiguity as to who bears the ultimate liability.

This conference is discussing many aspects which relate to pensions and to investment—questions such as the alpha and beta of investment strategies, measurements of risk, questions about private equity, etcetera.

These, no doubt, are interesting subjects. But I am more naturally drawn to issues which have the effect of bulking up savings and which lead to greater pension adequacy.

I think it is important to divine ways in which OECD countries and some developing countries might establish greater private provisioning and preservation in pension systems that can go on to produce adequate annuity incomes in retirement. Certainly, more fully funded ones.

Many countries within Europe are, in population terms, already contracting. That is, they are getting smaller, now. The intergenerational consequences of this are profound. Huge and growing retirement age populations voting with grey power to encourage governments to mount an unconscionable assault on the incomes of the young.

How, at this late stage, can countries begin to move towards greater adequacy of incomes in retirement when fiscal policy is liable to wilt under the load, particularly, with the plurality of our political systems making it so difficult to begin, in any meaningful way, on the pathways to higher levels of private funding?

Let me propose two ways: the wages system and the taxation system.

I have already mentioned the Australian experience with the wages system. While this began industrially, in a negotiation between unions and employers, under a policy encouraged by the government, it finished with the 9 per cent SGC, which is a legislated mandate obliging employers to withhold a proportion of wages and salaries and to deposit those withholdings into individual private pension accounts.

The agreement of the workforce materially helped in this. There is no doubt about that. And the leap in trend productivity also helped. It is easier to put money away if incomes are rising. But, in the end, without the government will, it would not have happened. This kind of mandated legislation can apply across most OECD countries and in some developing countries. It is worth doing even if it takes two years to put 1 per cent of wages and salaries into savings. That is, half a percentage point a year.

What is important here is not the quantum or the increments, but the beginning. Even if it took fifteen years to tuck away 10 per cent of wages as savings, it is worth it.

This would not amount to a dislocatory shift in profits any more than it would an unreasonable allocation of workers' cash to savings.

As with most things, this requires leadership. And what are the key ingredients in leadership? The answer is always the same: imagination and courage.

No point having the imagination without the courage and no point having the courage without the imagination. Political figures add value to the public system by decisiveness. They can cut through the procrastination and the nonsense by actually taking a decision. And by taking it, a lot of the inherent political risk evaporates.

But the problem of retirement savings will not be solved by useless politicians sitting on the egg hoping that before their time is up, someone else will come along to hatch it for them.

And this brings me to the tax system.

All governments by virtue of the impact of inflation on incomes find themselves in the position of collecting 'fiscal drag'. That is, the impact of even modest inflation in lifting incomes in a progressive tax system.

At some point, either through tax indexation with automaticity or by discretionary changes to tax rates, governments end up in the position of having to provide tax cuts. Often those tax cuts simply inflate demand. Often, as in the recent Australian experience, large tax cuts pump demand up such that the central bank is obliged to check the extra activity by imposing higher interest rates.

Those tax cuts would have been much better paid as savings rather than as cash. And in the Australian case, where the budget today is in structural surplus, those tax cuts should have been taken off the Cabinet table and the surplus, and preserved to age 60 years in every tax-paying individual's private pension account.

If one asks the question, in qualitative terms, where are national savings best left—on the Cabinet table for spending ministers to plunder or in the accounts of ordinary working people for their retirement—there is of course, only one answer. Preservation is king!

I suggest this, not for some idea that has never been tested. In fact, I proposed this as Prime Minister in the 1995–96 Australian Budget. In that Budget the government provided tax cuts, paid to the equivalent of 1 per cent of wages, in each of three consecutive years, into every taxpayer's superannuation account.

This would have had the effect of lifting the 9 per cent under my Superannuation Guarantee Charge to a total of 12 per cent. And, to cap it, I had the trade unions of Australia agree that they would oblige workers to make an equivalent payment of one percentage point of wages, in each of the same three years, bringing the total contribution to their pension account to 15 per cent: 9 + 3 + 3. This additional three percentage points from workers was called the 'Co-Payment'.

As it turned out, the incoming Howard government reneged on its promise to maintain the tax cuts. And when the tax cuts went, so too did the Co-Payment and Australia lost six percentage points of wages and wage equivalents in its national savings pool. Instead of being at one trillion dollars as now, we would have been at $1.3 trillion and rising rapidly.

There is, of course, a moral in this: if you want enlargement and innovation in economic ideas, don't go to a conservative government. However that may be, conservative governments are at least supposed to believe in thrift. God knows, they don't believe in much else. But Australia has a conservative government that believes that thrift and savings on this scale should not be within the ambit of worker preference no matter that that preference is actually managed by the 'for profit' financial investment services industry. The Howard government even has the blue suits under suspicion.

Nevertheless, governments around the world are able to direct tax cuts into savings. If one looks at the huge tax cuts under the Bush administration in America, imagine how much better those tax cuts would have been, qualitatively, if they had been paid as savings into the private pension accounts of Americans. With America's savings paucity and its current account imbalance, what a lost opportunity. And as those Americans of my age grow older and nearer retirement, how much more they might have appreciated those savings, had they not turned them to immediate expenditure.

I should make another point about the Australian experience.

The $1 trillion of mandated savings has completely turbocharged the Australian capital markets. You now see Australian institutions roaming the world looking for infrastructure and property deals to feed the growing need for volume and yield.

As Treasurer, in 1985, I removed the double taxation of dividends in Australia. Corporation tax is now paid by the company and the tax credited to the corporation is transferred to shareholders on receipt of their dividends, so as to relieve their personal taxation on that income.

This has completely changed the fashion for dividends in Australia. And if the dividends are substantial and regular, which they are, this naturally fixes the upside price of stock. It also fixes the down side. This has meant that the beta of the Australian stockmarket is far lower than stockmarkets of the United States and Europe.

Each year, an extra $100 billion drops into the lap of the financial investment industry in Australia from the superannuation system. A lot, for a workforce of ten million, but it has to be invested. This is another factor driving the sophistication of the financial services industry, as it looks for opportunities in Australia and, increasingly, around the world.

We always hear a lot from financial planners and investment strategists about savings and investment but it is the politicians who can make the real difference. And it is the politicians who need to grasp the relative immediacy of the coming demographic bulge, with its all too predictable dislocatory consequences.

That is what this debate must be about.

5

THE WORLD ECONOMY
The Narrow Escape
ACI—Financial Markets Association,
Sydney,
25 March 2010

The Financial Markets Association invited Paul Keating to provide his perspective on the world economy two years after the financial crisis, including the sustainability of Chinese growth and the portents for Australia in response to its heightened terms of trade. The speech offers a real-world view of prevailing international financial conditions as it does a revealing synopsis of China, especially the nature of its political economy and institutional management, including the imperative of a shift to consumption based on greater individual choice. Paul Keating paints a positive picture of Australia's immediate economic prospects but warns that unresolved fiscal scenarios worldwide, coupled with ongoing international financial imbalances threaten another global financial crisis—but this time without the fiscal room or ability to put counter-cyclical policies into place.

THE WORLD ECONOMY CONTINUES TO limp along.

The world escaped from the Global Financial Crisis, but only just. The most recognisable feature of the world economy today is that private investment and private borrowers have taken a back seat. Governments, to maintain demand, have been driven to massive dis-saving to substitute for an otherwise higher level of private expenditure.

The challenge is for debtor countries to stabilise their economies other than by resorting to another round of profligate private borrowing or a perpetual rise in government debt.

Neither of these paths is sustainable: another round of borrowing must lead to defaults, while an inexorable rise in government debt will, similarly, lead to defaults. Alternatively, one or both will lead to inflation.

As the study by the professors of economics at the universities of Maryland and Harvard, Messrs Reinhart and Rogoff, reveal, countries that see their national debt burdens move through the 90 per cent-to-GDP threshold find the trend ability of their economy to grow will be constrained by one percentage point of GDP. In other words, an economy that could once grow at 3 per cent per annum, finds itself speed-limited to 2 per cent. A large negative outcome.

What will have happened is that the public sector will have expanded, crowding out private investment.

The Reinhart and Rogoff study reveals that after a financial crisis, public debt rises by an average of over 80 per cent within three years; that is, it nearly doubles. This arises from the collapse in tax revenues from lower growth, the cost of the fiscal stimulus put in place to avoid a recession, and the direct public cost of the financial bailouts to banks and major industrial companies. And the higher taxes normally imposed later to deal with the growing debt have a further deleterious effect on growth.

This is, Australia being the exception, pretty much the picture of the advanced countries: North America, Britain, much of Europe and all emerging Europe. Fortunately, many emerging markets, particularly those in East Asia, are in better financial shape.

The way for advanced countries to stabilise their economies, other than by more profligate borrowing and more government debt, is to *earn* their way back to more balanced growth—and this means a big rise in net exports: import replacement and exports.

But for this to happen, the surplus countries like China and Germany must more strongly expand domestic demand. That is, move the driving character of their economies away from a preponderant reliance on investment to one of more consumption.

To get out of the general bind—to allow the debtor states to grow again—the surplus countries must facilitate a global adjustment in the balance of payments. But that facilitation has not been forthcoming. Germany wishes to continue running current-account surpluses with modest levels of domestic demand, while seeking to punish other European states which rely on its vendor financing. Germany wants people to continue buying its products but not borrow German savings to do it. It labels those states as profligate, yet relies on them to buy its prestige motor vehicles and machine tools.

On the other hand, China maintains its capital-intensive, export-led model by employing an undervalued, ultra-competitive exchange rate. It also heavily subsidises factor input costs.

So what is happening is that the surplus countries are absolutely insisting on the models that have worked for them before the crisis and now after it. Having learned nothing, they have forgotten nothing.

So the countries which ran large current-account deficits—the US, the UK, Spain, Ireland, etcetera—and which massively over-leveraged themselves can only deal with their now huge budget deficits by growth—by large resort to import replacement and exports.

But if the surplus countries like China and Germany refuse to facilitate a global shift in external balances, by expanding aggregate demand at home, the deficit countries can only make the adjustment through protectionism—imposing duties and quotas on the surplus production of those countries.

Talk of protectionism may seem alarmist or the prospects of it unlikely, but it could become a live option for the United States as it did during the Nixon administration of the 1970s at the end of Bretton Woods Mark I.

So the current game continues: the developed economies slow down while the 'developing' countries take up the slack: the BRICs, Brazil, Russia, India and China. Of those, China is the largest.

Let me say a few things about China.

The central question about China is the extent it remains a major engine of global growth, with its politically driven, top-down, capital-intensive, investment-cum-export model. Can its cycle of over-investment and excess capacity be broken in favour of a re-distributive, market-based system leading to a model of sustainable demand?

And can a major transition to a more vigorous domestic economy occur in a self-reinforcing one-party state, without the impulse of an enfranchised polity shaping consumerism and choice? In other words, without the individualist response, which is the hallmark of consumer economies and societies around the world.

If the answer to that question is in the negative, in the long term, can the cohesive, corporatist state of China continue to grow at rates of around 8 per cent or better, or will the leaden weight of China's corporatism drive the economic performance to increments of GDP of around 6 per cent?

The answer lies in China's willingness to reform itself—the willing-ness of the Communist party to embrace not simply state capitalism but consumerism of a more individualist kind—a policy which would have to reach out to embrace middle-class aspirations in a way which challenges the uniformist approach of the current political economy.

People should not think that China will simply turn in high rates of economic growth perpetually. We should remember that in the mother of all emerging economies, Japan, GDP growth averaged 10 per cent in the 1960s, 6 per cent in the 1970s and 4 per cent in the 1980s and as we know, around 1.5 per cent in the 1990s and since. These happy stories can eventually have unhappy endings.

It is instructive to recall the essence of Deng Xiaoping's 1978 modernisation strategy. It consisted of two elements: growth and reform—growth to provide a national revival and jobs, and reform to maximise the efficient use of resources, to make the growth sustainable.

The first element, growth, has been highly successful—remarkably so. The reform, however, after getting away to a good start, has broadly stalled. Socially, it ran into a wall after Tiananmen Square in 1989 and the social consequences had knock-on economic consequences for the way the economy worked.

The consequences of Tiananmen Square at the point where the social-cum-economic model was leavening was to consolidate political control and with that, to advance state corporatism.

This presented itself through the party-controlled economic apparatus: the state-owned enterprises. Under the Communist Party's management system, one agency is responsible for all key appointments, or, more particularly, for recommendations to the State Council for those appointments. This means that everyone, from the head of the National Development Commission, the governor of the central bank, the bank regulatory authority, the securities commission, the CEOs of the major banks, the CEOs of the state-owned enterprises, to the editors of the newspapers, are appointed under the one authority.

This process leads to a regular interchange of people between the party, the institutions of government and the state-owned enterprises, which implies that movement towards political change and to a more individualist, small-to-medium enterprise-based economy, is inhibited by a corporatist elite, perpetually refreshed by the inclusion of business leaders. Leaders with a vested interest in the continuity of the existing model.

The 'commanding heights' of the economy remain publicly owned and are shielded from market competition and market disciplines—like rates of return on capital; accountability to shareholders—the kinds of disciplines that are part of everyday commercial life in the developed world.

Coupled with this, factor input costs are subsidised by way of cheap capital, cheap land, cheap labour and cheap energy. This allows inefficient enterprises to survive, further driving the economy to even higher levels of investment.

These higher levels of investment have ensured that labour receives a declining proportion of national income. As a consequence, the wage share in national income fell from 53 per cent in 1997 to 40 per cent in 2007. This, in turn, has crimped consumption-led growth. Growth in consumption requires growing real wages leading to bigger private and service sectors, encouraged to grow in a reinforcing framework of competition.

But the state-owned enterprises also dominate the service sector, with forbidding barriers to entry. It is worth noting that industry and construction generated 50 per cent more jobs than services between 2003 and 2007. And the government stimulus, put in place in response to the global financial crisis, is simply reinforcing the impetus to investment, to industry and construction.

The huge funds the government urgently made available were channelled, chiefly through the state-controlled banks, in the main to finance fixed-asset investment by large state-owned corporations. So the long-standing imbalance in the economy in favour of investment over consumption was exacerbated as the banks poured more and more cheap capital into the state-owned enterprises.

And compounding this entrenchment is the fact that the retained earnings of state-owned enterprises (SOEs) now amount to a cumulatively higher level of national savings than savings by the household sector. Not only are these corporate savings unprecedented, the government gives the SOEs the dispensation of not being obliged to provide dividends to the national budget. So whereas in the developed world, corporations are obliged to distribute earnings to shareholders, this is not the case across the greater part of Chinese industry. The shareholder, the government, lets them retain the earnings. In the developed world, distributions to shareholders reinforce the propensity to consumption as shareholders spend their dividends—but this is not the case in China.

So unless there is a determined effort on the part of the government, the contribution to growth of consumption and its share of total output is set to remain broadly unchanged.

There is discussion within government circles that a more determined shift to consumption will have to be made within the new Five Year Plan. If such a shift does not happen, the current share of investment to GDP will see huge excess capacity in most industries across the Chinese landscape.

Unless China changes its model, unless it makes a determined effort to build private demand, until it appropriately prices the factor inputs to production, until it allows the real exchange rate to reveal itself,

China's economy will remain highly distorted and, in the medium term, its growth trajectory must suffer.

So, where does this leave Australia?

The developed world is slowing down but our largest customer, China, is growing well. But as I have said, on investment steroids. At US$6 trillion of GDP, China will be adding about US$550 billion of new wealth to the world economy. By way of contrast, the United States, at US$15 trillion of GDP and growing around 2 per cent, will add about US$300 billion of new wealth to the world economy. So it is easy to see where the kicker is coming from.

Australia survived the global financial crisis without a recession. And it did so because of the flexibility of the economy. Flexibility which came from the reform of Australia's financial, product and labour markets that began 25 years ago. This has given us one of the most flexible economies in the world—arguably the most flexible.

But further structural changes are ahead of us.

The terms of trade we currently enjoy, according to the budget forecasts, will be 35 per cent higher than the average of the last 50 years. This is an amazing statistic. And we have a very high level of remaining reserves of key mineral commodities.

But to draw the full benefit from these elevated terms of trade, a larger share of our factors of production will need to be allocated to the resources sector. Traditional industries like manufacturing and tourism, whose relative output prices are declining, will command less of a share of available capital. What will save those industries from absolute falls in output will be our expanding population and labour force. Nevertheless, the economy will be characterised by a higher general level of investment, lasting probably for some decades.

This means that the economy will be importing capital, thereby running a substantial current-account deficit over those same decades.

The funding of the current-account deficit has not been a difficulty for Australia—except through the global financial crisis. What the global financial crisis taught us is that markets break down. The term funding of our four major banks in the global financial markets was threatened and could only be rolled over during the crisis with and under the guarantee of the Commonwealth government. This means we have to be less sanguine about the current-account deficit and its funding. We need to think more and do more about national savings.

However, the size of the coming investment phase, the supply response to the elevated terms of trade, will be so large and ongoing, even a concerted effort to add to savings, like taking the Superannuation Guarantee from 9 per cent to 12 per cent of wages, will not be enough— but it will help. We cannot be in a position where, to finance ourselves, we are taking around the begging bowl in debt markets polluted by sovereign insecurities and sovereign defaults.

Australia has a clear and certain future but it must do things to consolidate it.

The sources of world growth will change but Australia should be well positioned to profit from it. But the international financial imbalances will have to be dealt with, as will the fiscal positions of the United States and significant parts of Europe.

Undealt with, these influences, taken together, threaten another financial crisis, but this time, without the fiscal room or ability, world-wide, to put countercyclical policies into place.

Australia, hopefully, can pick its way through this, but it should return to the 1990s savings and productivity agenda to make its future more certain.

6

FINANCIAL INNOVATION AND LABOUR REFORM IN THE POST-INDUSTRIAL AGE

Chosun Ilbo—Asian Leadership Conference,
Seoul,
21 February 2008

*Upon the election of the new government in South Korea, one of
the country's leading newspapers, Chosun Ilbo, asked a group of
international leaders to share their experiences in the quest for reform.
Paul Keating's address, albeit made in another country, is more
revealing than perhaps any he has given in Australia. The address
makes transparent his social and political philosophy. He says social
democratic states should commit to wage justice, including legislated
minimums for the low paid; that policy should never be about
buttressing top-end wealth off the back of a working poor; and that the
most vulnerable must be protected. He says decisive Cabinet government
with a competent bureaucracy is the highway to change. In the address
Paul Keating claims 'there is nothing more noble than lifting the great
body of a population into higher levels of income and employment'.*

CHOSUN ILBO HAS ASKED ME to address the subject of financial and
labour market reform. I have been asked to draw upon my experience
of introducing reforms to those markets in Australia during the period
I was Prime Minister and Treasurer of Australia.

In particular, I have been asked to reflect upon similar changes
made in Australia 25 years ago and more recently, fifteen years ago, to

provide some clue as to the importance of these reforms and how they might work in a South Korean context.

Perhaps I should make the overarching and key point first: any country has a right and can choose the economic pathway of economic nationalism and protectionism. But supporters of that policy have to know that such a pathway, while having some popular appeal, carries with it the choice of sub-optimal or lower rates of economic growth coupled with lower and slower rates of income growth.

Perhaps I could paraphrase it this way: open markets provide more opportunities, more growth and faster income growth. But they present greater challenges from the ensuing adjustments and put a greater requirement on the political system to respond to the need for those adjustments.

Open markets also do something else: by allowing competitive pricing, they make clear which parts of the economy are true profit centres and which, by contrast, are the parts which perform sub-optimally.

These outcomes inform investment choices such that capital is drawn to those parts of the economy where enhanced profitability lifts returns and with these returns, GDP growth. In other words, open markets identify the more likely and natural parts of the economy where scarce capital is best employed.

Impediments to trade, such as tariffs and quotas, financial regulation and labour-market rigidities falsely pump up particular sectors and industries, making them appear more attractive and profitable than they really are. Whereas those nominal attractions can only exist at the expense of the broader community by way of diminished incomes and lower GDP growth.

We have a choice. But if we have the option and the power, why would we take the low-income road over the high-income one, simply to satisfy entrenched interest groups or keep the political system free from trouble?

There is no revelation in this. But the fact that these truths are so often ignored or obscured makes their recital worthwhile.

Politicians and political parties exist for one purpose and one purpose only: to safeguard the people while improving their living standards, making the required changes to the fabric of their economies and their societies.

Politicians who are in the business of politics but not in the business of change let their communities down, and badly. The political game is about, and only about, getting the changes through. Bureaucracies are more than capable of running an existing system, but bureaucrats do not have the authority or generally the instinct to promote change.

The great curse of modern political life is incrementalism. Moving along, millimetre by millimetre, taking few political risks while pretending to be the elector's friend.

Mandates for paradigm shifts in an economy or society belong only to politicians and to the political system; they can never belong to bureaucracies. Bureaucracies have no political power on which to draw; what they do, sometimes well, is to filch morsels of power which they use to incrementally move along their own agendas.

It is no accident that in countries where bureaucracies have been in the ascendancy we find generally slower rates of economic growth and slower rates of income growth.

A decisive Cabinet government, aided and abetted by a competent bureaucracy, is the key to change.

With that in mind, your hosts have asked me to say something about the financial system and financial-market reform.

When I first began opening the financial markets in Australia in 1983 I used to speak in terms of a sclerosis which inhabited the Australian financial system. And I used apply the analogy that we needed to 'clear the financial arteries to get blood to the muscle of the economy'. That remark is as true today of unreformed financial systems as it was of Australia then. Open and porous financial markets bring financial resources to parts of the economy that were undreamt of even 30 years ago. Financial deregulation allows financial engineering and packaging of a kind which the old regulated and traditional financial system was unable to provide. And, more importantly, unwilling to try.

Most financial systems built around deposit-taking institutions were characterised as high-margin businesses, offering a relatively limited range of services. Institutions of this kind serve a society particularly badly by making people pay too high a margin for financial resources while limiting the size of the group who qualify to enjoy those resources. Low margin, big volume, fungible financial services are able to help the great body of the community into assets and services they require. In doing so, they promote higher GDP growth.

The absence of unnecessary financial regulation also underwrites the more rapid development of capital markets, those places where financial resources are available to industry and commerce other than through the intermediation of traditional banks. For instance, Japan is the model of a top-down, bank-intermediated financial economy whereas the United States has been the model of a much more horizontal financial structure where corporations and individuals have access to capital through a vibrant capital market. Where banks do what banks should do: look after the consumer, the householder and the small business entrepreneur.

Of its essence, financial regulation represents a set of structures most valuable to the already wealthy while deregulation, openness and fungibility present avenues which are most valuable to the clever and the imaginative. When a society leaves the door shut to the clever and the imaginative while leaving it open to those of established wealth, that society is heading for second-best outcomes.

That said, financial innovation also carries with it ongoing adjustment problems and distortions as we have seen in the United States more recently.

A sustained period of economic expansion like the one we have experienced since 1982 will generate an ever growing role for the financial economy in world economic affairs. A 25-year expansion characterised by low inflation and with less circumscribed financial markets will inevitably underwrite an expanding role for financial services in our economic life. Indeed, we have seen a proliferation of institutions and services of a kind never before witnessed. And this period, at least for half of it, has also been characterised by accommodating monetary conditions and high levels of liquidity induced, in the main, by central banks.

The outcome has been a *pot au feu*: a financial milieu without precedence in financial history. Financial innovation in this period has led to all sorts of financial engineering and packaging to get financial resources into every crack and crevice of the economy; while on the asset side, ownership of those resources has been spread to the four corners of the earth under every instrument imaginable. Each new instrument brings another new name: collateralised debt obligations or CDOs, derivatives, hedges, swaps, securitised bonds and all manner of financial units, be they in listed trusts or private portfolios.

The fact is, for the first time in modern history, we now have a financial system whose affairs and influences are beyond the reach and remedy of central banks.

However true this is, would we have turned our back on the financial innovation which has lubricated the last 25-year expansion, or would we have opted for the safe house of bank-intermediated economies run in clubby cabals by central banks, commercial banks and finance ministries?

The answer has to be that we should have preferred innovation over regulation, notwithstanding the problems that too often accompany innovation. The current sub-prime crisis in the United States teaches us, again, that no amount of financial slicing and dicing can turn a bad credit into a good credit.

If sub-prime loans were bad to begin with they remained bad even as they were sliced and diced into a collateralised security held by unsuspecting investors. And, let me add, that none of these tendencies have been helped by central banks who feel it is their bounden duty to underwrite the financial adventurism of investment banks and private equity funds, by putting onto the state the contingent cost of financial miscalculation.

I do not think it is too much to claim that as a consequence of the behaviour of central banks and their opportunistic clients, that 'moral hazard' has become the leitmotif of financial services.

This has to be a worry for all governments and all prudential supervisors. But it is a worry that we have to work our way through so that we can enjoy the advantageous aspects of financial innovation while seeking to limit the fallout to investors and the state alike.

North Asia, especially China and South Korea, have an enormous stake in getting the design of their financial systems right. With economies growing in the order of 8 to 11 per cent a year, the ongoing resourcing of these economies will not be possible unless their financial systems move in tandem, or are allowed to move in tandem, with economic expansion.

And what is true of financial markets is just as true of labour markets.

Policy toward labour markets should be such as to encourage labour to go to the most productive places in the economy to secure the greatest increments to income. Productivity-based wage adjustments therefore represent the best way of lifting incomes while holding down inflation. And this is best accomplished by labour-market mobility with workers free to switch to the best jobs.

Social democratic states very properly have another objective: to guarantee that working people are able to enjoy a living wage, one that lifts them and their families above the poverty line. This can take the form of a legislated minimum or a basic award but, in whatever form, it provides the foundation of a civil society. We should always remember that the point of economic policy is economic wealth and social progress. It should never be about top-end wealth provided off the back of an army of working poor, denied the kind of wages and conditions that are conducive to the sustenance of families.

We ought remember that in that great cauldron of opportunity, the United States, real wages have not risen since the early 1980s. That is, the huge increments to productivity from the late 1990s on have gone solely to profits and to those lucky individuals at the uppermost reaches of the corporate and financial system. This represents a massive indictment of the United States as the country of the fair society. This is not a model which will suit rising societies, particularly of the Asian variety, which rely upon the family unit, family cohesion and family income as their nation's basic building block.

What a country needs is wage justice with full employment, had by directing national financial resources to the appropriate and best parts of the economy, unfettered by the distortions of protection. Investment of the kind which, through productivity, is able to lift wages and profits simultaneously. Any fool can run a low-wage economy in the quest for low prices and competitiveness; what we need are clever people to run systems which are productivity-inducing, where real wages rise with GDP and where competitiveness is not had unfairly from the sweat of the low paid.

There will always be groups in the labour market whose positions are so weak that they are unable to bargain their way into higher wages, to garner a share of the productivity. This is invariably true for women and young people and the broadly unskilled. Policy has to work at protecting these vulnerable people from exploitation while the better off are able to reasonably enjoy their economic rewards.

There is a real challenge here: we want flexible and mobile labour markets with earnings related to productivity but decency demands that we should have this only in the context of safety nets for the disadvantaged.

Education provides the great springboard of opportunity, including into higher incomes. This is why an economy becoming more urbanised, with greater service orientation, has to have a premium on education. Education is the conduit through which higher levels of productivity are had.

Education has been a notable and strong trend in South Korea; it knows the way forward in the post-industrial age. A country like South Korea must continue to lift itself up the international division of labour and not be left behind to compete with low-wage countries.

There is nothing more noble than lifting the great body of a population to higher levels of income and employment: indeed, there can be nothing more noble for a political system than lifting the great body of a community. But this can only be done by governments competent in the ways of the world: knowing about the economy, knowing about business, knowing about the financial system, knowing about the workforce. Guiding policies with a kind and thoughtful hand.

Financial, product and labour market deregulation have brought much wealth to countries which have promoted these policies. Australia, as a case in point, has now experienced a continuous seventeen-year expansion averaging nearly 4 per cent GDP growth per annum with inflation at 2.5 per cent. In the 25 years since 1983, real incomes in Australia have risen by one third, over 30 per cent, the largest increment to incomes at any time in the twentieth century. These policies will work just as well for South Korea as they have worked for Australia.

Given that all societies are different, the variations on the theme in South Korea will of course have to be South Korean. But the underlying efficiency of the changes is guaranteed to lift people more rapidly up the income scale and to boost South Korean GDP more obviously on the international totem pole.

It is a very encouraging development indeed, that one of this country's premier newspapers, *Chosun Ilbo,* is committed to these kinds of outcomes and is prepared to meet the organisational responsibility of promoting a conference of this kind in pursuit of those outcomes.

7

DEVELOPING CHINA
The Continuing Story
SIBOS,
Sydney,
10 October 2006

Invited to provide an international audience with a contemporary overview of China, its development and impact on the world, Paul Keating rounds out the recent history of China, underlining the unprecedented nature of its modern rise from agrarian statehood to world manufacturing centre. He takes the opportunity to bring China's problems like urbanisation, productivity and its savings surplus into sharp relief, juxtaposing them with the other major industrial countries. Paul Keating also contextualises China's strategic circumstances arising from the transformation of its economy. The speech provides an important snapshot of China just before the onset of the global financial crisis and China's accession to membership of the Group of Twenty countries.

I HAVE BEEN ASKED TO talk to you about China, its problems and its impact on the world around it.

I think it is true to say that what is happening in China knows no precedence in world economic history. Never before have 1.25 billion people dragged themselves from poverty at such at pace.

The Industrial Revolution of the nineteenth century in the United States was built from a population of 40 to 60 million people. Britain's

Industrial Revolution before that was built on a population of less than half that.

The advent of an open and competitive China, this vast state, is a unique development.

But it should be remembered that China is still a developing country. And still a relatively poor one. Fifty per cent of its people are still engaged in agriculture. GDP per capita is still only US$1700 per annum. This means something like US$5000 per capita on the east coast of China equating to something in the order of US$1000 in the hinterland.

A key fact about China, not at all well understood, is that its economy and society resembles a patchwork quilt of varying prosperities, held together by social and political stitching. That stitching comes under strain every time the country develops disproportionately, one region to another.

This is why the government of China is always concerned with the centre and west of the country—and why the policy focus remains attuned to it.

Unlike Britain or the United States, which saw their predominantly rural populations drift to the cities and manufacturing centres in the eighteenth and nineteenth centuries, China will enjoy only some measure of this absorption and integration.

Its vast population will mean that roughly 400 million people in the countryside will be surplus to agricultural needs yet remain unable to be accommodated in the cities and industrial centres. This presents social-policy problems for China which no OECD government has had to grapple with.

China has managed its great surge in productivity by bringing people to manufacturing centres, displacing them from low-productivity agriculture—taking them from a bullock-drawn plough and putting them in front of a machine. As a result, productivity shot up and unit labour costs fell, as investment eked its reward.

But, as productivity increases, relatively fewer people are required in the productive process. Where do these otherwise displaced people go?

The first answer is that fewer of them will come from the country-side. The second is that more will be engaged in the service economy.

The good thing about service economies is that they are replete with people. But to have a burgeoning service economy, there has to be, especially in China, a big and sustained structural shift from investment to consumption.

Investment in China is growing at about 29 per cent this year while consumption is growing at 13 per cent. This growth in investment is underpinned by financial liquidity, with the major banks tripping over themselves to lend on virtually any new investment.

The huge level of Chinese domestic savings at 45 per cent of GDP and the managed exchange rate are among the reasons the economy is awash with money—the cost of capital is simply too low. Many still think that failing loans do not have to be repaid. That, like the old days, they are still part of state debt—or if not part, end up as state debt.

The result of this low cost of capital and indiscriminate lending is that a lot of the investment is irrational and sub-economic.

The central bank of China, the PBoC, is concerned about the quality of loans but it cannot see into what it refers to as the 'black box' of bank lending. The prudential supervisors try to get a grip on loan quality, while seeking to understand how loans might stand up to strain under certain sensitivity analysis.

There are four major commercial banks in China, but given that they are largely creatures of the managed system, we do not really know how commercial they are. In happy times they are very commercial. In the less happy times they may become mendicants, who without state assistance, may be a weight on Chinese growth and activity as Japanese banks were on Japan through the 1990s. Only time will tell.

The level of Chinese savings is itself a problem. That is, if from the West, we can regard savings of any kind as a problem. The fact is, China is saving more than it is investing, notwithstanding that investment has risen by 7 per cent of GDP to 41 per cent of GDP in the last five years. Gross saving has risen even faster.

The corporate sector in China, much of it formerly unreconstructed state-owned enterprises, has become amazingly profitable. Remarkably, it retains virtually all of its earnings—undistributed.

The problem with savings at this level and with consumption at only 40 per cent of GDP is that any reduction in investment flowing from concerns about poor loan quality and overheating will only see a higher level of savings. These, in turn, will amount to an even larger current-account surplus in the Chinese economy. For this year, even larger than the forecast 7 per cent of GDP.

The fact is, gross national savings at these very high levels lead to growing levels of investment unless more of the savings are consumed. Discretionary savings by households exist mainly due to notions of thrift held at large by the Chinese community, particularly in the absence of a national income support system and universal health care.

The Chinese plan on the fact that they will have to look after themselves and with life's exigencies, have money squirreled away to meet them. Over time, as the government provides more by way of income transfers, health care and aged care, discretionary savings may drop as people are encouraged to spend more of their savings.

The exchange-rate management system also presents major problems for China. Not only does it oblige the central bank to buy all the foreign exchange and then add the equivalent domestic currency to the money supply, with all the liquidity implications, the current rate of the renminbi is distorting the pattern of Chinese investment and consumption.

These days in China, no-one in the official family talks about growth being other than around 10 per cent. The 8 to 9 per cent growth of a few years ago is now a thing of the past.

The government of China has hocked itself politically to this 10 per cent growth tiger and is riding the tiger's back. This means that all must continue to go well.

Therefore, a shift to a quantity-based system for setting the exchange rate presents economic and political difficulties, especially if large slabs of the 'processing economy' become uncompetitive. And it should be remembered that about 80 per cent of China's foreign-exchange reserves, currently at US$914 billion have come from the 'processing economy'.

At the moment, many businesses in China, of the processing variety, are exporting at a loss. There is great debate about this! Companies can seek to reduce costs—unit labour costs—by putting in more machines. But in the short term, this does not do much for employment.

However over time, the nominal exchange rate needs to be in closer alignment with the real exchange rate if China is not to experience a burst of inflation.

China, not long ago, was purely an agrarian country. Within 25 years, it became the world centre of manufacturing. *Ipso facto*, its real exchange rate had to rise. Exporters in China, indeed, some members of the government, may wish the nominal exchange rate of the renminbi to remain low, in broad lockstep with the US dollar. But this simply means that attempts to camouflage the real exchange rate are likely to end in tears as the low nominal exchange rate induces higher inflation.

The authorities in China know and understand this, yet this remains a major problem for them. The fact is, China's State Council is gun shy when it comes to changing the exchange-rate system and, with it, the rate itself.

China's incremental contribution to world growth is now broadly in line with that made by the United States.

At US$12 trillion of GDP and growing at 3 per cent, the United States economy is producing roughly US$360 billion in new wealth. Japan, at US$6 trillion GDP and growing at 1.5 per cent, is producing about US$90 billion in new wealth, whereas China at US$3.5 trillion of GDP but growing at 10 per cent, is producing US$350 billion in new wealth—the same as the United States.

China, through its lower priced products, has also been exporting deflation at a time when oil and commodity prices have risen and as the real price of labour has picked up. It has given us what we mostly want: the price of wages going up with the price of widgets going down, with the gap between the two increasing our disposable income.

The key observation about the advent of China at this time is that it may prolong the current long wave of economic growth which began in 1982. This wave has been overlaid by two business or investment cycles: 1982 to 1990 and 1992 to 2000, while we are currently three years into the third business cycle, which began in 2003.

It is difficult to discern when the technology-inducing productivity starts to run out and where inflation—commodity price inflation and wage inflation—begin getting the upper hand.

At least we can say that the advent of China has made the current long wave richer by adding to supply while keeping prices in check, by bringing this extra productivity to the world economy.

But will it extend the current long wave beyond the normal 25 or 26 years, that is, beyond 2007 and 2008? For my own part, I doubt it.

Let me turn now to the strategic environment with special reference to China.

To all intents and purposes, in wealth and productive terms, China missed the twentieth century. It also missed the nineteenth century. The primary ambition of the government of China is to be left alone to 'grow out' its economy. It does not want or need strategic distractions. It does not want or need problems across the Straits of Taiwan. It presents no strategic competition to the United States, and it is not looking for any kind of showdown with Japan.

By and large, the Chinese are now setting in place a foreign policy which underpins its commercial and trading requirements. As a consequence, it is now establishing regional trade and strategic bodies. It will, by virtue of its size, be at the centre of an East Asian growth hemisphere which I believe it will cater to with prudence and sovereign regard.

As it gets larger, China will appreciate being more substantially involved in world affairs, for instance, playing a larger role with countries like India in areas formerly and exclusively run by bodies like the G8, the International Monetary Fund and the World Trade Organization.

The advent of China and India in their renaissance will break the template of 1947 set up by the victorious Allies to run the world. Their new age existence will make it more likely that globalisation will become an East Asian and developing country phenomenon, than it will remain a Western one. Hence these two great states are going to change the way the world functions.

The one dark cloud on the horizon remains the growing antipathy in China's relations with Japan. The postwar years have witnessed no real effort by Japan to live down its wartime history while accommodating itself within a growing body of East Asian states.

This is especially the case with China. This week Prime Minister Abe is paying a diplomatic visit to Beijing in the first days of his new prime ministership. This is laudable as far as it goes. But we must remember that the Liberal Democratic Party, Mr Abe's party, which has run Japan for nearly all the years since the war, are the Bourbons of the Pacific: learned nothing and forgotten nothing.

A concern is that Japan may use the current impasse with North Korea and its nuclear-weapon program to move into nuclear weapons itself—eschewing its peacetime constitution and the nuclear protection provided to it by the United States under the nuclear umbrella. In other words, in nuclear terms, going it alone. Such an outcome would be very affronting and confronting to the Chinese, encouraging China to adopt an altogether different posture as regards Japan.

It is to be hoped that problems on the North Korean peninsula can be more satisfactorily dealt with and that Japan, despite its insularity and deep-seated problems, will find common cause with its largest and nearest neighbour.

8

PICKING THE PEAK
25 Years of the Bull Market

China Development Bank, International Advisory Council,
Beijing,
20 September 2007

Paul Keating's chairman's address to the China Development Bank
underlined his earlier prediction that a peak in the world business
cycle was likely for 2009, which should otherwise mean a peak in the
stockmarket a year earlier in 2008. He reminds his audience that by
2008 the bull market will have run for 26 years, and warns of darker
clouds on the economic horizon: that a long period of monetary
accommodation in the United States had led to a boom in housing
prices and that the refinancing of mortgages had led to sub-optimal
lending. At the meeting, Paul Keating tells his Chinese hosts that
attempts by China to artificially hold down the real exchange are
ill-conceived, leading to a heavier burden of economic adjustment
falling on countries like Australia, which prices its exchange rate in the
market. The issues central to these remarks were brought into relief a
year later, with the Lehman Brothers bankruptcy of September 2008.

ON THE OCCASION OF THE seventh International Advisory Council meeting of the China Development Bank in October of 2005, each member of the Council was asked to give his views about the state of the international economy in general, with reference to China in particular.

At that meeting, I made the point that following a recession or substantial downturn, the second half of the subsequent up cycle was generally the strongest. I made the point that it takes time for consumers to regain confidence as it takes time for capacity utilisation rates to lift to levels where new spending on equipment is warranted. That during the second phase, everything kicks in: consumer spending as well as capital spending. Growth in capital spending typically results in over-spending and a cyclical recession generally ensues.

I pointed out that in the 1980s and 1990s, the second half of those decades was stronger than the first half and I told the meeting that I expected the second half of this decade to be stronger than the first half. Therefore, I said, most of 2006 and 2007 should be very strong years for the global economy and that I expected the global economy would be strong enough to push to a new cyclical high in 2007.

I made the point that given the slow start in the growth cycle of this decade which began in 2003, a peak in the business cycle was on the cards for 2009, which might mean a peak in the stockmarket a year earlier in 2008. I also made the point that by 2008, the bull market in stocks will have run for 26 years, meaning that we are at the wrong end of the bull market, a time when a bear market may first rear its ugly head.

Nothing which has happened in the two years since those remarks has altered my view as to how things are now panning out.

We can now discern a number of darker clouds on the horizon.

A long period of very accommodating monetary conditions in the United States kept consumption up through the American recession of 2000–03 and on into the middle of this decade. Part of that consumption saw a boom in housing prices and, with it, the refinancing of mortgages to lower repayment schedules, freeing up even more credit to be spent. The race to housing refinancing also occasioned sub-optimal lending which is now having the effect of recalibrating spreads to risk. This is having a deleterious effect on the value of the paper held by a good many financial institutions.

It is clear that without Alan Greenspan's monetary policy, US consumption would not have been in a position to tug the world out of recession and on to another cyclical high as the decade progressed. But the price of that consumption-led recovery has been high. Too much credit available at too low a price has dramatically diminished credit quality so as to put some institutions at risk. And an absence of prudential controls has mixed the fortunes of commercial banks and their normal lending books with their proprietary trading businesses.

I think it is fair to assume that we have seen the best of US consumption and we also have a fair idea that the investment cycle will soon taper off—if it is not tapering off already.

These eventualities will mean that national governments and their monetary authorities will need to respond to this changing dynamic in the world economy by commensurately promoting offsetting sources of activity. The chances are that the United States dollar will need to decline further if the United States trade account is to enjoy the benefits of a real depreciation against the rest of the world, which it sorely needs. We know that there is such a thing as the *shadow dollar* area, where large blocks of world GDP and their currencies have tended to follow the dollar down, thereby denying the United States the competitive advantage it needs, on a scale sufficient to change the pattern of its growth.

What this means is that the true floating currencies carry a disproportionate burden of the international adjustment, while the countries playing the *shadow dollar* game take unfair advantage while also distorting the pattern of their own growth.

These events will affect China and the management of its economy.

China has a number of issues on its plate at present. Concerns over the overheated economy have grown. Inflation is running at around 6.5 per cent and while a lot of this has to do with food prices, the old *hog cycle*, Chinese authorities have lifted interest rates and enforced higher reserve requirements on banks to curb lending enthusiasm, while engineering better provisioning.

The real problem is that the exchange-rate management system of the renminbi is far too rigid for the kind of conditions China's economy is experiencing. A managed exchange rate requires the central bank to buy all the foreign exchange with local currency—cash, thereby kicking along the money base of the economy, requiring an ambitious domestic bond-selling program running beside it to mop up the excess liquidity.

This is a very sub-optimal system for managing the currency, the monetary base and the economy. We may ask why governments do this. And the answer is by belief in the misplaced notion of helping exporters who pay nothing for the help.

In the case of China, in its transition from an agrarian to a much more sophisticated manufacturing and service economy, naturally, the real exchange rate must inevitably rise. Attempts by the government of China to sit on the real exchange rate with a tearaway economy producing a cornucopia of goods are, I believe, ill-conceived, militating seriously against growth in domestic consumption of the kind China desperately needs.

In short, the current Chinese system for managing the renminbi is storing up troubles for the government and people of China at a time when a huge shift in the pattern of growth is taking place in the United States.

Let me say, if China keeps up the policy of promoting net exports at the expense of domestic demand and consumption, the international burden of adjustment will fall very hard on those countries which have truly made their economies and exchange rates subject to market forces. Australia is one of them. It is episodes like these which underwrite regression against the otherwise, freer movement to openness and transparency—to protectionism.

Could I perhaps make a final point in relation to China's foreign-exchange reserves which have grown out of this policy?

We now read in the newspapers that the government of China is establishing investment funds to invest some of its reserves in assets other than American Treasury bonds.

These funds can serve China well but they will certainly serve China better if the funds are established truly at arm's length from the government.

Around this table we know that in China, the government has a position of primacy rarely seen in other places. That said, it should be possible for the government, in its own interests, to divine a structure for investment funds where governance arrangements, mandates, risk appetite and risk management are open and transparent.

Such a quality will not only serve China's government and citizens better, it will also inhibit the criticism that such funds will otherwise draw from recipient countries. If these funds behave like normal long-term investment businesses, then much of the suspicion about them being sovereign funds is likely to abate. And why should China not be looking for capital growth as well as healthy returns when its investments in US financial assets so far have seen a steady and large decline in value in line with the fall in the US dollar? We all know it is hard enough to make money without unnecessarily losing it.

9

THE NEW GLOBAL MOSAIC

Local Government Unlimited Conference,
Queenstown, New Zealand,
28 July 2003

Paul Keating's 'The New Global Mosaic' was an up-to-the-moment yet
sweeping analysis of the global scene. At the time of the speech, the US
economy had been in recession for three years. In it he predicts the US
will come out of recession 'from about now'—and further predicts that
the new investment cycle might have 'half a dozen productive years'
in it, ending in 2009 after a stockmarket peak in 2008. The speech is
prophetic in a number of other respects. Paul Keating says East Asia
was likely to mark itself out as a growth engine of the world; China has
the promise, geostrategically, of becoming the 'second pole'; he questions
whether Europe's one-size-fits-all fiscal and monetary union will work
smoothly and says that US unipolarity is unsustainable, that its wars
against errant states will lead to American exhaustion. He concludes
with the view that the United States has to return to a policy of
liberal internationalism.

IN THE BUSINESS OF NATION-BUILDING—which is the business of all
of us in public life—we are creatures of our time and circumstances.
Of the prevailing geopolitical and geoeconomic moods. And we are
always searching for the Rosetta stone, that code stone that tells us how
best to find that happy mix between what should be rendered unto
Caesar—and what may properly be left to the individual.

New Zealand and Australia have much in common, including a very serious effort on the part of each of us in remodelling our economies. With a notion that markets, more efficiently organised, could deliver better outcomes, we each attempted to change our old, protected and closeted industrial societies into more outward-looking, competitive and innovative ones.

The interesting thing about both our countries is that these efforts were, in the main, undertaken by Labor governments. It was once par for the course that Labor governments tended to centralisation and protection, eschewing openness and competition of a kind that, in the event, we both chose. If I could say where I think this process has been different between Australia and New Zealand—in Australia, these things were done in the context of a formal set of long-run consensual policies set out between the trade unions and the government of the day.

While the great wish and want of society will be for economic growth and the pursuit of income, people always yearn for something else as well; and that is to belong, to be included. A sense of nation and well-placed patriotism, based on the family of the country. A sense that change is directed to a point, which extends beyond economic growth to individual and community happiness and fulfilment. It is why those of us in the nation-building business always keep an eye out for the country in the broad, and for those at risk of missing out. It is why the bindings that come with good social policy end up being good economic policy.

The question is, where do we go from here? Much has been achieved, but what do we do now? How do we do things better? How do we move on a wider front, yet move together, and how do we make the interests of any one of us work for all of us?

I have never been in local government in an elective sense, but I have always had a great regard for it, for the authenticity that comes from proximity to the people and their very real problems. Local government in most countries is at the coalface of government and any system which improves the representativeness and effectiveness of government will make society that much better and stronger. So I am pleased to be with this distinguished group of local government representatives gathered to think about their country, to share ideas and consider the future.

I suppose the first trick for you, indeed for all of us, as we survey the world, is to find our coordinates—the degree of strategic longitude and the degree of commercial latitude which reveal exactly where we are. Perhaps, in this discussion, I should deal with the economic latitude first. I will return to the strategic dimension in a few moments.

It is worth noting that there were three economic long waves in the twentieth century—1904 to 1929, 1947 to 1974, and 1982 until now. Each had a duration of about 25 years, and each was technology driven.

The first wave, from 1904 to 1929, was driven by breakthroughs in petrochemicals, industrial production and transportation.

The second wave, the postwar wave, was driven by the economic rebuilding of Japan and Europe, along with technological breakthroughs in areas like plastics and aviation, and, of course, motor vehicles.

The wave we are currently living through, the third wave, has been driven by telecommunications and microprocessing. By all reckoning, if the past is to be any guide, this wave should run until about 2007 or 2008. We have already had two legs, two business cycles, 1982 to 1990 and 1992 to 2000. The second one saw an enormous increase in stockmarket values around the world and in personal incomes and real wealth.

The good news is, I believe that there will be a third business cycle. From about now. The bad news is that it will not be so richly laden as the second one and we are beginning it at relatively high valuations for equities compared with those which obtained in 1982 or 1992. Or those which obtained at about this same point in the second long wave, which would have been about 1965. What will be different about this leg compared to the last two is that towards its end, the technological edge may have dissipated and the demographics will have acted to reduce unemployment substantially. Towards the end of this cycle, in say five to six years from now, we may see a pick up in real wages and with it wage inflation of a kind which may encourage central banks to do what they have traditionally done, and that is, cool the economy to keep wages and prices under control.

Where the last wave ended with an exogenous shock, from the inflationary OPEC pricing of the early 1970s, and the one before that with the Depression in 1929, this one may actually go down for endogenous reasons as we struggle to maintain workforce growth in countries like our own. At any rate, we've probably got half a dozen years left in this cycle before more negative economic forces materialise.

One of the caveats, which could affect this scenario, is the potential for East Asia to mark itself out as the growth engine of the world. China, with its World Trade Organization (WTO) mandates, holds out the promise of being the most important growth economy in the world outside the United States. And China is no typical East Asian top-down command economy of the kind we see in Japan or South Korea, where financial intermediation is managed largely by banks in the absence of efficient capital markets. China will, over time, have a range of financial markets and instruments. As it grows, it will reveal itself to be an economy built around the individual and small-to-medium enterprises—an economy far more reminiscent of New Zealand's and Australia's than Japan's. It will become, I believe, a place with which New Zealand and Australia, in a corporate sense, will want to do business. It is also likely to become, in geostrategic terms, the second pole in what has become a unipolar world. China has the certainty of knowing who and what it is, and the cultural confidence to cope and deal with the United States.

Japan, a great trading partner of both our countries, has been in a structural recession for fourteen years and there is a distinct possibility that its financial system will be subject to seismic fractures of a kind that could bring its economy to its knees. There is also an acceleration in the deterioration of its demographics.

Whether North Asia and its poorer cousins in Southeast Asia can make a difference as to how the world behaves economically five years from now remains open to conjecture. But it is the part of the world in which we live, and its future matters mightily to us, because more of our bread is going to be buttered by what happens there than in any other place.

Some believe that Europe's aggregation of populations and economies would make it a logical alternative pole to the United States. But it is yet to be seen whether the one-size-fits-all fiscal and monetary policies agreed under the Treaty on European Union will be capable of working smoothly. The arrangements are providing financial management at the broad fiscal and monetary level, but at an obvious cost. We can already see how they are limiting Germany's capacity to restimulate its economy through fiscal policy or to run a monetary policy more appropriate to German conditions.

Perhaps more importantly, Europe remains diverse and politically fractured. It simply does not possess the coherent cultural confidence of, say, the United States or China. It may have a common market and a common currency, but it is burdened by centuries of ethnic and national suspicions. It also lacks the force projection and the arsenal of conventional and nuclear weapons enjoyed by the United States.

Let me now say a few things about the American economy. The first thing is its absolute size. At US$10 trillion, its GDP is twenty times larger than Australia's and about 150 times larger than New Zealand's.

The United States has pulled the world economy along for over a decade. The American consumer, in effect, saved the rest of us. Its great strength is that it has a fungible capital market which can take capital from less productive places and put it into more productive places in its economy, faster than in any economy in the world. The administration of President Clinton also took the United States from historically large central government deficits to large central government surpluses. By reducing the relative size of the public sector in America, *ipso facto*, the private sector became that much bigger.

But another very important thing happened. The governor of its central bank, Alan Greenspan, uncharacteristically for central bank governors, pursued a policy of growth to maximise wealth and incomes. Most central bankers of his standing and responsibilities would normally keep a baton of price stability in the knapsack and not much else.

Greenspan thought he could and, in the end, did see a paradigm shift in productivity of a scale which he knew could deliver rising real incomes in the context of falling unit labour costs. So he kept monetary conditions accommodating to growth through the 1990s, believing that the productivity wedge would pay for the wages growth which in other times would have come at the expense of profits. He had the golden circle working for him—rising real wages, rising profits, falling unit labour costs and falling inflation. The consequence of this extended period of his management was to increase the capacity of the American economy to grow at a rate faster by half than we had formerly witnessed.

Notwithstanding this achievement, Alan Greenspan is not without his critics. Some say he should have dealt with the asset price bubble of the Dow and NASDAQ even after his warning in 1996 about 'irrational exuberance'.

But this opens an old argument. Should central banks focus solely on activity in the real economy and inflation or should they also attempt to operate policy to deal with asset prices? Personally, I have always seen activity, inflation and the real economy as being the monetary touchstones. In the end, high stock prices imply low dividend yields and these, over time, correct themselves. Investors can turn to bonds. And in the United States, you can purchase Treasury bonds which are indexed for inflation—where the real interest rate is constant and known at the time of purchase. Markets do work as prices adjust to yields.

Greenspan, I believe, saw the main chance to move his economy up a notch to a sustainable new plateau of activity, having its inflation rate protected by productivity.

In the past quarter century, the speed limit for American GDP growth was of the order of 2.0 to 2.5 per cent or thereabouts. That limit now has a substantial 3 in front of it. And to have a base of $10,000 billion growing at an extra 1 per cent in the context of continuing low inflation is a mighty achievement. And a lot of new wealth.

These are some of the reasons why America has been the motor economy and why we owe Clinton and Greenspan, in these respects, so much. I might say, but only in passing, that following the microeconomic reforms in Australia over the same period, the Australian economy grew by an even greater degree—from an average of 1.7 per cent in the decade to the mid-1980s to an average now of over 3.5 per cent—with endemically low inflation made possible by a doubling of trend productivity. Put in place by a Labor government. That productivity wedge is, in the end, what the game is all about. It is not just the icing on the cake—it is the cake. It is the reason why real incomes in Australia grew by 20 per cent across the 1990s—the fastest real income growth in any decade of Australia's history. It did for Australian competitiveness the very same thing that Mr Greenspan and his productivity dividend did for the United States and its consumers.

But America has been in a growth recession for the last couple of years. It has not experienced negative growth, but its growth has been much slower—something like 1.5 per cent—because its investment cycle topped out in 1997. Business cycles are, of their essence, investment cycles, and there has been an investment drought in America now for just on six years. That's why we owe the American consumer so much for taking up the slack. But even the American consumer couldn't keep it up forever.

So now we await the upturn in the American investment cycle. The question is, when will that occur? My best guess is, any time now. Stockmarkets invariably pick the turn well before the real economy, and faster than the rest of us, and such a turn normally leads the investment cycle by nine to twelve months. When we look back I think that we will find that the stockmarket turn, this time, came between November last year and March, heralding a turn in the business cycle for later this year.

Now, there have been, as the Americans call it, headwinds. These are not necessarily economic forces but they do matter—things such as the corporate scandals (the Enrons, the WorldComs), the war in Iraq and other negatives. But the fundamentals out themselves in the end. The cycle turns.

So let me recap: I think there is going to be a third leg, a third business cycle. The downside is that it will not be as rich as the last one. But a third leg anyway.

The real imponderable is the geostrategic setting. We should know, if we have forgotten, that the strategic climate governs everything. We should never forget that globalisation started in earnest in the last quarter of the nineteenth century when the biggest sinew of trade was between Great Britain and Germany. This did not stop either country drifting into the First World War, the repercussions of which only saw the world economy get back to sustainable growth as late as 1947 and to strategic equilibrium in 1989.

We are, they tell us, living in a unipolar moment, when the US has decided to eschew liberal internationalism and multilateralism for a winner-take-all, me-first strategy. The whole political and strategic framework of containment has been tipped over for an aggressive pre-emptive first-strike doctrine which gives the rest of us very little to be part of, or little to attach ourselves to.

I think what happened is that when the Cold War finished and the Berlin Wall came down, the Americans cried victory and walked off the field. You might remember the slogan that Clinton used against George Herbert Bush, 'It's the economy, stupid'. Clinton was scathing at Bush's adventurism, as he saw it, in Iraq in 1991. And before the investment cycle kicked back for the second leg in 1992, George Herbert Bush was defeated and American public policy focused on a peace dividend. It also focused on its economy and the magic of the Internet. It seemed as though the Cold War had not ended for the Americans, but simply faded away.

Of course, it did end for the Americans. It ended when the Twin Towers came down in September 2001. It ended with a bang. Clinton and Gore would have handled this strategic moment very differently from Bush, Cheney, Rumsfeld and Wolfowitz. The current admin-istration has responded by jerking American policy into a unilateral response, rejecting in its application any notion of cooperation or resort to multilateral frameworks.

The real question is whether this policy is rewarding or sustain-able or whether it will leave America exhausted by the self-wrought responsibility of dealing with errant states and groups which it deems to be a threat to its security. This policy comes, I believe, at a very high price. It has fractured the 50-year-long spell of Atlantic unity and tugs away at the notion of America's 'righteous might', a notion to which President Franklin Roosevelt so often referred.

Churchill said in 1940 that Britain was 'fighting by ourselves alone, but not for ourselves alone'. A lot of people, I am sure, think today that the United States is fighting by itself alone, for itself alone. This is not good. The big question is: can the world be run from one city? Does the American Congress have the wit and the wisdom—let alone the resources—to run the globe?

I, for one, do not believe it does. For all of its glory, indeed its past magnanimity, any attempt by America to take on the mantle of Empire is to deny the very precepts of its founding.

The really bad news in all of this is that by walking away from multilateral arrangements such as the Comprehensive Test Ban Treaty and the Anti-Ballistic Missile Treaty, and by their failure to live up to commitments made under the Non-Proliferation Treaty, the Americans have given a signal to the rest of the world that they too can be part of a resumed nuclear arms race. Believe you me, this has well and truly begun. Not just in India or Pakistan, or Iran and North Korea or even Israel, but in lesser states which believe they need their pocket nuke to make the world deal with them respectfully. I hope the Americans have not led us into a *Mad Max* world while they seek to shield themselves in the cocoon of national missile defence.

All of this has let a lot of hares run—and as relatively small states with a broadly European complexion tucked away in the bottom of Asia, none of it is much good to us.

Nationalism is generally built on arbitrary and parochial distinctions between the civic and the human community; why we are worthy, and someone else is not. The interests of the human community, I believe, deign that the world must be run cooperatively. This period of strident American unilateralism and militarism cuts across this notion while putting no adequate or alternative framework into place.

Let me conclude then, by returning to the positive things. There are, I believe, half a dozen quite productive years left in the international economy and it might be longer if the North Asians can keep their act together. But unless the current American administration returns to a more liberal notion of internationalism we will overlay these positive economic prospects with geostrategic uncertainty of a kind that is debilitating and broadly unnecessary.

All of this may seem a long way from the considerations of local government. But, as I said, you need to take your coordinates before you start any journey. I wish you all the best for your deliberations over the next few days.

VOCATIONAL EDUCATION AND TRAINING
The Oft-Forgotten Tier
Skilling Australia Forum,
Surfers Paradise,
10 September 2003

*Paul Keating completed his Higher School Certificate at a TAFE
college. In the course of his political life and as a constituency member,
he maintained a close interest in technical and further education. As
Prime Minister he established a new national vocational education
and training system under a new Commonwealth–State authority—the
Australian National Training Authority, investing the authority with an
additional $720 million in growth funding. This address to a TAFE and
training forum allows him to reflect upon the development of TAFE,
and training generally, since his reforms of 1992. In the address he
urges the continued replenishment of the formal public-sector vocational
institutions, saying the Commonwealth government should be rendering
to Caesar the things which remain Caesar's.*

I AM DELIGHTED TO BE involved again in a discussion on vocational
education and training, and to be here with the people who matter
mightily to this sector of Australian education.

It strikes me as apt that we meet in Surfers Paradise on the Gold
Coast because the dramatic changes that have taken place in this part
of the country tell the story, in microcosm, of the profound changes
to our entire nation.

I doubt the locals of Elston had any idea what was in store when, in the 1920s, they optimistically renamed their town Surfers Paradise in honour of the most successful local pub. I doubt they ever envisaged the massive growth of domestic and international tourism to their region, or the huge numbers of service jobs that would become necessary to support it.

They could not have predicted the massive building boom. They certainly could not have foreseen that the beach counter-culture would trigger a mini-boom in surf and leisurewear. Or imagined the massive uptake of alternative health and fitness products and services. Or foresaw the evolution of a fit, active and ageing population of Australians looking to spend their later years in productive work or pleasure in this splendid part of Queensland.

And, as all of you will know, for every single one of these changes, the critical facilitating factor—the element that made such social and economic change possible—was the skill levels of Australians.

Australians with qualifications in everything from tourism, hospitality or transport to design or business administration; land or marine resource management; health services or engineering or surveying. Australians with the opportunity to acquire market-relevant skills in their younger years; Australians with the opportunity to upskill or retrain in their older years.

Only through developing our skills as a people have we been able to respond to a very fast-changing world. Australian skills have turned the sleepy town of Surfers Paradise into this modern tourism and lifestyle powerhouse.

And only by continuing to invest in our skills can we give ourselves the capacity to control and create the best possible future.

In February 1992, just two months after becoming Prime Minister, I delivered my first major economic statement. It was actually my fourteenth, but my first as Prime Minister. In that statement, I was able to point to the Labor government's outstanding record in education. Of course, governments always say they are committed to education. Who would say otherwise? But we had the results to prove it, including that huge increase in secondary school retention rates (from three in ten students finishing high school to nine in ten), and an historic and matching expansion in university places (200,000, or the equivalent of twenty new universities).

But in that speech I acknowledged that Australia had one weak strand in education. Our technical and vocational training sector. This sector was under-resourced and therefore under-performing. And I committed myself to raise the quality and status of vocational education and training to the level of the other tiers of education in this country. In this sector we needed both expansion and improvement.

My passion for vocational education and training was—and is—not a matter of sentiment, or of misplaced egalitarianism. The Japanese and German economies trained their way to global manufacturing prosperity in the second half of the twentieth century. For Australia to prosper, we must have a high quality and flexible vocational education and training regime, a system which will equip Australians with the skills for today and tomorrow, and more than this, a system which can identify and plan for the emerging skills requirements as the new century reveals itself.

It is not enough to be a clever country; we must be a capable one too.

In June 1992, I delivered on that promise. After long rounds of negotiations with the state Premiers, we had finally put together an agreement. And so we announced a whole range of new initiatives to give heft and heart to the vocational education and training sector, with the centrepiece being the establishment of the Australian National Training Authority—or ANTA, as it is now known.

I wanted the Commonwealth to focus on universities and vocational education, leaving the states to deal with secondary education. That is, to deal with it after we had funded the tripling of Years 11 and 12 retention rates.

In this country, approximately 40 per cent of secondary school students go to tertiary institutions. But when we tripled the output of Year 12 we had to do the same for universities, to maintain the same 40 per cent transition rate. So accordingly, we funded over 200,000 new university places. Apart from the enormity of this task the problem was: what were we to do with the other 60 per cent of kids, many of whom often cascaded into nothing?

The answer was for the Commonwealth to involve itself directly in funding the growth of TAFE. To develop a national system in order that the aspirations and needs of those who, for one reason or another, had bypassed the university system or who had no training opportunity at all, could be met by adequate levels of teaching in the one system which enjoyed such a close profile to the real economy and to the workplace.

And the results achieved since then have been substantial. From 1992 to 2001, the number of students in the public vocational education and training system increased by 68.5 per cent. But even this number, large as it is, disguises the 82.9 per cent increase in the numbers of women participating in VET. Around 1.76 million students undertook training in the public VET system in 2001. Between 1990 and 2000 the proportion of people aged 25 to 64 years with a vocational or higher education qualification rose from 46 per cent to 50 per cent. And something like 35 per cent of students enrolled in the public VET system in 2001 had completed some kind of secondary education prior to starting their training, suggesting that the perceived value of VET to students has risen over time.

These figures are impressive, but the real achievement of vocational education and training lies in its extraordinary capacity to meet changing national requirements. We certainly ask more from this area of our education sector than any other. Vocational education and training was once all about men in manufacturing; now it also caters to women and a vast range of industry sectors. It used to be about young people and first-time training; now it is adapting to support the training and retraining needs of an aging population. It used to be a stand-alone system, linked at best with some of the major employers; now you will find VET enmeshed in school curricula, universities and workplaces.

In 2001, 8.6 per cent of students in the public VET system undertook some vocational education and training while still at school. And 7 per cent of graduates undertook their study with the aim of getting into another course in future. In other words, young people are being given the opportunity to fit themselves to the appropriate education model for their stage of development. Many use vocational education and training as a way of gaining confidence and insight into their own abilities and move their educational attainments at a pace and by steps that provides them with educational and career opportunities that they might not otherwise enjoy. Another reason why formal linkages between VET institutions and universities is a good thing, allowing students to plot their way to attainments with vocational education so that they might be streamed within an associated university. This kind of streaming is, I think, very desirable.

Vocational education and training is one of this nation's greatest assets: an adaptive, dynamic and responsive training system.

But right now, there are, I believe, real problems within the sector and real risks. The priority that I ascribed to vocational education and training as Prime Minister has not been maintained. The momentum has slowed.

Vocational education and training is, of course, maintained primarily as a state-government responsibility. But state governments can be accomplished backsliders. State-government funding performances for vocational education and training are quite varied. Some states are coasting, some are not doing enough, while others are actively diminishing their systems. If we take Victoria as an example, as a result of so-called 'productivity improvements' since the late 1980s, a total of $120 million is now being taken each year from the VET sector. A huge sum. Taken as a cumulative amount, just over $1 billion has been sucked away from the education and training of people in that state during this period. A substantial under-investment in their creativity.

At the Commonwealth level, the emphasis has subtly changed. Since 1997, the Howard government has trebled payouts in subsidies to the private sector for training. With the kick-along of $365.5 million in 2001–02 (mostly subsidies to the new apprenticeship schemes) the private sector is now, on paper at least, likely to be spending more than $4 billion per year on various forms of education and training.

Some people say considerably more. In fact, private-employer funding today is at least roughly equal to the total funding of public vocational education and training.

Private-sector involvement is not to be disparaged. The problem is that there has been a relative decline in Commonwealth government expenditure on the public vocational education and training system between 1997 and 2001.

The Commonwealth proportion of total public VET funding, both by way of recurrent and capital spending, is about 28 per cent. If you put employer and public spending on VET together, you get a total of around $8 billion of which the Commonwealth contributes something like 18 per cent. In other words, the Commonwealth under Howard is diminishing its place in the total national vocational education and training system. And while money is being spent on private training, the standards of accountability are markedly different from those expected from the public institutions and the output is harder to measure.

A recitation of the importance of vocational education and renewal in its organic development is required.

When it comes to the big themes in national life, one cannot look for leadership from the middle and you cannot expect it from the bottom of any system. Leadership has to come from those who sit on top of the system. And in post-secondary education, the Commonwealth should always be taking the lead. It is the Commonwealth which should set the priorities, articulate the values, and finance the new directions. And bring the states along.

Australia has been through a very great economic transformation. The reforms from 1983 began with the rollback of the old Australian Defence Model where, before, Australia sat closeted, ring-fenced by tariffs with a sclerotic financial market, depending upon declining terms of trade.

Now the economy is open and much more competitive, with a floating exchange rate taking the external shocks and higher productivity delivering rising real incomes and endemically low inflation.

With the region to our north growing faster, and with China growing rapidly and off a much bigger base, there is some real likelihood that natural resource values will strengthen as we take a higher proportion of Chinese and other North-Asian finished products. These trends will only propel us further towards the higher ends of technology and manufacturing while underwriting an even larger service sector. At the same time, a rapidly changing demographic will be putting real pressure on the labour market. All of this will mean that job training and retraining will be more important than it has ever been.

A competent and competitive set of vocational education institutions becomes an imperative. Adequacy of resources and levels of output quality can only be seriously contemplated within a national system. This is why ANTA was established: to provide funding and a system with overarching standards and mechanisms to improve quality. What was also required was the maintenance of state effort.

We have made substantial gains, but more has to be done.

I am pleased to see the involvement of business in vocational education and training, but the truth is, individual businesses cannot see, or affect, the whole picture. And government oversight of taxpayers' subsidies to business is necessarily limited. In this environment, the onus for leadership or momentum cannot be put onto business. And it must be acknowledged that many business programs focus on short time-lines. Business is unlikely to see itself as responsible for the long-term developmental needs of workers other than where the interests of the business and the broader national training interest is likely to coincide.

When Labor put in place a national training levy, part of the purpose was to tempt business into a dialogue with government, to bring business with a real financial stake in vocational education to the table and to share, and work out, national training issues. And much has happened since then. As a result of the levy, privately provided training is well and truly part of the landscape. Now it is the public system which is in need of a larger role in the training story.

At the moment, this sector is at risk of failing to meet Australia's needs. Supply of public places is not keeping up with the demand.

Organisations like, for instance, the Northern Melbourne Institute of TAFE literally cannot keep up with the training requirements of its diverse community. In 1995, NMIT was funded for 5.228 million student contact hours. Today, in 2003, it is funded for 5.207 million student contact hours. Slightly less than eight years ago.

Meanwhile, private providers of vocational education and training are receiving substantial support. A full 50 per cent of growth in ANTA funding to Victoria from 1992 to 2003 has gone to private-sector providers. One thing to remember is that private providers are not asked to provide the same communal facilities as the TAFEs, they face less stringent accountability requirements, and are not asked to provide support for students in housing, counselling and student life.

And sometimes our public institutions face outbreaks of government-sponsored managerialism which is dispiriting to them. One of the performance measurements faced by one TAFE was based on student contact hours per square metre of facility. This particular institution has 2000 acres of farmland, which is used for the teaching of various programs. To meet the SCH/square metre requirements it would need to enrol a further 618,000 students. At which point it would be entitled to an extra $4.7 billion of extra funding.

None of this is to say that a healthy level of private-sector funding is not desirable. It is. But one must render to Caesar the things that are Caesar's. Public institutions in relative or absolute decline are never a pretty sight. Institutionally, only the Commonwealth government can provide the wherewithal to get the balance right and to keep it there.

Perhaps a word here about conditionality might be appropriate. In the old days conditionality identified itself as matching grants. The Commonwealth underwrote programs, but the funding had to be matched by participating states.

In this way, ANTA could be more handsomely funded by the Commonwealth, knowing there would be no decline in the effort of recipient states.

This would also allow disparities of quality to be addressed with a much more even system emerging.

Such a policy would soon stimulate all states to consider their VET budgets more carefully and move towards a healthy expansion of the entire system.

If matching funding from the Commonwealth were made open-ended, as it is, for instance, with additions to the private-school stock, growth in the quality and availability of vocational education and training could move rapidly to attain the levels we need to underpin the continuing productivity growth on which our whole economy depends.

Education is the centrepiece of any modern economy. It is how we keep the culture of our productivity alive and well; it is the key to personal mobility and one of the important ways we promote individual self-regard and esteem.

I look at young people today and I am struck by their cheerful acceptance of a commitment-free world, their seeming comfort with an era in which most things, including employment, are provisional and almost certainly impermanent. They know they have to live off their wits, and rely on their skills, that they are to be granted very little.

It is up to those in leadership to keep the pressure on for an education and training system which, at least, will give these young people the tools, the skills, the attitudes and the confidence to carry on and to thrive. For their own sakes, and for all our sakes.

HUMAN RESOURCE MANAGEMENT
The Role of Leadership
Australian Human Resources Institute,
Melbourne,
11 May 2004

Paul Keating's address to the Australian Human Resources Institute
provides an insight as to the roles of individuals and leadership in
the transformation of the Australian economy: a program of changes
which he says were conceived radically, coming other than by way of
some bureaucratic master plan. In the address he makes the case for
the construction of frameworks within which paradigm shifts may be
divined, while abhorring what he calls the safe house of incrementalism.
Paul Keating says in the post-industrial age, in the new age of
uncertainty, young people in the workforce now live their lives far
more autonomously than those of any generation—being obliged to
carry modules of experience from job to job, as they manage their own
careers. He says their commitment is not to institutions, as was their
parents, but to good management and leadership.

THIS NATIONAL CONVENTION OF THE Australian Human Resources
Institute has been held under the theme of 'people leading business'
and its emphasis is on the management of human resources. The
conference organisers want to emphasise qualities of 'management'
and have asked me to reflect upon the role of leadership, how it is
employed and why it matters.

We are all people of our time and are influenced by the vagaries of our time. There is no doubt we are all subject to prevailing trends, strategic circumstances and orthodoxies but that said, we can make the best of our times and actually reshape them or we can take the determinist view that all is preordained and that we should 'go with the flow'.

I belong to the school which says that individuals cannot only make a difference but, with inspiration, make all the difference.

I have always been one who believed in frameworks. Get the framework right and problems can be seen within relativities. They can be calibrated. And when one is able to reach that point, problems appear more resolvable—they tend to arrive in slow motion rather than present as a series of rapid changes or events.

So it is important that we are able to see the world as it really is—to have a wider comprehension of it; see it in a framework or, as I have often said, 'in the big picture'. Because once you have a picture, you are able to get the coordinates of your circumstances right. The latitude and longitude by which we focus on a problem, but a problem in context, in a framework or wider picture.

I believe these settings are imperative whether you are running an enterprise, participating in public life or, in an individual sense, making your way around and through the world.

But leadership requires something over and above this; something extra. Leadership is about interpreting the future to the present; having the ability to see over the horizon; letting those wider coordinates inform one's thinking. Giving one the ability to move forward more profoundly, and by moving forward I mean not having one foot in the safe house of incrementalism.

Incrementalism is the house of indifferent outcomes: we are not actually stuck, we are moving forward but only a little bit forward, taking little or no risk but garnering little or no real advance. There are so many people who live their lives through the credo of incrementalism; it represents a modality of thinking I have always abhorred.

In a world constantly changing under influences like globalisation and rapid communications, the premium has to be on quantum changes;

quantum leaps and leaders are the instruments by which such changes occur. The new world belongs to paradigm shifts in thinking and flexibility in management.

Elements of leadership are latent in all of us. Necessity brings those elements to the fore. But more often than not, those elements come by way of inspiration. Something that, by its example, model or excitement even, lifts us up to make us do things. To call the shot and take the risk.

The great 'value-add' in running anything is decisiveness. Making the decision to do something. It saves so much time and wasted energy; not directing people to do things which are inconclusive, perpetually chasing down hares.

Today we are living in the post-industrial age. These days the premium is on knowledge and creativity. Commerce is no longer dominated by capital-intensive, single-product behemoths. The weight now belongs to a mosaic of broadly funded businesses of diverse products much more heavily weighted in services.

It is worth recalling that in the United States today, manufacturing employment is at the same level it was in 1958; yet output is up 370 per cent. That is four times the output coming from roughly the same body of people.

Changes in the nature of work and in workforce composition have had a profound effect on individuals and their work expectations.

Individuals are now far more autonomous than individuals of any generation. Young people these days see their lives in modules; they are much less committed to institutions in a way my generation was committed. In this the, 'age of uncertainty', individuals carry modules of experience along to the next engagement as they manage their own careers.

Their loyalty and commitment is garnered not by a promise of lifelong employment or institutional commitment, it is earned by good management and leadership, being part of a cooperative undertaking, where flexibility and reward are clear, where they grow better as a person, where they exist in a milieu of real *esprit de corps*.

In these settings, productivity reveals itself in ideas and in an intellectual commitment to a set of common goals. These kinds of work structures place a much larger premium on leadership and human resource management. Labour productivity improvement has been the clear outcome from the movement away from pay and work rigidities of the old centralised kind.

Factor productivity is, of course, significant in the exercise. Investment plays to the new workplace flexibility; indeed it facilitates it. In the post-industrial age, productivity has been driven by investment in telecommunications, by advances in microprocessing and by the connectivity facilitated by the Internet. These productivity-laden advances have induced large increases in trend productivity which has given us what we mostly aim for: rising real wages in the context of falling unit labour costs. Falling unit labour costs have lifted business profitability while rising real wages have fuelled consumption. And consumption has seen large service economies sophisticate themselves further, providing even more employment.

These trends are also changing the way we live. The Fordist model of industrial production with centralised plants providing the employment centres for clusters of suburbs has given way to decentralised modes of production, where the information economy allows people to work in myriad places, including from their homes.

The technology is now being widely employed: small and medium enterprises are now yielding a factor productivity dividend and so is the whole economy. Secular increases in trend productivity allow economies to grow faster without exacerbating inflation. This is exactly what has happened in Australia.

The Australian economy can now grow at more than double the rate it once used to, while maintaining a low rate of inflation.

In the ten years to when I became Treasurer in 1983, the Australian economy grew at an average rate of around 1.8 per cent. These days it grows at 3.8 to 4 per cent. And any economy which had doubled its capacity to grow sustainably, with low inflation, spins off massive increments of wealth. It also spins off a lot of employment, notwithstanding the higher levels of productivity.

In the ten years to 1983, trend productivity in Australia was a modest 1.25 per cent per annum. As a result of the structural changes I presided over as both Prime Minister and Treasurer, that trend rate increased to 3 per cent. Indeed, the Productivity Commission told us authoritatively last week that trend productivity in Australia at 3 per cent per annum across the decade of the 1990s made Australia the highest productivity country within the OECD developed world.

This 3 per cent productivity in the context of the enterprise-bargaining system introduced by the Keating government has allowed wages to grow at around 5 per cent per annum, giving Australia an inflation rate of around 2 to 2.5 per cent. A world of difference from the 8 to 10 per cent inflation outcomes of the period when John Howard was Malcolm Fraser's Treasurer.

The 1980s and 1990s structural changes took Australia from its insular economy to an open competitive one. The old economy was ring-fenced by tariffs, had sclerotic financial markets and a rigid labour market. The changes opened the financial, product and labour markets, bringing financial blood to the muscle of the economy, while delivering 'within sector' wage flexibility.

The changes brought competitive financial flows, effective external price competition and productivity bargained wage settlements at the enterprise level.

Importantly, in human capital terms, these changes were conceived *radically*, not incrementally. They came as individual parts of a wider schematic that took a decade and a half to put into place.

The new paradigm was conceived by ministers; it did not arrive by way of some bureaucratic master plan. It was delivered politically by a leadership which was determined not to be determinist. One that would not accept the orthodoxy that events were predetermined—and that we were governed by the immutable destiny of incrementalism.

Modern Australia is very much a case in point around the theme of this convention: people leading business—with the emphasis on leadership.

The world-leading changes effected in Australia between 1983 and 1996 did not have to happen. They were not slated to occur. They occurred because a handful of politicians—individuals—recognised that the old paradigm had outlived its usefulness, had come to its end. A new paradigm had to be put into place. And it was—an outcome of leadership, and only leadership.

Today, arguably, Australia has the most flexible economy in the developed world. In 1997 and 1998, we saw it withstand the enormous forces unleashed by the East Asian financial crisis. At other times, and under the earlier model, the economic consequences of that crisis would have smashed the country, giving it a huge and prolonged recession. Instead, Australia skipped through; its exchange rate falling by half, its new wages system immediately adapting, the absence of protection leaving our businesses free to search for efficiency and productivity.

People matter. Shifts in thinking and flexibility in management are the key. I have no doubt that wherever we look, groups of employees are looking for the signals to follow an alert and creative management to the next order of enterprise growth.

Successful human resource management must be about harnessing their ideas and managing their expectations. If this convention can move even a few people down that pathway, its staging will have been worthwhile.

12

THE COMPASSIONATE AGENDA

Jesuit Social Services,
Melbourne,
29 May 2004

*Paul Keating was asked by Jesuit Social Services to tell them how
he saw the imperatives of economic change in Australia and how
this related to the social wage as remodelled by Labor. He used the
opportunity to explain how the closed Australian Defence Model had
broken down and had to be replaced with an open competitive one
built around productivity. Paul Keating used the address to tell the
story of Labor's graft of an efficient and open economy to an inclusive
social wage. He went on to say the Labor policy tradition was built
fundamentally around employment but that he recognised other
demands associated with those 'unconnected' with this agenda. He is
especially sympathetic to the young who he says cheerfully manage their
own careers, moving from job to job, in a world of uncertainty.*

THE WORK OF WELFARE AGENCIES has changed, as the economy and
society have changed.

The certainties of the old or pre-1980s and 1990s structure have
gone; the binding bits of the old order have either gone or have changed.

The former 'Australian Defence Model' or, as it is sometimes called,
the 'Australian Settlement', was all about appropriating bits of prosperity
to particular groups. And at the heart of the 'settlement' was the issue of
employment; or if we extrapolate that, income adequacy. The model of

its essence was industrial, or more particularly, the agenda was industrial. The old Defence Model was built on three legs: high terms of trade coming from gold, wool, wheat and minerals; paying for a very high tariff, which protected employment, remunerated at equitable levels by government-appointed arbitrary tribunals. The model ran, more or less, from 1900 to 1985.

But as the secular decline in Australia's terms of trade accelerated from about 1965, in the end we had an industrial structure which was not only archaic but unaffordable. The terms of trade could not pay for the weight of the tariff or the real price of labour. Our national income had been permanently cut but we were still seeking the employment and income guarantees which had obtained earlier.

The whole structure was collapsing and it had embedded within it an industrial culture in business which lacked innovation or quality or price competitiveness. Finally, it could not produce the investment or the employment required to sustain itself.

My job as Treasurer, and later as Prime Minister, was to dismantle it and put in its place a sustainable structure. In effect, I blew the whistle on it with my 'banana republic' remark of 1986.

The economic changes from 1983 onwards peeled back the layers of regulation and protection. The financial markets were opened up, turning banks from rationers of credit to creators of credit. The product markets were opened by the progressive dismantling of tariffs while the labour market was invested with flexibility by the dismantlement of the centralised wage-fixing system. While this was being accomplished, there was a dramatic improvement in levels of education. When I became Treasurer, three children in ten completed Year 12; when I finished as Prime Minister, nine children in ten completed Year 12 and with that trebling of high-school retention rates came a trebling of university places.

These changes made the country more porous, let competitive breezes through, allowing latent cleverness and innovation to find a place for itself. Regulation was a yoke on the clever and the innovative, and was, in effect, a levy for and by the wealthy.

But the changes did end the old certainties and verities. People were no longer 'tucked in'. A transition had been made from the age of certainty to the age of relative uncertainty.

However, in macro or broad terms, the construction of the new open economic model has been a resounding success. Between 1992 and 2002 real wages, as distinct from nominal wages, grew by over 20 per cent, the highest rate of growth of any decade of the twentieth century. And with the enhanced economic growth, cyclical unemployment is at a new low. In twenty years, nominal GDP has doubled and as a consequence, the wealth of the country has been massively improved. But more than that, these changes included a profound and historic development: the breaking of the back of inflation—the influence which cut people's saving to pieces and put massive mortgages on their backs.

But importantly, with this policy of fundamental economic adjustment came a concomitant commitment to a kindly and universal social wage. It had these important elements: access and equity in health through Medicare; access and equity in education; the establishment of a safety net for the low paid to sit beneath enterprise bargaining; a safety net with a comprehensive system of minimum award rates.

On top of this, first through a system of award-based superannuation and then through the universal system of the Superannuation Guaranteed Charge, 9 per cent of all wages and salaries were diverted to savings and vested in every working Australian's individual account. As a result, great sectors of Australian society are much better off—better than they have been at any time in the past.

Most people's real incomes have grown—but for some off a low base, who rely on the social safety nets of Medicare, family payments and education to sustain them.

But that said, the new economic structure is characterised by impermanence and uncertainty, especially for those who are not in a position to secure a larger piece of the economic pie. For instance, those whose life is characterised by casual employment, relying on the social struts to get them by, those who have been locked out of shelter—or property owning at least, by the large increments to property values. And those who feel that they are not part of society or who have been, to some real extent, alienated from it.

This is especially true of the young. A group I often describe these days as being the new poor. At least two million of them between eighteen years of age and their early thirties. A group who, more cheerfully than I could have imagined, get along in a world without institutional loyalties, without lifelong employment, whose lives are led in the uncertainty of temporary employment and who pay for their own education.

These young people are more often than not locked out of the property market and are slated to rent, often in substandard accommodation, or rely on the camaraderie of mutual friends in similar circumstances. Indeed, unless they can prevail upon the goodwill of their parents for sustenance and support, many look forward to being nothing more than renters for all their lives. No wonder they are wary of marriage and financial obligations.

And given how the labour market is disproportionately rewarding some, these people have to watch the already well-off become wealthier. In the new divisions of labour, even young people with university degrees find it difficult to get permanent, well-paid jobs. Many join the army of casuals who do a number of jobs in a week.

There is no effective advocacy group for young people. As a group, they are on their own.

Without institutional bonding, they are left to manage their own careers, working out how to retrain and re-equip themselves. Most begin their working lives with a substantial debt to the state for their education—or they pay for it out of earnings in TAFE fees and to other non-tertiary institutions.

And as their work and their labour productivity has risen, a large part of the productivity dividend has been appropriated to the old—to their parents' generation. The productivity dividend has been capitalised into the housing assets of the middle-aged who later in life will rely upon their children for income support and geriatric care.

The fact is, the young are up against it. The break for them may come with Australia's deteriorating demographics. As workforce requirements put pressure on labour supply, in time, the real price of labour is likely to rise. As demand for labour puts pressure on the labour market, wages growth may carve out some wealth for them. Some effective progression in the tax system may be needed to help those in the lower income deciles. Further provisioning of employer-funded productivity-based superannuation to at least 12 per cent of wages and salaries could also make arrangements more equitable for them.

But this agenda, the agenda of the young, is fundamentally an employment agenda. An agenda of the connected, if not well provided for.

There is another agenda, the agenda of which people here are familiar—the agenda of the unconnected. Those who, for one reason or another, are not part of the labour force, not part of the mainstream. Who, for reasons of family or circumstances or geography, simply miss out.

The traditional Labor Party agenda has, more or less, been about employment and equal opportunity. Of its essence, it has been industrial—its objectives have been those of its industrial constituency, the trade unions and the workforce at large. It has very much been about putting into place the macro building blocks of opportunity. As I mentioned earlier, income adequacy and income supplementation, like minimum rates and supplementary payments connected to the care and maintenance of children. Access to education, enhanced secondary retentions and tertiary places, health protection, trade training, income support for disabilities, and support for women with children at home.

Labor has always been about workers: wage adequacy, bargaining, income support, labour-market programs. One way or another, it has been connected to employment.

The new agenda must include these things but should extend itself to those not employed or conventionally unemployed. People who do not care about employment—in short, those who are disconnected.

What to do about alcohol abuse or substance abuse or violence in the home is much more challenging than building a universal health system or even universal education—no matter how necessary these are.

These are issues I know Jesuit Social Services are interested in.

But, in national terms, where do we start with these problems?

I think it must be with children: dealing with child neglect and connecting them to education and to a job. The fabric, I think, very much depends on whether we look after kids or whether we allow them to drop through. That question and how we approach it is a measure of us and of the kind of society we are. There are those who believe we should deal with the 'problems at source'—the alcoholism, the drug dependency, the psychiatric illnesses, the disabilities.

Some organisations and individuals are set up to tackle these issues. From a Commonwealth perspective, I should prefer to go after the kids, make a beeline for them and try to lift them out of it; to move them into the main game.

Whatever the views about it, it is an agenda which is central to the quality of the nation's fabric—to our sense of inclusion, indeed, to our charity. But to take these issues on, and be effective with them, does not require a denunciation of the economic reformist agenda as the misplaced zeal of misdirected economic rationalists. So many people in the welfare community have this view.

The Australian Defence Model had to go. It had outlived its usefulness; it was making us the poorer while robbing us of hope. Now, in a wealthier country, we have the resources to do better. What is required are acts of recognition and of indignation at social plight. We have the wherewithal and the instruments, but we must have the leadership and the will to use them.

13

THE IRRESISTIBLE EMERGENCE OF EMERGING MARKETS

Alliance Bernstein Symposium,
Sydney,
16 August 2010

Paul Keating was invited to address a symposium on emerging markets attended by investment funds and asset managers. He was asked to reflect upon the rapidly growing developing markets of the world, to juxtapose them with their developed counterparts. In the address, Paul Keating makes points salient to the evolving international commercial order, including how early investors in developing markets are likely to be rewarded as the weight of mobile investment funds validate their initial market choices.

STOCKMARKET INDEXES HAVE DIVIDED THE world into two segments: 'developed' and 'emerging' markets. This division broadly, though not completely, corresponds with the membership outline of the OECD, that is, between its members and the rest of the world.

But while this distinction is arbitrary, it is also too static. While more or less fixed for most of the postwar years, in the last decade the distinction has been changing and changing fast. What distinguishes the so-called 'developed' markets is that they enjoy per capita incomes that are considerably higher than those in emerging markets. But comparing per capita incomes does not adequately deal with the purchasing power parities of emerging countries, for the simple reason that a unit of currency buys more at home than it will buy in the United States.

As well, emerging economies are catching up rapidly with the incomes of the developed world. For instance, South Korea, South Africa, Mexico, China, Russia and India all have quite sharply rising per capita incomes and, of course, better ones on a purchasing power basis. This arises from the fact that the rate of growth of those countries now surpasses that of the developed world by a wide margin. And that margin has grown wider since the global financial crisis.

So, by 2050, the order of countries in terms of total GDP will look something like this: (1) China, (2) United States, (3) India, (4) Japan, (5) Brazil, (6) Russia, (7) United Kingdom, (8) Germany, (9) France and (10) Italy.

And even within this list, compared to China, the United States and India, Japan would be a *distant* fourth, well behind the race leaders.

The fact is, market capitalisations usually underestimate both the present importance and future dynamics of emerging markets. Indeed, the future dynamics of emerging markets is poorly reflected in the market capitalisation of their stockmarkets compared to those in the developed world. Currently, emerging markets represent roughly 29.5 per cent of world market capitalisation.

On a straightforward GDP basis, the present weight of emerging markets well outstrips their share of world stockmarket capitalisation and this is more the case if the GDP numbers are purchasing power parity adjusted.

It goes without saying, but is worth saying, that market capitalisation levels reflect two factors:

(i) the extent to which an economy is represented by non-government enterprises, listed on public stock exchanges, and
(ii) the valuations attached to those enterprises by investors.

But, if an economy has a large government sector and a large business sector which is not financed through public capital markets, the market capitalisation of that country's stockmarket would be commensurately smaller. The same would also be true if valuation levels were measured by price/earnings multiples, as these are also relatively low.

In fact, modest valuation levels have been a major reason the weight of emerging markets has been low. Yet emerging market returns on equity is now higher than that of the United States and has been for most of the last decade. So, what is the reason for the modest valuation levels? The answer is risk. More particularly, perceived risk.

Traditionally, investors have considered emerging markets to be more risky. This is why valuations are so much lower than in the developed world. And it is true a lot of things can go wrong in the emerging world: fires this week in Russia, a disastrous flood in Pakistan, terrorist attacks in a host of countries from India to Indonesia. And in earlier times, financial market crises of a kind we saw in Thailand and Indonesia, Mexico and Brazil.

But the risks in emerging markets, in recent years, have been overstated.

After financial crises, particularly the East Asia crisis of 1997, the debt-to-GDP ratios of emerging countries have been pulled down considerably. Many now have huge foreign exchange reserves and run substantial current-account surpluses. Indeed, emerging economies meet a large proportion of the financial obligations of the United States and not the other way around.

And this is not only about exports.

While exports have been the main driver of economic growth in emerging markets, as the level of national incomes increases, domestic spending in these markets also becomes more important.

If we take China as a case in point, it is clear that Chinese prosperity cannot be permanently garnered by more investment and more exports to the developed world. Household consumption in the West is now coming back and as we have recently noticed, US household savings have now risen to 6.2 per cent, the highest level in fifteen years. Those same households are de-leveraging, as are industrial companies. So the idea that China and a number of other countries can base their prosperity on a growing level of exports to developed countries is an unreal one. Domestic spending and domestic consumption will become more important in China's case and in countries with a development profile similar to China.

In Japan, the mother of today's emerging economies, exports are now reduced to a mere 10 per cent of GDP.

I should say something here about demographics.

Demographics is another reason the economic importance of emerging markets will grow. Europe's and Japan's populations are in decline, China's and India's will grow to 1.4 billion each. In fact, between 2000 and 2025 the world will grow from 6 to 8 billion people. But, importantly, the developed world's share of this population will decline. For instance, North America will decline from 5.2 per cent of world population in 2000 to 4.9 per cent in 2025. Europe will decline from 12 per cent in 2000 to 8.9 per cent in 2025, while Japan will decline from 2.1 per cent in 2000 to 1.6 per cent in 2025.

We should remember that Japan was once an emerging market.

During the postwar period Japan was to the world what China is today, described as an emerging market. Japan's GDP growth rates were similar to those of China; in fact in some periods they were even higher. Despite all the risk that investing in Japan involved in the 1950s, 1960s, 1970s and 1980s, its equity market turned out to be the best in the world for those four straight decades. In retrospect, investors could have gone to Japan and have kept all their money there for 40 years and been well in front. In no other country would they have done better. The reason? Japan's superior economic performance.

Japan: real equity returns 1950–90

	1950s	1960s	1970s	1980s	1950–90
Japan	27.5%	8.5%	3.4%	18.2%	14.0%
US	15.7%	5.6%	−0.7%	11.0%	7.7%

And these returns were adjusted for local inflation.

Which brings me to the point about index investing. What I call the self-fulfilling prophecy of index investing.

We all know that the bigger the weight of a particular item or country in a stockmarket index, the more investors it will attract. Thus, as Japan's weight in the global indices went up and up in the 1960s, 1970s and 1980s, more and more international investors had to own a piece of Japan. The same will happen with today's groups of emerging markets. As their economic importance grows, their weight in the indices will rise. Underweight as they presently are, overweighting emerging markets looks pretty much a one-way bet. All the investor has to do is be ahead of the index-following crowd and stay ahead. We know their appetite for market weight will have them surely follow—thereby validating early decisions to invest.

A reason so many investors remain doubtful about emerging markets is their past bad experiences with investing in them. If we compare the American S&P 500 index over the 40 years between 1960 and 2000, it shows that, on balance, it out-performed emerging markets over the period. Indeed, the entire game was lost after 1985 following the Mexico crisis, the Argentine crisis, the Russian crisis and the Asian crisis. But the fact is that, as a group these days, emerging economies are in much better shape than during the 1990s. Their economies have grown stronger off a much broader domestic base, their public finances are much improved and they are politically more stable than before. In other words, the risk of investing in them has sharply reduced. This is why many emerging markets have seen their indexes move to new all-time highs.

Emerging markets, by the nature of their sensitivity to the global business cycles, are high beta markets—they oscillate. During market corrections they have tended to fall deeper than the more defensive Western markets. Following negative international events they tend to sink more sharply but they then out-perform developed markets when things look up, offering very attractive absolute returns.

Perhaps I should conclude on this point. There is no doubt that the economic weight and importance of emerging markets will rise over the next ten to twenty years. Being the true growth regions of the world, the number of emerging market companies and their listings will rise as their valuations will also rise.

International index-following investors will chase emerging market equities just as they have always chased winners. Therefore, an investment in emerging markets is a sure bet as long as one is willing to commit money for a considerable period of time in order to overcome inevitable streaks of under-performance. A buy-and-hold strategy would therefore seem best.

However, the most important point is that eventually the distinction between 'developed' and 'emerging' will disappear. Given the manner in which the global economy will grow over the next twenty years, the current distinction will no longer be relevant.

14

THE RE-EMERGING CRISIS
The World Malaise—Mid-2011

Price Waterhouse Coopers,
GWS Giants Lunch,
Sydney,
28 July 2011

In this address Paul Keating paints a readily discernible picture of the current world economic malaise and its antecedents. He traces the economic decline of the United States back to the inequity and income inequality that displaced the American prosperity compact of the 1947–77 period. He lays the blame at the feet of the conservatives. In the address he also explores the gloomy portents within Europe and explains why the European project is at risk. Finally, he contrasts these outcomes with the advantageous position of Australia after its long period of radical structural adjustment under the Hawke and Keating governments. Paul Keating concludes by saying that leaders who baulk at using their power or taking responsibility do not deserve to have their jobs.

THE CONTINUING EUROPEAN DEBT CRISIS and the slowdown in United States growth to half its recent estimate tells us the world economy has not recovered from the 2008 crisis and that it is still plagued by the huge overhangs of private and public debt. These are the lingering manifestations of the 2008 calamity, but to understand how it arose, and its long antecedents, requires a deeper sense of the influences and their wider context.

Let me sketch out the backdrop.

The two great discontinuities of the last twenty years were the ending of the Cold War and the Global Financial Crisis of 2008. But there was a third discontinuity. Real but rarely articulated, this was the shift to conservatism in the United States after Ronald Reagan's election as President in 1980. This was the movement that set off the fracture of the binding social philosophy of the United States, the fracture that began the unravelling of 30 years' prosperity obtained between 1947 and 1977.

By the end of Ronald Reagan's term as President, with Mikhail Gorbachev's *perestroika* pulling away the struts of the Soviet Empire, a conservative philosophic movement had emerged and taken on a substantial momentum. This movement brought on the decisive break within the Republican Party of the United States, breaking it from its traditional, centre-ground, nation-building ethos.

By 1990 we had heard two thunderclaps: the fall and dismemberment of the Soviet Union and a distant one, the not-so-loud but significant radicalisation of American conservatism.

President George Herbert Walker Bush's subsequent defeat by Bill Clinton in 1992 brought two further large changes. The first was that the President of the United States was no longer a member of that heroic generation who had fought through the First and Second World Wars and survived the Depression. These people were as worldly as they were wary. They were, every one of them save for Ronald Reagan, committed to the fundamental American bargain: that the relativity between the pay of American workers and the value of their output would be maintained. This commitment was true of Presidents Carter, Nixon, Johnson, Kennedy, Eisenhower, Truman and Roosevelt.

Then came an historic break. The first baby-boomer US President, Bill Clinton, unburdened by the history of the first half of the twentieth century, presided over a different America. One participating in a national celebration: the end of the Cold War with the collapse of its bipolarity, and the switch into the first investment phase of the digital revolution. Strategically, America cried victory and walked off the field. It did this at the moment it should have begun exploiting the opportunity of establishing a new world order to embrace open regionalism and the inclusion of great states like China and India and the then loitering Russia.

The lift in American wealth, the dotcom boom, which was part of it, and the peace dividend brought the American budget back to fiscal surplus. But the shift from the pre-war generation of American leaders also did something else: it brought onto the scene an altogether different kind of Republican, one completely at odds with those who had been committed to the postwar prosperity compact—the American bargain—Newt Gingrich.

Gingrich pursued a crusade to lower taxes on the rich while dismantling the paternalism of the welfare state. And he did what the Tea Party Republicans attempted this year: he wilfully shut down the government in 1995 in the ultimate political confrontation. His leitmotiv for the welfare state was Medicare, and he did everything conceivable to destroy its financial viability and universality. He did the same with President Clinton's health-care reform, which he saw as a renaissance of the centralised welfare state.

With conservative ideologues like Irving Kristol and William Buckley he argued, without a shred of empirical evidence, that, under so-called supply-side economics, tax cuts for the wealthy would not only lift economic activity, but do so without detriment to the federal budget. This was the trickle-down theory: give more money to the wealthy and through their investments, everyone will be better off.

Gingrich and his movement conservative friends put the cleaver through American polity—including most obviously in their attempted impeachment of Clinton himself.

The key point here is that politics, not economics, changed the nature and underpinnings of the American social compact, by seeking to put structural inequality into a respectable intellectual framework. From thereon, the rot sets in.

Between the election of Ronald Reagan in 1980 and the Global Financial Crisis of 2008; in those 30 years, the wages and benefits of the bottom 90 per cent of American workers have either been held flat or have fallen. By contrast, the top 1 per cent saw an increase of about 50 per cent in income while the gains for the top 0.1 per cent were stratospheric. So, of that great burst in American productivity between 1990 and 2008; of that massive increment to national income, none of it went to wages. By contrast, in Australia, real wages over the same period had risen by 30 per cent, including with it universal health protection for every Australian working person.

The subsequent election of George W Bush in 2000 witnessed an outright victory for Republican radicals. The government walked away from the prosperity compact, slashing public investment in schools, higher education, public transport, training and aid to the unemployed, including those with children. Bush even attempted to privatise social security. To stave off declining living standards, women in working families joined the workforce, with a fourfold increase in their participation in the 30 years to 2008. And, not earning enough to sustain them, American workers were obliged to work longer hours. Typically, by 2008 they were working 50 to 60 hours a week.

Even that was not enough to allow them to afford their piece of the national pie, so they began running down their savings and borrowing. By 2008 the average American owed around 135 per cent of their after-tax income while their savings had fallen from around 10 per cent a year in the 1970s to zero by 2008. The wind-down to the debt wreck was underway.

Meanwhile, the loan sharks of Wall Street had geared up to augment the lost purchasing power of the workforce. A combination of the accommodating monetary policy and low interest rates of Alan Greenspan and the surfeit of savings from the surplus countries like China, Japan and Germany allowed the likes of Lehman Brothers and Bear Stearns to gear up at ratios as high as 45 to one, to provide a financial increment to working Americans from their housing mortgages and their credit cards.

The rest is history.

America has paid an enormous price for the breakdown of its fundamental bargain, its national compact. It has created a small group of super-rich off the back of the great mass of a depressed working and middle class. No wonder philanthropy has taken off; the wealthy have the largest part of the money that should have belonged to working Americans.

The financial collapse of 2008 and its aftermath have witnessed falls in confidence and consumption which have held unemployment at around 9 per cent, coupled with a huge deterioration in the budget balance. George W Bush's tax cuts for the wealthy and his two wars in the Middle East added over US$6 trillion to America's government debt. Now, the same Republican radicals—perhaps a more viral variant, the Tea Party—refuse to rein in the Bush tax expenditures while seeking to cut social programs for the middle class and the poor. On current projections, without large discretionary policy changes, American public debt is heading towards 110 per cent of GDP.

This almighty economic cloud gathering fundamentally from the politically inspired inequality of the 30 years to 2008 now hangs over the world. America is hugely indebted and its economic growth is structurally constrained.

But American friends are not solely to blame for the current international malaise.

The Europeans, not to be outdone, have pumped up their own black cloud in the form of an ultra-stressed monetary union. The European monetary union, with its single currency, started out in 2000 with all the bonhomie of inclusion that had eluded Europe since 1871. The Union and its single currency, the euro, is a political project designed to embed Germany in a wider European landscape. Most notably in a symbiotic relationship with France, but particularly in a wider construct designed to bring about a fiscal union. At the inception there was wide debate as to whether the euro should be founded around the principal economies of Western Europe: Germany and France, with the Benelux countries as outriders. At the same time an altogether bigger idea set itself in motion: that the euro should displace the currencies of Italy, Spain, Portugal, Greece and Ireland.

As it turned out, the bigger idea won.

Importantly, it won as a political idea, not an economic one. But the political idea was never validated by a political union. And, in the event, not even a fiscal one.

From its inception in 2000, countries like Italy, Spain and Portugal were relieved of their higher domestic interest-rate structures as they were invested with interest rates associated with the recently replaced deutschmark. And the major European banks, believing they enjoyed an implicit cross-border guarantee by virtue of the single currency, took their new low-interest loans and lent like fury.

The property and credit boom around the Mediterranean and up into places like Ireland was the consequence. When the reckoning began in 2008 we found there was no Pan-European supervision of banks; while all went abroad to grow, banks returned home to die.

The process of their decline has seen the bare transfer of private debt to public budgets, now of a scale endangering the sovereign viability of a number of countries, starting with Greece but moving to countries like Portugal and Italy. The yield or borrowing cost on Italian government ten-year bonds is now 6 per cent; the yield in Germany is 2.3 per cent. The 4.7 per cent spread or difference simply reflects perceived sovereign risk in lending to the Italian government, and the rates are worse for Greece and Portugal.

This carnage within the euro sovereign bond market is not only sharply lifting the budgetary cost of funding the mountainous levels of sovereign debt, it is also lifting private borrowing costs which sharply militate against economic growth. Without economic growth, these countries cannot repair their debt. Yet while they remain within the single currency, its value and rigidity prevents them from improving growth through import replacement and exports.

In the old days an external shock or internal adjustment could be met with a discretionary depreciation of the exchange rate, but that remedy is lost to the countries within the single currency, within the euro. Marooned, they are damned to low growth. And as their loss of competitiveness will not be remedied by the rigid exchange rate, it will manifest itself by a sharp fall in prices. It goes without saying that a sharp fall in prices, whether it be in property or goods, makes the credit crisis even worse. This story has a moral: the state's first obligation is to its own sovereignty and quality, not to relieve the problems of careless lenders.

So we have two-thirds of the world's economy in an economic hole and half of that bound up in a sovereign debt crisis. The United States, one-third of the world's economy, is growing at a snail's pace while the ability to deal with its medium-term fiscal trajectory is hampered by its acute political paralysis. Europe, also a third of the world economy, is barely growing, with its leadership preoccupied by a structural debt crisis.

There is little room to manoeuvre. Resort to debt and fiscal stimuli is beyond most countries. Interest rates, already at very low levels, leave little space for further stimulatory adjustment. Even the US Federal Reserve's two monetary quantitative easings have run their course. This leaves minimal room on the fiscal and monetary front on over two-thirds of the world economy.

We can be glad China and the emerging countries continue to grow strongly. China still looks like turning out 9 per cent growth this year, off the second-largest individual economic base in the world. China at around US$7 trillion of GDP and growing at 9 per cent implies an increment of US$600 billion to new wealth. Combined, the United States and Europe look like turning in an exceptionally modest US$400 billion in new value. This year, with emerging markets accounting for about 60 per cent of global expansion, we can be grateful that fewer of our eggs are in the North Atlantic basket.

It is important to underline that there is nothing preordained about American decline any more than the European project is destined to fail. But the portents are not good. Despite the rhetoric, President Obama conducts himself as an arbitrator or mediator between the competing strands of American economic and political ideology. In market terms he is a price taker not a price maker. He repeatedly eschews striking out, snatching the naked flame and hanging on. But the cost of this strategy is not simply a cost to him; it is a cost to the whole world and to the confidence that it is being confidently run. On the other hand, Chancellor Merkel is the archetypal worry-wart. She does not lead; she assesses. Each iteration of the euro zone crisis is met with studious hesitations as she scrambles, always belatedly, to the next rung of crisis resolution.

You really wonder why leaders want these jobs when they do not really want to lead. And what is their risk? That Barack Obama will not get a second term? Or that Angela Merkel's coalition might finally end up on the rocks? If they actually made the leap they might astound themselves. Because, in the end, everyone in political life gets carried out—the only relevant question is whether the pallbearers will be crying.

In this ocean of ordinariness, let me say a couple of things about Australia. This economy is now in the twentieth year of its expansion. This is unprecedented. Not only is it unprecedented for Australia, it is unprecedented, for a country of this size in the developed world since the Second World War.

This expansion has been underwritten by the flexibility of the Australian economy induced by one-and-a-half decades of reform by the Hawke and Keating Labor governments. Their unique graft of an open, competitive economy to a generous and inclusive social wage paved the way for textbook changes to Australia's financial, product and labour markets.

Between 1991 and this year, the Australian economy tripled in size. Annual GDP growth has averaged 3.5 per cent while inflation averaged 2.6 per cent. In the same period unemployment fell by more than half from 10.5 per cent to 4.9 per cent.

Seminal to this story was a productivity revolution arising from the reforms of the 1980s and 1990s. Trend productivity more than doubled to 3 per cent over the period to 2002. This led to a unique outcome: rising real wages with falling unit labour costs. Uniquely, the reforms led to an increase in wages and profits simultaneously. Of the three percentage points of productivity, two percentage points went annually to wages, while one percentage point went to profits. Twenty years of this since 1991 have given the Australian worker a 30-plus per cent increase in real wages.

At the same time, real disposable income grew even faster than wages. A national competition policy and the abolition of tariffs also drove down prices. Indeed, every whiff of deflation coming from China has been taken to the pockets of the Australian workforce. We have had real wages rising strongly with prices falling markedly. The gap—disposable income growth—has been unprecedented. But now, as productivity has fallen back to under 1 per cent after twelve years of structural inaction by the Howard government, its negative impact on Australian wealth has been camouflaged. It has been camouflaged by the massive increase in export values associated with the terms-of-trade lift coming out of China and North Asia.

Australia's terms of trade, remarkably, are 40 per cent higher than the average of the last 50 years. And they look like continuing for at least the next decade or two. The vast reserves of Australia's mineral and hydrocarbon endowments are sufficient to meet current levels of production way into the future.

So, in a very ordinary world, Australia has been set up to do well. Not only do the structural reforms of the 1980s and 1990s and the elevated terms of trade continue to work in its favour, it also has low levels of government debt, a solid and viable banking system and, through superannuation, an accumulation of A$1.2 trillion or 110 per cent of GDP. This savings pool, designed to meet the need of retirement incomes, is unique among countries of comparable scale and size. The problem of ageing that is now to beset the United States and the countries of Western Europe will, in large measure, have been met by the Keating government's universal superannuation system in Australia.

As in everything, leadership is key. Australia's economic position dramatically improved with the adoption of a set of structural changes radically conceived and politically constructed. Conceived not by way of some bureaucratic masterplan or process of increments, but by imagination and insight.

Leaders must sketch out the landscape and then move the nation forward. Those who do not want to do this, who baulk at exercising power or accepting responsibility, do not deserve to have the jobs.

ACKNOWLEDGEMENTS

As the speeches contained here are but a fraction of those written and given, I should like to acknowledge and thank my two private secretaries over the period, Susan Grusovin and Cheryl Griffiths, for their sustained commitment to the quality of the work. In a policy sense, I owe a particular debt of gratitude to Allan Gyngell, my foreign policy adviser in office, who worked with me between 1996 and 2003 before taking up the inaugural executive directorship of the Lowy Institute for International Policy. Allan's judgement on the big strategic issues of the day is invariably unerringly right.

I should also thank Colleen Cory from my office for her patient work on the book, as I do Isabella Penna, who assisted me in the initial compilation of material.

INDEX